Cost-Benefit Analysis

Cost-benefit analysis (CBA) is the systematic and analytical process of comparing benefits and costs in evaluating the desirability of a project or programme – often of a social nature. It attempts to answer such questions as whether a proposed project is worthwhile, the optimal scale of a proposed project and the relevant constraints. CBA is fundamental to government decision making and is established as a formal technique for making informed decisions on the use of society's scarce resources.

This timely sixth edition of the classic *Cost-Benefit Analysis* text continues to build on the successful approach of previous editions, with lucid explanation of key ideas, simple but effective expository short chapters and an appendix on various useful statistical and mathematical concepts and derivatives. The book examines important developments in the discipline, with relevant examples and illustrations as well as new and expanded chapters which build upon standard materials on CBA. Highlights include:

- updated historical background of CBA
- extended non-market goods valuation methods
- the impact of uncertainty
- evaluation of programmes and services
- behavioural economics
- decision rules and heuristics
- CBA and regulatory reforms
- CBA in developed and developing countries
- value of household production
- other topics frequently encountered in CBA, such as costs of diseases and air pollution, and value of statistical life.

This book is a valuable source and guide to international funding agencies, governments, interested professional economists and senior undergraduate and graduate students.

The text is supported by online resources with discussion questions and Power-Point slides for each chapter.

E.J. Mishan was Professor of Economics at the London School of Economics, UK, from 1956 to 1977.

Euston Quah is Albert Winsemius Chair Professor of Economics at Nanyang Technological University, Singapore.

'Cost-benefit analysis is as important as ever in assessing projects, whether in private business, transportation, health and agriculture, or urban and regional planning. This book will be of great use to students, economists, business people and government planners. A welcome new edition from the maestro, Euston Quah, and a tribute to his late coauthor, Ezra Mishan'.

– **W. Brian Arthur, Center for Advanced Study in the Behavioral Sciences, Stanford University, USA**

'In this sixth edition of his classic treatise, *Cost-Benefit Analysis*, Professor Euston Quah provides an up-to-date rendering of the fundamental concepts that constitute the foundation of this important analytical tool, as well as the essential empirical methods, ranging from the basics of discounting to the latest methods of valuing externalities. This book can function as a comprehensive text in an appropriate college course, and as a key reference for practitioners. As such, it belongs on the shelf of scholars, policy analysts, and policy makers'.

– **Robert N. Stavins, A. J. Meyer Professor of Energy and Economic Development at Harvard University, USA**

'Building on the earlier eminent work with E.J. Mishan, the sixth newly updated edition of Euston Quah's continues to improve what has been referred to as a classic work in cost-benefit analysis. It is a very important book for both practitioners and academics. I strongly recommend it as a reference book for all of us interested in public policy'.

– **Richard L. Sandor, Aaron Director Lecturer at Ronald Coase and Richard Sandor Institute of Law and Economics of the University of Chicago, USA**

'This timely sixth edition builds on the success of previous editions. The key economic tools are lucidly explained and the new themes explored. The case studies are up-to-date and cover a wide range of potential applications. It will be an indispensable source and guide to government and international agencies as well as to students and professional economists'.

– **Cheng Hsiao, Former Editor of the *Journal of Econometrics* and Professor of Economics at University of Southern California, USA**

'Increasingly, calculations of gains and losses if made for communities and societies have to take into account a contextualized and scale-sensitive economic order. This sixth updated edition offers an excellent guide by integrating investment criteria, uncertainty and frequently encountered issues in the actual use of CBA while examining the continued validity of key concepts, the limitations of the criteria used and the consistency of techniques. It is highly recommended to everyone making informed decisions when resources are scarce'.

– **Helga Nowotny, Former President of the European Research Council**

'As a text, Mishan and Quah's *Cost-Benefit Analysis* shows the intuition of how to use economics as it instructs how to do CBA. As a reference, from the first edition it has been within easy reach of my desk'.

– **Jack L. Knetsch, Emeritus Professor of Economics at Simon Fraser University, Canada**

'Cost-benefit analysis is the most well known word in economics. However, it is not deeply understood what the analysis is, how to measure it and to what kind of conditions it can be applied. The analysis can be used in many different projects not only in public and private projects but also in our daily lives. Economists often discuss the cost-benefits, however engineers and medical doctors also have to pay attention to cost-benefit analysis results. Otherwise, various policies which may incur huge costs would be proposed and cost of burden to the general public may be very high in the future. This book explains very simply the essence of cost-benefit analysis and its applications in many different areas. The book is recommended not only to students in economics and business, but also to a general audience who wish to understand public decision-making. This book will help you think and make better decisions in your daily life'.
  – Naoyuki Yoshino, Dean/CEO of Asian Development Bank Institute, Japan, and
Professor Emeritus of Economics at Keio University, Japan

'Cost-benefit analyses have seen a revival during the last years. This book is a must-have for all researchers and policy-makers interested in taking measures to solve important problems like global climate change, avoiding a digital divide, making people behave more sustainably etc. Every measure comes along with costs and benefits. This book gives theoretical background and practical advice on how to assess and counterbalance them in order to make the resource use highly efficient'.
  – Renate Schubert, Professor of Economics and Associate Vice President
of ETH Zurich, Switzerland

Cost-Benefit Analysis

Sixth edition

E.J. Mishan and Euston Quah

Routledge
Taylor & Francis Group

LONDON AND NEW YORK

Sixth edition published 2021
by Routledge
2 Park Square, Milton Park, Abingdon, Oxon, OX14 4RN

and by Routledge
52 Vanderbilt Avenue, New York, NY 10017

Routledge is an imprint of the Taylor & Francis Group, an informa business

© 2021 E.J. Mishan and Euston Quah

First edition published by Allen & Unwin 1976

Fifth edition published by Routledge 2007

British Library Cataloguing-in-Publication Data
A catalogue record for this book is available from the British Library

Library of Congress Cataloging-in-Publication Data
Names: Mishan, E. J., 1917-2014, author. | Quah, Euston, author.
Title: Cost-benefit analysis / E.J. Mishan and Euston Quah.
Description: Sixth edition. | Milton Park, Abingdon, Oxon ; New York : Routledge,
2020. | Includes bibliographical references and index.
Identifiers: LCCN 2020009842 (print) | LCCN 2020009843 (ebook) |
ISBN 9781138492745 (hardback) | ISBN 9781138492752 (paperback) |
ISBN 9781351029780 (ebook)
Subjects: LCSH: Cost effectiveness. | Welfare economics.
Classification: LCC HD47.5 .M53 2020 (print) | LCC HD47.5 (ebook) |
DDC 658.15/54–dc23 LC record available at https://lccn.loc.gov/2020009842
LC ebook record available at https://lccn.loc.gov/2020009843

ISBN: 978-1-138-49274-5 (hbk)
ISBN: 978-1-138-49275-2 (pbk)
ISBN: 978-1-351-02978-0 (ebk)

Typeset in Sabon
by Swales & Willis, Exeter, Devon, UK

Visit the eResources: www.routledge.com/9781138492752

In memory of Ezra and Ray Mishan

This sixth edition is dedicated to the good memory of Ezra J. Mishan who was not only a great scholar and prolific writer but also a good friend who had shown much warmth, intellectual wit and genuine friendship. Ray Mishan was a good host and often gave good advice in all matters.

For an extended review on Professor E.J. Mishan's contribution to economics, especially welfare economics and cost-benefit analysis, see Quah (2016) and Ng (2016) in *Singapore Economic Review* and also E.J. Mishan obituary by Euston Quah (*The Guardian*, 7 November 2014).

To my wife, Juat Mei and my children, Josh and Jo-Ann.

Contents

xii   *Contents*

Preface to the sixth edition

In this new edition, we have kept to the more traditional practice of beginning a textbook with an introductory Part I on Scope and method; a decision that has required, *inter alia*, the removal of some chapters of the fifth edition, and parts of some other chapters, to this introductory Part I, where they are now more comfortably lodged, for it is incumbent in this Part I that the authors make clear just how the economist's conceptions of costs and benefits differ from those employed in the business world. To the layman and the politician, the notion of gains and losses may seem evident enough for transactions between a limited number of people. It is far from evident, however, when calculations of gains and losses have to be made for whole communities and society, whether or not the individuals are directly engaged in some project or programme. A new chapter on the framework of cost-benefit analysis (CBA) summarizing the steps necessary to conduct a CBA is presented.

As for the remaining parts in this sixth edition, apart from correcting some minor errors in the fifth edition, some rearrangement of the chapters has taken place and, occasionally, what appeared there as two consecutive chapters has been combined here to form a single chapter: all this, and more, in the endeavour to make the exposition in this new edition more lucid and concise.

It may be noted, in particular, that Part IV (on 'External effects') ends with an extended chapter in which the possibly quite different outcomes from using a calculation based on the CV^{21} measure, instead of the CV^{12} measure, are elaborated and illustrated. Again, in our Part V (on 'Investment criteria'), a searching comparison of the implications and the limitations of the various criteria in common use cannot be undertaken without taking up far more space than any of the other parts. In this connection, the two chapters devoted to explaining the proposed normalization procedure (in compounding net benefits forward to a terminal date), regarded as a technique superior to any of the popular discounted-present-value criteria for evaluating a stream of net benefits, have been entirely re-written to make it more comprehensible.

The chapter on cost-effectiveness analysis is now relegated to the expanded appendices. There they are included with a number of other appendices that, although not central to a proper exposition of CBA, touch on sources of misunderstanding or of common error in some popular treatments of the subject.

We also note that, in some of the more ambitious textbooks, there are extended reports of cost-benefit studies already undertaken for existing programmes or projects. Their value, however, is limited unless the methods used in such studies are also subjected to fastidious examination, and validity to the concepts of CBA.

In this sixth edition however, we have provided one new section on the topics frequently encountered in the use of CBA. These topics include valuation methods of non-market goods in particular, the value of statistical life, CBA and public health, the use of benefit transfers, and an exposition of fairly new techniques and rankings of qualitative CBA and the application of CBA to less developed countries is also a new topic added.

It may be unnecessary to remark that no significant theoretical novelty is to be found in this edition, or indeed in earlier editions. Inasmuch as CBA is, in fact, no more than an assembly of concepts and techniques culled from mainstream economic theory, in particular from that branch known as Welfare Economics, it is not surprising that the subject itself cannot boast of theoretical innovation.

Apart from proposals for the gathering and refinement of data, the development of CBA over the years has centred, in the main, on controversies over the propriety of concepts, over proxies for their measurement and over the appropriateness of the techniques employed to determine the ranking of alternative public projects. With regard to all such issues, our overriding concern remains that of examining the validity of the key concepts in use, of making explicit the limitations of the usual proxies adopted for their measurement and of checking for consistency the various techniques employed in any cost-benefit calculation.

No textbook can provide detailed guidance on every aspect of gathering and processing data on the variety of programmes and projects in which CBA may be employed. Indeed, attempts by authors to put together increasingly comprehensive textbooks on the subject result is so overloading the students' minds that they 'cannot see the wood for the trees'.

In this introductory text, however, we continue the policy of earlier editions in focusing the student's attention on the crucial concepts and, unavoidably, also on the controversies they engender. The purpose of this stratagem is to enable the conscientious student initially to understand what ideally he should be seeking to measure before resorting to a considered choice among the proxies available or contrived. Our aim, that is, is primarily to sharpen the student's insight into the rationale of the basic fundamental concepts, in the endeavour to develop his judgement in appraising the validity and the usefulness of the diverse techniques employed or proposed in the economic valuation of projects.

Acknowledgements

This sixth edition has greatly benefited from the meticulous and painstaking research assistance provided by Iuldashov Nursultan and Tsiat Siong, Tan, both research associates and former graduate students of mine at the Nanyang Technological University, Singapore.

It has also benefited from discussions with colleagues at both the National University of Singapore and the Nanyang Technological University. The latter, in particular, Wai Mun, Chia who had also contributed to the chapters on the cost of air pollution, and diseases and the value of statistical life. My former teacher at Simon Fraser University, Canada, Jack L. Knetsch had also contributed to earlier ideas, comments and feedback as well as contributed to the chapter on behavioural economics and CBA.

I also thank colleagues who had written to me suggesting improvements in some parts of the previous fifth edition and seeking clarity in other parts. One mention of this came from Professor Pierre Lemieux, at the University of Quebec, Canada.

Mention must also be made of the various cohorts of students at both the National University of Singapore and the Nanyang Technological University who had been exposed to much of the materials found in this sixth edition as well as the earlier fifth edition of the book.

Finally, I wish to record my deep appreciation to my former administrative assistant Zach Lee, who is now Research Associate with the Technical University of Munich-Nanyang Technological University project who had with me many good discussions on the subject; Jackson Teh, Research Associate and Dr Shan Xin, Research Fellow for assisting with the several rounds of checking and proof-reading of the final manuscript and not forgetting my able and efficient secretary, Shida Baji who coordinated many working meetings.

I would also like to acknowledge the team from Routledge, Andy Humphries and Emma Morley for their editorial support.

To all the above, my intellectual and organizational debts. As is normal, all remaining errors are with the authors.

Euston Quah

Part I
Scope and method

1 Brief historical background to cost-benefit analysis

1   Cost-benefit analysis (CBA) is currently an established technique that is widely used in both governments and international organizations. Although certain under-lying concepts of the technique originated from Europe in the 1840s, the use of CBA in environmental economics is a relatively new occurrence, becoming estab-lished only after regulations were set by the US government which made the use of CBA mandatory in certain circumstances in the 1930s.

The two underlying concepts which originated from Europe are the concept of con-sumer surplus and the concept of externality. These concepts are the main aspects that distinguish CBA from traditional profit-and-loss accounting. The concept of consumer surplus was argued by Jules Dupuit in 1844, when he pointed out that the users of roads and bridges in France enjoyed benefits in excess of the tolls they paid for the usage (Dupuit, 1844). Dupuit named this additional enjoyment 'relative utility' which later became known as Alfred Marshall's consumer surplus. In the 1920s, Pigou (1952: 183–192) effectively developed the concept of externality by arguing that there is a difference between private economic production and public economic product, citing child labour, maternity leave for working mothers, alcohol, war and factory pol-lution. The key relation of the above two concepts to CBA was that they identified how social welfare could be measured (consumer surplus) and how previously ignored factors could contribute to or subtract from it (externalities).

2   CBA in environmental applications took on a significant role with the enact-ment of the US Flood Control Act of 1936 which, among other things, stated that any flood control project should be deemed desirable if the benefits to whomsoever they may accrue are in excess of the estimated cost. Although no specific guidelines were given on the implementation of the standard, the Act effectively paved the way for the assessment of projects on the basis of calculating their net benefits and the entire social assessment of the net benefits instead of solely basing it on the financial appraisal, which looks at the interests of only the producers.

Owing to the lack of specific and concrete guidelines, inconsistent sets of stand-ards and procedures were developed and implemented by the various agencies involved in the development of water resources. This gave the impression that each agency's main objective of the CBA was to justify the projects that each agency wanted to carry out instead of providing critical evaluations of the merits of the projects.

In order to ensure consistent and standardized practices and guidelines across dif-ferent agencies, an inter-agency group was formed in 1946. Called the US Federal

Inter-Agency River Basin Committee's Subcommittee on Benefits and Costs, it produced the *Proposed Practices for Economic Analysis of River Basin Projects* (1950; revised 1958) or more commonly known as the *Green Book*. This publication, together with the *Budget Circular A-47* by the Bureau of Budget in 1952, not only attempted to standardize practices among the agencies and bring them in line with economic theories but they also caught and encouraged academic interest.

3   A firm theoretical *framework* for CBA was finally established with works by three eminent economists (Eckstein, 1958; Krutilla and Eckstein, 1958; McKean, 1958) which methodically utilized neoclassical welfare economics in relation with CBA. The 1960s and 1970s saw the rapid development of CBA as numerous books and papers on the topic appeared, all trying to accomplish the deceptively simple objective of determining whether a proposed project's benefits exceeded costs and, if so, by how much.

While the valuation theories and techniques were still undergoing refinement in the 1970s, the criterion by which proposed projects might pass was well established by the 1930s. Nowadays known as the Kaldor–Hicks criterion[1] it required the net money measure of gains, from a proposed project, to be positive, regardless of the effects of distribution. Otherwise known as a potential Pareto improvement, the criterion was developed after a prolonged debate amongst welfare economists about the viability of inter-personal comparisons of utility triggered by the repealing of the Corn Laws and in recognition of the impossibility (or at least, great unlikelihood) of achieving Pareto improvements (Mishan, 1981).

4   Use of CBA became more institutionalized and widespread from 1960 onwards, as governments in the US, Canada and the UK required formal CBA before the commencement of certain policies and projects. In the US, President Lyndon Johnson implemented a planning-program-budget system (PPBS) throughout the federal government in 1965 which contributed to the widespread use of CBA. In Canada, Sewell *et al.*'s *Guide to Benefit–Cost Analysis* (1965) and the implementation of a PPBS system in 1967 led to popular use of CBA. In the UK, the institutionalization of CBA took place after the release of the 1967 *Government White Paper*, and CBA was used for the M1 motorway project, the 1970s Channel Tunnel Proposals and the Third London Airport, among many other projects. The academic contributions by Mishan (1971a, 1971b) on CBA and normative economics (1980a, 1980b) added significantly to the growing literature.

In addition to being used by governments, CBA was also formally adopted by several international organizations – the OECD in 1969, the UN in 1972 and the World Bank in 1975 (Squire and van der Tak, 1975). At the Earth Summit in Rio de Janeiro in 1992, it was agreed that country application of financial support for public sector projects be subjected to passing the cost-benefit test as far as possible.

In 1980, US President Ronald Reagan signed Executive Order 12291, in which the efficiency criterion was explicitly required in the preparation of Regulatory Impact Analysis for regulations that are expected to have an annual effect of $100 million or more on the economy. This executive order was replaced by Executive Order 12866, signed by President Clinton in 1993. This new order is similar to the former, requiring that all the costs and benefits of available regulatory alternatives be considered in the process of deciding whether to proceed with certain regulations. This order has continued to remain relevant and in force. Additions to Executive Order 12866 such as Executive Orders 13422 and 13563 have been made by both President Bush and Obama respectively. President Bush's presidency was focused on cost reduction by removing burdensome government regulations that 'impede' economic growth but few amendments of Executive Order 12866 were done with the benefit–cost analysis framework mostly left in place. Under President Obama, Executive Order 13563 places greater emphasis on equity and distributive impacts in conducting cost-benefit analysis and more attention to 'material failures of private markets'. In President Trump's presidency, Executive Order 13771 emphasized reducing regulatory costs, meaning that for one new regulation to be imposed two other costly and ineffective regulations must be cancelled. This dramatic shift of attention from benefits to costs may either decrease possible overregulation, refine analytical tools for government agencies or result in even more methodological challenges in the long run. In implementing his regulatory rollbacks, President Trump used controversial calculations in CBA. For example, in calculating the cost of greenhouse gas emissions, President Trump included only the environmental cost to the USA, rather than the global impact. Critics have argued that this is inadequate as global warming is a global, multigenerational issue. This highlights the difficulty in defining not just the scope of CBA but also the usage of different valuation methodology in real-world applications.

In recent times, as more organizations adopt a triple bottom line[2] approach, cost, not just benefit, analysis has become more pervasive, especially in the corporate sphere. In addition, after the financial crisis of 2007, there have also been calls to extend the requirements of CBA to financial regulators to increase accountability.

5   In more recent history, two developments that could have potentially far-reaching effects on CBA have emerged. The first is the growing number of valuation databases; the second is the development of a new branch of economics – behavioural economics.

The establishment of valuation databases, where the results of valuation studies are meticulously recorded, has thus far been limited to valuation studies of environmental goods. At present, there appear to be at least four databases of this sort, the most comprehensive being the Environmental Valuation Reference Inventory (EVRI) which was established in the late 1990s. Other databases also seem to have been established around this period or later.

The databases were set up to facilitate a valuation method known as benefit transfer that rose to prominence, not coincidentally, in the early 1990s. Benefit transfer is, in essence, the practice of assigning a value to an item based on the established value of another similar item. The exact methodology and associated issues are covered in the later chapter on benefit transfers.

Nonetheless, from the brief description, it should be clear that the method required an origin from which values could be 'transferred'. That is where the databases entered the picture. The databases provided a ready source from which CBA practitioners could derive values for items in their studies without employing any of the conventional methods.

Most experts still agree that the conventional methods yield more accurate value estimates. However, with the increased ease of obtaining transferred values, one can reasonably expect that future CBAs will utilize fewer conventional methods and more benefit transfers. As such, it is not improbable that future CBA develop- ments will occur along the lines of developing more accurate transfer techniques as opposed to further refinement of the conventional methods. Increasingly too, there have been calls for concern over the use of cost-benefit analysis in less developed coun- tries, that the method may require some adjustments to accommodate and recognize differences between these countries and developed countries (Quah, 2013). A new chapter has been added in this edition dealing with this issue (see Chapter 45).

The other recent development that has had an impact on CBA is the growth in the relatively young branch of behavioural economics. Studies in behavioural economics have sparked off new controversies regarding the validity of certain CBA techniques, with valuation methods being the most readily debated topic. The more technical nature of the issue will be further explored in Chapter 10, which discusses behavioural economics and CBA. Suffice to say, such challenges will provide an impetus for the further development and refinement of methods and techniques that account for behavioural biases and, more importantly, answer the central and seemingly innocuous question at the heart of all CBA – do the benefits of a proposed project outweigh its cost and if so, by how much would society benefit?

Notes

1 The term was coined in the late 1930s from the writings of two eminent welfare econo- mists, Sir John Hicks (1939) and Nicholas Kaldor (1939).
2 The triple bottom line approach involves the consideration of social and environmental performance in addition to the traditional financial performance.

2 What is cost-benefit analysis?

1 Let us be clear from the start that the sort of question a CBA sets out to answer is whether one or a number of projects or programmes should be undertaken and, if investable funds are limited, which one, two or more among these specific projects that would otherwise qualify for admission should be selected. Another question that CBA sometimes addresses is that of determining the level at which a plant should operate or the combination of outputs it should produce. In this introductory volume, however, we follow custom in confining our attention chiefly to the former question, about the choice of investment projects.

But why bother with CBA at all? What is wrong with deciding whether to undertake any specific investment or to choose among a number of specific investment opportunities, guided simply by proper accounting practices and, therefore, guided ultimately by reference to profitability? The answer is provided by the familiar thesis that what counts as benefits (or profits) and costs to personnel engaged in the activity of a particular segment of the economy – be it a firm, an industry or any private or public organization – does not necessarily coincide with, indeed, is unlikely to coincide with, all the benefits and costs experienced by the individuals residing within an area subject to a CBA. The economy of a whole country or nation state should often be analysed. However, it can also be a region that encompasses a number of contiguous countries or, alternatively, one or more provinces of a country or even a single town or city. This problem is called the accounting stance. In order to avoid unnecessary verbiage, however, we shall assume henceforth that the area in question is that of the whole country and therefore speak of 'the economy as a whole' or 'society as a whole'.

A private enterprise, or even a public enterprise, comprises only a segment of the economy, often a very small segment. More importantly, whatever the means it employs in pursuing its objectives – whether rules of thumb or more formalized techniques such as mathematical programming or operations research – the private enterprise, at least, is guided by ordinary commercial criteria that require revenues to exceed costs. The fact that its activities are guided by the profit motive, however, is not to deny that it confers benefits on a large number of people other than its shareholders. It also confers benefits on its employees, on consumers and – through the taxes it pays – on the public. Yet the benefits enjoyed by these four groups continue to exist only for as long as they coincide with the yielding of profits to the enterprise. If it makes losses, the enterprise cannot survive unless it receives a public subsidy. If it is to survive unaided as a private concern and to expand the scale of its operations, it must produce profits large enough either to attract investors or to finance its own expansion.

There is, of course, the metaphor of the 'invisible hand'; the *deus ex machina* discovered by Adam Smith that so directs the self-seeking proclivities of the business world that it confers benefits on society as a whole. Moreover, one can, indeed, lay down simple and sufficient conditions under which the uncompromising pursuit of profits acts always to serve the public interest. These conditions can be boiled down to two: that all effects relevant to the welfare of all individuals be properly priced on the market, and that perfect competition prevails in all economic activities.

2   Once we depart from this ideal economic setting, however, the set of outputs and prices to which the economy tends may not serve the public as well as some other set of outputs and prices. In addition to this possible misallocation of resources among the goods being produced, it is also possible that certain goods that can be economically justified are not produced at all, while others that cannot be economically justified continue to be produced. If, for example, technical conditions and the size of the market are such that a number of goods can be produced only under conditions of increasing returns to scale (falling average cost), it is possible that, although some of these goods will be produced by monopolies charging prices above marginal cost, other such goods will not be produced, as there is no single price at which the monopolist can make any profit. Nevertheless, the production of these latter goods is not necessarily uneconomic. It may simply be the case that the monopolist who sells each good at a single price cannot transfer enough of the benefits from his potential customers to make the venture worthwhile.

Again, certain goods with beneficial, though unpriced, spillover effects also qualify for production on economic grounds; but they cannot be produced at a profit as long as the beneficial spillovers remain unpriced. The reverse is also true and more significant: profitable commercial activities sometimes produce noxious spillover effects to such an extent that, on a more comprehensive pricing criterion, they would be regarded as uneconomic.

The economist engaged in the cost-benefit appraisal of a project is, in essence, asking similar questions from that being asked by the accountant of a private firm. Rather, the same sort of question is being asked about a wider group of people – who comprise society – and is being asked more searchingly. Instead of asking whether the owners of the enterprise will become better off by the firm's engaging in one activity rather than another, the economist asks whether, by undertaking this project rather than not undertaking it, or by undertaking instead any of a number of alternative projects, net benefits will accrue to a society consisting of all the individuals who reside or work within the area in question.

Broadly speaking, for the more precise concept of revenue to the private firm, the economist substitutes the less precise yet meaningful concept of *social benefit*. For the costs of the private firm, the economist substitutes the concept of *opportunity cost* – the social value foregone when the resources in question are moved away from alternative economic activities into the specific project. For the profit of the firm, the economist substitutes the concept of *excess social benefit over cost* or, in short, net social benefit.

It may be mentioned in passing that it is just possible that within the accounting stance in question the economist is instructed to include benefits that accrue only to a specific group, say to those who are disabled, indigent or single parent families.

Irrespective, however, of the political desirability of such an objective, collecting such specific data alone may prove so costly as to raise questions about its feasibility.

Again, it may be held that there are difficulties in calculating the value of benefits that accrue to individuals, or to those members of a family who do not themselves make economic decisions. Yet the economist may reasonably accept as the value of such benefits those that may be calculated from the decisions on their behalf taken by others.

3 Returning to the notion of net social benefit, or excess social benefit over cost which is to be estimated by a CBA, it may be recognized as one referred to in the literature on welfare economics as a *potential* Pareto improvement or, earlier still, as a 'test of hypothetical compensation'. The project in question, that is, may be regarded as an economic improvement if its implementation produces an excess of benefits over losses for the community: one, that is, for which a costless redistribution of the benefits could make everyone affected by the project better off.[1]

More formally, however, the cost-benefit criterion to be adopted can be expressed in simple notation form as $\Sigma V_i > 0$, where V_1, V_2, ..., V_n are the net valuations of each of the n persons affected by the project, where a positive V valuation indicates a net benefit and a negative V valuation a net loss to the person. Clearly, if the aggregate valuations sum to a positive figure, the aggregate of benefits exceeds the losses, and a potential Pareto improvement is realized. (More precise measures of such valuations in the form of compensating variations will be introduced later.)

The above criterion is better regarded as necessary though perhaps not sufficient, inasmuch as it may have to meet some additional political requirement, say, that ΣV exceed a certain figure or else exceed a given benefit–cost ratio.

Another reason why our $\Sigma V > 0$ above may be deemed insufficient is that, as it stands, it makes no provision for the distributional impact of the project. Since a number of ways have been proposed for attaching distributional or other weights to the valuations, none of which, however, we find acceptable, we defer these proposals, and our objections to them, to Chapter 33.

In the meantime, although the criterion we have adopted (simply that the sum of all valuations be positive) is straightforward enough,[2] our difficulties begin once we start to trace all the repercussions and bring them into the calculations. These difficulties, which require extended treatment, are to be found chiefly in the concepts and measurement of consumer surplus and rent, in the distinctions between shadow prices and transfer payments, in evaluating a range of spillover effects, in the choice of investment criteria and in proposals for dealing with future uncertainty. They are dealt with in that order in the parts that follow.

4 Finally, the reader will appreciate that the techniques employed in CBA can be put to related uses. Public funds used for the financing of education or medical services, recreational facilities, the building of dams or irrigation works, the provision of tools, technical equipment and advice, and the establishing of industries or information centres are different ways in which the state can help others to help themselves. Of course, none of these ways might meet a strict cost-benefit criterion. Yet, some or all of them might be regarded by society as superior to direct cash transfers. The economist can then contribute to such decisions to the extent of selecting – within the limits of a number of seemingly equally appropriate ways of helping

these less privileged groups – those opportunities that yield the maximum social benefit per dollar transferred in such ways to these groups. Clearly, the discounted present value (DPV) of the maximum benefit per dollar invested in these socially approved ways may turn out to be less than a dollar. But such projects do have the merit of encouraging people to help themselves – an intangible benefit, no less important just because it cannot easily be quantified.

Similar calculations arise when transfers in kind are not the immediate goal, the beneficiaries being a mixed income group or the greater part of the community. The economist in such cases is required to restrict his estimates to the 'cost-effectiveness' of a number of alternative projects, any one of which is thought to be politically desirable. Should the government wish to discover the resource costs involved (though *not* the benefits) of maintaining alternative standards of water purity along different stretches of the Delaware Estuary, the economist would be able to provide cost estimates, leaving it to the community to decide, through the political process, just which standards to adopt. Another example of cost-effectiveness would be the comparison of the social costs of alternative airport sites, on the assumption – possibly unwarranted – that the airport site confers benefits that more than cover all the social costs.

Notes

1   Although this potential Pareto improvement involves no more than an exercise in positive economics, some economists would regard it as having normative implications independent of any political decision. Both the reasons that may be advanced for this view and those for rejecting it will be discussed in Chapter 33.
2   It has frequently been alleged that the Arrow Theorem invalidates the validity of welfare economics and, by extension, that also of CBA. This is a misunderstanding of the scope of that theorem. The intransitivity that may occur when majority decisions are used to rank alternative policies – an intransitivity easily demonstrated by an example, say, of three alternative policies, A, B, C, to be ranked by three persons (or groups) – can have political implications for countries where decisions are reached by majority rule. But in economics, where persons are assumed not merely to be able to rank alternatives, but also to assign money valuations to units of goods and bads, this sort of intransitivity does not arise. The possible contradiction in the so-called Kaldor–Hicks test, first pointed out by Scitovsky (1941), however, has no affinity with the above theorem. It arises rather from the relationship between the set of market prices and the distribution of the community's income, as explained in Appendix 2.

3   Framework to cost-benefit analysis

In CBA, it is not a final answer that is the most important. It is the process of getting to the answer that matters more. Essentially, an analyst must respond to seven questions in CBA:

1   Who should be the reference target group?
2   What are the benefits and costs?
3   How to measure these benefits and costs?
4   What should be the discount rate?
5   Are there equity considerations?
6   How do we deal with uncertainties?
7   What investment decision criteria do we use?

For each of these questions, an analyst must provide a transparent elucidation of his/her approach including clarity, choice of methodology and any other value judgements.

1 Who should be the reference target group?

It is clear that the reference target group must always be a society at large. CBA is not financial appraisal as it is much broader in its impact and its effects. Thus, where the concerns of the firm impact its shareholders and owners, CBA looks at how the proposed project policy or programmes affects society. But society can also encompass cities, provincial or state and country-level. It must be clear which society we are targeting. Who has standing is thus answered by a society that we are interested in. At times, we can even have a larger society to include, as in a global CBA where the society becomes an entire world. Where CBA extends beyond international borders such as a region, then benefits and costs will have to include impacts on societies outside one's own country. Thus, when for example China builds a dam upstream of the river, the impacts may be felt by residents outside China who are downstream users. If the target reference group is only on China, then the benefits of an otherwise worthwhile project may not be realized. Where the dam is concerned, increased electrical output and control of a river flooding and irrigation will only be attributed to those residents living in China. This is similar to accounting where the social cost of the dam is to be restricted to only impacts on residents within China. In CBA, this issue of who has standing is sometimes referred to as the accounting stance.

2 What are the benefits and costs?

This question requires a listing of all the effects and impacts of a proposed project. Naturally, any effect that produces a positive outcome such as savings in time, money, higher productivity, increased electricity generation, savings in lives, more output produced and so on will be counted as benefits. The converse will be counted as costs. However, care must be taken to not count some costs and benefits twice or more. Such issues are known as double counting problems. The government project that reduces time and costs for farmers to obtain water for their crops, all thing being equal, would result in a higher profit for the farmers. If, when estimating the benefit, an analyst were to add these savings in costs to the increased profit generated, then it will be a clear case of the double counting. Another issue has to do with transfer payments, where taxes are paid and return to the government by a designated firm in a sub-contracted project. The benefits of the project should not exclude the taxes paid. Similarly, where subsidies are given to a project, such subsidies should not be counted as benefits of the project. Both taxes and subsidies are transfer payments and thus in accounting for each benefit and cost, one must be cautious to distinguish what are the real benefits and costs from transfers. However, where taxes are paid to a foreign country, when doing a CBA, where the standing is residents of one's own country, such taxes are to be counted as costs. Similarly, where subsidies are received from the foreign country, then these contributions are to be counted as benefits.

3 How to measure these benefits and costs?

Once benefits and costs are systematically identified and double accounting, transfer payments issues are addressed, the next question is how to put a monetary value to such benefits and costs. This question in turn requires answers to several following questions. Are market prices readily available? If market prices exist, to what extent do they reflect true social values? If market prices do not exist, can we create surrogate prices? At times, there are monopoly or oligopolistic elements in the market that make market prices questionable. There are also negative externalities, such as pollution, which market prices do not fully account for. Subsidized fuel prices also need to be adjusted to reflect the true price of the fuel. Where market prices do not exist, this is a challenge for CBA as it would require methods to estimate people's willingness to pay for such non-market goods. The willingness to pay is one indicator, there is also the willingness to accept losses of non-market goods. Such non-market goods include peace and quietude, aesthetics, air and water quality, time costs and lives saved. Fortunately, there are many non-market techniques that can be used by analysts in valuing non-market goods.

4 What should be the discount rate?

Because benefits and costs are accrued over time and decisions, however, need to be made today, such benefits and costs will have to be discounted. The $100 benefit in the future is not $100 today. While the process of discounting is straightforward, the choice of discount rate is not. There are several schools of thought on the choice of the discount rate and much controversial discussion has been made in the literature. There are essentially two schools of thought, one is the idea that because funds invested into the public sector can also be used for the private sector, the returns to a public sector project should not be any lower than the returns from the private sector. This Chicago school of thought measures the opportunity cost of the funds used and often the choice of the discount rate reflects prevailing market interest rates. But because private sector interest rates tend to be short-run, market interest rates tend to be higher and because public sector investments tend to take a longer time horizon and also encompass more in society, there is a search for a discount rate that reflects society's future trade-offs between future and present consumption.

The social time preference rate is another choice of the discount rate. A combination of private and public sectors' concern can be used to calculate the hybrid discount rate. Such hybrid rate will take into account where the funds of the public sector come from such as whether the funds will be raised through taxes and hence displace present consumption now or from the issue of bonds which displaces private sector investments. But such hybrid rates are difficult to estimate. Another approach which is much more practical is to look at how governments made investment decisions in the past. Thus if 5–7 per cent discount rate has been used, then the present choice of discount rate should be within the same range.

5 Are there equity considerations?

Some public sector projects may impact equity and income distribution. Thus, adjustments to benefits and costs must be made because the same $1 may not be the same for a rich and a poor person. In CBA a set of weights are usually used to either increase or decrease the estimation of benefits and costs. There are of course some controversies in the use of weights. This will be discussed in a later chapter.

6 How do we deal with uncertainties?

Because benefits and costs are accrued in the long-run, the longer the time, the estimation of costs and benefits may need to be adjusted. Global warming implications for example may distort benefits and costs in the far future. Methods to account for uncertainty are often used. Such methods often involve expected value calculations, inferring from historical precedence and even some heuristic methods.

7 What investment decision criteria do we use?

The choice of investment decision criteria includes net present value, internal rate of return, benefit–cost ratio and net terminal value. By far, the net present value is the most easily understood investment decision criterion as it uses quantum of benefits over costs unlike the other criteria. Each of these investment decision criteria will be discussed in full in later chapters.

8   CBA is a rational, logical process which if done properly provides an asset to informed decision making. The above seven questions must be answered in a systematic way. Criticisms of CBA that it has been vague, elusive and manipulative are often exaggerated. This is simply because of the process which requires answering the seven questions above. Should an analyst try to be manipulative for

example, he/she would find it futile because readers could easily see how the seven questions are answered. Finally, where the choice of discount rates, investment decision criteria, methods to value non-market goods, set of weights to be used and methods of accounting of uncertainties is challenging, the use of sensitivity analysis where several alternative numbers/methods are evaluated separately can often be used.

In the final report, the options are compared but it is to be noted that CBA is only one approach to a normative question of allocative efficiency in the use of scarce resources. But CBA does provide a rigorous framework. It is not the job of a cost-benefit analyst to make decisions for the government because the government may have other holistic considerations beyond CBA.

For each of these questions, separate chapters are dedicated to discuss in full.

Part II

Basic concepts of benefits and costs

4 Measurements of consumer surplus

1 Notwithstanding some ill-considered judgements about the uses of consumer surplus by some highly regarded economists some three score years ago,[1,2] it is a concept so crucial to allocative economics generally, and CBA in particular, that there is everything to be said for clarifying the concept itself and the ways it can be measured.

Thus, if a man is willing to pay as much as $25 for a litre of cider, the economist has to concede that it is worth no less to him than $25. If, however, he buys that litre at $15, he is obviously better off than if he had indeed to pay the $25 that he is willing to pay. And it makes sense to say that, when he buys the litre of cider at $15, which is $10 less than the $25 he is willing to pay, he makes a saving of $10 which may properly be regarded as a measure of his gain – that is, of his consumer surplus.

Again, if we now suppose that, at the price of $15, the man buys 10 litres of cider each month, and the price is then lowered to $10 a litre, there is a cost-saving of $5 on each of the 10 litres he habitually bought. Thus, in the limiting case in which he continues to buy only 10 litres at the lower price, he will find himself with an additional sum of $50 (10 × $5) each month, which he can spend on other goods. Such an example alone is enough to vindicate the concept of consumer surplus. There can, however, be arguments about how exactly to measure it.

2 Let us put these arguments aside for the present and adopt in this and the following two chapters a simple common-sense definition of consumer surplus, traceable to the French engineer Dupuit (1844): the consumer surplus of a person is measured by the most he would pay for a thing less the amount he actually pays for it.

Let us now consider a single person's demand curve for a good x. In the ordinary way, we interpret this curve as a locus of the maximum amount of x that the person will want to buy at any given price. This demand curve, however, may just as well be interpreted differently – as the most the person will pay for each successive unit of x. If the good x is a litre of milk, we can ask what is the most the person will pay for one litre of milk per week: then, what is the most he will pay for a second litre and so on, as depicted in Figure 4.1 for the first 10 litres.

These successive amounts of money, which we can speak of as marginal valuations, are plotted in the figure as the heights of successive columns. If the price of a litre of milk is equal to P, say 20 cents, then the person makes a gain or surplus on each successive litre of milk bought per week up to and including the seventh

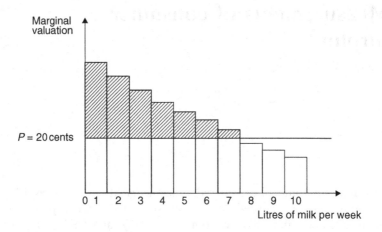

Figure 4.1

litre. He does not buy an eighth litre, since it's worth to him is less than the price he would have to pay for it. Thus, the figure illustrates the case in which the man makes the largest consumer surplus by buying 7 litres of milk at 20 cents, so spending $1.40 per week on milk. The area contained in the shaded parts of the columns above the price line is a sum of money equal to the person's consumer surplus.

3   Once perfect divisibility is assumed, the stepped outline of the columns gives way to a smooth demand curve. From a point on the vertical or price axis the horizontal distance to the curve measures the maximum amount of the good the person will buy at that price. The market demand curve, being a horizontal summation of all the individual demand curves, can be regarded as the marginal valuation curve for society. For example, the height QR in Figure 4.2, corresponding to output OQ, gives the maximum value some person in society is willing to pay for the Qth unit of the good – which, for that person, may be the first, second or nth unit of the good bought. But to each of the total number of units purchased, which total is measured as a distance along the quantity axis, there corresponds some individual's maximum valuation. The whole area under the demand curve, therefore, corresponds to society's maximum valuation for the quantity in question. If, say, OQ is bought, the maximum worth of OQ units to society is given by the trapezoid area $ODRQ$. Now the quantity OQ is bought by the market at price OP. Total expenditure by the buyers is, therefore, represented by the area $OPRQ$ (price OP times quantity OQ). Subtracting from the maximum worth of buyers ($ODRQ$) what they have to pay ($OPRQ$) leaves us with a total consumers' surplus equal to triangle DRP.

If an entirely new good x is introduced into the economy and is made available to all and sundry free of charge, the area under the resulting demand curve, ODE (given that prices of all other goods are unaffected), is a good enough measure of the gain to the community in its capacity as consumer. The services provided by a new bridge or a new park would be familiar examples. Again, however, if a price OP for the service is introduced, the amount OQ will be bought, leaving the

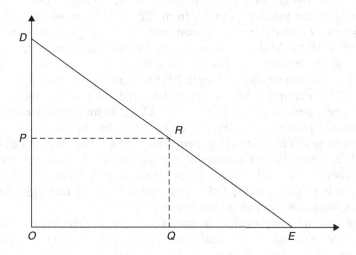

Figure 4.2

triangular area *PDR* in Figure 4.2 as the consumer surplus. Estimates of consumer surplus, it need hardly be said, are to be entered as benefits in all cost-benefit calculations. Alternatively, it represents a welfare gain from consumption.

4 Any investment with the object of reducing the cost of a product or service is deemed to confer a benefit on the community, which benefit is often referred to as a 'cost-difference' or a 'cost-saving'. The benefit of a new motorway or flyover is estimated by reference to the expected savings in time and in the cost of fuel by all motorists who will make use of the new road or flyover. As already indicated, however, the concept of cost-saving is derived directly from the concept of consumer surplus, as shown in Figure 4.3. Thus, prior to the introduction of, say, the new flyover in question, the consumer surplus from using this particular route (being the maximum sum motorists are willing to pay above the amount they currently spend on

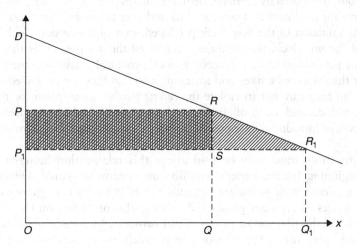

Figure 4.3

the journey – an average of OP per journey) is the triangle PDR. If the flyover halves the cost of the journey to them, from OP to OP_1, at which lower cost the number of journeys undertaken is increased from OQ to OQ_1, the consumer surplus increases from PDR to P_1DR_1, an increase equal to the shaded strip PP_1R_1R.

This increase in consumer surplus can be split up into two parts. There is, first, the cost-saving component, the rectangle PP_1SR, which is calculated as the savings per journey, PP_1, multiplied by the original number of journeys made, OQ. The other component, represented by the triangle SRR_1, is the consumer surplus made on the additional journeys undertaken, QQ_1, either by the same motorists or by additional motorists. The cost-saving item that enters a cost-benefit calculation is, as indicated, no more than a portion of the increment of consumer surplus from a fall in the cost of the good. Since it takes no account of the additional goods that will be bought in response to the fall in cost, the cost-saving rectangle alone can be accepted as a *minimum* estimate of the benefit.

We might call this explanation a casual account of the matter, though not a misleading one. Nothing need be said about *utility*, as we are not going to translate our money magnitudes into utility terms: the area under the market demand curve, that is, does not become translated into a sum of individual utilities, but remains simply as a sum of their valuations. The extent of the collective improvement from the introduction of a good is, then, expressed in terms of a sum of money which is measured by a triangle of consumer surplus, such as PDR in Figure 4.2. Its interpretation is simply the maximum amount of money the group as a whole would offer in order to be able to buy OQ of this new good at price P. The extent of the collective improvement from a reduction in its price, however, is expressed as an increment of consumer surplus, as for example the strip PP_1R_1R in Figure 4.3. The strip can be interpreted as the maximum amount of money the group as a whole would offer in order to have the price reduced from OP to OP_1.

5   So far, the consumer surplus analysis has had reference to the demand for a final good, say a clock, although it can also be extended to the derived demand for some input or intermediate good, such as the steel that is used in the manufacture of clocks.

The appropriate consumer surplus measure for steel, or steel of a particular kind, is obtained from the correctly *derived* demand curves for steel. Thus, the short-run demand curve for steel derived from the clock industry is obtained by subtracting from the marginal valuation of the first clock produced, that of the second clock and so on until that of the nth clock, the combined cost of all the a inputs other than steel that enter into the production of each successive clock produced – assuming the prices of all inputs other than steel to be fixed and assuming also that they are combined efficiently.[3] We are also to take care not to violate the *ceteris paribus assumption* for the demand curves for steel derived from all other steel-using goods, which requires that such demand curves be introduced in sequence, as will be explained in the following chapter.

6   Something more must now be said about this relationship between price and quantity. Beginning from a general equilibrium system, we could deduce that the amount of a good x that is bought depends not only on its own price but, in general, on the prices of all other goods and factors; also on tastes, on technical knowledge and on the distribution of resource endowments. In statistical estimates of the price demand curve for x, the relationship is much more restricted. We might, for

example, try to gather enough data so as to derive a specific equation from the relationship $X = F(P_x, P_y, P_z, M)$, where X is the maximum amount of good x demanded, P_x, P_y, P_z are the prices respectively of the goods x, y and z, and M is the aggregate real income. Goods y and z could be chosen as being close and important substitutes for x, or else y could be a close substitute and z a close complement of x, the relative prices of all other goods being ignored. Sometimes the price of one or more factors is to be included in the function. If, for example, the good x is taken as being farm tractors, the income of the farm population would obviously be a significant variable in the demand for tractors. In any statistical estimate of the price–demand curve for x, the *ceteris paribus* clause will operate to hold constant only those variables, other than P_x, that are included in function F. All those variables that are not included in function F – an almost unlimited number of goods and factor prices – are assumed, provisionally at least, to be of negligible importance.

In CBA, however, the emphasis in the *ceteris paribus* clause of the market demand curve for good x is on the constancy of the *prices* of goods closely related to good x. So although the *amounts* bought of all the other goods in the economy, including the amounts of closely related goods y and z, are likely to alter in response to a change in the price of good x, the measure of the consumer surplus arising from the change in the price of x is not thereby affected.[4] Only if, for any reason, alterations in the *prices* of related goods y and z take place following a fall or a rise in the price of good x does the measure of consumer surplus from the initial change in the price of x have to be qualified, as we shall see in the next chapter.

7   This injunction to ignore consequent shifts in the *ceteris paribus* demand curves for other goods does not, however, preclude an interpretation of the resulting areas under such demand curves. Assuming provisionally constant costs in the production of all goods in the economy, a fall in the price of x will cause a shift to the left of the *ceteris paribus* demand curve for good y, which is, we assume, an important substitute for x. The now smaller area under this demand curve for y is the consumer surplus enjoyed from the availability of y, at the unchanged price of y, when the price of x is lower than before. This smaller area of consumer surplus for y accords with common sense, for with the fall in the price of its close substitute x, the existing level of welfare will depend less on good y than before. Thus, if y were now to be totally withdrawn from the market, the welfare loss suffered by society would be smaller, simply because the substitute x has become available at a lower price than before.

To illustrate, in Figures 4.4 and 4.5, the initial *ceteris paribus* demand curve for each good is the solid line. D_xE_x is the demand curve for x (when the price of good y is held constant at p_y); D_yE_y is the demand curve for y (when the price of good x is held constant at p_{x_1}). If now, as a result of some improved method of production, the price of x falls from p_{x_1} to p_{x_2}, the demand curve for y falls from D_yE_y to $D'_yE'_y$, as shown in Figure 4.5. At the unchanged price p_y, the smaller quantity of y (OB) is demanded instead of the quantity OC that was demanded before the fall in the price of x.

With a lower price of x, consumers are obviously better off. They would, of course, be better off even if they had to buy exactly the same amounts of x and y as they did before the fall in the price of x. But they further improve their welfare by buying more of x and buying less of y. Once they have made these changes in their purchases of x and y, how do we interpret these consumer surpluses? First, the measure of the gain

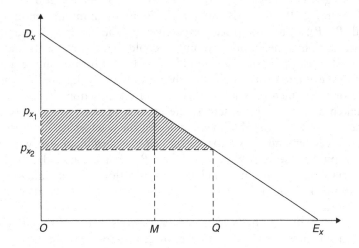

Figure 4.4

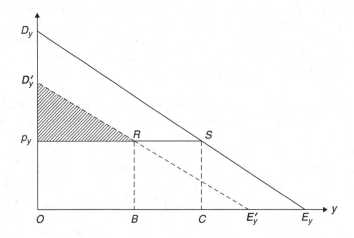

Figure 4.5

in consumers' surplus is represented wholly by the shaded strip in Figure 4.4 between the original price p_{x_1} and the new price p_{x_2}. Provided all other goods prices remain unchanged – and in particular that of the close substitute y – this shaded strip measures the most that consumers will pay to have the reduction in the price of x.

Second, the shaded triangle shown in Figure 4.5 represents the consumer surplus in having a price p_y when the price of x is now p_{x_2}. (This triangle is the difference between the most they would pay for OB of $y\left(OD_y'RB\right)$ when x is priced at p_{x_2} and what they have to pay for OB of y (OP_yRB).

Note particularly the interpretation of this reduced triangle of consumer surplus – that where the demand curve for y shifts inward in response to a fall in the price of x. The reduction of the *initial* area of consumer surplus p_yD_yS (corresponding to the original price of x, p_{x_1}) to this smaller area of consumer surplus $p_y D'_y$ R (corresponding to the lower price of x, p_{x_2}) – a reduction in area equal to $D'_y D_y$ SR – *is* not to be regarded as a loss of consumer surplus consequent upon the fall in the price of x from p_{x_1} to p_{x_2}. This reduction in area is simply the consequence of consumers' bettering themselves by switching from good y to the new lower-priced good x. Provided supply prices are constant, and we assume they are, the *ceteris paribus* conditions are met, and the partial analysis depicts the consumers' gains wholly within the area of the demand curve of the good, the price of which has fallen – irrespective, that is, of the resulting magnitude and direction of the shifts in demand for all other goods in the economy.

It follows that, if we are focusing our attention on the consumer surplus of the good x, and it appears to increase in response to a rise in the price of the substitute good y, this larger area under the demand curve for x is to be interpreted as the maximum amount of money that people are now willing to pay for having x available at its unchanged price when all other prices are given and the price of the substitute good y is higher.

8   No exception to this analysis occurs if the rise in the price of a good y, or of any other good related to x, is a result of direct government intervention. If the government levies an excise tax on y or adopts a policy of withdrawing y from the market, the economist is always at liberty to point out the lack of economic justification for such policies, and the consequences that are likely to follow from their implementation. But assuming these policies are to prevail over the relevant time period, he has no choice but to measure the changes in the consumer surpluses of good x in the usual way.

Only if the economist is engaged in a cost-benefit study that encompasses a number of closely related goods is he in a position to pronounce on actions to change other relevant prices from some generally acceptable pattern, say from that corresponding to marginal social costs. A transport economist, for example, would wish to point out that the apparent increase in the consumer surplus of private traffic, which *seems* to warrant investment in road-widening schemes, is the result simply of a reduction in the availability of public transport, a reduction that is itself the result of traffic congestion on existing roads. The imposition of a toll on traffic designed to produce an *optimal* flow of vehicles on the existing road will, of itself, also increase the efficiency along it of public transport. Moreover, with such a toll in place, the resulting consumer surplus may no longer warrant investment in road-widening. Such a solution is clearly the more efficient, and that which, in the circumstances, the economist will propose.[5] In contrast, if the economist is required to advise on road-widening schemes but is allowed no control whatsoever on the existing volume of private traffic (which may well be greatly in excess of an optimal flow), he has no choice but to accept such political constraints and to calculate the benefits of a road-widening scheme under the existing conditions.

9   We have stated that, in the construction of the demand curve for a good x, the comprehensive *ceteris paribus* pound contains all other product prices, all factor prices, tastes, technology and resource endowments. Since changes in resource endowments can imply changes in distribution or in the size of population, and changes in technology can imply changes in real income per capita, the *ceteris paribus* clause can be expressed in an alternative form that requires constancy of product prices, population, per capita income, distribution and tastes. We shall now go

on to consider the treatment of consumer surplus when each of these items is no longer held constant, beginning in the next chapter with the treatment of consumer surplus when the prices of related goods are altered.

Notes

1 There have been critiques based on inconsistency, intransitivity and multiplicity. An appraisal of the main critiques can be found in Mishan (1977a).
2 For instance, Little (1957) stated that it was no more than 'a theoretical toy' (p. 180) and, according to Samuelson (1963), 'The subject is of historical and doctrinal interest with a limited amount of appeal as a purely mathematical puzzle' (p. 195). This latter remark could be said with some truth about quite a number of topics in contemporary economics, but it certainly cannot be accepted as sound judgement of the consumer surplus concept. Without it, how can the economist rationalize the free use of parks, bridges or roads, or the use of two-part tariffs?
3 The first-order conditions for productive efficiency require that input rates of substitution be inverse to the ratio of input prices. The elasticity of the derived demand for an intermediate good such as steel varies *inter alia* with the elasticity of substitution between this intermediate good and others, and also with the elasticity of the demand for the final goods using the intermediate good.
4 If the demand curve for x has an elasticity greater than unity along the relevant range, the expenditure on all other goods taken together will fall, and (assuming full employment) some of the factors released will move into the production of good x, the converse being true if the elasticity of demand for x is below unity.

   In the limiting case of unity elasticity of the demand for x, there will be no change in the total cost of producing the additional amount of x and no change in the total expenditure on good x. Consequently, there is no change in the total expenditure on all other goods taken together.
5 This analysis is used by Mishan (1967a) in connection with the misuse of consumer surplus in road-building proposals.

5 Consumer surplus when several prices change

1 This chapter is a simple exercise in partial equilibrium analysis: in the adding and subtracting of consumer surpluses arising from sequential or simultaneous changes in the prices of two or more related goods.

2 Hicks (1956) has shown how the consumer surplus on two or more substitute goods, say gas and electricity, that are introduced simultaneously can be measured. Suppose that gas is introduced at a given price p_g into an area that has no electricity. The shaded triangle of Figure 5.1 can be taken as a measure of the resulting consumer surplus. If, following this event, electricity is introduced at a price p_e, the demand curve for electricity $D_e E_e$, is obviously smaller when gas is available at a fixed price p_g than it would be in the absence of gas, for the consumers already derive much benefit from gas, and the introduction of a fairly close substitute is not so great a boon as it would be if, instead, there had been no gas in the first place. The additional gain to consumers from introducing electricity into a gas-using area is given by the shaded triangle in Figure 5.2. The sum of these two triangles together measures the consumer surplus from providing both gas and electricity at prices p_g and p_e, respectively.

Should the economist elect to measure the simultaneous introduction of gas and electricity using the same sequential device but in the reverse order (that is, first measuring the consumer surplus for introducing electricity when gas is assumed to be unavailable, and then measuring the consumer surplus for gas on the assumption that electricity is already available), the sum of these two component surpluses should, theoretically, be exactly the same.

This method of adding consumer surpluses can, of course, be extended to three or more goods, and is just as valid if the goods in question are complements rather than substitutes. If, for example, gas and electricity were complements – as they would be if the only use of electricity were the heating of electric pokers for lighting gas fires – a fall in the price of gas would raise the demand curve for electricity.

The analysis is, of course, symmetrical for simultaneous *withdrawal* of two or more goods. Thus, assuming again that gas and electricity are close substitutes, if electricity is first withdrawn from the market while gas remains as readily available at its old price p_g the loss of consumer surplus is given by the shaded triangle in Figure 5.2. Since gas is a substitute, the demand curve for gas shifts to the right following the withdrawal of electricity. The resulting or final consumer surplus for gas then becomes the shaded triangle in Figure 5.1, and is the measure of the loss sustained if gas, previously available at p_g, is also withdrawn from the market.

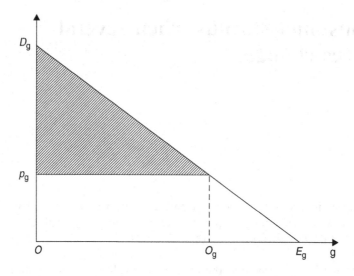

Figure 5.1

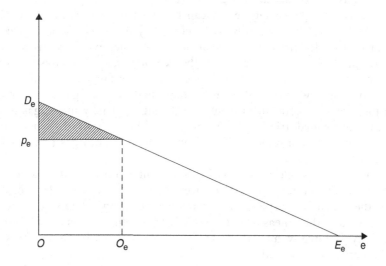

Figure 5.2

3   The further extension of the method to simultaneous *price* changes poses no problems. Suppose once more that electricity and gas are close substitutes and that the prices of both rise. The loss of consumer surplus arising from the rise in the price of gas from p_{g_1} to p_{g_2}, the price of electricity being (provisionally) unchanged, is shown by the shaded strip in Figure 5.3. As a direct result of the rise in the price of gas, the demand curve for electricity now moves outward from $D_e E_e$ to $D_e' E_e'$ in Figure 5.4. If, following this adjustment, the price of electricity rises from p_{e_1} to p_{e_2}, the further loss of consumer surplus is given by the shaded area in Figure 5.4. It is hardly surprising, after all, that the loss of consumer surplus from a rise in the

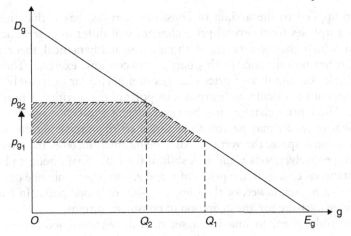

Figure 5.3

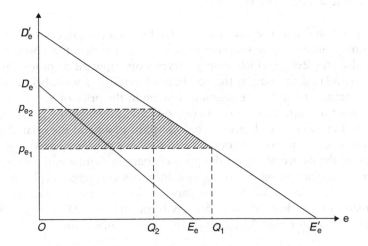

Figure 5.4

price of electricity becomes greater when the price of its substitute good has become higher. The less available or the more expensive substitute goods are, the more it matters if the price of the good in question rises, and vice versa.

If, instead, gas and electricity happen to be complementary goods, a rise in the price of gas causes an inward shift of the demand curve for electricity. The additional loss of consumer surplus of any concomitant rise in the price of electricity is then smaller than if the price of gas had not risen in the first place. This also makes good sense, as an initial rise in the price of gas makes electricity *less* useful when it is complementary to gas – and not more useful as it will be when it is a substitute for gas.

4   The reader can soon convince himself that the analysis is symmetric for a sequential or simultaneous fall in the prices of two or more goods. A brief caveat is called for in this context because of the much-touted 'path-dependence' problem

which, when applied to the adding of consumer surplus, has it that the aggregate of consumer surpluses from several price changes will differ in general according to the order in which they are taken. Although the mathematical theorem is itself a valid one, it has no relevance to this particular economic exercise. The economist is obliged to take the number of price changes in a particular order only because he finds it convenient for calculation purposes to portray them within a partial equilibrium setting. These price changes are, however, deemed to occur simultaneously.

The imaginative reader may be able to picture a set of concave indifference surfaces in three-dimensional space, the vertical axis y being (real) income, the two horizontal axes being, respectively, goods x and z. A shift of the individual's budget plane, arising from a simultaneous change in the prices of x and z, will touch only one of the indifference surfaces – a higher, lower, or the same one – at only one point. In consequence, there is a unique measure for any definition of consumer surplus.[1]

Were it possible, then, to imagine a set of n-dimensional indifference surfaces, a simultaneous change in any or all of the goods prices, represented now by a change in the n-dimensional plane, would again reveal a unique equilibrium and, therefore, a unique consumer surplus.

5   For expositional purposes, we have so far held supply prices of all goods constant. By now removing this simplification, we can see that the above analysis is applicable also to cases in which supply curves slope upward or downward. For, if any good y is related to good x, the equilibrium price of y will also be affected if, in the first instance, there is an exogenous change in the price of x.

Let us restrict our attention to the two-good case, in which the good that has an exogenous fall in price, say electricity, has constant costs and the related good, say gas, which is a substitute for electricity, does not have constant costs.

Again, using the device of taking the price changes in sequence, the exogenous fall in the price of electricity from p_{e_1} to p_{e_2} first increases consumer surplus in electricity by the shaded area in Figure 5.5. But this fall in the price of electricity induces a leftward shift of the demand curve for gas from DD to $D'D'$ in Figure 5.6. If we assume first that, as in Figure 5.6, gas has an upward-sloping supply curve, there will

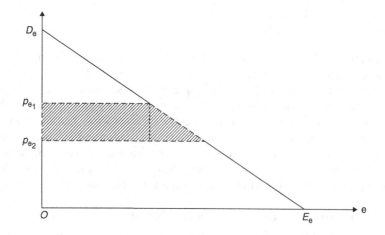

Figure 5.5

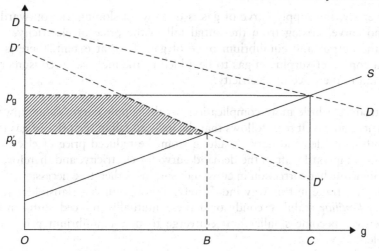

Figure 5.6

be a fall in the equilibrium price of gas from p_g to p_g'. In consequence, there will also be a small leftward shift in the downward curve for electricity which, however, we provisionally ignore.

The total increment of welfare arising from the initial fall in the price of electricity *plus* the further induced fall in the equilibrium price of gas is calculated by adding the shaded strip in Figure 5.6 to the shaded strip in Figure 5.5. The interpretation of this procedure is straightforward enough.

First, the shaded strip in Figure 5.5 represents the increment of consumer surplus arising from the fall in the price of electricity *with the price of gas at* p_g. Second, the shaded strip in Figure 5.6 represents the further increment of consumer surplus for a fall in the equilibrium price of gas from p_g to p_g' *with the price of electricity remaining at* p_{e_2}. The sum of these two areas is then a measure of the amount that consumers are willing to pay for reducing the price of electricity from p_{e_1} to p_{e_2} when, as a result, the price of gas to them will also fall from p_g to p_g'. An extension of the analysis reveals that if gas has, instead, a *downward*-sloping supply curve, the leftward shift in its demand curve which is associated with the fall in the price of electricity results in a higher equilibrium price for gas and therefore entails the loss of a strip of consumer surplus – consequently a *subtraction* of that strip from the shaded area in Figure 5.5. The resulting difference between the two areas is then a measure of the amount consumers are willing to pay when the price of electricity falls from p_{e_1} to p_{e_2} and, as a result, the price of gas is increased.[2]

Symmetrical reasoning applies also to goods that are complements. If, for example, gas were now complementary with electricity, a fall in the price of electricity would cause an *outward* shift in the demand curve for gas. First, assume the supply curve of gas to be upward sloping. The outward shift in its demand curve increases the equilibrium output and price of gas. This rise in the price of gas entails a consumer loss which must be subtracted from the consumer gain arising from the initial fall in the price of electricity.

If, conversely, the supply curve of gas is downward sloping, the outward shift in its demand curve, arising from the initial fall in the price of electricity, results in a fall in the output and equilibrium price of gas. To that extent, there is now an additional consumer surplus in gas to be added to the increase in consumer surplus from the fall in the price of electricity.

6   To introduce a little more complication, let the supply curves slope upward both for electricity and gas. It now follows that the induced fall in the price of gas (from the inward shift of its demand curve resulting from the reduced price of electricity) will itself induce an inward shift in the demand curve for electricity, and therefore a *fall* in its price. Some further correction in consumer surplus is therefore necessary.

One may continue in this way indefinitely, although under plausible assumptions (related to *familiar* stability conditions) these mutually induced shifts in the two demand curves become smaller and converge to new equilibrium prices for both gas and electricity.

However, since the errors in estimating the relevant demand curves – in the above example, the initial demand curve for electricity and the inwardly shifted demand curve for gas, following a fall in the price of electricity – are likely to be large enough to swamp the refinements from further mutually induced shifts in the demand curves, some attempted corrections are best ignored. They would be worthwhile only if the initial price change was unusually large.

Notes

1 Although, as affirmed in the text, the theorem is without application to the simultaneous change in a number of goods prices, it is of passing interest to remark that the necessary and sufficient condition for path *in*dependence with respect to any pair of prices pi and pj is that $\partial qj/\partial pi = \partial qi/\partial pj$ (where qi and qj are the corresponding quantities), a condition that is explicit in the Hicksian system (see Hicks, 1939: Appendix).
2 The measure of simultaneous changes, whether of prices or availabilities, can have particular importance when measuring the community's loss or benefit from alterations in the amounts of collective goods or bads. To illustrate with a case of related sources of dis-amenity, say two chief sources of noise in a given area, that from cars and that from aircraft.

   For each source of noise, we have an *individual*'s downward-sloping marginal valuation curve which measures the maximum sum he would pay to be rid of successive units of noise, beginning with some almost unbearable volume of noise, given – and this is critical – the existing large volume of noise from the other source.

   With this sort of *ceteris paribus*, consider the marginal valuation curve for reducing car noise. Since there is not that much benefit to the individual from reducing car noise while aircraft noise continues at its high level, such a marginal valuation curve would not be very high. The same is true of the marginal valuation curve for reductions in aircraft noise.

   Obviously, the benefit to the individual of a simultaneous reduction in the noise of both would be considerable: certainly more than the sum of the valuation as measured by the areas under the two *ceteris paribus* marginal valuation curves.

   The correct measure of the benefit of removing both sources of noise is derived by adding to the benefit (or consumer surplus) as measured under the marginal valuation curve for car-noise riddance, *given the existing high volume of aircraft noise*, the subsequent benefit (or consumer surplus) as measured by the area under the now much higher marginal valuation curve for aircraft-noise reduction. This latter curve is now much higher, simply because the relevant *ceteris paribus* contains the information that all car noise has been removed. Consequently, removal of aircraft noise now does make a real difference to the individual's amenity.

6 Consumer surplus when other things change

1   We now consider the treatment and interpretation of consumer surplus when there are changes in population size and in per capita real income, when enterprises producing similar goods already exist and when there are changes in people's taste over time.

2   When estimating the demand curves over the future for goods to be provided by new investment projects we must make allowance for the growth in aggregate real income and its distribution.

Ignoring considerations of military or political power, a rise in population without any rise in real per capita income is not generally thought of today as conferring an increase in social welfare. Nonetheless, the resulting rise in demand for goods does operate to increase consumer surplus as defined and, consequently, may eventually make economically feasible particular projects that would, in the absence of population growth, remain economically unfeasible.

In fact, population growth and growth of per capita real income are the two components of aggregate economic growth and, together, contribute over time to the apparent growth of social benefits arising from any investment project that is currently undertaken. Clearly, the expectations of such growth-induced benefits must be taken into account by the economist, who is required to declare in advance the average rate or future pattern of aggregate economic growth on which his calculations are to be predicated. Having adopted some acceptable pattern over time of aggregate economic growth, he must then determine the way in which this economic growth will affect the magnitude of the benefits conferred by the goods that are to be produced by the investment project(s) under examination.

For example, in the *absence* of any expected growth in the economy, a hypothetical investment of 100 this year is expected to yield an annual stream of real benefits of 10, 10, 10, ..., 10, ignoring the question of uncertainty. Allowing for an annual average growth rate of aggregate real income of 4 per cent, and assuming an income elasticity of unity for the goods produced by this investment, it becomes necessary to revise the annual stream of benefits to something like 10.4, 10.8, ..., $10 (1.04)^n$, the nth year being the terminal year. Indeed, as indicated, the investment may prove to be economically unacceptable in the absence of such a rate of growth of aggregate demand.

This appears to be straightforward enough wherever a unique project is at issue such as a tunnel under the Severn River, a bridge over the Channel or a new national park. For such projects will not, over the foreseeable future, be 'threatened' by rival projects of a like nature. In such cases, growth in population alone (ignoring, that is, any increase in per capita income) will act to increase the demand for the services of such projects. The value of such services will grow, then, simply because the same service is being provided to more people. The bridge or tunnel or national park will accommodate an increasing number of travellers or visitors per annum – up to some point without an increase in current costs of upkeep.[1]

As for growth in per capita income in the absence of population growth, the increase in the usage of such newly created assets is less certain. For example, it may be the case that very few people will demand more park visits in response to a continuing rise in their incomes. Nevertheless, even if a person pays no more visits to a national park as he becomes richer, the value he places on the same number of visits will 'normally' – that is, if his income (or welfare) effect is positive – increase over time. This is not because his annual visits to the national park necessarily provide him with more utility as he becomes richer, but simply because the maximum sum he is prepared to pay for the same number of visits is higher when his real income is higher. Making our calculations on the basis of constant money prices over time, any rise in the value of benefits over time for all such reasons must be entered into the calculations.

3   Consider now the situation when one or more enterprises are similar to that being contemplated. The demand for the goods from, and the returns to, the existing enterprise(s) will be diminished by the introduction of the project in question. In what way should we allow for this?

Suppose the issue is that of building a bridge A now, bearing in mind that another such bridge B may be built a few years hence. If this later bridge B is built in response only to the growth in traffic – itself a result of the growth in population and in per capita real income – no problem arises. But if bridge B is to some extent competitive with the original bridge A, two questions must be faced: first, whether bridge A should be built at all if it is expected that a competitive, and possibly superior, bridge B will be built at a later date. Second, if it does appear economically feasible to build bridge A today, notwithstanding the later introduction of bridge B, when should bridge B be introduced?

Concerning the first question, the alternatives to be considered are those of introducing bridge A today and of building bridge B at some later date, where the sizes or construction of the two bridges can be varied, as can also the date at which the chosen bridge B is to be introduced. If the number of discrete variations in the timing and the size of the bridges is large, so also will be the alternative combinations, each such combination being regarded as a distinct and separate investment project. The object of the exercise – obviously, a somewhat tedious and time–consuming business – is to choose that combination which, on a net benefit criterion, is ranked above all others.

As for the second question, once bridge A is already in existence, the building of bridge B can be justified only when the benefits over time from building it – as measured by the expected consumer surplus of its users – exceed its capital costs. And it does not matter whether the traffic expected to make use of the new bridge B is so great as to leave bridge A devoid of traffic. In economics, bygones are bygones. Bridge A has already been built; the capital sunk into its construction is irrecoverable. What matters now is whether the variable costs of bridge A could still be covered, otherwise bridge A should close. We need compare only the capital cost of building a new bridge B with the expected benefits over time, given that bridge A is still available.

The demand schedule for the use of bridge B is that which provides us with a measure of the community's benefit to be reaped by incurring the required capital expenditure. The area under the relevant demand curve that is above the variable cost of maintaining the bridge can be taken as a measure of the consumer surplus conferred by bridge B – being interpreted as the maximum sum above this variable cost that users of the bridge are ready to pay when they already have bridge A at their disposal.

4 Let us now move on to consider shifts in demand, and therefore of consumer surpluses, when there is a movement over time from one area to another, say from London to the Brighton area. Clearly, an increase in the investment in social capital, especially in public utilities, *will* be required in the Brighton area at the same time as existing social capital in London falls into disuse. If we suppose that, prior to the exodus, the amount of social capital was just right in both places, a prospective shortage of 100,000 houses in Brighton would be matched by a prospective vacancy of 100,000 houses in London. There would also be a need to extend schools, build roads, invest more in transport, electricity, gas, water and telephones, and provide additional distributional services in Brighton, all of which would require additional capital, while the equivalent capital investment in London would become superfluous. Clearly, it would have been more economical of society's scarce resources if the desire to move to Brighton had not occurred, for then the existing social capital stock would have sufficed.

But, once this change has occurred, the economist is concerned only with ways of meeting it efficiently.

Once social capital is irretrievably sunk in the London area, nothing can be done about it. In the light of existing demands, unwanted capital facilities become useless. All that matters now is the economic feasibility of building a new social capital in Brighton, where it is wanted. We must, therefore, compare only the additional capital outlays in Brighton with the magnitude of the expected benefits over the future as measured by the demand schedules for the extra services in question.

However, what the migrants into the Brighton area are willing to pay for the services will depend, among other things, on what they are compelled to pay for them in the London area. Only if they had to pay more than the marginal costs of public services in London could the amounts they would be willing to pay in Brighton be accepted as a correct measure of the benefits there. Indeed, an ideal allocative procedure would require that the managers of these service industries (public utilities and the like) be ready at all times to reduce the charges for such services to no more than the current marginal costs of providing them, rather than lose a customer. If the economy actually worked in this way, the services of the economist could be dispensed with in such circumstances. But as it is difficult to discriminate between customers in this way, and as extending a reduction in charges made on behalf of one customer to all other customers involves the company in losses of revenue – such losses being, in effect, transfer payments from the company to its customers – the customary charges (which are generally in excess of marginal cost) are generally maintained.

If this is so, however, it follows that the choice of moving from London to Brighton is being made on the wrong terms, for if, by reducing the charges of one or more of such public services until it is nearer to the marginal cost of its provision, a number of such 'emigrant' families can be induced to stay on in London, then a potential Pareto improvement can be effected: everyone concerned can be made better off as compared with the alternative situation in which such families move to Brighton.[2] The ideal experiment is not to allow any family to move from London to Brighton without first offering it the option of buying all such existing services at their marginal running costs. If, when such terms are offered to potential migrants, they are still willing to move and to pay for all newly required public services prices which cover their inclusive costs, all well and good.

Unless marginal cost pricing is already established in the public utility sector, such an ideal experiment – call it option 1 – is likely to run into administrative and political objections. For the costs of discovering potential migrants and of offering those special marginal cost terms without arousing the suspicion and hostility of other households can be prohibitive. If, however, option 1 is adopted, and all potential emigrants from the London area are presented with special permits enabling them to buy public utility services at their marginal costs, their demand schedules for any such service, say electricity, in Brighton will be based on a *ceteris paribus* clause that includes a price for electricity in London equal to its marginal cost.

If this condition can be met, the installation of an (additional) electricity plant in Brighton can be justified only if (measured, say, on an annual basis) the total revenue from the sale of the additional electricity along with the consumer surplus exceeds in total both current and overhead costs.

The economist, however, may well have to accept as a political constraint the existing prices set by public utilities in London and to calculate the benefits from extending them in Brighton by reference only to the resulting demand schedules.

5   Life would be less trying for the economist if people did not change their tastes so often over even short periods of time, as they habitually do in a modern economy. Such changes are not always rational: they may spring from trivial causes or be inspired by ignoble motives – greed, envy, the desire for attention or for being in fashion. It is no part of the economist's brief, however, to uncover or to judge people's motives in this respect. He has perforce to accept as basic data the individual's choices or revealed preferences at any particular time.

As already indicated, allowance can be made for a growth in benefits over time arising from increases in population and real income per capita and also for the introduction or withdrawal (when they can be foreseen) of goods or bads associated with the operation of subsequent enterprises. Tastes may also change spontaneously or in response to advertising campaigns.

In so far as he cannot foretell such changes, the economist, if he is to make estimates at all, *has perforce to project current valuations* into the future in the knowledge that (to that extent) they are vulnerable. However, for public projects designed to improve the environment, to reduce pollution or to increase amenity, the valuation of their benefits is not likely to change significantly – at least not to fall significantly – with the passage of time. What is more, the economist's confidence in his findings will grow if his calculations of the criterion $\Sigma V > 0$ are met in a so-called sensitivity analysis that involves variation in the magnitude of key parameters.

6   Although there can be justification for a programme that spreads accurate and useful information within the community, it is doubtful whether such justification can be extended to campaigns designed to change people's tastes for no good reason. Part, at least, of the expenses of a commercial advertising agency is directed

into an attempt to alter the existing patterns of tastes among potential buyers so as to favour the sale of goods supplied by their clients. Can there be any benefit to society of employing resources for this purpose?

If purely spontaneous changes in people's tastes that are in no way related to dependable information necessarily incur wastage of resources, so *a fortiori* do commercially induced changes. And if, under existing political institutions, society permits scarce resources to be used expressly for the purpose of inducing changes in taste, then society is indeed countenancing the incurring of avoidable waste. In a dynamic economy where tastes are being manipulated by agencies, success in shifting the demand for a good x to that for good y, then from y to z, then from z to w and, possibly, from w back to the original good x – which changes, we can suppose, would not have occurred in the absence of advertising expenditures – then idle capacity is prematurely brought about in the production of each of these goods. An unnecessary rate of obsolescence is created. The economist who remains neutral in the matter of people's tastes may properly conclude that avoidable waste is the price paid for the acceptance of persuasive advertising. This wastage of resources is, of course, passed on to the community at large through the higher prices needed to cover the higher cost of more rapid obsolescence.

Notes

1 We are ignoring the eventual costs of congestion as numbers increase. These are adverse spillover effects or external diseconomies that fall on the users themselves of tunnels, bridges and national parks, and they are discussed in some detail in Part IV.

2 If the price per unit of electricity charged by the London supplier yielded an excess over its variable cost of $100 for the amount used by family A, an effective bribe of less than $100 that induced family A to remain in London would make both parties better off than they would be if family A moved to Brighton.

7 Introduction to the compensating variation

1   So far, we have used a single value V to be the measure of a good or bad. But following the Hicksian definition of consumer surplus (Hicks, 1939), we must recognize that, in general, there can be two useful ways of valuing a good or bad. First, there is a compensating variation (CV), which measures the largest sum a person is willing to pay for a good (or for the removal of a bad). Then there is what Hicks called an equivalent variation (EV), which measures the smallest sum a person will accept to forego a good (or to accept a bad).

The CV or EV measure can, however, be used as a measure either of a gain or a loss of the individual's welfare. And it transpires that the so–called EV measure is, in fact, no more than the CV measure for the reverse movement. That is to say, if CV^2 measures the individual's compensatory sum, as in the change from state 1 to state 2, then EV^{12} is exactly equal, in fact, to CV^{21}, the compensating variation for the movement from state 2 to state 1, all things being equal and subject to zero income effect.

2   In more general terms, we can define CV^{12} as the sum of money (or numeraire) paid or received by the individual following the movement from state 1 to state 2 (according to whether it raises or lowers his welfare, respectively) that would exactly maintain that individual's original level of welfare – the state 1 level of welfare. We can then define the CV^{21} measure as the sum of money paid or received by the individual that, in a movement from state 2 to state 1, would maintain his welfare at the state 2 level. To illustrate, if the change to state 2 is a fall in price of a good (or alternatively a rise in the price of his services) *ceteris paribus*, and therefore a rise in the individual's welfare, his CV^{12} is positive, being the most he would pay for this movement from state 1 to state 2 – which, if paid, would restore his to his original or state 1 level of welfare. Per contra, if the change to state 2 is a rise in the price of a good (or alternatively a fall in the price of his services), *ceteris paribus*, and therefore a fall in his level of welfare, his CV is negative, being the minimum sum he would have to receive in this movement to state 2 – which sum, if received, would restore him to his original or state 1 level of welfare.

To be tedious about it, if we now go on to suppose that, having moved to state 2, the individual is to contemplate a return to state 1, the relevant measure is the CV^{21}. And if the original movement to state 2 raised his welfare, this movement back to state 1 must lower it. Consequently, his CV^{21} is *negative*, being the minimum sum he must receive if he is to maintain his state 2 level of welfare. It follows that if, instead, the movement from state 2 to state 1 raises the individual's welfare, his CV^{21} is *positive*, being the most he would pay for the movement.

3   Is the most an individual would pay for a good always less than the smallest sum he will accept to go without it? The short answer is almost always.[1]

To be more precise, it is so for what is sometimes called a *normal* good – one of which more is bought when the individual's real income, or more generally his welfare, is increased. The so–called *inferior* good, of which less is bought when his welfare is increased, is exceptional (a favourite example is margarine, at least when it is regarded as a poor man's substitute for butter) and, unless otherwise stated, we may consider only normal goods, which will, of course, include collective goods.

Why this must be so can be understood if we bear in mind that the CV^{12} is the maximum a person would pay for a good that would increase his welfare, say, from his original indifference curve I_1 to a higher indifference curve I_2. This maximum sum he would pay will therefore be such as to return him to his original indifference curve I_1. Conversely, his CV^{21} is the minimum sum he must receive, this being the (larger) sum that will maintain him on his I_2 indifference curve.

Now, if the welfare effect is normal (as posited), then whatever the price of the good x, the individual buys more of it the higher his real income, which – on a diagram with real income y on the vertical axis and good x on the horizontal axis – would show that, for a given slope of the indifference curves, the amount of x taken on the higher indifference curve is larger. Therefore for the *same* amount of good x taken, the slope on the I_2 curve is steeper than that on the I_1 curve.

It follows that if, with respect to each of these two indifference curves in turn, we were to plot the increments of y, or real income, that have to be given up for successive and equal increments of x, the resulting 'marginal indifference curve' or what we may call the marginal valuation curve MV_2, that is derived from the I_2 indifference curve will at all points be above the MV_1 curve derived, that is, from the I_1 indifference curve.

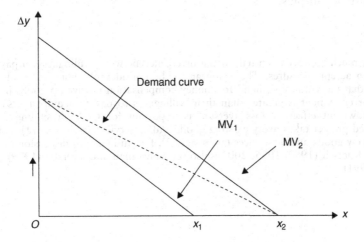

Figure 7.1

The area below the MV_2 curve in Figure 7.1 is, of course, the measure of the minimum sum a person would accept for having to part with the x_2 amount of x, the corresponding smaller area below the MV_1 curve being the measure of the largest sum he would pay for the x_1 amount of x.

This figure can also be used to trace the locus of amounts of x a person would buy as the price of x, from being so high that no x at all is bought, is gradually lowered to zero. This price–quantity locus is clearly that of the individual's demand curve and, for all normal goods, it will lie diagonally between two marginal valuation curves, as shown: the higher MV_2 curve being appropriate to the level of welfare reached when a person has, at the zero price, taken all the x that he wants; the lower MV_1 curve being appropriate to his welfare before he buys any x at all.

4   In the light of the above, the measurement of consumer surplus we have been using in the previous two chapters – the area under the demand curve that is above the price line – is seen to be an overstatement of the maximum sum the buyers will pay to be able to buy a good x at the market price. It is also an understatement of the minimum sum required to compensate them if that price is no longer available.

Such refinement of the measure of consumer surplus that emerges from the implications of CV^{12} and CV^{21} might be of some use if we were able to obtain exact measures of individual and collective demand curves. Alas, the errors in any actual statistical estimates of demand curves are such as are more than likely to swamp these theoretical refinements we would seek to impose on a (hypothetically) perfect estimate of a demand curve. For all practical purposes, then, the economist perforce continues to measure the consumer surplus from the area under these unavoidably imperfect estimates of demand curves (sometimes called the ordinary or Marshallian demand curve).

Yet, our treatment of the measures of compensating variation has more than an academic value, albeit a heuristic one. In particular, the differences between CV^{12} and CV^{21} measures can be important in other cost-benefit measurements, chiefly in connection with the measurement of spillover effects, as we shall see in Part IV. Check Appendices 5 and 6 for more information on Hicksian and marginal measures of consumer surplus.

Note

1 Recently, much has been written on the divergence between willingness to pay and willingness to accept measures. There appears to be considerable empirical evidence which suggests that individuals' demand for money compensation to give up goods in their possession or enjoyment is greater than their willingness to pay to acquire the same goods. This endowment effect or loss aversion is important for CBA, depending on whether a proposed project takes away existing goods and/or services (as in state 1) or introduces or adds new goods and/or services (as in state 2). For an in–depth discussion on loss aversion, see Knetsch (1989, 1995, 2003); also see Kahneman and Tversky (1979) and Hanemann (1991).

8 Measurements of rent

1 Rent may be defined as the difference between what the owner of factors of production – say, a worker or a landowner – earns by employing his factors in producing some current good(s) and the minimum sum he would accept to keep them there.[1] It is then a measure of the resource-owner's gain from the opportunity he has of placing his factors in this chosen occupation – given, of course, the opportunity of placing them in any other occupation.

It is the proper counterpart for the gain to factor-owners of a consumer surplus, the latter being regarded as the measure of gain to the consumer from the opportunity of buying some good(s) at the existing price(s). In general, then, rent is in tandem with consumer surplus in as much as it is a measure of his change in welfare when the relevant prices or opportunities facing him are changed. The only distinction between the two is that, whereas an increase in consumer surplus is a measure of gain in welfare for a fall in one or more prices of goods, an increase in rent is the measure of his gain in welfare for a rise in one or more of his factors of production. In both cases, however, the introduction of new opportunities in place of, or in addition to, favourable price changes will also raise his welfare and is measured by an increase in consumer surplus or rent.

This much understood, it has now also to be said that the area below the demand curve provides a good enough measure of consumer surplus (indeed, the only practicable measure); we cannot go on to suppose that the area above the supply curve of factors, say the supply curve of labour, offers a good measure of the labourer's rent. Let us see why.

2 It is usual to draw a person's price–demand curve as sloping downward from left to right and his supply curve for labour or other services sloping upward. If his welfare effect (or 'income effect') is normal, the individual's demand curve has to be downward sloping. (It can slope upward only if the welfare effect is negative and is large relative to the substitution effect – the characteristics of the so-called Giffen good.) Analogous remarks apply to the individual's supply curve. If the 'welfare effect'[2] is zero, the individual supply curve must slope upward: it can slope downward or become 'backward-bending' only if the welfare effect is positive and large relative to the substitution effect.[3]

In general, the smaller these welfare effects that accompany price changes, the more accurate as an estimate of consumer surplus or rent will be the relevant area derived, respectively, from the individual's demand or supply schedule. In the case of a person's demand curve, there is a presumption that the welfare effects are small, for a man's current expenditure is commonly spread over a wide variety of goods each of which – with, perhaps, the exception of housing – absorbs only a small proportion of his total income. Indeed, as living standards rise, the variety of goods offered by the market increases along with the increase in a man's real income. One might surmise, therefore, that the welfare effect will become less important an ingredient in his price–demand curve for any single good.

The case is otherwise for the individual's supply curve, in particular for his supply of productive services, say the supply of labour, skilled or unskilled. If he supplies to the market only one sort of labour, the impact of the welfare effect arising from a change in the price of this labour falls entirely on the amount of it supplied. It then exerts a preponderant effect. Backward-bending supply curves for individual workers are not regarded as curiosa, a fact which would seem to make the measurement of economic rent rather awkward.

But there is a countervailing feature in connection with individual supply curves, which tends to restore measurability. Notwithstanding the mathematical convenience in postulating an economy in which each individual contributes, in general, to all goods in the economy, spreading his total effort among them – as he spreads his income among all goods – on the equi-marginal principle, this postulate is recognized as unrealistic. Nor is it a necessary condition for the model of perfect competition, which model is quite consistent with the more realistic assumption that the worker is constrained in his chosen employment to work a given number of hours, and between stated times. (He may, of course, be offered overtime work, though again it will be subject to constraints on the days and times.) For this reason, there is little point in conceiving of the worker's rent from his employment in precisely analogous terms as his consumer surplus.

3   In depicting any consumer surplus for a good x in terms of the CV[12], we may derive an MV_1 curve, as in Figure 8.1 to show the excess of marginal valuation over price of the first unit of x bought, of the second unit of x bought and so on until, with the purchase of the nth unit of x, this excess valuation is zero. By again explicitly ignoring welfare effects, the analogous way of measuring rent is by

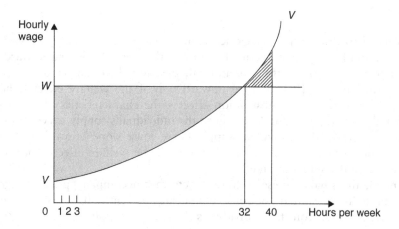

Figure 8.1

reference to an upward-sloping MV curve, and would amount to the excess of the price offered for the factor over its marginal valuation for all the factors supplied at that price: for a worker, these marginal valuations are now the minimum sums acceptable to him for successive units of labour provided. Clearly, the amount of labour he chooses to provide will be that at which the (rising) marginal valuation of his labour is equal to the prevailing wage rate. This measure of the resulting rent – the area above his MV_1 supply curve of labour and below the wage rate – is to be interpreted as the maximum sum he would pay to remain in this chosen occupation at the prevailing wage rate, given the existing pattern of prices and wages.

As mentioned above, however, the worker does not choose to spread his hours of work among different firms and occupations on the equi-marginal principle. If the contrary were the case or if, at least, the worker were free to set the hours he would choose to work in a given enterprise, he would, given his rising MV_1 supply curve VV in Figure 8.1, choose to work 32 hours only each week, the amount of time for which his VV curve intersects the horizontal W line, measuring the wage rate. His rent would then be equal to the shaded area above the VV curve. But if, as is likely, the working day were fixed and he had to work, say, a 40-hour week to get the job, he would be obliged to work eight hours longer than the 32 hours that he himself would choose. For each of these additional hours he has to work, the wage he receives is below his successive marginal valuations. On these eight extra unwanted hours, he suffers a loss equal to the striped triangle. His net rent is therefore the shaded area minus the striped area. And, as he is offered the job as an all-or-nothing proposition, he will accept the job only if the difference between these two areas is positive.

As all workers finding employment in this occupation will be obliged to work the 40-hour week, irrespective of whether they would prefer to work fewer or more hours, the net rent from working the 40-hour week is, for any one of them, the first area less the second area (if any). Letting the worker's weekly (disposable) pay be represented as the area of a unit column with height equal to this weekly wage, as in Figure 8.2, the rent is the shaded rectangle measured from the top of the column.[4] By gradually raising the weekly wage and observing the numbers that

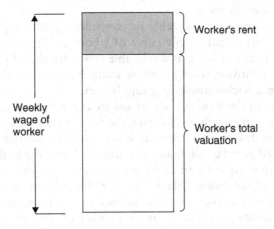

Figure 8.2

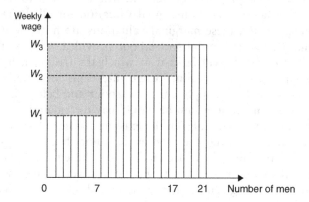

Figure 8.3

enter the industry in response to the higher wage, a supply curve of labour to the industry is generated, and from this we are able to identify the rent of those employed. Thus in Figure 8.3, if at the lowest wage, W_1, seven men just agreed to work, they make no rent. If now the wage rises to W_2, and, in response, another ten men are just willing to enter the industry, the first seven enjoy between them a rent equal to the shaded rectangle (W_2-W_1) *times* the distance 0–7. If the wage rises to W_3, and four more men enter, the first seven men between them make a rent equal to (W_3-W_1) *times* the distance 0–7, and the next ten men between them make a rent equal to (W_3-W_2) *times* the distance 7–17, and so on. We are able to do this simply because no worker is allowed to alter the number of hours he works in that occupation.

As the number of workers grows, the stepped supply curve becomes closer to a smooth curve, the corresponding area above it being the measure of the aggregate of rents enjoyed by the workers employed in that occupation. And this aggregate rent is to be interpreted as the largest sum they would, in aggregate, be willing to pay to remain in this occupation at the prevailing wage rate, given all other prices and opportunities open to them.

To be sure, it is virtually impossible to construct an MV supply curve for the individual worker. His actual supply curve of labour could perhaps be discovered, but such a curve would not serve as a tolerable proxy for the MV_1 curve in view of the operation of a relatively strong positive welfare effect, one that may result (as indicated earlier) in a backward-sloping supply curve.

Without recourse to the worker's actual supply curve, however, the difficulty can be overcome if we can somehow discover the least sum the worker is willing to accept to remain in his chosen occupation on an all-or-nothing basis; accepting, that is, the required number of hours per day and per week along with all the other constraints that go with the job. Such a sum may then be represented as equal to the area of the lower (blank) part of the column in Figure 8.2, which becomes a unit in the construction of the stepped supply curve of Figure 8.3, which again becomes a smooth supply curve as the number of workers grows.[5]

4   This workers' rent as measured by the area above the aggregate supply curve of labour is one thing. The rent that is sometimes measured as the area above the supply curve of a good *x* for a firm or an industry is another. This latter may be accepted as valid only in either of two cases.

First, there is what we may call Ricardian rent, in which labour and capital, both of them available in any amounts at constant prices, are applied in fixed proportions to a given quantity of land. The supply curve of the resulting product, say corn, rises, not because of any changes in the supply prices of the variable factors, labour and capital, since, as just stated, their supply prices remain unchanged. The supply curve of corn rises simply because the best land is limited in supply, and, as the price of corn rises with an expanding demand, it becomes worthwhile to bring inferior land into cultivation. Even if there is only one quality of land, though limited in amount relative to demand, rent will accrue to it once the marginal cost of a bushel of corn rises above its average cost – as it eventually will, because of diminishing average returns to additional 'doses' of labour and capital. In these circumstances, the area between such a supply curve and the price of the product provides a measure of the rent accruing to the owner of the fixed factor, land. Increases in such rents arising from the introduction of an investment project are accordingly entered on the benefit side of the analysis.

Second, there is the case in which the area above the supply, or cost, curve has to be identified as what Marshall (1924) called *quasi-rent*. For over a short period, during which the capital employed by the industry or firm is in the specific form of plant or machinery, it is deemed to be fixed in amount and to have no alternative use. In this short period, then, it partakes of the nature of land, and all its earnings *above* those necessary to induce it to remain in the occupation (zero in the strict Marshallian quasi-rent concept) are to be regarded as rent. In this short period, then, if the price of the product rises above the per unit variable cost of the product, the resulting excess receipts over the total of these variable costs are quasi-rents; such positive sums make a contribution to the industry's or firm's overheads or capital costs.

The above two instances are clear examples of economic rent to a scarce factor. They enter as part of the benefit of producing a given amount of goods during either a short or a long period. Thus, if a given piece of land is used to grow a new crop or to site some new project, any rise in the rent of the land is to be entered on the benefit side of the scheme. If, within a short period, some investment in the industry or firm causes its variable costs to fall, the additional quasi-rents that result are also to be entered on the benefit side.

Notes

1   A more detailed elaboration of the measurement of the concept of rent will be found in Appendix 6, again employing the CV^{12} and CV^{21} measures.

2   Assuming that his money income is constant, a fall in the price of a good which makes a person better off can be regarded as an increase in his real income, for there is some rise in his money income which (given all other prices constant) will be accepted by him as equivalent to a fall in the price of that good. Here, no difficulty arises in identifying the increase in his welfare with the income effect so measured.

In the case of his supplying a service to the market, however, his money income cannot be assumed constant, as, obviously, it varies with the amount of the service he elects to supply at the price offered. What is more, a rise or fall in the resulting money income does not necessarily correspond to a rise or fall in his welfare (or 'real' income). A rise in the wage rate, for instance, may result in the worker's choosing so to reduce hours as to maintain money income constant, notwithstanding which his welfare has increased: for his income is the same, while he enjoys additional leisure. A positive welfare effect, that is, can be associated with no change in his money income or even with a reduction of his money income. For this reason, it is more sensible to talk of the 'welfare effect', resulting from a change in the supply price.

3 An increase of welfare has a 'normal', or positive, welfare effect if the person offers *less* at any given price – if, that is, he keeps more of the good he is offering for himself. A worker who came into an inheritance would supply less labour (or take more leisure). Hence, if the price of the good a person supplies is raised, the substitution effect induces him to supply more, while a positive welfare effect causes him to supply less. As distinct, then, from the 'welfare effect' on the demand side, the 'welfare effect' on the supply side, if it is positive or 'normal', works *against* the substitution effect.

4 This minimal wage necessary to attract the worker into the industry or project will be greater, by the costs of movement (pecuniary and psychic), than the hypothetical minimum wage where movement costs are zero. *Per contra*, once the worker has moved into the industry, the minimal wage he will accept to remain there is equal to this hypothetical minimum wage *less* the full costs of movement.

   In considering a possible introduction of a new project, however, it is the former minimal wage that is relevant.

5 In calculating the rent to the aggregate number of workers from such a supply curve, it is not necessary that all workers be equally efficient. If additional workers that are hired were less efficient than the original ones, the cost of production would indeed rise. But the measure of workers' rent would not thereby be affected.

9   Is producer surplus a rent?

1   Given a fully employed economy in which the supplies of the various factors are fixed, the long-period supply curve for a good x is generally conceived to be upward sloping. Indeed, if production functions are homogeneous and linear,[1] and each good combines factors in different proportions, upward-sloping supply curves for all goods become a necessary implication.

The question is then whether the area above such an upward-sloping long-period supply price for a good, often referred to as a producer surplus, can be interpreted as a gain to some members of society, being then on a par with such measures of gain to society members as those discussed in the preceding chapters on rents and consumer surplus. The short answer is no.

2   In order to appreciate the difference between the valid measures of gain such as consumer surplus or rent, and the spurious measure of gain, producer surplus, let us follow standard textbook procedure and assume, first, that all firms in the particular industry are of equal size and efficiency. In that case, the rising supply price of the industry's output of good x has to be attributed to the growing scarcity of the factor that is intensively used in the production of good x. In an economy with only two factors, say capital and labour, we may suppose that good x uses a larger proportion of capital to labour than does the only other good y. If the amount of good x produced is increased at the expense of good y, an initial shortage of capital in the economy relative to labour will result in a rise in the price of capital and fall in the price of labour. The cost of a unit of x, being capital intensive, will therefore rise as more of x is produced and that of a unit of y, which is labour intensive, will fall as less of y is produced.[2]

Any point along this rising supply price for the product indicates the minimum average (inclusive) cost for each of the firms in the industry and, therefore, the minimum average (inclusive) cost for that output. Thus, at output Ox_1 in Figure 9.1, the minimum average inclusive cost for all firms is given by x_1m_1. A typical long-period envelope curve for such a firm is represented as S_1S_1. At the larger output Ox_2, the minimum average inclusive cost for the industry is given by x_2m_2, and the typical long-period envelope curve for the firm is represented by S_2S_2. Clearly then, this long-period industry supply curve cannot be interpreted as a net gain by the producers of this particular good, as each of them makes zero (Knightian) profit[3] in long-period equilibrium. It is, in fact, a curve of average cost *including* rent.

Since real rentals (the price of units of capital) rise and – unless there are increasing returns to scale – real wages fall as the output of x is expanded, we are able, under

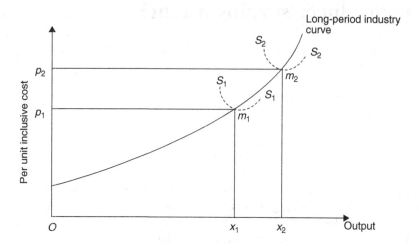

Figure 9.1

particular monetary assumptions, to calculate the rise in money rentals and the fall in money wages corresponding to increased amounts of capital and labour required by some given increase in the quantity of the product x. We can then associate the increase in the area above the supply curve of x with the increased amounts of the two factors employed in the x industry when each factor is multiplied by the increase or decrease in its income. More specifically, the addition to the area above the supply curve for x is made up of the gains of *only* those units of capital now employed in x *less* the losses of only those workers now employed there. These gains and losses in x alone are clearly only a small part of the total gains and losses accruing to the factor classes as a whole, since they are also employed in other industries.

It is certain, therefore, that any increase in the area above the supply curve for x is *not* to be associated with a net gain by either factor or by both factors taken together or by the producers.[4]

Thus, so far as shifts of demand curves are concerned, say from product y to product x, attempts to measure net benefits arising in the x industry – or, to be more ambitious, net benefits arising in all industries that use the two (or more) factors – are hardly practicable, especially where, as is likely, a larger number of factors are involved. Indeed, such a shift in production implies no more than a movement from one part of the production boundary to another. It is a movement that, in general, raises the earnings of some factor classes and lowers those of others. But one cannot infer that there are net gains to society as a whole.

If, however, the area above the supply curve of x were to increase solely in consequence of a downward shift in this curve, the result, say, of an improvement in technology, it need have no effect on factor prices. In this technically 'neutral' case, the increased area does indeed count as a benefit. Insofar as the reduction in the cost of producing x is wholly passed on to consumers, the gain will be measured as an increase in consumer surplus. In so far as some part of this gain is withheld by the producer, for a time at least, it partakes of monopoly rent.

Essentially, producer surplus is not to be included as it is mere pecuniary profit and does not arise from any scarcity rent. Anything that increases profit whether government or firms arising from increases in price must take into account whether this comes from real changes in the supply curve. If it is only pecuniary, then this profit should not be counted as benefits.

A more advanced treatment of the concept of rent can be found in Appendix 8.

Notes

1 A homogeneous linear production function is one where the output x increases by the proportion c, if each of the inputs is increased by c.
2 Only in a full-employment economy in which all goods (with homogeneous production functions of degree one) use factors in the same proportion as their availability will the long-period supply curves of goods be horizontal.
3 Normal return on capital is not 'profit' any more than normal return on labour. In the long-period equilibrium, at any point on the industry supply curve, expenditure on factors (both labour and capital) is deemed to be just covered by revenue, leaving no profit, positive or negative, to induce firms to move into or out of the industry.
4 This long-period supply curve cannot, that is, be regarded as an average cost curve that includes the rent of a *fixed* factor, for in that case the curve would also be one that is a marginal cost of the good x *excluding* rent – as, say, in Ricardian rent or Marshallian quasi-rent.

   It might seem, however, that this long-period supply curve for a good x, arising as it does from varying combinations of two or more factors, could be treated as a marginal curve by a perfectly discriminating monopsonist. For, by paying more only to any additional factors he may require in expanding production, he would be able to appropriate a sum equal to the area above the supply curve.

   Such a discriminating monopsonist would, however, have to be the sole buyer of the factors he employed, else he would be unable to employ them at prices lower than those prevailing in the rest of the economy.

   So singular a case may hardly be considered seriously as a possible exception. We are justified, therefore, in treating the long-period supply curve for a good as no more than an average cost to the one or more firms producing it.

Part III

Shadow prices and transfer payments

10 Introductory remarks

1   Broadly speaking, a 'shadow' or 'accounting' price – the terms are interchangeable – is the price the economist attributes to a good or factor on the argument that it is more appropriate for the purpose of economic calculation than its existing price, if any. There is nothing very special about the notion of a shadow price. In evaluating any project, the economist may effectively 'correct' a number of market prices and also attribute prices to unpriced gains and losses that it is expected to generate. He will, for example, add to the cost of a factor or subtract from the cost of a good in making allowance for some external diseconomy. Wherever the amounts of a good to be added to or subtracted from the existing consumption are large enough, the economist will substitute for price the more discriminating measure of benefit, consumer surplus. Certain gains or losses to an enterprise he will value as zero, because, for the economy at large, they are only transfer payments. The cost of labour he must value at its opportunity cost, not at its wage, and so on.

Nonetheless, the term has been used more specifically in a number of connections, and it will, perhaps, avoid confusion if these are briefly indicated.

2   First, the term has long been used in mathematical programming, a technique in which the value, at given prices, of an 'objective function' is, say, maximized, subject to certain amounts of inputs and a number of technologically feasible factor combinations. From this 'primal' problem, a 'dual' problem can be derived, with a corresponding objective function which is to be minimized. It transpires that, for a wide class of problems, the variables in the dual solution can be interpreted as shadow prices or accounting prices, inasmuch as they are the 'correct' input prices – being consistent with the maximum value of the primal objective function.[1] We shall not, however, be using the term shadow price in connection with this technique.

Second, the term has been extended to estimates of social benefits or social losses that are either unpriced or not satisfactorily priced. Unpriced or inadequately priced benefits or losses may be valued by (i) adopting the prices of similar things elsewhere or (ii) calculating the price for a good or a 'bad' that is *implicit* in government decisions to undertake particular projects or (iii) calculating the spillover effects by reference to market prices, or by some other method. Consider each method in turn.

(i) The price adopted for some public good, or service, may be based on that at which it is sold in some other region of the country. Thus, the value of a public amenity such as a beach, a park or a museum, to be established, say, in New York may be estimated by reference to the prices charged for similar beaches, parks or museums, in other parts of the United States. Such prices, even when attempts are made to allow for differences in circumstances, are not very satisfactory. The prices that are set elsewhere for such things are not likely to be optimal prices, and are sometimes set arbitrarily or, rather, by reference only to political considerations. Since a correct measure of the benefit is the maximum that people would pay for the service rather than go without, one cannot hope for much from this device. At any rate, no generalization that is useful, and also not obvious, can be made with respect to this practice, and we need say no more about it here.

(ii) Wherever there is an uncalculated benefit B associated with an authorized public project which, on a CBA that is confined to *measurable* benefits, reveals an excess of costs over benefits ΔK, it can be argued that the implicit value, or shadow price, of this uncalculated benefit B is equal to ΔK or, rather, that it is at least equal to ΔK.[2] One of the difficulties of this argument is that one cannot hope for a deliberate and systematic criterion to be invoked in such a case. There can be, and there usually are, the widest discrepancies between these implicit valuations, though even if this were not the case, the validity of this procedure is open to methodological criticism.[3]

(iii) The existence of spillover effects requires that market prices be corrected *inter alia* for incidental losses and gains falling on persons other than the producers or users of goods. These incidental social losses or gains can sometimes be valued by reference to market prices, though not without difficulty. Prices of such goods, once corrected for the spillover effects they produce, are also spoken of as shadow prices. However, we shall defer the discussion of spillover effects to Part IV. Finally, and most commonly in a CBA, shadow prices are associated with the calculation of opportunity costs of the materials or productive factors used in the building and operation of the project in question, whether they are transferred from domestic sources or from abroad. It is in this latter opportunity-cost sense that we shall discuss them, and with particular reference to the opportunity cost of labour and the opportunity cost of imports.

Notes

1 When these shadow prices are imputed to the given inputs, the value of the dual objective function is minimized. It can then be interpreted as the minimum input cost, subject to the constraints and to the requirement that no profits (excess revenues) be made. These shadow prices are, therefore, no different from the factor prices that would emerge in a perfectly competitive equilibrium in which product prices are exogenously determined. An unusually clear introduction to the uses of mathematical programming is provided in Throsby's book (1970). See also Takayama (1994) and Sydsaeter and Hammond (2005).

2 If, instead, there happens to be an *uncalculated* social loss D, arising from an authorized public project which shows an excess of measured benefit over measured cost ΔB, then, on the same argument, the implicit value, or shadow price, of this uncalculated loss D can be taken to equal ΔB – or, rather, as not greater then ΔB.

3 For arguments tending to reject the validity of this procedure for deriving implicit valuations, the reader is referred to the chapter 'The value of statistical life' in Part VII.

11 Opportunity cost of labour

1   So far, we have been using the abbreviated notation ΣV to denote the aggregate of the valuations created by the project over time to its terminal period T, omitting, for the time being, the discounting or compounding procedure necessary to reduce the ΣV to a single figure.

However, we may write $V_t = (v_t^b - v_t^c)$, where V_t is the *net* benefit in the year t (which could be positive or negative), v_t^b is the valuation of the benefit in year t, while v_t^c is the valuation of the cost in the year.[1]

The calculation of v_t^b presents no problem, at least in so far as the goods produced by the project are marketable. In the earlier chapters in Part II, we perforce had to adopt, as an adequate measure of consumer surplus, the area under the demand curve for a good x *less* the amount the consumers have to pay for the amount, OQ, they buy. Thus, the *full* valuation for the total value OQ amount of x is the area under the demand curve (without any subtraction of the sum paid by the consumers). And it is from this valuation v_t^b of the benefit of the project's output of the good x that we now have to subtract the real cost, the v_t^c.

In a cost-benefit calculation, however, costs are not, in general, equal to the costs of the materials and productive factors used by the project in the ordinary sense; say, as they would be calculated by a private enterprise from their market prices. The relevant costs in a CBA are what are known as 'opportunity' costs – a term which serves to indicate the valuations forgone when the materials or factors are transferred from other employments.

2   In general, then, this key concept of opportunity cost to the project is the worth of that particular input in some alternative use. Yet, so defined, there will be ambiguity wherever there is more than one alternative use. In such cases, the definition adopted may refer to the alternative use that yields the highest value. And were the economist at liberty to choose from which use the material or factor should be transferred, such a definition would be valid. In so far as the economist is, in this respect, subject to political constraints, he has no choice but to calculate the opportunity cost of anything as the value it created in that particular (politically determined) use from which it is to be transferred. It will simplify the exposition if, henceforth, we think of opportunity cost in terms of a particular designated alternative use.

Although the concept of opportunity cost, using this definition, can be extended to any material or productive factor that is to be used in a project, either for its initial construction or for its operation up to some terminal year T, nothing is lost in our understanding of its nature and method of calculation if, in the main, we confine our treatment of it to labour or to labour of a particular skill.

In respect of labour, however, we should be aware that the calculation of its opportunity cost must also take into account any occupational preference the worker has when comparing the employment conditions offered by the project and those in his existing occupation. We may also have to take account of any costs of movement the worker may have to incur in moving from his present employment to employment in the new project.

In the absence of either of these, however, the opportunity cost of a unit of labour – say, a 40-hour working week of that labour – to the project is no more than the value it can create in the production of the amount of a good x from which it is to be transferred. In more familiar jargon, its opportunity cost is equal to the value of its marginal product in x, abbreviated to VMP_x, this being the value forgone when the unit of labour is moved from producing x to producing alternative goods – say, y and/or z – in the project.

In a cost-benefit calculation, this VMP_x figure must, in general, be adjusted to make allowance for any externalities associated with the production or consumption of the amount of good produced by the unit of labour. If, in that labour's unit of production of good x, a positive externality of $50 is conferred on the community, this $50 is added to the VMP_x. Conversely, if the community suffers a loss valued at $80, that much has to be subtracted from VMP_x. The adjusted VMP_x may be referred to as the *social* value of the marginal product of labour in producing the good x, or $SVMP_x$, and is therefore the appropriate opportunity cost of that labour to the project.

3   In order to fix our ideas, we may suppose that a unit of labour is to be transferred from the production of good x to producing something else in the project. If this unit of labour produces ten units of x during a week, each unit of x having a social value of $50, its $SVMP_x$ is $500, which is then the appropriate opportunity cost per week to the project – *provided* the worker is indifferent between producing good x and working in the project and provided also there are no costs of movement when he transfers his labour from producing good x to working for the project.

If the worker is not indifferent between occupations; if, say, he would require no less than $75 per week additional to his wage in x to induce him to work for the project, the opportunity cost of his labour to the project becomes $575 or $SVMP_x$ plus *op* (*op* being shorthand for the occupational preference premium of the worker). Were the reverse to be the case, the opportunity cost, $SVMP_x$ *minus op*, becomes $425 per week.

A further adjustment to the opportunity cost is required if the worker incurs costs in moving from the production of x into the project, where the costs include both the money costs of relocation and the less tangible 'psychic' costs experienced by him, his family and friends, when he departs from an area in which he had settled. Although the physical costs of the relocation are easily ascertained, the 'psychic' costs can be estimated only from the worker himself. Consequently, there can be difficulties in eliciting the true figure. Whatever the total of these costs is, however, they will occur only once and they are, therefore, to be spread over the entire period of the worker's employment in the project.

It will be noticed that, in the above examples, no mention has been made of the wage rate or the worker's rent either in the production of x or in the project. Calculation of their magnitudes is unnecessary in estimating the opportunity cost, for the wage paid and the worker's rent are properly conceived as transfer payments from the rest of the community to the worker.

4   Calculating the opportunity cost of the entire output produced by all the factors during a period of, say, a year, is a straightforward business. If the only factor used during the year in project *w* were 2,000 workers transferred from *x*, their opportunity cost to project *w* would be equal to the social value of the amount of the good *x* they produce in a year, say $25 million, corrected, however, for their occupational preference for working in *x* rather than in *w* (which we may suppose to be measured by an average of $75 a week). The full opportunity cost is therefore equal to this $25 million *plus* the measure of occupational preference, which is equal to (2,000 × 50 × $75) for a 50-week working year.

This social value of *x*, assumed above to be $25 million is, of course, equal to the most the community is willing to pay for it, adjusted for externalities in its production or consumption. And the most people are willing to pay for that annual amount is adequately measured by the area under the demand curve for *x*. Nor is there any difficulty if the workers employed in project *w* are transferred from the production of a number of different goods. If, say, 1,200 workers are transferred from producing good *x* and the remaining 800 from producing good *y*, the social value forgone is simply the sum of the area under the demand curve for the amount of *x* produced by 1,200 workers over the year *plus* the area under the demand curve for the amount of *y* produced by the 800 workers over the year – again, adjusted for any incidental externalities.[2]

5   Nor is any revision required if the inputs required by the project are materials imported from abroad (as we shall see in Chapter 14) or materials that have to be transferred from a domestic non-augmentable stock.

An example of a non-augmentable stock would be the total oil reserves in a country that has no prospect of increasing the amount of oil at home or abroad in the foreseeable future. The opportunity cost of the amount of oil required by the project is equal to the domestic social value of the oil currently being used in the economy.

As for the opportunity costs of other inputs such as plant, equipment and machinery, their calculation follows that of labour. They are not, that is, the prices that are paid for them, but calculated by reference to the social value forgone when they are transferred to the project in question.

If, for example, some particular equipment has to be produced specifically for the project, its opportunity cost, say it comes to $10,000, is calculated by reference to the opportunity cost of labour and other inputs required, whether imported or not. Investment in such a piece of equipment would, of course, be made in anticipation of its contributing to the social value of the project's annual product.

However, the required equipment may not be specific to the project, but one that currently has a social value of other goods being produced in the economy. Its opportunity cost is then calculated as the social value it contributes annually in producing these other goods. This opportunity cost could, for example, be $1,500 per annum for ten consecutive years.

6   As for the opportunity cost of a significant area of land required by the project, this is sometimes entered as the DPV of the expected net benefits over the future that would otherwise accrue to this area of land if it remained in its current use; or sometimes, this is worth simply as the market value of the land.

It may then seem that its opportunity cost may be properly calculated as the DPV or, rather, the compounded terminal value (CTV),[3] of the net contribution of the land to the annual social value since these annual contributions have to be forgone when the land is transferred to the project. However, the contribution made to the social value of the product by the land itself may not be possible where it is combined in fixed proportion with the other inputs. In addition, transferring the land from its current use to the project entails a dismantling of the whole of the existing concern and also, therefore, the disposal of the various sorts of labour, machinery and equipment used in producing its goods. Such losses must also be counted. Yet, it would be erroneous to cost such losses arising, say, from the disposal of labour or machines once used by the concern as equal to their resulting opportunity costs. For it may well be that the machines have only scrap value, and the discarded labour has no use, or little use, elsewhere.

On such a reckoning, the cost to the project of taking over the land, and therefore the consequent disposal of the labour and machinery involved, would be understated. For these other factors would, if the land remained in its original use, continue to contribute to the full social value there.

It must be concluded that, wherever a significant area of land is involved (significant in that the area of land has value in some other use), it is virtually impossible to assign to it an opportunity cost. The only valid procedure then available to the economist entrusted with the CBA of a project is that of comparing the social value of the land in its current use with its use in the proposed project.

In each of the two alternative uses to be considered, the fixed factor, land, is combined with other factors to yield a stream of net social benefits – the social value of the annual benefits *less* the opportunity costs of the other inputs required. The project meets the economist's criterion if the DPV, or preferably the CTV, of the net social benefits from using the land for the project exceeds that from continuing the current use of the land.

In the particular case where the project being mooted is that of restoring an area of land to its original wilderness state or creating a designed wilderness area, additional costs may be incurred if demolition has to be employed; apart, that is, from the opportunity costs of labour and other inputs required initially in restoring or designing a wilderness area and, subsequently, in maintaining and monitoring the area.

Notes

1 It will be convenient, nonetheless, to continue to use ΣV as shorthand for the aggregate of valuations (both positive and negative to the end of the period T), although it is more revealing to use notation $\sum^{V_t}$ or $\sum^{(v_t^b - v_t^f)}$. In either case, if the aggregate is positive – at least when reduced by discounting to a present sum – it must be concluded that all the factors and materials used in the project over time have a higher value in aggregate than the value they created in the uses from which they are transferred.
2 No problem arises if the economist wishes to calculate opportunity costs in terms of goods rather than in terms of factors. For example, the opportunity cost of a good w is simply equal to the opportunity cost of a unit of labour (or other x-producing factor) divided by the number of w goods it produces.
3 As will be indicated in Part V on 'Investment criteria', our critique of the popular DPV for evaluating net benefit streams is a prelude to our proposal that it be supplanted by our proposed CTV.

12 Opportunity cost of unemployed labour

1 The method of calculating opportunity cost continues, in the main, to be serviceable when extended to unemployed labour. In a less than fully employed economy, that is, the opportunity cost of such labour to the project is, again, equal to the social value of a worker's labour in its existing use, allowance also being made for the worker's occupational preference.

Should the worker place some value on the leisure perforce available to him while unemployed, which value has to be forgone when he takes up employment, that is indeed the value which must be attributed by society to his being in the unemployed state, as he himself is a member of society. Thus, if the minimum sum he would accept to move into employment generally were $50, this $50 has to be accepted as the appropriate opportunity cost. If, however, he is not indifferent to the occupation and to the organization that offers him employment, an adjustment will again have to be made for occupational preference. In other words, this minimal sum acceptable to him will vary with the sort of work he will be required to do and the organization with which he will have to work. For the work he is required to perform in project w, for example, it may be as high as $80.

However, his enforced leisure may be burdensome to him, so much so that he is prepared to pay to be employed even where no wage at all is offered to him. If he would pay as much as $20 a week – from his assets or from sums borrowed – to be employed in project w, even where he receives nothing in return, the opportunity cost to the project is equal to *minus* $20, This can be regarded as a benefit to the community of $20, even if he produces nothing of value. By his being no worse off when he pays the rest of the community $20, and their being better off by the $20 he pays them, the *net* benefit V to the community is $20.

More generally, to the value the worker attaches to his enforced leisure[1] must be added the value of the externalities consequent upon his leisure activities and behaviour, in particular the effects on his friends (or enemies) and members of his family. If, on balance, these externalities are positive in value, this value must be added to the $80 minimum he would accept to work in the project in calculating his opportunity cost.

2 Let us disregard these externalities, however, and therefore continue to calculate his opportunity cost to the project as equal to $80. If we now introduce unemployment benefit, say $100 a week, then by taking up employment in the project, he will have to forgo this sum. The minimal sum he will then accept to agree to work in the project must now be $180. Does the introduction of unemployment benefit

make any difference to the opportunity cost, calculated above as $80? The answer is no. The opportunity cost is still no more than the $80 value he places on the 'leisure' of being unemployed.

Thus, if working in the project he produces goods worth exactly $80, the net gain to society V, equal to $(v^b - v^c)$ – equal therefore to $80 *minus* $80 – is zero. Let us check this carefully.

To employ the worker, the project must transfer $180 to him. Of this amount, $100 represents the transfer to him of the unemployment benefit – originally assumed by the rest of society but, when employed, undertaken by the project. So far as this $100 of payment to the worker is at issue, there is neither gain nor loss to society as a whole: the $100 gain to the worker is offset by the $100 loss to the rest of society. But the project pays the worker $180. The additional $80 received by the worker represents a net loss to the project (and to society as a whole) in as much as the $80 received by the worker is no gain at all: simply a compensation for his work that leaves him no better off than he was when unemployed. But this net loss of $80 to society is exactly offset if the worker produces goods worth $80, leaving the net gain to society equal to zero.

It is much more likely, however, that the worker will produce goods worth more than $80. If he produces goods valued at $500, V becomes equal to $500 – $80, or $420.

3   However, the calculation of opportunity cost of labour in conditions of what is sometimes called 'disguised unemployment' is no different from that of labour when employed in creating goods of value to the community, as in the preceding chapter. The fact, then, that the marginal product of labour in, say, agriculture in some parts of Africa or Asia is zero may well warrant its opportunity cost to the project being equal to zero.

We may suppose that the worker values his leisure when unemployed at $2 a week when the alternative is that of working in agriculture; this $2 being the opportunity cost of his labour to agriculture. But working in a commune of village workers, he receives $3 a week, this being the *average* product of labour when it happens that the *marginal* product of labour is zero. Our worker therefore enjoys a rent of $3 minus $2, or $1 a week. If he has no occupational preference or costs of movement, he will not move out of the commune to take up employment in the project unless he receives more than $3 a week there.

Since his opportunity cost, equal to the value of his marginal product in agriculture, is zero, it follows that were he to move to the project but again produces nothing of value, society would neither lose nor gain from his employment in the project; V is equal to zero. This is so, no matter what wage the project pays him, but it will be easier to check this result if we assume that he receives exactly $3 in the project, the same as he received in agriculture.

Bear in mind that the worker himself is no better off (or worse off) with the $3 wage that he receives from the project than with the $3 he receives from the agricultural commune. The agricultural commune, however, is made better off by the $3 a week, since it no longer has to pay, for his departure does not reduce the amount of the crop produced. The project, on the other hand, is worse off by the $3 a week it now pays the worker who produces nothing of value. Taken together, society as a whole is neither better nor worse off.

Put otherwise, the $3 a week received by the worker continues to be a transfer from the rest of society, whether from the agricultural community or from the project so that, for society as a whole (including the worker), there is neither a gain nor a loss. And, since he works either in agriculture or in the project, the worker produces nothing of value, the conclusion that the net gain V to society is zero remains.

Should the worker indeed produce some social value when working in the project, say $5, then $5 becomes the net gain V to society.

We may therefore confidently conclude that the calculation of the opportunity cost to the project of labour moving from *disguised* unemployment – from some economic activity where his output is either zero or some low figure (less than his wage there) – is the same as that if, instead, he moves from an activity in which he is profitably employed; equal, that is, to his $SVMP_x$ where x is the good in whose production he was employed before moving to the project in question (adjusted for occupational preference and costs of moving, if necessary).

Note

1 What we call his leisure may be complete idleness or it may be, wholly or in part, recreational, educational or productive (the production of some goods that brings him in some income). But whatever he chooses to do with this 'leisure', the economist has to accept the worker's own valuation of it in calculating his opportunity cost.

13 The additional benefits of using unemployed labour

1   In times of low employment, there is obviously a stronger case to be made for implementing public projects, since they not only act to absorb otherwise idle resources, but also generate additional income and employment. It follows that public projects that would not be economically feasible under conditions of high employment may be economically feasible under conditions of low employment. In this chapter, we explore the effect of such benefits on the calculation of the opportunity cost of labour.

In the preceding two chapters, we addressed the calculation of the opportunity cost of labour to the project, first, within a fully employed economy and, second, when the labour required is drawn entirely from the unemployed – the latter being calculated, however, without any reference to the additional benefits arising from the multiplier effects generated.

In the more general case, of course, a proportion of the workers required by the project will be drawn from the ranks of the unemployed, the remainder from those already productively employed. This presents no difficulty. It should be manifest that the total opportunity cost of the labour required by the project is simply the sum of two parts: the opportunity cost of those workers productively employed elsewhere in the economy and that of the unemployed workers.

To illustrate a case where the opportunity cost of a construction worker drawn from his existing employment is calculated to be, on average, $12,000 per annum and that calculated for a construction worker from the unemployment pool to be, on average, $4,000 per annum, the total opportunity cost to the project of employing 1,000 workers, of which 625 are drawn from their existing employment and the remaining 375 from the unemployment pool, is – provisionally ignoring multiplier effects – equal to ($12,000 × 625) *plus* ($4,000 × 375); that is $7.5 million plus $1.5 million, or $9 million in total.

2   However, before adjusting this opportunity cost for multiplier effects, we may as well recognize the existence of a self-evident relationship between, on the one hand, the proportion of unemployed workers likely to be found among the total required by the project and, on the other hand, the extent of the unemployment in the economy as a whole. Although this relationship will differ somewhat for each particular skill, in every case, the greater the degree of unemployment in the economy, the larger the likelihood that the worker will be drawn from the unemployment pool.

Such a relationship can be plotted on a diagram in which the probability of the worker's coming from the unemployment pool is measured along the vertical axis and the percentage unemployment in the economy along the horizontal axis, as in Figure 13.1.

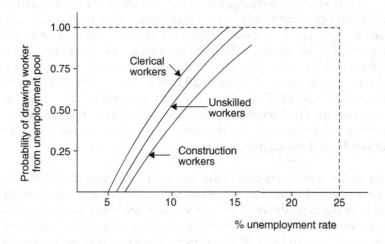

Figure 13.1

Although an attempt has been made to establish such a relationship for a number of different skills,[1] it is uncertain how useful the results would be to an economist engaged in CBA. The amount of empirical work to be undertaken in plotting such a relationship for even a small number of skills could be justified only if it could be assumed that they would remain constant over the years, which is highly unlikely in a modern economy. In any case, the economist should be able, without undue effort, to ascertain at the time the likely number of workers of a particular skill that the project will be drawing from the unemployment pool.

3   This much said, we may finally address ourselves to the additional benefits to society conferred by a project that uses labour from the ranks of the unemployed, bearing in mind that, for additional income and unemployment to be generated, additional money must be activated or otherwise made available. Put otherwise, in order to create additional aggregate expenditure in the economy, there must be no offsetting reduction of expenditure elsewhere. Should the funds necessary to finance the project be raised by a loan, say by an issue of bonds floated on the stock market, hitherto idle bank balances are directly or indirectly activated. Alternatively, the money required may be created by the banking system: the government may, for instance, choose to finance the public project, not from revenues raised by additional taxes,[2] but by borrowing from the central bank which creates the additional money required.

If an additional $1 billion is created, or activated, to be spent on bringing into employment hitherto unemployed workers – therefore without reducing income and employment elsewhere in the economy – the expenditure of the newly employed on currently produced domestic goods (equal to $1 billion *times* their marginal propensity to consume *domestic* goods) adds further to the increase in aggregate income, and so on. With a Keynesian multiplier of 5, the eventual increase in aggregate income becomes $5 billion.[3]

4   Let us now return to the example used in section 1 above, in which, of the total opportunity cost to the project of $9 million, $1.5 million was that of the 375

workers drawn from the unemployment pool. The effect on the calculation of the latter part of this opportunity cost – and, therefore, on the total opportunity cost – of the multiplier-generated increase in aggregate income must now be considered.

If the wage paid by the project is $20,000 per annum to each of the 1,000 construction workers it employs, the 375 workers drawn from the unemployment pool will together receive an income of 375 *times* $20,000, or $7.5 million.[4] With a multiplier of 5, this initial increase of $7.5 million will go on to add an *additional* increase in aggregate income equal to 4 *times* $7.5 million, or $30 million, this sum being the additional benefit to society created by the initial employment of the 375 construction workers drawn from the unemployment pool.

5   In so far as the opportunity cost to the project of employing the 1,000 construction workers was calculated in the absence of this $30 million of additional benefit to society, arising from the expenditure of the 375 workers newly employed, its inclusion will constitute a subtraction from the original calculation of $9 million.[5] The properly corrected opportunity cost of the 1,000 construction workers is therefore $9 million less $30 million, or minus $21 million.

Although it comes to the same thing, it is obviously easier to leave the original calculation of opportunity cost at $9 million, leaving the additional benefit of $30 million to be added to the benefit side of the project.[6]

6   It may first be thought that an addition to this benefit should be made in the belief that an additional $30 million of expenditure generates a consumer surplus on the goods bought. But any attempt to measure additional consumer surplus in these circumstances is misguided in view of the accepted definitions of consumer surplus. As indicated in the chapter on consumer surplus, an economic surplus (positive or negative) to the individual can be calculated only for a *change* in his situation. Thus the CV^{12} is a measure of his gain, or loss, from moving from an initial state 1 to an alternative state 2; the reverse being true for the CV^{21}.

Were we to ask what consumer surplus a person derives from his existing income, the only sense one can make of the question is by a comparison of two situations: a state 1, in which the individual has no income at all, and a state 2, in which the individual has his existing income. The CV^{12} measure is calculated by asking what is the most that the individual would offer for a movement from the zero-income state 1 to the full-income state 2. And the answer is unambiguously, the whole of his income. And the CV^{21} measure gives the same answer, since the question is now: what is the smallest sum the individual would accept to induce him to move from state 2, in which he enjoys his full income, to state 1 in which he would have nothing.

The same reasoning applies to a consumer surplus of an addition to his income, say from, $4,000 per annum to $12,000 per annum. Accepting the $4,000 as state 1, the CV^{12} measures the most he would pay for moving from $4,000 per annum to $12,000 per annum, which is obviously equal to $8,000 per annum. The CV^{21} is also equal to $8,000 per annum being the minimum annual sum he would accept to forgo $8,000 per annum.

We may conclude, then, that the only conceivable measure of a consumer surplus of the benefit of the $30 million additional aggregate expenditure is no less than the $30 million itself.

Notes

1 See Haveman and Krutilla (1968).
2 Were the government to raise an additional $1 billion in taxes in order to spend it entirely on the public project, the additional aggregate income generated would just be $1 billion, irrespective of the multiplier, a result that follows from the so-called balanced-budget multiplier.
3 A multiplier of 5 assumes that of an additional $1 of income, 80 cents is spent on domestically produced goods, and the remaining 20 cents on saving, on imports and taxes.
4 To be sure, if the unemployed construction worker received $100 dole/charity money each week, his *net* income when employed is reduced by this $100 per week. But the $100 he forgoes when employed is transferred back to the rest of the community, whose disposable income is increased to that extent, the multiplier of 5 being unaffected.
5 Regarding the additional benefit of $30 million as equal to the addition of $30 million to aggregate income is warranted in as much as the additional expenditure on *all* goods – including personal savings (expenditure on additional bonds or equities), imported goods and additional taxes for (hopefully) additional government services – is also equal to $30 million.
6 It may be as well to remind the reader that the rent enjoyed by each of the 625 construction workers (on average equal to $20,000 less $12,000, or $8,000 per annum) and the rent enjoyed by each of the 375 newly employed construction workers(on average equal to $20,000 less $4,000,or $16,000 per annum)are not net benefits to the community but only transfers from the rest of the community to the 1,000 workers.

14 The opportunity costs of imports

1 In the literature on project evaluation, it is common enough to present formulae for calculating the shadow price, or opportunity cost, of any imports to be used in the construction or operation of the project. We shall, however, continue to adhere to our method of using simple examples to illustrate the basic logic that informs a valid formula for the opportunity cost to the project of the required imports in particular circumstances or, for that matter, a more general one for all circumstances.[1]

Before embarking, it will make for smoother sailing if first we make a number of easily removed assumptions which in no way affect the basic logic

  (i) that the exchange rate between trading countries remains constant, so enabling us to use a common currency, say the US dollar, in all transactions;
 (ii) that the amounts of the additional imports or exports to be considered are such as not to affect the prevailing prices;
(iii) that no spillovers are present, which assumption allows us to equate the social value of any goods with its market price;
(iv) that the foreign prices which the country has to pay for its imported goods include the costs of freight, insurance, loading and unloading, etc.

It should be manifest that the removal, later, of the first three assumptions adds something to the workload of the economists, though without in any way modifying the principle ideas. If, for instance, exchange rates are likely to vary over time, the economist must evidently adopt the exchange rate that is expected to prevail at the time the project will require the imports. Clearly, he can only guess what the exchange rate will be in future years[2] and perhaps his best stratagem will be to set upper and lower limits to the expected exchange rate, these limits being farther apart for farther years. Recourse to this stratagem produces a lower and a higher opportunity cost of the goods to be imported by the project in any year t.

Again, if the amounts of the goods to be imported or exported are large enough to affect their market prices, the valuations of such goods are taken to equal the relevant areas under the downward-sloping demand curves.

Finally, adjustment for possible positive or negative spillovers, discussed in detail in Part IV, although time-consuming, requires us to add or subtract from existing market prices in order to produce the *social* valuation of the relevant goods.

2 It may be thought that matters could be greatly simplified by ignoring domestic prices in the importing country by restricting ourselves instead to world prices of

all traded goods, which prices may then serve as opportunity costs. Grounds offered for recourse to this expedient include:

(i) that everything produced and consumed domestically has an effect (via the availabilities argument) on the balance of payments;
(ii) that, because of substitution possibilities, we can compare one thing with another and, in particular, we can conveniently compare any good with foreign exchange;
(iii) because world prices express their real cost or benefit to a country in terms of foreign exchange; and
(iv) free foreign exchange is a good yardstick, as it can be used to satisfy almost any need.[3]

These arguments are far from compelling. The employment of world prices, where they do exist, as a proxy for the opportunity costs to a country of its imports could be valid only in exceptional cases. They are certainly not valid for an importing country in which the production of some goods is taxed or subsidized or in which some imports are regulated by quotas or subjected to tariffs, or where goods exported are regulated by quotas or subjected to taxes or subsidies.

In general, that is, the economist must accept the effect on all prices of government policies, and to accept also any constraints imposed by the government in any operations involved in the paying for goods or materials required by the project.

Bearing this in mind, let us consider the calculation of the opportunity cost of the import of an additional 100 tons of copper for a project in India, the copper being supplied by some foreign country at a price of $1,000 a ton. We shall do so under the assumed existence of two limiting circumstances: first, that India cannot increase the value of its exports, or else does not wish to do so; and second, that India is, indeed, willing to increase its exports, at least to the extent necessary to pay for the additional imports required by the project.

Before we start, however, it is as well for the student to be aware of a familiar microeconomic proposition, namely, the equivalence of a quota and a tax or tariff in respect of their impact on the price and quantity demanded of the good in question.

If, for instance, there is a 200 per cent *ad valorem* tariff on the imports of copper, which has the effect of reducing the annual amount imported by India to, say, 1,500 tons, an annual import quota of 1,500 tons of copper will also have the effect of raising the domestic equilibrium price by 200 per cent.

In either case, a transfer payment takes place within the Indian economy. A 200 per cent rise in the initial price of $1,000 per ton of copper will yield the government a revenue of 2 *times* ($1,000 × 1,500 tons), or $3 million. And this is the sum that is, in the new equilibrium, transferred from the consumers of copper-containing goods to the government, in the first instance, whether the government uses a tariff or a quota system to limit the imports of copper to 1,500 tons – provided that the government charges $2,000 for a licence to buy a ton of copper or else auctions such licences in a competitive market.

Should the government distribute such licences as a sort of perk among particular firms for political reasons, the additional profits made by these favoured firms would also amount to $3 million, being now a transfer to them of $3 million from the consumers of copper-containing goods.

This much granted, we may confine ourselves to assuming a tariff, regardless of whether the government uses a tariff or an equivalent quota – at least in so far as we are addressing ourselves to the calculation of the opportunity costs of imports. For what is essential to our understanding is a recognition that, when the government receives an *additional* revenue of $200,000 on the additional 100 tons of copper that is imported, the transfer of this sum is, itself, of no consequence to the calculation. What one segment of society (the government) gains is equal to the loss sustained by another segment (the consumers of goods containing copper). The economy as a whole is no better or worse off.

What is of consequence, whether the government uses a tariff or the equivalent quota, is the rise in the scarcity value of the copper resulting from the imposition of the tariff or quota. In our example, the resulting rise in the market price of a ton of copper to $3,000 is the social value that is now placed on it by the Indian community.

If, therefore, the *additional* 100 tons of copper required by the project were, in fact, *not imported* but instead bought from the domestic market at the prevailing price or, indeed, appropriated without compensation by a tyrannical government, the opportunity cost to the project would have to be $300,000, this being the value of the 100 tons of copper that would be lost to the rest of the economy when it was transferred to the project.

3   Once we return to our initial assumption, that the value of India's exports cannot be increased, the only way we can now *import* the 100 tons of copper from abroad at the foreign supply price of $1,000 a ton is by reducing the amounts of other imported goods that could be bought from abroad for $100,000. Were the government to decree that the $100,000 needed for the 100 tons of copper become available by a reduction only in its imports of manganese, all we have to know is the value on the domestic market in India of the amount of it, say 200 tons that can be bought abroad for $100,000. If the domestic market value of these 200 tons of manganese is $200,000 (this $200,000 that has to be forgone in order to make the 100 tons of copper available to the project), then $200,000 is the opportunity cost to the project of the 100 tons of copper.

True, if the economist were permitted to choose the amounts of imported goods to be reduced so as to make available the $100,000 of foreign exchange required to buy the additional copper, we should expect him to choose those imports that have the lowest value on the domestic market, so minimizing the opportunity cost of the 100 tons of copper. This could be as low as $100,000. And it could, indeed, be lower if some goods in India were subsidized.

Nor is it entirely inconceivable that, for political reasons of its own, the government should decree that the $100,000 needed for the import of an additional 100 tons of copper be made available by reducing the required amount of some goods on which it pays a subsidy, say, of 40 per cent. The domestic value of this amount of imports (which saves the country $100,000 of foreign exchange) would therefore be no more than $60,000. Again, the transfer – this time from the government to the consumers of this good – is immaterial to the calculation. What is material is the $60,000 that is the value lost in that market, notwithstanding that the scarcity value of the good in question has been depressed by an expansion of its consumption consequent upon the subsidy. In these circumstances, the opportunity cost of the 100 tons of copper to the project is equal to $60,000.[4]

4   We now remove the restriction on exports. The additional imports of our 100 tons of copper can be paid for by exporting domestically produced goods that will fetch $100,000 on the world market or, to be more precise, will fetch $100,000 in the foreign country that is prepared to buy them.

From what has been said above, the reader will immediately appreciate that the opportunity cost of the 100 tons of copper to the project is now equal to the domestic value of the goods that are exported to pay for it. True, in the real world, there may be some difficulty in determining which those particular exports are. But the economist should at least know just what he is after – what, ideally, he should be calculating if all the relevant data were available.

If the economist is not permitted to select the batch of goods to be exported to pay for the copper (that having the lowest domestic value), he will discover, if he can, the domestically produced goods that the government has elected to export. In our example of the additional 100 tons of copper, the government may decide to export Indian jute worth $100,000 to the foreign importer. At, say, $4 per pound of jute to the foreign buyer, $25,000 pounds of it has to be exported to pay for the 100 tons of copper. And if, for any reason – for instance, a tax on its production or a monopoly that controls the sale of jute – the domestic price in India is $6 per pound, the opportunity cost of the 100 tons of copper is equal to $150,000.

Clearly, if the Indian government were to export, instead, an amount of jute that could be sold to the foreigner for $60,000, the remaining $40,000 needed by selling cotton, the opportunity cost of the 100 tons of copper becomes equal to the domestic value of the jute exported *plus* the domestic value of the cotton exported, and so on for three or more goods exported.

More generally yet, the 100 tons of copper required by the project may be made available by both reducing some imports and expanding some exports. Where this is the case, the calculation of the relevant opportunity cost becomes somewhat more tedious but, in essence, it comes to no more than an addition of sub-calculations.

5   It remains to deal briefly with the social value of any good exported by the project itself. If the project sells one of its goods, say w, to a foreign country for $5, so enabling the country to use the $5 of foreign exchange to import an additional $5 of goods from abroad, such imported goods are to be valued by the project at their domestic value in India. Assuming the goods sell at $8 in India, then that is their value to the project.

In sum, the social value *to the project* of the goods that it exports during a given year is equal to the domestic value of the additional goods such exports enable it to import.

Notes

1 A good example of the latter can be found in Dasgupta *et al.* (1972: 216) and Boardman *et al.* (2006).
2 The opportunities for hedging against adverse movements of the exchange rate, by selling or buying currencies in the forward exchange market, are limited to a couple of years at most.
3 Such reasons are those given by Little and Mirrlees (1968).

4 It may be unnecessary to remind the reader that, although the prevalence of taxes, tariffs, quotas, subsidies and any other regulation, in addition to the prevalence of monopolies, is associated with a sub-optimal position for the economy as a whole, a CBA is an exercise in partial economic analysis. The economist has to calculate gains and losses starting from the prevailing sub-optimal position that is reflected in the resulting prices. See Appendix 4.

15 Transfer payments and double counting

1   So far, the transfer payments discussed have been of the (disguised) unemployment benefits received by workers in connection with the calculation of the opportunity costs of labour. We now turn our attention to the other sorts of transfer payments.

2   The obverse of the benefits or direct subsidies received by unemployed persons are the direct taxes paid by employed persons. While a private firm properly calculates profit as *net* of all taxes it has to pay, the economist interested in social net benefit properly values such benefits as *gross* of tax. If, out of $100,000 annual net benefit from the operation of a dam, $35,000 is paid as tax to the government, this amount is to be regarded as a transfer to other nationals via the government, not as a loss to society as a whole; in effect, a form of redistribution of the net social gain of $100,000.

Similarly, tariffs that have to be paid by citizens on imported goods – or subsidies on them received by citizens – are also no more than inter-community transfer payments.

There is, however, a caveat to be made if foreigners are involved. If, for instance, the project in question is financed by an issue of shares on which shareholders receive a dividend, although the amount of tax paid to the home government is, as indicated, a transfer payment (from shareholders to other nationals), any *additional* tax paid by foreign shareholders to their own government is obviously *not* a transfer to nationals: it is a transfer abroad of part of the annual benefit produced by the project. Hence, the tax paid by resident foreigners to their own government constitutes a loss to the home economy and must therefore be subtracted in that year from the value of the project's benefits.

3   Are transfers involved in a shift in the demand for goods from area A to area B consequent upon a shift in population from the former to the latter area? We need not enquire into the reasons for the movement of people from A to B. If we discovered that they moved because they thought the climate in area B was more salubrious or that the tap water tasted better, the benefit would be calculated as the CV^{12} of those who chose to move over and above their costs of movement, but for the rest, the consequent increase in the demand for goods in area B does not of itself produce a benefit. Allowing that the additional goods bought in area B after people moved there are no different from those they bought in area A, *qua* consumers, nothing is gained or lost.

Existing storekeepers in area B will, of course, gain, but such gains will be offset by the losses suffered by storekeepers in area A. Yet this may not be a simple transfer of gain from one area to another. Over time, costs may arise. Service personnel may be willing enough to move from area A where they are no longer needed to area B where they are needed, notwithstanding which costs are incurred in their moving. Again, extended store capacity will have to be built in area B while such capacity has to be reduced in area A. But it would be a rare coincidence if, in the very year that, say, $1 million was to be spent in extending store capacity in area B, $1 million was no longer needed to be spent in area A to replace obsolete store capacity. Chances are that the $1 million of additional store capacity needed in area B will be spent soon, and only some years later will area A save $1 million from not having to replace that much store capacity. The resulting cost being equal to the potential return lost in delaying the recoupment of the $1 million spent in extending store capacity. In other words, the $1 million spent in area B may not be exactly offset by the reduction in expenditure in area A, owing to this lagged effect.

4   A caveat may now be entered against the possibility of counting a project's benefits twice.

Consider, first, the proposed construction of a railway linking a suburban area A with a big city, one that will offer an hourly service from six in the morning to midnight. The social value of the rail link is to be calculated, as usual, by the most potential users are willing to pay for it *less* any negative externalities the construction and service may incur. From this figure, the value of the net benefits is obtained by subtracting the opportunity costs of its construction and operation.

In consideration of the variety of advantages conferred by the rail link on the residents of area A, house prices there are apt to rise, the increase in the price of any particular house being, possibly, an indicator of the benefits expected to accrue to those occupying it: in effect, the capitalized value of the expected benefits. But only under special conditions may the rise in house prices in the area be accepted as a valid measure of the benefits over time from the introduction of the rail service. One of these conditions is that the size of area A be large – large enough to accommodate residents that are so far distant from the location of the railway station that the rail link offers them no advantages at all. The houses of such residents will therefore not rise at all in consequence of the rail link to the city. For the remaining houses, the closer to the railway station, the greater the benefit of the railway service and the greater the rise in the house price. Yet even were this condition met, people's uncertainty about the future usefulness of the rail link in view of possible later developments, to say nothing of the possible irrelevance of the implicit rates of discount involved, make it apparent that the differential rise in house prices in the area that may be attributed to the introduction of the rail link is a poor indicator of the extent of the benefits conferred.

This is particularly so when area A is such that all residents find the rail link to be an advantage. And this is likely to be the case. Even for a resident that will continue to drive into the city, the existence of a rail connection to the city has a contingent or insurance value; his automobile may be damaged, the weather may make driving risky, he may have damaged his wrists or otherwise feel disinclined to drive.

When all residents derive some benefit from the introduction of a rail link, a zero increase in the price of a house cannot be taken to mean that the residents derive zero benefit from the rail link. Indeed, the limiting case is where area A is such that, irrespective of the location of the house, accessibility to the railway station is much the same for everyone. For in that case, there can be no differential rise in house prices. In fact, house prices do not increase at all in consequence of the introduction of the rail link, no matter how advantageous.

One can only conclude that the only accurate way of measuring the social benefits of the rail link is by direct calculation of the magnitudes: that is, by calculating the CV[12] for every one affected by the change. On an annual basis, this amounts to ascertaining the largest sum the residents of area A are willing to pay for the rail services *less* the costs of any unwanted spillovers, and subtracting from this figure the annual opportunity costs of constructing and servicing the railway.

5   Although, in the above example of a rail link, there is no risk that the economist engaged in evaluating a project will double-count benefits, once as a flow of benefits and again as a capitalized value of expected benefits, there is a possibility that a double-counting of the flow of benefits may occur in some circumstances.

For example, consider an irrigation project that reduces the costs of grain production over the area of cultivation. The value of the benefit created by the project is to be reckoned, ultimately, as a consumer surplus – as a 'cost-saving' to the consumer arising from a reduction in the price of the grain. There will also be, initially, a rise in the profits of the cultivators or farmers, a rise in the profits of grain merchants, a rise in the profits of bankers, and so on. But these gains, no matter how long they continue, are not to be entered as benefits to the project – at least not as benefits *additional* to the cost-saving of the consumers of grain. Such extra profits are to be conceived as transfer of a part of this benefit to consumers of grain to the farmers, grain-merchants, banks and other middle men – at least during the period of adjustment in a competitive economy. Put more generally, the total benefit of the project which, as mentioned, is equal to no more than the gain to consumers from a lower price of grain, is distributed over a varying period of time among consumers, farmers and middlemen according to the operation of market forces and institutions.

Clearly, double-counting would be involved if, to this 'cost-saving' to consumers, we were also to add (temporary) gains by middlemen. Easier to understand if we use the example of cost-saving which is a benefit and we add to that the profits of farmers. This is double counting, all other things being equal.

Part IV
External effects

16 Introduction to external effects

1 External effects, an abbreviation for external economies and diseconomies –
sometimes referred to as 'externalities', more picturesquely as 'neighbourhood
effects', somewhat vapidly as 'side effects' and more suggestively as 'spillover
effects', or briefly, 'spillovers' – first appear as 'external economies' in Alfred
Marshall's *Principles* (1924) in connection with a competitive industry's downward-sloping supply curve. Marshall's argument is that, as industry expands by,
say, an additional firm, any resulting reduction in the average costs of production accrues to all the firms in the industry. The total reduction in costs experienced by all the intra-marginal firms is to be attributed to the entry of the
additional firm. The true or 'social' cost of the additional output produced by
this marginal firm is not the total cost of it as calculated by that firm, but this
cost *less* the total savings in costs by all the intra-marginal firms. This proposition is important in determining the 'correct' or 'optimal' output of the industry. For in practice, the additional firm makes no allowance for the savings in
costs it contributes to the rest of the industry. If, therefore, firms continue to
enter the competitive industry until, at the going price of the product, the total
cost of the firm is equal to its total revenue, the equilibrium size of the industry
will be that at which the market demand price is equal to the average (inclusive)
cost of the good in question. But the marginal cost, or total cost of the incremental firm, will be below average cost by the amount of the total cost-savings
it confers on the intra-marginal firms. Therefore, marginal cost will, to the same
extent, be below the market price and, abiding by the marginal-cost pricing rule,
output should be extended beyond the competitive equilibrium until marginal
cost is equal to price. The existence of external economies in a competitive
industry, Marshall concludes, entails an equilibrium output that is below
optimal.

Constructing a curve marginal to the industry's downward-sloping supply curve,
the point at which this marginal curve cuts the demand curve identifies the 'ideal'
or optimal output. This concept, and its corresponding construction, was extended
in a symmetrical manner to external diseconomies, to reveal that the optimal
output of a competitive industry was below the equilibrium output.

When such externalities first appeared in the literature, they tended to be
regarded, if not quite as curiosa, as in the nature of a refinement of economic analysis, one having limited applications. For among the older textbooks, at least, as
among the population at large, there was a tacit presumption in favour of the

spread of industry, the prevailing conviction being that, although the establishment of additional plant and equipment might cause some local inconvenience, the growth of industry would, on balance, confer economic benefits to society as a whole.

With the passage of time, it was realized that externalities had wide application, not simply as between firms in connection with the optimal size of an industry – which may be referred to as external effects *internal* to the industry – but also as between industries themselves or, more generally, as between different economic activities in which the gains of one or more groups are at the expense of others.

2   Familiar examples of negative spillovers include the manifold adverse ecological repercussions on flora and fauna, and on the climate and soil, in clearing the trees of forest land.[1]

Other examples within urban areas include the traffic congestion suffered by all drivers along roads and highways, the noise or pollution suffered by people in the vicinity from the operation of industry or of its products, and the consequent effects on people's health and longevity. Even the offence to citizens given by the erection of some tasteless or incongruous building or other structure may properly be regarded as a spillover – as, indeed, would the reverse of this, the pleasure in a beautiful building enjoyed by citizens being properly regarded as a positive spillover.

From a little reflection on examples such as these, it emerges that one characteristic common to all of them is the incidental or unintentional nature of the effect produced. The person or industry engaged, say, in logging may or may not have any idea of the consequences on the profits or welfare of others. But it is certain that they do not enter into his calculations. The factory owners, whose plant produces smoke as well as other things, are concerned only to produce the other things that can be sold on the market. They have no interest in producing the smoke, even though they may be fully aware of it. But so long as their own productivity does not suffer thereby, and they themselves are not penalized in any way, they will regard the smoke as an unfortunate by-product.

If these external effects are not deliberately produced, however, neither are they willingly absorbed by others. Such effects may add to the enjoyment of life, as does the smell of fresh-cut grass, or else add to life's vexations as does the noise, stench and danger of increasing car traffic. But they are not within the control of the persons who are absorbing them – at least not without their incurring expenses.[2] However, a definition of external effects that gives prominence to these aspects – that a person's welfare or a firm's profits depends upon things that are initially outside his control, which things are incidental to the activity of others – is by itself insufficient and may, indeed, lead to confusion. Let us see how.

3   The statement that a firm's or industry's outputs or profits or a person's welfare can be influenced by the activities of others is true, apparently, within the context of any general equilibrium system. In particular, it is true within a general equilibrium system that has no external effects of the sort illustrated above.[3] The familiar interdependent system of Leon Walras is a case in point. Among the set of equations posited are those for individuals regarded as consumers and owners of productive services. All the *variables* in each person's utility function – whether they

refer to the amounts of finished goods bought or the amounts of productive services offered – are deemed to be entirely within his control. The parameters within each person's utility function, however, are the set of prices; and these are determined by the system as a whole.

Thus, for each person, the quantities of the things that he is willing to buy or to sell depend, *inter alia*, on the set of market prices of these things. The amounts of goods supplied by perfectly competing firms also depend upon the market prices. These sets of market prices can, in general, be altered by any changes in technology, in people's tastes, or in the accumulation and redistribution of assets. It follows that the activities of persons and firms, in response to these sorts of changes, also have incidental effects on the welfare of others. If, to take a simple example, people start changing from tea to coffee, the price of tea will at first tend to fall and that of coffee to rise. The producers of tea will initially suffer and those of coffee benefit, while the consumers of tea will be better off and the consumers of coffee worse off.

But in this general equilibrium system, in the absence of all external effects as commonly understood, such interdependence operates *indirectly* through changes in market prices. Each and every exogenous change mentioned – a change in techniques, in tastes or in factor endowment – entails a corresponding change in the equilibrium set of prices. Since, in general, every price is affected, every person's welfare is affected also, and this can be very important.[4] Nevertheless, given perfectly competitive markets and no external effects, each general equilibrium position meets the requirement of a Pareto optimum, i.e. one in which it is not possible to make one or more persons better off without making at least one person worse off.[5] In contrast, the concern with external effects arises just because their existence implies that, unless special arrangements are made, the equilibrium solutions attainable may *not* be Pareto optimal.

We may, then, infer that external effects are effects on others that are conveyed directly and not indirectly through prices. If we allow that these effects on people's welfare matter in principle no less than do the priced products and services, it follows that it is just because these external effects, these by-products of the activities of others, are not properly priced or not priced at all, that the equilibrium solution is not Pareto optimal. To illustrate, the competitive equilibrium price of steel spades is $10, price being equal to long-run average and marginal cost. In their production, however, noise is produced, this being the only external effect in the economy. The noise created in producing the marginal spade would be tolerated without complaint only on receipt of, say, $7 by those disturbed by the noise. The social cost of the marginal spade is, therefore, $10 plus $7, or $17 altogether.

If we produced one spade less to start with, the factors released would, assuming universal perfect competition, create $10 of goods elsewhere. But the accompanying removal of noise is tantamount to a gain of $7. Society as a whole is better off to the extent of $7. The original output is then clearly in excess of the optimal output.

If all external effects, both positive and negative, could somehow be properly priced by a universal system of property rights,[6] then any perfectly competitive equilibrium would, indeed, be optimal. In fact, if every external effect, positive or negative were to be properly priced within a competitive market along with other goods and bads, it would cease to be an external effect: it would have been 'internalized' into the competitive economic system – as expressed, say, in the Walrasian system of equations. This will be fully appreciated once we have satisfactorily defined an externality.

4   Let us begin by writing the equation

$$U^1 = U^1(x_1^1, x_2^1, x_3^1, \ldots) \tag{16.1}$$

where U^1 is the utility, or welfare, of person 1, and x_1^1, x_2^1, x_3^1, are the amounts he has (flows or stocks, according to the problem) of three of the goods, x_1, x_2, x_3, on which his utility or welfare depends. Equation (16.1) is no more than the statement that person 1's utility or welfare depends on the quantities he has of those goods: no external effects are implied by the equation. If, instead, we write the equation as

$$U^1 = U^1(x_1^2; x_1^1, x_2^1, x_3^1) \tag{16.2}$$

the possibility of external effect is implied. The term x_1^2 gives the additional information that person 1's utility, U^1, depends not only on his own quantities of a number of goods, but also on x_1^2 person 2's quantity of x_1. If x_1 were flowers, then person 1's welfare would be affected not only by the flowers in his own garden, but also by those in his neighbour's garden. We could also interpret equation (16.2) as a production function, U^1 being the output of good 1, and the xs as the inputs used in the production of good 1. Equation (16.2) is now interpreted as saying that the amount of good 1 depends directly on the inputs x_1, x_2, x_3, etc., used directly in the production of good 1, and depends also on the amount of input l used in the production of good 2. The amount of the ith input used in the production of good 2 (this amount being under the control of the producers of good 2, *not* of the producers of good 1) is therefore regarded as imposing external effects on the output of good 1 and also, therefore, on the price of good 1 and the profits of the producers of good 1.

Such notational definitions are common enough in the literature. Another would be $\delta U^1/\delta x_i^2 \neq 0$, which can be interpreted as saying that a small change in person 2's quantity of good i will *not* leave person 1's utility unchanged. For the external effect to *exist*, however, we should have to add the information that $x_i^2 \neq 0$. Thus, $x_i^2 > 0$ implies that person 2 purchases some of the ith good; $x_i^2 < 0$ implies that he sells some of the ith good. If we write $\delta U^1/\delta x_i^2 > 0$, then person 2's external effect is one that raises person 1's welfare, the converse being true for a reversal of the inequality sign. Notation of this sort is helpful, but there are limitations. Thus, if x_i^2 refers to person 2's purchase of, say, a lawnmower, it is not possible to infer from the notation alone whether person 1's welfare is reduced (a) by his envy of person 2's new lawnmower, (b) by its being a noise nuisance, (c) by the extra smoke suffered by person 1 among others (including person 2) in consequence of the factory's production of an extra lawnmower or (d) by a combination of any or all of these. We return to these possibilities in the following section.

Again, the fact that person 1 reacts to the amount of good i taken or produced by person 2, without his being able to control person 2's consumption or production of good i – which information is imparted by the notation above – does not suffice to define an external effect in the economist's sense. My wealthy aunt's welfare (as well as my own) depends unambiguously on the amount of arsenic I put into her tea. If it was discovered that, in my impatience to inherit her fortune, I had used arsenic to accelerate the natural process of ageing, the coroner would be unlikely to refer to the results of my enterprise as an external effect. Yet, if person 1 is my aunt, person 2 is myself, x_i^2 is the amount of arsenic that I use, $\delta U^1/\delta x_i^2 < 0$, 0 expresses the proposition that my aunt's welfare varies inversely with the amount of arsenic that I use. It would therefore fit the situation just depicted. In contrast, an alternative interpretation of the external effect indicated by the same term, $\delta U^1/\delta x_i^2 < 0$,, would be that of my good aunt suffering at the thought of my injudicious consumption of arsenic, in small doses, as a stimulant. In order, therefore, to comply with the conventional meaning of external effect, the x_i^2 notation is to be interpreted strictly as person 2's consumption or production of good x_i which is determined solely by reference to his immediate interest, and in disregard of the effects it may have on the welfare of others.

5   Once the reader has a clear idea of what an externality is,[7] a little reflection will convince him that the number of external effects in the real world is virtually unlimited. If my wife is envious of her friend's new fur coat, her friend's wearing it in my wife's presence has an adverse external effect on at least one person. A cigar smoked in the presence of non-smokers has adverse external effects. Attractive short-skirted women may generate adverse external effects on other women and favourable external effects on men. A's promotion causes B to rejoice and C to curse. And so one could go on.

But should they all be taken into account by the economist? No, for there are at least two qualifications to consider.

First, there must obviously be a very large number of spillover effects that, if not trivial, would certainly be uneconomic to correct: the administrative costs and other expenses necessary to ensure compliance would exceed the social benefit of correcting the spillover effect. Because of the incidence of such 'transactions' costs, however, it may also appear uneconomic to correct even significant spillover! It may, nonetheless, transpire that some adverse spillovers may be eliminated or reduced either by alteration in the mode of production or in the use of the good in question or else by the employment of some technical device (which we discuss in later chapters).

Second, the question of the 'legitimacy' of certain spillovers has to be faced. For among all those spillovers that could, in fact, be economically corrected by one means or another, not all may be worthy of social recognition. Economists, and society at large, might wish to distinguish and, in practice, do distinguish, between external effects that are a source of 'legitimate' satisfaction or grievance, and those that are not. Among the latter is the resentment or envy felt by some people at the achievement or possessions of others.[8] But though such reactions may elicit sympathy and qualify for psychiatry, they are unlikely to command moral approval. Once ethics are bought into external effects in this way, the question of which effects are to count and which are not must, in the last resort, depend upon a consensus in the particular society. Since ethical distinctions of this sort are consistently made and acted by society, the economist is justified in following suit.

Though perhaps not formally embodied in legal documents, no economic policy that caters to these 'negative feelings' of people has ever been introduced.

In contrast, there is no lack of evidence that society does take seriously all tangible damage inflicted on people in the pursuit by others of pleasure or profit. As adverse environmental effects provide, today, the most important instances of damage inadvertently inflicted on other people, they will feature prominently in our discussion of methods of evaluating them.

Notes

1 Again, the adverse spillovers from creating a dam or artificial lake, include the erosion of fertile soil, the reduction of fish in the river, the silting of the river or canal, the spread of water-borne diseases and of breeding grounds for mosquitoes and locusts.
2 If an adverse spillover effect could be avoided without incurring any costs, it could hardly be called an adverse spillover. Certainly, no problem would arise
3 This system is, of course, a theoretical construct only. Engineers affirm that in all input–output activities there is wastage, and therefore waste material is absorbed into the air, the earth or its waters, so creating the potential for external effects.
4 For instance in appraising welfare criteria. See Mishan (1957).
5 If every relevant effect in the economy is properly priced, the economy is in an optimal position. The reverse, however, is not true, since optimality can be consistent with unpriced spillovers. See the example in Chapter 17.
6 A proposition initially stated by Coase (1960), one that apparently gave immense satisfaction to the business community in as much as it was assumed that such a system was feasible enough to vindicate unfettered free enterprise. The sobering fact, however, is that a universal system of property rights is far from being feasible. Were it otherwise, there would certainly be no need for CBAs. In this connection, see Appendix 7.
7 There are quite a number of economic phenomena – all, perhaps, relevant to considerations of optimality – masquerading in the literature as external effects that cannot be admitted on the interpretation in the text. Common among these are such developments as the pooling of risks, improved training facilities and other cost-saving arrangements. Such arbitrary extensions of the original concept, and the consequent ambiguity generated, are discussed in Mishan (1965a).
8 This is all-too-common phenomenon, envy of the greater income or wealth of others, is often referred to in the literature as the 'Jones effect' (the obsession with 'keeping up with the Joneses'). The more prevalent it is, the less can economic growth be held to increase society's welfare.

17 Adverse spillovers

1 We now turn to a more detailed consideration of adverse environmental spillovers. The warrant for doing so does not derive simply from their rapid growth,
especially in the post-war period, nor simply from their frequent neglect, but from
the evaluative problems that arise whenever an adverse spillover effect has a large
effect on the welfare of a number of people. If the judgement that adverse environmental spillovers have become more important since the war than favourable spillovers is questioned by the reader, he need not complain of bias.

The analysis of favourable spillovers is quite symmetrical, and economy in exposition suggests that a thorough treatment of either type of spillover alone, favourable
or unfavourable, will suffice to demonstrate the principles.

2 We have taken it for granted that spillovers have to be evaluated, ultimately, by
reference to the subjective estimates of the victims of spillover effects. One can go
further. One can argue for these compensatory sums being actually paid to the victims in the event of a project being introduced that generates adverse spillovers.
Indeed, this view of the matter would seem to follow from the classical liberal doc-
trines as expounded by John Stuart Mill, in contradistinction to a Pareto economic
decision based simply on the determination of a net balance of gain or loss, one in
which the question of actual compensation is disregarded. A fortiori, the liberal
doctrine would reject the 'social engineering' approach to the spillover problem, an
approach that seeks to formulate 'tolerance levels' for society. True, the upper limit
of the tolerable degree of, say, noise may be so chosen as to preclude ascertainable,
physical damage or bodily hurt, given our present knowledge of the effects of noise
on people and property. Yet, noise below that limit can be highly irritating to a lot
of people. If a man were subjected at regular intervals to the gentlest tap on the
back of his head, his subsequent exasperation would hardly surprise us. Neither the
fact that he emerged from the treatment without bruises nor the affirmation that
this head-tapping business was, in some mysterious way, an unavoidable by-
product of the operation of modern industry and, indeed, could be counted on to
promote exports, would assure us about its moral justification. And if the occasional or frequent bombarding of a man's ears with noise, as a consequence of
other people's pursuit of pleasure or profit, can be said to differ from this imagin-
ary case, it is not so much that, over time, people become less physically sensitive
to its incidence but rather that, of necessity, we have learned to curb our desire to
give expression to our annoyance, in the belief that there is little we can do to prevent or reduce its omnipresence.

Yet, granted that the growing incidence of noise does reduce people's well-being, if the true liberal would reject the adoption of some maximum tolerable levels of noise at different times of the day, it is not merely because such a policy is necessarily arbitrary. It is because the adoption, of such tolerance norms runs counter to the doctrine that each man is to be deemed the best judge of his own interests – no less so in matters that affect him directly and intimately.

3   It must be acknowledged, however, that economists are seen as more eager to defend men's interests in cases where they are beneficiaries of privately produced goods than when they are the victims of those adverse spillovers created by the production or consumption of privately produced goods. The proposal by high-minded members of society that, say, provocative lace underwear should be withdrawn from production, or at least not advertised in the media, would be sure to provoke condemnation by free-enterprise economists, notwithstanding that provocative lace underwear is not a requisite of the good life. Yet, when it comes to the distress that many people suffer in consequence of the destruction of environmental amenity – something, it can be argued, that is indeed a prerequisite of the good life – the response, until very recently, has not been impressive. At all events, for decades, citizens had submitted to being continually robbed of choice in respect of amenities such as clean air, quietude, green space and other collective goods that vitally enhance their sense of well-being. They tended to accept the spoliation of the physical environment in which they were immersed much as they might accept climatic changes, as a phenomenon to which they can perhaps adapt, but which, in itself, is outside the control of men.

Such an attitude, however, is not justifiable. Some framework of law is necessary if markets are to function in an orderly fashion, and if trade and enterprise are to flourish. But not all laws are equally effective in harmonizing the search for commercial gain with the welfare of society. The economist's interest in social welfare or, more simply, in extending the citizen's area of choice, can do more than offer suggestions to promote a smoother functioning of the existing economic mechanisms. At a time of rapid deterioration of the environment, he can propose alterations in the legal framework itself as something that can make significant contributions to social welfare.

Prior to such proposals, however, let us summarize three aspects of the approach to adverse spillovers still popular among those economists who argue for a presumption in favour of competitive enterprise.

4   (i) First, granted that, for any good x that incidentally also creates measurable adverse spillovers that vary with the output of x, there exists a uniquely determined optimal output, which is that at which the price of x is equal to its social marginal cost (the latter term being the sum of the private marginal cost of x and the marginal cost of its spillovers).

It is easily demonstrated that this optimal output can just as well be reached by levying an excise tax on good x as by offering an excise subsidy for reducing the output of x – for the purpose, in either case, of inducing producers to supply the optimal output of good x. This same optimal output can also be reached either by compelling the producers of x to compensate all those who suffer from the incidental adverse spillovers or else by such victims themselves bribing the producers of x to reduce its output.

One is supposed to conclude that the question of responsibility for the reduction of the spillover – the question of who compensates whom – in these cases of manifest conflict of interest has no bearing on the allocative problem of determining the optimal output. From such a conclusion, it follows that differences in the ways by which this optimal output may be reached affect only the distribution of welfare in the community.

(ii) Nor, apparently, can this question of which party should compensate the other, be settled by considerations of equity. To be sure, it may be argued that, although the smoke produced by a soap factory does indeed damage the welfare of many of the inhabitants living in the vicinity, so also can the required curtailment of the smoke-producing output (or the required installation of anti-smoke devices) be said to damage the interests of the manufacturers. The fact is simply that the interests of the two groups – the soap manufacturers (or beneficiaries from soap production), on the one hand, and the victims of their smoke pollution, on the other – are mutually opposed, and only a misuse of language can detract from the essential symmetry in respect of equity.[1]

(iii) Finally, whatever the institutional framework, the party suffering from the spillovers in question has a clear interest in bribing the other party to reduce the initial (uncorrected) output in the direction of the optimal output. But recognition of the opportunity for mutual gain in moving to an optimal output leads to a consideration of the costs of negotiating an agreement between the two parties.

For instance, *in the absence of such negotiating costs*, the potential gain in reducing the output of x by successive units can be reckoned as the excess of the most the inhabitants will pay for the reduction of that particular unit of x less the minimum sum the manufacturer will accept for agreeing to the reduction. And if this potential gain is, say, $100, its division between the two parties will depend upon their respective bargaining power.[2]

If, now, negotiating costs amount to $120, they will exceed the $100 of potential mutual gain. The contemplated reduction in the output of x is, therefore, no longer mutually advantageous. With this consideration in mind, an observed absence of negotiation to reduce the particular spillover is explained by the argument that the potential mutual gain in the movement towards an optimal output must be smaller than the costs of negotiating it. Since these negotiating costs are real enough, involving as they do the use of scarce resources, they may be supposed frequently to swamp the (costless) mutual gains of a movement toward an optimum position.

By such reasoning, some economists found themselves perilously close to an ultra-conservative doctrine that, in respect of spillovers at least, what is already in existence is best. And for the rest, one can do no more than await the advent of innovations, technical or institutional, that reduce the costs of preventive devices or the costs of negotiation and administration.

5   This complacent, though fairly widespread, doctrine has been challenged in the literature on externalities.[3] But it must also be challenged in the cost-benefit literature. It may be thought that, whereas the externality literature is concerned primarily with optimal outputs, CBA addresses itself, in the main, to the question of the economic justification of a specific project taken as a whole (or the selection of several from a large number of technically feasible projects) and only in

a secondary way to the question of optimal outputs of projects once they are established. But the arguments about optimal outputs summarized above, dealing as they do with compensatory payments, with equity and with negotiation costs – or transactions costs as they are more generally called – can just as well be extended to the issue of the acceptance or rejection of a specific project.

Having said this much to affirm the relevance of considerations (i), (ii) and (iii) to CBA, a brief word on each is appropriate before concluding the chapter.

(i) The alleged uniqueness of the optimal solution rests on the implied assumption of zero welfare effects. Once the assumption is removed, as it has to be wherever the project in question has significant effects on welfare, optimality becomes ambiguous. This aspect of the problem is treated in some detail in Chapter 20.

(ii) The freedom of one group to pursue its own interests or enjoyment, it is alleged, necessarily interferes with that of the other group once the externality situation is created. For example, the inhabitants of an area being polluted by the smoke emitted from a soap-works suffer accordingly, but so also does the soap-works (and its beneficiaries) if its operations are curtailed. The question, then, of which of the two parties should have the property rights in the airshed over the area – in effect, the question of which party has legally to compensate the other for forgoing some of the advantages it enjoyed before the externality appeared – may be settled by reference to the alternative distributional implications.

To be sure, distributional considerations ought properly to be taken into account in a social decision. But they are not the only considerations. Although such externality situations are indeed Pareto-symmetric, as described above, they are not, in general, symmetric with respect to ethical merit. In accordance with the classical liberal dictum, the freedom of a man to pursue his own interests has to be qualified in so far as it reduces the freedom or welfare of others. And the freedom of the soap manufacturer to spread smoke over the inhabitants of the area will conflict with the freedom of the inhabitants to continue to enjoy unpolluted air. For the mere action of the inhabitants in enjoying the unpolluted air does not *of itself* cause any damage to the soap works beneficiaries, whereas the action of the soap works – the emission of smoke – does *of itself* reduce the welfare of the inhabitants. The conflict, that is, is initiated directly by the action of the soap works: it is not initiated by the inhabitants breathing the unpolluted air. To take an extreme example, a conflict of interests between a householder A and a burglar B is indeed Pareto-symmetric and, of course, an optimal solution is possible. But the conflict of interests is clearly not ethically symmetric. The conflict is initiated by B's action and is manifestly culpable.

(iii) The argument that the existence of negotiating costs, or transaction costs as they are sometimes called, act to support the *status quo*, or at least the presumption in favour of unconstrained private enterprise, may be valid under existing legal institutions. But in the light of the ethical considerations discussed above, it is manifest that transaction costs are more justly to be borne by the party that inflicts the damage on others. Once the law clearly recognizes this, the existence of transaction costs no longer acts to strengthen the *status quo* in so far as it favours unconstrained private enterprise but, instead, must act to strengthen the *status quo ante* – the original state that was free of smoke or noise nuisance or other adverse spillover, prior to the introduction of the enterprise in question.

Notes

1 This proposition gathers plausibility from habitual attention given to the spillovers generated between two firms or industries.
2 The loss to the manufacturer from reducing the output of x by a unit is calculated as the profit forgone. Where, however, we are thinking in terms of the long-period supply curve of a competitive industry and ignore the costs of adjustment, the loss is calculated as that of a consumer surplus.
3 Mishan (1967b, 1971b); Cropper and Oates (1992).

18 Internalizing externalities

1   The verbal description of an external effect – that is, a direct effect on another's profit or welfare arising as an incidental by-product of some other person's or firm's legitimate activity – would seem adequate to convey its meaning. Its nature is made yet clearer, however, by examining the notion of 'internalizing' the external effect. The basic idea is that of transforming the incidental by-product into a joint product that is priced on the market. As told by a number of Argentinians, before the turn of the century cattle were slain on the ranches for their leather only. Their flayed carcasses were left to rot but, if found in time, they could be used as fresh meat by the poor peasants. Apparently, only the leather had a market price, the meat being a by-product, or external effect, of leather production – a favourable spillover of the leather industry for those peasants who happened to be in the vicinity.[1]

Suppose, however, that the human population began to multiply more rapidly than the cattle population, that the taste for meat grew, that meat began to be stored in refrigerators and that, most important of all perhaps, the meat could be exported to distant markets. Domestic meat would become scarce and, therefore, a market for it would come into being. It would then cease to be a spillover, an unintended by-product in the process of obtaining hides for leather. It would take its place as a good in its own right, a joint product with leather. Whatever the separate demands for meat and leather are like, the long-run competitive equilibrium output is optimal, as the cattle population is expanded to the point at which the sum of the market prices are equal to the marginal cost of cattle production. The external effect has been internalized into the pricing system.[2]

Internalizing spillover effects arises also in the case of external diseconomies that are internal to the industry. Common examples of the latter category are deep-sea fishing, in which any additional fishing boat above a certain number reduces the catch of each of the existing fishing boats in the fishing grounds, or traffic congestion, in which every additional vehicle above a certain number causes delay to each of the existing number of vehicles using a given highway system. Internalizing this sort of spillover would require that a positive market price be imputed to the currently unpriced though scarce resource – the area of the sea in the first case, the highway in the second. Once such a resource is priced, it will be used more economically. The analogy of scarce land used in the production of, say, corn is exact. If priced correctly, which implies that in a competitive industry the rent of this scarce resource be maximized, the competitive equilibrium output that emerges is also the optimal output.[3]

Another example, though one in which internal accounting prices are substituted for market prices, is that of two separately owned but adjacent factories, A and B. Factory A produces shoes and is powered by an old-fashioned coal engine, which emits so much smoke as to seriously affect the output of factory B, which produces chocolate bars. The manager of factory B remonstrates with manager A, but to no effect. The daughter of the owner of factory A and the son of the owner of factory B decide to get married, in consequence of which the two factories come under common ownership and control, and the couple live together happily ever after. The cost of the smoke, reckoned in terms of the damage inflicted on the output of factory B, is no longer a spillover generated by A and suffered by B. It is now unambiguously a cost to the joint A–B enterprise and, as such, ways and means of reducing it will be sought. Either antismoke devices will be installed in factory A, or else, if cheaper (and assuming the smoke damage to B's output varies directly with A's output), A's output will be reduced to the point at which the value of the marginal damage to B's output, added to the marginal cost of shoe production in A, is equal to the market price of A's shoes. Thus, the smoke ceases to become a spillover effect, but becomes a properly costed item that is internalized into the costing system of the A–B merger.

2   The number of spillover effects that can be internalized into the pricing mechanism or into the costing systems of firms is, however, limited. Among those that cannot easily be internalized through the market are many of the by-products of modern industry and of the hardware it produces. One thinks, in this connection, of traffic noise and various forms of pollution arising from the spread of sewage, garbage and radioactive wastes; also of the post-war phenomenal growth of diseases of the nerves, heart and stomach, caused by high-tension living, the most ubiquitous by-product of sustained technological advance. Why cannot such spillovers be so internalized? The answer is simple: in order for a competitive market for such spillovers to emerge, certain conditions have to be met which, in the nature of the physical universe, cannot be met. First, the potential victim of these adverse spillover effects must have legal 'property rights' in, say, their ownership of some quantum of quiet and clean air which, if such rights were enjoyed, they could choose to sell to others. Second, in order for such rights to be enforceable, it would be necessary to demarcate a three-dimensional 'territory' about the person of each potential victim in order to identify the intrusions of others and take appropriate legal action. Third, in order for a monopolistic situation not to arise, each of these three-dimensional properties within a given area, which can be rented for particular purposes (say, to accommodate the noise or pollution of someone's activity), must be a close substitute for the others.

The first condition could, of course, be met in the sense that all forms of pollution could be outlawed in the absence of specific agreements between the parties concerned. But because the second condition cannot be met in the world we inhabit, there is difficulty in demarcating each person's property, and a consequent difficulty in identifying the trespasser and the extent of the trespass. Nor can the third condition be met, for, in this hypothetical scheme of things, the right to use one man's 'territory', within some given area, is no substitute for that of another man. Each man within the area has his own three-dimensional territory and, since the noise to be created by the new activity enters in some degree into all of such territories, the enterprise has to reach agreement with each one of them. None can substitute for the other. Unless all agree, the permission of those who do is worthless.

If it were otherwise, if one territory could be substituted freely for another, as could plots of land in an agricultural area, an appropriate market price would arise from the competition of the sellers. The physical universe being what it is, however, each potential seller is in a completely monopolistic position for, without his particular consent, the necessary arrangement for the whole of the affected area cannot be concluded. The reader will detect a similarity between this hypothetical problem, posed by the third condition, and that facing a railroad company having to buy every mile of land through which the track has to run. The cost of acquiring rights where a large number of landowners are involved could be prohibitive were it not for legislation compelling the sale of rights on terms which the courts decide are reasonable. Another instance, occasionally reported by the press, is that of a single householder or small business holding out against a property company that is attempting to buy up a specific area of land as part of some new development scheme.

We must, then, resign ourselves to the prospect of never being able to internalize these important environmental spillovers within the market economy; that is, of not being able to create a market for them – which is, of course, one of the reasons why cost-benefit methods are required to evaluate them.

3   Some further light is cast on the nature of spillover effects by briefly observing the connection between them and collective or public goods. Environmental spillovers usually affect a large number of people within an area. But whereas the positive spillover has been defined as an unintended beneficial effect on others arising from some legitimate economic activity, the benefits conferred on the community by a collective good are those that are deliberately created. It may be noted, moreover, that the collective good may be optional for members of the community, an example being a public park which allows each person to choose how many hours, if any, he wishes to spend there.[4] A non-optional collective good, in contrast is one in which each person perforce receives some amount of it, an example being the rainfall over a certain area that is caused by 'seeding' the clouds above it. In such a case, the amount of rain falling on the land of each person can be more or less than he would prefer. It may even be so large an amount that, on balance, it becomes a net loss to the recipient – an adverse spillover.[5]

4   It is not to be supposed, however, that the evaluation of positive spillovers in a cost-benefit calculation is confined to collective goods. What are often referred to as public goods – whether or not they are publicly financed – need not also be a collective good as defined. A hospital or a railroad is not, strictly speaking, a collective good: once constructed, the services produced by either can be separately allocated to each of a number of persons for their own particular use.

For the collective good, the benefit in any period of any one unit of the good is equal to the aggregate of the benefits enjoyed by all affected by it. If, therefore, the amount of the collective good is variable, the net benefit to the community is maximized by increasing the amount of it until its marginal (aggregate) benefit is equal to its opportunity cost.

The same is true if, instead, we are initially addressing ourselves to the construction of some public good that is not, strictly speaking, a collective good. For instance, if we are to determine the longest distance to be covered by a proposed rail link that would connect a number of towns and villages over the time span contemplated, we have to aggregate the benefits of each potential passenger over that time span for each alternative length of the railroad – adequately measured in each case by the areas under the expected future demand curves – and compare them with their relevant opportunity costs.

Once the chosen rail link has been established, however, the service it provides has to be treated as a private good. Hence, in operating the service, net benefits are maximized if every person pays the marginal cost he incurs which, in the absence of congestion, could be zero, provided that the daily or weekly overheads are covered by the consumer surplus.

In the case of a public good such as a hospital, in contrast, once the optimal size of the hospital has been constructed, the marginal cost of each patient is positive and will generally vary between one patient and another.

Notes

1 Notwithstanding which the number of cattle slain could be optimal if, at the margin, the value of the meat was zero. We discuss this point further in the next chapter in terms of 'allocative significance'.
2 It may seem unnecessary to remark that the possibility of internalizing an external effect (or, in the absence of internalization, correcting for optimal outputs) does not mean that the creation of an *adverse* external effect need not make things worse. Yet, students do sometimes argue as though this is so; as though, so long as optimizing by one method or another takes place, the creation of adverse external effects may be viewed with equanimity. The introduction of an adverse external effect into the economy is a bad thing no matter how the economy adapts to it. By internalizing the bad, or by optimizing the output that produces the bad, we are doing no more than making the best of a bad job. We are certainly not as well off as we should be if this bad had not appeared on the economic scene.
3 Assuming a period during which there is one scarce fixed factor and one factor that is variable in supply at a constant price, the average cost curve eventually slopes upward. A curve drawn marginal to this average cost curve cuts the demand curve at the optimal output. At this output, the difference between average cost and marginal cost *times* output gives the amount of the rent to the fixed factor – the maximum rent possible in a perfectly competitive market in which the price of the product is treated as a parameter.
4 There can, however, be a problem of congestion if the number of people increases relative to the number, or the size, of the facilities provided.
5 Among those who on balance gain from the given artificial rainfall, there can be those farmers whose crops receive too much rain, in the sense that the benefit to them of the marginal inch of rain is negative. The optimal condition, however, requires that rain be increased until the sum of the benefits and losses of the marginal inch of rain is equal to the cost of producing it.

19 Evaluating spillovers

1   In principle, the method of evaluating spillovers arising from the construction or operation of a project is straightforward enough. For the given amount of any spillovers created by a project during a specified period, either everyone affected by it benefits (unambiguously a positive spillover) or everyone affected loses (unambiguously a negative spillover) or else some gain by it and some lose. In the last case, the net effect of the spillover is, of course, the algebraic sum of all the individual valuations and can, therefore be, on balance, either positive or negative. There will be instances when part or all of a community's valuation of a spillover can properly be calculated by reference to prevailing market prices. The cost of any person's additional laundry bill arising from industrial smoke in the vicinity is a good example. So also is the cost of the damage resulting from cattle straying onto adjacent farmland. But in the last resort, there may be no alternative but to value the spillover as equal to the subjective valuations of those who suffer or benefit from its effects. In terms of the Kaldor–Hicks criterion, the relevant subjective measure is conceived as that sum of money (to be paid by the individual if the spillover raises his welfare; to be received by him if it lowers his welfare) that would restore his welfare to its original pre-spillover level.

Thus, an algebraic aggregate of all the individual valuations of a spillover that is positive is one that meets the Kaldor–Hicks criterion for the community. It may then be inferred that a costless distribution of the gains could make everyone in the community better off, the reverse being true for an algebraic aggregate that is negative.

If, for instance, the building of a dam for irrigational purposes creates only two spillovers: (i) the creation of an artificial lake in which people can swim or boat, and (ii) a body of stagnant water which causes a vast increase in the insect population, each spillover is to be evaluated in the manner stated above and then added, to result in either an excess of benefits or an excess of costs attributable to the project.

2   A common proposal for dealing with the conflict of interest arising, say, from the proposed use of some natural resource is that of auctioning the property rights, a solution that does not comport with our adopted potential Pareto-improvement criterion. This can be illustrated by a proposal to build a dye-works that pours its effluent into the otherwise clear waters of a lake along which it is to be situated. People living close to the lake shore are incensed, as the resulting effluent would ruin their customary recreations that depend upon the lake's pristine waters.

True, it can be argued that, of the two conflicting parties (the owners of the dye-works and the lake-shore community), the one offering the highest sum for use of the lake should be assigned the property rights to it. Such a solution meets the principle that any scarce resource should be allocated to the organization that can use it to produce the greatest value for society.

Yet, it is also true that the auctioning method is one that may not be able to meet the potential Pareto criterion. In our example, we can suppose that the expectant owners of the dye-works are able to offer, at most, $45 million, whereas the lakeside community could manage, at most, but $35 million, in consequence of which the dye-works is given the go-ahead. But it may also transpire that the smallest sum that would reconcile the lake-side inhabitants to the establishing of the dye-works by the lake far exceeds the $45 million that the dye-works' owners can afford. If, say, the smallest acceptable sum were $65 million, then certainly the use of the lake by the dye-works would fail the Kaldor–Hicks test: the loss to society as a whole (including the dye-works' owners) would be such that a costless distribution of the $20 million loss could make everyone in society worse off.

3   In evaluating the costs of adverse spillover effects, the economist engaged in a cost-benefit calculation also has a duty to seek ways of minimizing their costs by proposing recourse to whatever technology is currently available. This search to reduce spillover costs is of the highest importance, as it can make all the difference to whether the project in question meets the cost-benefit criterion.

Whether the adverse spillover is, so to speak, an overhead in the productive process – an example being the power required to drive the machinery in a weaving shed, where the volume of noise created by it is quite independent of the number of looms, if any, in operation – or whether, instead, the amount of the spillover effect varies directly with the amount of the goods produced will make little difference to the analysis. But the exposition is simplified by addressing ourselves, first, to the latter case and also by provisionally assuming that the cost suffered by the community from the unit of spillover generated is uniquely determined. Thus, in Figure 19.1, the cost of the spillovers created by successive units of the good x being produced is measured by the height of the EE_1 curve increasing from left to right. The figure also shows that, *in the absence of all spillovers*, there is an excess (consumer) benefit-over-cost curve BB_1 that slopes downward from left to

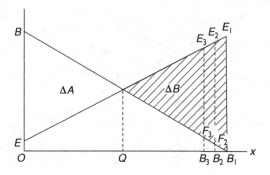

Figure 19.1

right so that the optimal output (again, in the absence of all spillover effects) is seen to be equal to OB_1, the amount of this excess benefit being measured as the area of the triangle OBB_1.

We must now consider ways of dealing with the cost of the spillovers, represented in the figure as the area under the EE_1 slope. Let us first illustrate three alternative methods.

4   *Method I*: If the only available method of reducing the spillover is to reduce the output of good x, we should want to reduce that output to OQ as, beyond output OQ, each additional unit of x produced results in an excess benefit that is, increasingly, below the cost of the concomitant spillover.

In other words, we may start with the output OB_1. On this last unit of x produced, the spillover cost is equal to B_1E_1, whereas the consumer gain is zero, leaving a net social loss equal to B_1E_1. Proceeding in this way, moving toward the left, as we cease to produce successive units of x, we reduce ever smaller amounts of net social loss until we reach output OQ. It follows that the measure of net gain to society from reducing output of x from OB_1 to OQ is equal to the striped triangle area indicated by ΔB in Figure 19.1.

It also follows that if, instead, we begin with zero output of x and then start producing x, the net social gain of successive units of x produced can be measured as the excess of the height of the BB_1 curve above the corresponding height of the EE_1 curve, which excess height is zero at output OQ. Thus, by producing, the output OQ of x, we secure the maximum social net gain, one equal to the area of triangle ΔA.

Whichever way we look at it – whether we begin with the commercially determined output OB_1 of x, or whether we begin with zero output of x – the net social gain can be maximized by producing output OQ of x.

5   *Method II*: Using the same sort of figure (Figure 19.2), we again measure the excess benefit curve and the corresponding EE_1 curve that measures the cost of the spillovers created by successive units of x.

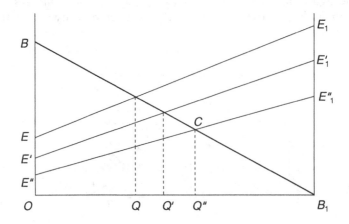

Figure 19.2

But now, rather than reducing the spillovers by reducing the market output of x by B_1Q, we begin by maintaining the market output OB_1 and reduce the spillover effects by the employment of some technical device, say the fitting of some antinoise device to aircraft, where OB_1 is to measure the number of flights per annum to some given destination.

Suppose that an initial expenditure of $100,000 per annum in muffling the noise on all the aircraft to that destination reduces the cost of the noise to people living within the relevant area by $180,000, the original curve EE_1 has to be lowered, say to $E'E'_1$. Each of the OB_1 flights, that is, now inflicts less noise on the community, the reduction in cost for any one flight being measured by the vertical distance at that point between the original EE_1 curve and the $E'E'_1$ curve. The area or the strip between the two curves, $EE_1E'E'_1$ is, therefore, equal to the benefit of $180,000 (or reduced cost) from the resulting reduction in noise.

A further expenditure of $100,000 on muffling aircraft noise has the effect of reducing the cost of noise by, say an additional $140,000, lowering the cost curve to $E''E''_1$. Clearly, we can continue in this way until the value to people of a further reduction in aircraft noise is no greater than the expenditure required to produce that reduction.

If we assume that the curve $E''E''_1$ is as far as we can go in increasing the net social gain by the method of noise muffling, it will be observed that there are still a number of flights, measured as the number from Q'' to B_1, that will continue to create noise whose cost is above the excess benefit from the flights. Therefore, by eliminating $Q''B_1$ flights per annum, we can secure a further net social gain which can be measured as equal to the area of the triangle E''_1CB_1.

It may be concluded that the more effective is this second method of muffling aircraft noise, the greater will be the reduction of the cost-of-noise curve EE_1. Consequently, the fewer will be the number of flights that have to be eliminated in order to reach an optimal reduction in aircraft noise when using both methods I and II.

6 Now it need hardly be remarked that these two methods, among others that are possible, are available to be used at the same time, that is, in combination. This being the general case, we have devised a method for determining an optimal combination of all methods that are feasible.

The diagram by which the optimal solution, using only method II, can be more neatly exhibited is that shown in Figure 19.3. Along the horizontal axis, we measure, from left to right, successive units of pollution. Along the vertical axis, we measure two things: (i) the social value (or cost) of any unit of pollution and (ii) the opportunity cost of eliminating that unit of pollution.

This (i) value (or cost) of pollution curve, which we may more suggestively refer to as the marginal social damage curve, rises with the amount of pollution generated. Up to OV' units of pollution that are generated by the production of the good, or goods, in question, no perceptible effect on people's welfare is registered, after which it is shown that successive units of pollution entail increasing social loss – each being measured, say, by the maximum sum people affected are willing to pay to eliminate that unit of pollution. Thus the Nth unit of pollution suffered is valued, or costed, at NV.

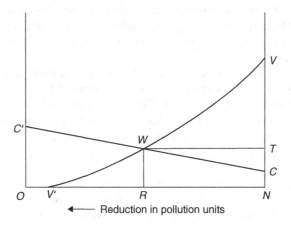

Figure 19.3

The total amount of pollution created by the production of the goods in question being equal to ON, the opportunity cost of removing successive units of pollution can be measured from right to left along the rising CC' curve.

Figure 19.3 clearly suggests that the net social gain from reducing pollution is maximized by a reduction of NR pollution units, at which point the (falling) marginal gain from pollution reduction is equal to the (rising) marginal cost of pollution reduction. A tax of TN per unit of pollution would therefore be 'optimal', as without knowledge of, or reference to, the VV' curve, the levying of such a tax will impel the industry to reduce pollution by NR. For up to the first NR units of pollution, it is cheaper to reduce pollution than pay the tax. After NR units, the reverse is true. The optimal amount of pollution remaining is, therefore, equal to OR, and this much pollution has to be borne, in as much as the loss sustained, as measured by the area $V'RW$, is well below the opportunity cost of its removal, a cost equal to the area $ORWC'$.

Looking at the matter otherwise, the net social benefit from reducing the initial amount of pollution ON by NR units is the excess of the social gain from reducing NR pollution over the opportunity cost of its removal, this net social gain being equal to the area bounded by CVW.

7   *Method III*: As an alternative method of reducing pollution, we may consider moving a smoky pottery-works away from a populated area. Along the horizontal axis of Figure 19.3, we now measure the distance in miles that the pottery-works can be moved from its initial position N, the CC' curve being the marginal opportunity cost per mile of moving the works[1] and the VV' curve the marginal social gain per mile of moving the works further from its initial location. It may then be concluded that the optimal distance the works should be moved is equal to NR miles.

For direct comparison with method II, it will be convenient to posit a unique transformation of the distance from N in miles into the number of pollution units that are eliminated, for once the number of miles distant from the original location of the works has been transformed into the corresponding number of units of pollution removed that were adopted in method II, we are able to superimpose the resulting CC' and VV' curves of this third method on those resulting from method II.

So much by way of demonstration. We shall now, however, restrict the analysis to a direct comparison of the first three methods of pollution reduction, one that is applicable to any given sort of pollution. Thus, in Figure 19.4, which has the same axes as Figure 19.3 and the same VV' social damage curve, C_aC_a' is the marginal opportunity curve for method I,[2] C_bC_b' is that corresponding to method II, while C_bC_c' is that corresponding to method III.

In general, and as can be seen from Figure 19.4, the optimal level of pollution reduction when any one method is used alone differs from that of the others. In the figure, these three optimal levels of pollution reductions are OR_a, OR_b, OR_c, corresponding to methods I, II and III, respectively. Used alone, their corresponding optimal pollution taxes must also differ. If instead of using only one method singly, all three methods are to be simultaneously employed, economy requires that the amount reduced by each method is such that the marginal cost of each method is the same. This result follows from the idea of reducing the first, second, third, ..., nth unit of pollution by whichever method is the cheapest for that unit, bearing in mind that, eventually, each of the methods is used increasingly. The succession of lowest incremental costs so derived forms a composite marginal cost curve, and the true optimal pollution-reduction is determined where this curve cuts the VV' curve at R''.

For simplicity of construction, we assume the marginal cost curve of each of our three methods is independent of the costs, if any, incurred by the other two methods (an assumption that is unnecessary but facilitates the geometry). We can

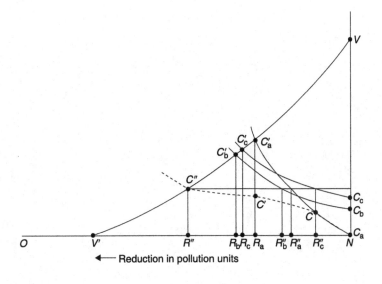

Figure 19.4

then construct the composite marginal cost curve for pollution reduction $C_aCC'C''$ by 'horizontally adding together' the three separate marginal cost curves. From C_a to C on this composite curve, method I alone is used to reduce pollution. From C to C', some reduction is effected by both methods I and II. From C' onward, further reductions receive a contribution from each of the three methods.

The reader will at once observe that the composite optimal pollution $V'R''$ that remains is smaller than the 'optimal' pollution determined by the employment of any one method alone. Consequently, the composite pollution tax $C''R''$ is also smaller than a pollution tax determined by reference to any single method of pollution reduction. Since the magnitude of the composite pollution tax is to be adopted by each of the three methods when they are used together, the pollution reduction contributed by each of the methods when they are used together is smaller than the 'optimal' pollution reduction effected by that method when it is used alone. Thus, of the total pollution reduced jointly, NR'', methods I, II and III are responsible, respectively, for amounts NR''_a, NR''_b and NR''_c. Clearly, each of these amounts is smaller than NR_a, NR_b and NR_c, these being respectively the 'optimal' pollution reductions of methods I, II and III, when each method is used alone.

Notes

1 The rising CC' curve measures the rising marginal cost of transporting the pottery-works products over an increasing distance to sales outlets in the populated area.
2 The $C_aC'_a$ curve corresponding to method I can be derived from the excess benefit curve B $'B$ in Figure 19.1, as the amount of excess benefit that is foregone increases with successive units of pollution eliminated.

20 Compensating for environmental damage

1   In demonstrating the determination of an optimal output of a good in the presence of the spillover effects that it generates, economists have seemingly been unaware or, if aware, have failed to make explicit that a conclusion of the uniqueness of the optimal position depends upon the assumption of zero welfare (or income) effects and zero budgetary restrictions.[1] It may, however, also be possible that some economists, although aware of these welfare and budgetary effects, believe that attention to them would serve only to clutter up the analysis without adding anything of much value to the result of the analysis.

There may be cases where the analysis that determines a unique optimal output is valid. But the welfare effects and budgetary restrictions may not be ignored when we are to consider those spillovers that make a substantial difference to people's welfare – substantial enough, at any rate, to make the question of whether the cost-benefit criterion is met depend crucially upon which of the conflicting groups is the one entitled to compensation.

In general, wherever the adverse spillover takes the form of a pollutant that cannot be entirely or economically removed by technological means, the residual amount of the pollutant must be costed by recourse to compensatory payments. Concentrating for the present on this residual amount of pollution that cannot economically be removed by any feasible technology, its pertinent cost can be valued as a compensating variation in either of two alternative ways: as the most that a group B, suffering from the pollutant, is willing to pay for its elimination, or else the smallest sum that this group will accept to bear with it. A comparison of the cos-benefit calculations from using each of these two alternative ways of evaluating the damage can, not surprisingly, result in contradictory outcomes.[2]

2   Once the reader is familiar with the CV^{12} and CV^{21} measures of benefits and losses, his attention may be drawn to the differences in the application of these alternative measures. In all normal circumstances – those in which welfare effects are positive, as they will almost certainly be for environmental goods or bads – the least sum a person is willing to accept (to forego a good or to bear with a bad) will, as stated earlier, exceed the largest sum he is willing to pay (to forego a bad or to enjoy a good). And the difference between the two is magnified when we bring a budgetary constraint into the picture. For, in the absence of any welfare effects, the most a person is able to pay for a good, or for the avoidance of a bad, no matter how important it is for his well-being, is limited by his budget – by his

present and expected future income, his assets and by what he can borrow. To illustrate by an extreme example, if he were compelled to undertake a dangerous mission in which his chances of survival were slight, but from which obligation he would be freed if he could offer a large enough sum of money to induce some other person to undertake the mission, the largest sum he could scrape together would be finite and limited. The limit might be, say, $2.5 million. Conversely, if he were asked to name the smallest sum he would accept for voluntarily accepting to undertake the mission, we would not be surprised if there was no sum large enough to tempt him to do so.

In general, then, the more important to his well-being the item in question, the greater the difference between the most he would pay for it and the smallest sum he would accept to go without it. And it is this phenomenon, the large magnitude of the difference between these two sums that, as we shall see, presents the economist with a problem. For the choice of using the CV^{12} measure or the CV^{21} measure in evaluating the spillovers can determine whether or not the project is able to meet the cost-benefit criterion.

Bearing in mind that the economic activity involved during, say, the operation of the project that unavoidably damages the interests of group B also produces benefits, else it would not be undertaken. And since these benefits, however valued, are reaped by another group, group A, there is clearly a conflict of interest between the two groups.[3] Therefore, in illustrating the alternative uses of CV^{12} and CV^{21}, we shall compare the value to each of the two groups of that operation of the project producing the damaging spillover effects.

3   The cost-benefit criterion introduced in Part I of this book, that $\Sigma V > 0$, was identified as the Kaldor–Hicks test, sometimes also referred to as a potential Pareto improvement. It may now be more precisely expressed as $\Sigma CV^{12} > 0$. This is properly interpreted as requiring for its fulfilment that everyone in the community could be made better off by a costless distribution of the gains in moving from state 1 to 2.

Yet, it is no less compelling to employ, instead, the alternative criterion, $\Sigma CV^{21} < 0$, which is properly interpreted as requiring for its fulfilment that everyone in the community could be made *worse off* by a costless distribution of the losses that are incurred in moving from state 2 back again to state 1.

Admittedly, a superficial reflection would suggest that, if $\Sigma CV^{12} > 0$, then indeed $\Sigma CV^{21} < 0$ and vice versa. After all, if it is true that everyone can indeed be made better or worse off by a movement from state 1 to state 2, then the return to state 1 must be able, respectively, to make everyone worse or better off. Yet, it is easy to show that having regard now that in *absolute* magnitude, ΣCV^{21} can exceed ΣCV^{12} or vice versa, for each person affected, this superficial reflection referred to is far from certain.

Granted that the choice of the calculation ΣCV^{12} rather than the calculation of the ΣCV^{21} or vice versa can make a crucial difference, the question arises: which of these alternative criteria should the economist adopt? On economic grounds alone, there can be no convincing answer.[4] It follows that if, for any reason, the political decision makers were to require the economist to employ the $\Sigma CV^{12} > 0$ criterion rather than the alternative $\Sigma CV^{21} < 0$ criterion, or the reverse of this, the economist would have no grounds for demurring. He may accept the decision as a valid political constraint.

It is, perhaps, unnecessary to remark that one cannot altogether rule out the possibility that, for every person affected, CV^{12} is (ignoring the sign) exactly equal to the magnitude of CV^{21}, in which case the ΣCV^{12} calculation is exactly equal (save for the sign) to the ΣCV^{21} calculation and, if the one criterion is met, so will be the other. But once the magnitude of ΣCV^{12} and ΣCV^{21} differs for each person, as they generally would, the magnitude of the ΣCV^{12} calculation will differ from that of the ΣCV^{21} and, which is more important, it becomes possible for the $\Sigma CV^{12} > 0$ criterion to fail, while the $\Sigma CV^{21} < 0$ criterion to succeed. It also becomes possible for both $\Sigma CV^{21} < 0$ and $\Sigma CV^{12} < 0$.

4 Bearing in mind the conflict between group A and group B for operations of the project that generate environmental spillovers, if we suppose that the movement from a state 1 to a state 2, one that also damages the environment, is one that involves group B in a loss, then the movement from state 2 to state 1 that, instead, *improves* the environment is one that confers a benefit on group B – the opposite being true for group A. Since for each of these four possibilities we can use either the ΣCV^{12} calculation or the ΣCV^{21} calculation, we shall use each case to illustrate a distinct proposition. The four propositions are as follows:

(i) If $\Sigma CV^{12} > 0$, and therefore the project is accepted on that criterion, it necessarily follows that $\Sigma CV^{21} < 0$, which confirms the acceptability of the project.

(ii) If $\Sigma CV^{21} > 0$, and therefore on that criterion, the project is rejected, it necessarily follows that $\Sigma CV^{12} < 0$, which confirms the rejection of the project.

(iii) If $\Sigma CV^{12} < 0$, and therefore the project is rejected on that criterion, it is possible that $\Sigma CV^{21} > 0$, so confirming the rejection of the project. But it is also possible that $\Sigma CV^{21} < 0$, so that, on this latter criterion, the project is *accepted*, contrary to the ΣCV^{12} criterion.

(iv) If $\Sigma CV^{21} < 0$, and therefore on that criterion the project is accepted, again it is possible that $\Sigma CV^{12} > 0$, so confirming the acceptance of the project. But it is also possible that $\Sigma CV^{12} < 0$ which, on that criterion, *rejects* the project, contrary to the acceptance by the ΣCV^{21} criterion.

5 We now use four simple examples that will illustrate the validity of each of these four propositions in the order stated above.

(i) The first example is that of the introduction of a project – the movement from state 1 to state 2 – that eliminates the effluent that hitherto existed in that area, this being a gain to group B while incidentally causing a loss to group A. Using the ΣCV^{12} measure, we shall suppose that the most that group B would pay to move to state 2, one that eliminates the effluent, is (in million dollars) equal to 100, while the smallest amount acceptable to group A which has to suffer a loss in moving to state 2 is equal to 80. The ΣCV^{12} of both groups taken together is then equal to +100, −80 or +20 (bearing in mind our convention of a plus sign for a payment and a minus sign for a receipt). Since $\Sigma CV^{12} > 0$, the ΣCV^{12} criterion sanctions the project. If, instead we employ the ΣCV^{21} criterion, which addresses itself to the relevant sums for a return from state 2 to the original state 1, group B will lose in now having to put up with the effluent, while group A will gain. Since the least sum that group B will accept to move back to state 1 must exceed the most it would pay to move to state 2, we may suppose its ΣCV^{21} to be equal to 110. As for group A, which loses in the movement to state 2, it gains if the movement is back to the original state 1. But the most it will pay for the return to state 1 must be less than the least sum it required in moving to state 2. It will therefore be less than 80; say it is equal to 70. The ΣCV^{21} of both groups taken together is then equal to -110, $+70$ or -40. Thus the $\Sigma CV^{21} < 0$ criterion is met and, *a fortiori* the project is accepted. (This example, illustrating proposition (i) is summarized in Table 20.1.)

(ii) In order to illustrate the second proposition in which $\Sigma CV^{21} > 0$ rejects the project, we shall suppose that the movement from state 1 to state 2 is one that creates effluent so that, if the project is adopted, group B will lose and group A will gain.

In order for ΣCV^{21} to be positive, the most that group B is willing to pay for a return to the original (no effluent) state 1, must exceed in magnitude the smallest sum acceptable to group A for this return to state 1. We may therefore suppose these sums to be $+100$ for group B and -80 for group A, taken together equal to $+20$.

The alternative ΣCV^{12} measure for group B, being the smallest sum acceptable for moving to the effluent state 2, must, however, exceed the most it would pay, 100, to avoid the effluent, say it is 110. As for group A, since it would accept no less than 80 to agree to move back to the non-effluent state 1, it would pay less than this to move to the effluent state 2, say 70.

It follows that the total ΣCV^{12} of the two groups comes to -110, $+70$ or -40. Consequently, it transpires that *a fortiori* $\Sigma CV^{12} < 0$, which confirms the initial rejection of the project by $\Sigma CV^{21} > 0$.

This example, which illustrates our second proposition, is summarized in Table 20.2.

Table 20.1

	A	B	(A+B)	
ΣCV^{12}	-80	100	20	(project accepted)
ΣCV^{21}	70	-110	-40	(project accepted)

Table 20.2

	A	B	(A+B)	
ΣCV^{21}	-80	100	20	(project rejected)
ΣCV^{12}	70	-110	-40	(project rejected)

Table 20.3

		A	B	(A+B)	
(a)	ΣCV^{12}	100	-120	-20	(project rejected)
(b)	ΣCV^{21}	-110	115	5	(project rejected)
(c)	ΣCV^{21}	-130	120	-10	(project accepted)

Table 20.4

		A	B	(A+B)	
(a)	ΣCV^{21}	−120	100	−20	(project accepted)
(b)	ΣCV^{12}	110	−105	5	(project accepted)
(c)	ΣCV^{12}	100	−120	−20	(project rejected)

6 The two remaining propositions (iii) and (iv) are illustrated in Tables 20.3 and 20.4, respectively, without further explanation, provided the reader bears in mind that the minimum sum acceptable to either group to forgo a good (or to bear with a bad) is always larger than the maximum sum it is willing to pay for the good or the removal of the bad. These are the two ambiguous cases, and the ambiguity is revealed in each case by the fact that, in each of these tables, use of the identical criterion in rows (b) and (c) can be shown to confirm and to contradict, respectively, the result of the criterion in row (a).

It may be noted in passing that, when the project in question is one that creates, or increases pollution, the employment of the $\Sigma CV^{12} > 0$ criterion tends to act against adopting the project, as group B has recourse to the larger sum, the minimum acceptable, rather than to the smaller sum, the most it could pay to avoid the pollution. *Per contra*, when the project is one that improves the environment, the $\Sigma CV^{12} > 0$ will tell against group B, because it is the smaller sum, the most it can afford to pay for the improvement, that is to count. In that case, the employment instead of the $\Sigma CV^{21} < 0$ criterion will act to favour group B, because the sum involved becomes the larger one – the least it would accept for returning to the original state 1 (which existed prior to the removal of the pollution).

7 To be sure, those spillovers, positive or negative, that cannot be uniquely priced by reference to the market, and for which, therefore, we have to resort to evaluating by either ΣCV^{21} or ΣCV^{12}, may be a relatively small component of the total effects produced by the project. In such cases, the rejection or acceptance of the project as a whole by either criterion will be unaffected by the evaluation of the spillovers in question. But as the spillover component of the project assumes greater proportions, the choice of the $\Sigma CV^{12} > 0$ or the $\Sigma CV^{21} < 0$ can be the decisive factor in the acceptance or rejection of the project.

Consider, for example a proposal to clear 100,000 acres of forest land in order to use the land for agricultural purposes. The benefits over the future would be reckoned as the discounted sum of the annual excess of the value of crops to the consumers *less* the opportunity costs of producing them for each of the next *m* years. If, however, the farmers were to bid for the land or to be compensated for being denied its use, they would reckon the benefits in terms of expected profits. Conversely, the loss to the community if such a project were implemented would take into account the irrevocable loss for present and future generations arising from the destruction of a variety of species of flora and fauna and the recreational facilities the forest provides.

On the $\Sigma CV^{21} < 0$ criterion that would be used under a ruling or order that requires those who oppose the scheme to recompense those prepared to cultivate the land, producing goods of real value that would augment GNP, it is highly likely that the criterion would be met, and the scheme approved. Yet, as we know from proposition (iv), this result could be contradicted if, instead, we employed the $\Sigma CV^{12} > 0$ criterion, this possible contradiction being that illustrated in row (c) of Table 20.4. For using the $\Sigma CV^{12} > 0$ criterion in this instance, the minimal sum demanded by the community to suffer the loss of this vast forest land is almost sure to be far in excess of any sum the farmers could offer. The scheme, then, could not be vindicated by a CBA.

The same argument would, of course, apply to the activities of logging companies devoted to cutting down many thousands of acres of tropical woodlands each year. For all practical purposes, the loss to society is irrevocable because, given that such trees generally require hundreds of years to reach their full stature, the re-planting of such trees is hardly an attractive economic proposition. Such activities, it may be concluded with confidence, would never be able to meet the ΣCV^{12} criterion.

Finally, in order to illustrate proposition (iii), in particular the possibility exemplified by row (c) in Table 20.3, we may suppose that, two decades ago, a small workshop for producing bicycle tyres was established within a residential area currently inhabited by 5,000 families. The enterprise so prospered that the original small shed gave way to a large factory producing car tyres and housed in an over-towering building, one that was not only an eyesore to the residents, but was also spewing clouds of black smoke from its twin chimneys and creating a foul smell that spread over most of the area.

The residents – desperate to move from the existing pollution state 1 to a nonpollution state 2 – offered as much as \$200 million to the factory owner to site his works elsewhere. The latter made it clear, however, that he would require at least \$250 million to cover the full costs of such re-siting of his works. The $\Sigma CV^{12} > 0$ criterion cannot therefore be met, as the ΣCV^{12} aggregate amounted to –\$50 million.

If, now, on appeal to the courts, the property rights in the ambient air, in and above the residential area, were granted to the residents who, coming together, agreed they would no longer tolerate this blight on their lives unless they received in compensation no less than \$500 million – just enough to enable families to move elsewhere – the factory owner would have no choice but to site his works in some other area.

Thus, once the property rights to the ambient air are ceded to the residents, the relevant calculation becomes that of ΣCV^{21} – the sums involved in moving from the proposed non-pollution state 2 back to the original pollution state 1 – which is decidedly negative, being in fact equal to –\$250 million. The criterion, $\Sigma CV^{21} < 0$ is met and, therefore, the movement back to the non-pollution state 2 is sanctioned.[5]

The above two examples, both of them highly plausible, should convince the reader of the crucial importance on occasions of the choice between adopting the $\Sigma CV^{12} > 0$ criterion or the $\Sigma CV^{21} < 0$ criterion.

Notes

1   This is certainly the case in the well-known article by Coase (1960), and is illustrated by his initial example of cattle straying into neighbouring agricultural land, the optimal position (whether in terms of the number of cattle admissible or the cost of fencing) being uniquely determined by existing market prices.

2 The seeming contradiction that is possible in applying the Kaldor–Hicks criterion first revealed by Scitovsky (1941) arises in a different economic context; that of a general equilibrium analysis in which the distribution of the available goods is related to their market prices. (See Appendix 3,'The alleged contradiction of the Kaldor–Hicks criterion'.) Also, recent empirical studies seem to find a consistent divergence between the willingness to pay and the willingness to accept measures. While there are good reasons for this disparity of measures, it appears that the consensus has been that, if there is a welfare loss (as in the case of environmental damage), the choice measure is that of willingness to accept (compensation demanded), while if a project results in a welfare gain (as in the case of environmental improvements), the choice measure is that of willingness to pay. For more on this literature, see Knetsch and Sinden (1984) and Hanemann (1991).

3 It is not impossible that some people will be in both groups; as a gainer from the good being produced by the project and also a loser from the spillover it generates. This possibility, however, in no way makes any difference to the analysis.

4 Any proposal that we use the ΣCV^{21} calculation for some items and the ΣCV^{12} calculation for others has to be vetoed, as no clear interpretation could be made of the resulting combined calculation.

5 Even if, on the one hand, the resident is willing to pay all the costs of movement to another area in order to obtain some relief (that is, some marginal increase in the welfare level pertaining to the existing state 1), the fact that his house is located in the heavily polluted area will have reduced this value of his (possibly) most important asset to virtually nothing, must drastically reduce the most he is able to pay either to persuade the factory to move or to move himself to another area. On the other hand, if he is allowed full compensation for having to remain in the polluted area, the level of welfare which he will have to sacrifice will be that which he would enjoy in the non-polluted state 2 – clearly far above his welfare level in state 1, and reflected therefore in the large minimum compensation acceptable.

Part V
Investment criteria

21 Introduction to investment criteria

1 Investment criteria are the *bêtes noires* of the economist. Although we shall begin by examining the more familiar proposals in the following chapters in order to reveal the particular difficulties inherent in proposals to reduce a flow of values over some time span to a single figure, we may as well mention such difficulties briefly at the start.

First, the data are much harder to gather, or rather to predict, over future years than are currently available data. The unavoidable uncertainty of future benefits, disbenefits and outlays, may be dealt with in various ways. Yet, they are all somewhat arbitrary inasmuch as none can be anchored in the subjective preferences of those affected by the project being evaluated. Therefore, the treatment used to cope with uncertainty cannot be assumed, strictly speaking, to accord with a potential Pareto criterion.

Second, even if it were the case that all the magnitudes for future benefits, disbenefits and outlays were absolutely certain, no investment criterion, no matter how sophisticated, can be sure of meeting a potential Pareto criterion.

What is invariably being suppressed in the popular treatment of such investment criteria as discounted present value, or internal rate of return, is the basic economic rationale involved: what economic meaning can be attached to the magnitude arising from the application of any of these investment criteria?

2 Let us first be quite clear about the nature of these benefits and costs. An investment in, say, a railroad requires an initial outlay of capital to be spread over the first one or two years. These expenditures are clearly costs. So also are the anticipated outlays at future periods of time, whether for repairs, maintenance or for adding equipment, though their magnitudes are usually smaller than the initial outlays. Benefits are understood in the most comprehensive sense to include all additions to social welfare that can, in Pigou's words, 'be brought into relation with the measuring rod of money'.

Benefits should therefore include not only expected *receipts* over time, as the services produced may not, in fact, be sold to the public but provided free, or sold at a price below their cost (underground rail travel could, for instance, be made free). Even if the good produced is sold at a price that covers its cost, the revenue collected is almost always less than the full amounts people would be willing to pay rather than go without. For, as indicated earlier, an estimate of the full benefit to the buyers of the good is roughly equal to the area under the market demand curve, rather than its price times quantity.

Again, there are positive and negative spillover effects to be evaluated and added, algebraically, to the benefits of the direct recipients of the goods that are purposely produced by the project. For example, the very existence of the railroad is a form of insurance even to those who use other means of transport, a form of insurance for which they would presumably be willing to pay something. Such sums, the estimated value of indirect benefits, are to be added to the direct benefits. On the other hand, any compensatory sums called for by those people whose assets or whose welfare decline as a result of the noise or pollution, or any other disamenity associated with the railroad service, are to be subtracted from the benefits.

We remind ourselves in passing that if we correct the benefit calculation for all spillover effects in order to come up with a net figure *for social benefits*, we *cannot* also invoke the concept of *social costs* – else we should be entering the same spillover effects *twice*, i.e. on the cost side as well as on the benefit side. By convention, therefore, outlays will be calculated as the actual money disbursements – the sums spent on the project at any time during its life, all the incidental spillover effects on society that arise either in the building or in the operation of the project being added to, or subtracted from, the direct benefits at the time they appear.

3   A distinction is sometimes made between 'capital costs' and 'operating costs', the former being the sums needed to build the project, the plant machinery and the like, the latter being the sums to be disbursed at regular intervals in order to maintain the flow of products or services. Such sums or 'operating costs' can be met from what is sometimes called a revolving fund, which can take the form of a line of credit from a bank which may be drawn upon as needed in order to meet the wage bill, maintenance, repairs, and payments for materials. Indebtedness to the bank or other financial institution, however, may be eliminated altogether or else limited as a result of a stream of cash receipts from the sale of the goods being produced by the project.

In calculating the magnitude of these operating costs, only as a first approximation may they be set to the actual disbursements to be made for repairs, maintenance, and materials. Ideally, however, we should have to calculate the opportunity costs of the resources used for these things by the project – that is, the social benefits that would have occurred if, instead, these resources were left in their current uses. In particular, it is not the wage bill that is to be included in the operating costs but the opportunity costs of the labour employed by the project (as defined and measured in Chapter 11).

Again, if regular borrowings from banks are anticipated, a first approximation to the value of these outlays over the future would be set equal to the interest payments that have to be made in subsequent years. More accurately, however, we should calculate the annual opportunity costs (or net social benefits foregone) whenever the banks lend the required sums to the project managers.

Finally in this connection, it is important to bear in mind that, inasmuch as we are concerned with net *social* benefits, all taxes paid from the revenues of the project are *not* to be subtracted from the value of such benefits given that both tax payers and the government are within the target reference group (see Chapter 3). The taxes that are paid from the revenues declared by the project are transferred to the government and have to be valued according to how the government disposes of them.

4   The social benefits, on their own, in each period are to be calculated as the sum of (i) the value of the project's marketable goods (equal to the cash receipts from the sale of those goods *plus* their consumer surplus), (ii) the value of all unpriced benefits conferred on some segment of society, and (iii) the algebraic sum of all externalities, positive and negative, created in each period by the project.

By subtracting the opportunity costs of the factors employed in each period from the value of these social benefits in each period, we derive a stream of *net* social benefits over the relevant time span – some positive, some negative and possibly also some that are zero. And it is to this stream of net social benefits that we can apply our adopted investment criterion.

It is advisable, first, to set out these social benefit figures and their corresponding opportunity costs, period by period – more commonly year by year. For a four-year time span, we might set out our data as in the following example:

Social benefits	0	0	150	260
Opportunity Costs	100	130	135	0

The successive annual *net* social benefits are therefore –100, –130, 15 and 260.

In general, we can summarize the stream of expected gross benefits less their costs as $(b_0 - k_0)$, $(b_1 - k_1)$, $(b_2 - k_2)$,...,$(b_n - k_n)$, where b_0 and k_0 are the social benefits and opportunity costs, respectively, of the initial period, b_1 and k_1 are the social benefits and opportunity costs of the first period, and so on, the subscript always referring to the period or year. If we now define the *net*, or excess, social benefit in any t^{th} period or year, B_t as equal to $(b_t - k_t)$ we can write the above as a stream of net social benefits: B_0, B_1, B_2, ..., B_n, where the Bs can be negative, zero or positive. This is the stream to which an investment criterion is usually applied.

5   It may sometimes be proposed that the economist himself make available the results of his cost-benefit calculation in the form of an actual stream of net social benefits, B_0, B_1, ..., B_t, thus allowing the decision makers themselves to cast their eyes over the time-profiles of the various projects being mooted, in preference to, or in addition to, their being ranked by the economist on some investment criterion or other.

Yet, in the absence of guidance from the economist, political decision makers cannot be depended upon either to rank alternative projects in a consistent manner on any acceptable principle, simply by contemplating their time-profile, or to judge whether any single one is economically acceptable. There is, indeed, no more warrant for decision makers' drawing conclusions about the acceptability or ranking of alternative projects from their study of the relevant time-profiles than there is for their imposing their political judgements on the valuation of the economic data used in a cost-benefit calculation. If it is economic expertise they are requesting, they are implicitly accepting strictly economic methods of calculation.

And in a CBA based on the Pareto criterion, the economist necessarily has to compare alternative investment streams by reducing each to a single figure at a common point of time – the discounted present value (DPV) criterion being currently favoured. Certainly, if we have to use some one rule for the appraisal or ranking of investment streams, this favoured criterion is generally superior to the somewhat crude criteria commonly employed by business concerns.

There is, nonetheless, some pedagogic value in briefly describing the latter, as we do in the following chapter, if only to highlight their weaknesses and so pave the way for an understanding of the standard DPV methods and, later, for more sophisticated investment criteria.

In sum, the search for an investment criterion involves us in a search to discover an answer to the question: what single figure best summarizes the net social benefits of each of the investment streams under consideration? If we are able to find a satisfactory answer to that question, we shall have no difficulty in finding a solution to another common question: given funds that will enable us to finance one, two or more projects, which of these projects, if any, should we choose?

22 Crude investment criteria

1 Suppose we are faced with a choice of four investment options with the net benefits shown in Table 22.1. Which, if any, do we choose if our budget is limited to 100?

If we had to choose *only* one from the four, we could be sure that it would never be A_4, irrespective of the criterion used. For A_3 is as good as, or better than, A_4 period for period. In the jargon, investment option A_3 'dominates' A_4. Thus, if we subtract A_4's net benefit stream from that of A_3, the difference is a series, 0, 20, 0, 0,10, these figures showing the amounts by which A_3's net benefits exceed those of A_4 in successive periods. In no period is A_3's net benefit less than that of A_4.[1]

Let us now consider three rather crude investment criteria, which, however, are commonly employed in the business sector, especially where the venture contemplated is risky.

2 The *cut-off period* is perhaps the crudest possible criterion that is used in business in order to decide whether or not to invest in a project. A suitable period is chosen over which the money invested must be fully recouped. The period could be ten years, though usually a shorter period such as five years or even less is chosen. Such a criterion may be justified in cases of low barriers to entry, innovation in products or methods that cannot be protected by a patent, and which innovations are likely to be copied by competing firms within two or three years. A cut-off period of three years, for instance, may be chosen in the belief that, after three years, further profits are uncertain and increasingly unlikely. Glancing down the table, it is clear that a cut-off period of three years *after* the initial outlay would admit the A_1 investment option. Indeed, more than the initial 100 is recouped in the first year after the outlay. The A_2 option only just scrapes home. A_3 would be able to recoup as much as 160 in the three years, while A_4 would recoup 140.

Table 22.1

	0	1	2	3	4
A_1	−100	115	0	0	0
A_2	−100	20	30	50	170
A_3	−100	100	110	−50	0
A_4	−100	80	110	−50	−10

The shortcomings of this criterion are easy to perceive. If the returns were not expected to accrue mainly in the first few years but mainly after the first few years, worthwhile projects would be rejected. A stream – 100, 0, 0, 20, 40, 60, 80, 120, ... would be rejected. So also would a stream – 100, 20, 20, 20, 20, 20, 20, ...

3 *Pay-off period (or capital recovery method)*: instead of choosing an arbitrary cut-off period, we may rank the investment options according to the number of years necessary to recoup the initial outlay. Clearly, project A_1 would be ranked first, as its pay-off period is less than a year. For project A_2 it is exactly three years. If we ignore subsequent *outlays* in the last two projects, it is one year for A_3 and more than one year for A_4.

The *pay-off period rate of return* is but another way of expressing the above results. It is obtained simply by dividing 100 by the number of years in the pay-off period. Since the A_1 investment option pays off the initial outlay in less than a year, we divide 100 by something less than a year, which yields a pay-off period rate of return of more than 100 per cent. For project A_2, the pay-off period rate of return is equal to 100 divided by three, or 33.33 per cent. For the A_3 project, it is exactly 100 per cent, and for project A_4, it is somewhat less than 100 per cent.

The justification for either form of this ranking device is similar to that for the cut-off period. When imitation by competitors or rapid obsolescence is anticipated, or in circumstances of political uncertainty, one of the overriding considerations is safety. One looks for quick returns and prepares for a hasty exit. A project such as A_1, which pays 115 within a year of 100 being invested, is likely, in such circumstances, to be looked on with greater favour than option A_2, which would not show any profit until the fourth year. The method is easy to understand and gives a decision quickly without much further analysis.

In the complete absence of uncertainty, however, it would be impossible to justify either of the above rules-of-thumb. If interest rates happened to be low, A_2 would be far more profitable than A_1 and more profitable than A_3 for that matter. And like the cut-off period, the method takes no account of the time value of money, and favours short-term investment over long-term ones.

4 *The average rate of return* is the simplest way of taking account of all the figures in the investment stream. Just because all the figures are taken at face value in calculating the average rate of return, there is an implied assumption that all the figures have been corrected for uncertainty.

For all investment options with only an initial outlay of 100 and no subsequent outlays, such as A_1 and A_2 in Table 22.1, there is no ambiguity in the method. One simply adds together all the subsequent positive net benefits, divides this sum by the number of years and expresses the resulting figure as a percentage of the initial investment outlay. For option A_1, the sum of positive benefits is 115. This sum divided by the number of years, in this case only one year, gives an average net benefit of 115 per annum. Expressed as a percentage of the outlay of 100, it is 115 per cent. For A_2, the sum of positive net benefits over four years is 270 and, dividing by four, gives an annual average return of 67.5. Expressed again as a percentage of the outlay of 100, it is 67.5 per cent.

For investment options A_3 and A_4, which happen to have outlays also in later years, we add together all the figures, both positive and negative, after the initial outlay of 100 and proceed as before. For A_3, the algebraic sum of net benefits over three years (years 1, 2 and 3) comes to 160. This sum divided by three yields an average of 53.33 per cent per annum. Similarly for option A_4 which yields an average return of 32.5 per cent per annum.

The weakness of this method is apparent at once, for it is by no means evident to anyone thinking of investing 100 that A_1 with an average of return of 115 per cent is superior to A_2. It might be added in passing, however, that the weakness is not particular to this method, but arises also in the more familiar internal-rate-of-return method, which will be treated later. Note that comparisons on projects with different life spans, such as A_1 with one year and A_2 with four years, are not ideal due to opportunities of reinvestments, but is made here for illustrative purposes.

5 *The average rate of return including the initial outlay* is an obvious modification of the preceding criterion. The average rate of return is calculated in the same way *except* that the initial outlay of 100 has to be included as a negative net benefit before dividing by the number of years.

Thus, in option A_1, we subtract the outlay of 100 from 115 to give 15, this being a 15 per cent net benefit on the outlay of 100. In A_2, subtracting the 100 outlay from the 270 net benefits leaves us with 170 net benefits, and dividing by four yields a net average return of 42.5 per cent per annum on the outlay of 100. Similar calculations yield a net average return of 20 per cent per annum for three years on the 100 outlay for the A_3 option, and an average of 7.5 per cent per annum for the four years for option A_4.

Under conditions of certainty, at least, this criterion, although clearly superior to the others, is unsatisfactory for two reasons. First, the results depend critically upon the number of years counted on this criterion. But determining the length of the investment stream by reference to the number of years for which there is a net benefit, positive or negative, is arbitrary. If, for example, option A_1 were altered so as to yield a slight positive net benefit, say 0.1, in year 2, the annual net benefit, spread over two years, would be little more than 7.5 per cent on the outlay of 100, which makes this slightly altered A_1 option far less attractive.

Second, a less apparent but no less serious defect is that this criterion takes no cognizance of the *profile* of the net benefits over time. Given the algebraic aggregate of all the net benefits following the initial outlay of 100, it makes no difference to the calculation whether the net benefits are bunched together over the first years, spread evenly over the time span, or are bunched together toward the end of the time span. Thus, an investment stream of –100, 5, 20, 25, 250 is valued as highly on this criterion as one of –100, 250, 25, 20, 5; or, for that matter, an investment stream of –100, 1, 1, 1, 297 is valued as highly as an investment stream of –100, 297, 1, 1, 1.

Yet, who would not prefer the latter stream to the former! People do indeed take account of the timing of benefits: they are not indifferent as between receiving 100 now and 100 in ten years' time, the former is preferred to the latter. Once we take account of the time dimension of the net-benefit stream, we are impelled to move away from these rather primitive investment criteria and move on to those that are more familiar to economists – those in which 100 in any year is valued more than 100 in any subsequent year.

6 Although all investment criteria resort to the common procedure of reducing a stream of net benefits to a single figure at one point in time, usually the present time,[2] the economist invariably uses some rate of interest (or some combination of rates) as a means of weighting the net benefits in successive years.

The more familiar criteria fall into two categories: (i) those that draw on a given rate (or rates) of interest in reducing the investment stream to a present discounted value, and (ii) those that, in contrast, are used to discover just what is the average rate of return on the initial outlay. This latter criterion, known as the internal rate of return, may be defined as that rate of discount which reduces the entire investment stream (including the initial outlay) to zero.

These two popular criteria, the present discounted value and the internal rate of return, will be compared in the following two chapters.

Notes

1 If, however, we had funds enabling us to choose two or more of these investment options, we might choose both A_3 and A_4. But we should never include A_4 while rejecting A_3.
2 However, as we shall propose later, the future compounded value, taken at a terminal year, offers certain advantages.

23 The discounted present value criterion

1 If we have an investment –100, 50, 150, and we are given a rate of interest or discount rate of 10 per cent per annum, the DPV of the net benefits alone that are generated by the initial outlay of 100, 50 at the end of the first year, and 150 after the second year is given by the calculation

$$\frac{50}{(1+0.1)} + \frac{150}{(1+0.1)^2} = 169.4$$

In this connection, an initial outlay of 100 has a present value also of 100, being incurred at the end of the zeroth year.

The DPV of the *entire* stream, –100, 50, 150, is equal to the DPV of the net benefits (positive or negative): here, 169.4, *minus* the DPV of the outlays, here 100, and is therefore equal to 169.4–100, or 69.4.

In more general terms, given a stream of benefits generated by only a single initial outlay K_0, but which for the time being may be designated as B_0, so enabling us to represent the entire stream as B_0, B_1, B_2, ..., B_n, where the Bs are positive, negative or zero, its net DPV is given by

$$B_0 + \frac{B_1}{(1+r)} + \frac{B_2}{(1+r)^2} + \cdots \frac{B_n}{(1+r)^n}$$

or more briefly by

$$\sum_{t=0}^{t=n} \frac{B_t}{(1+r)^t}$$

where r is the rate of discount.

The necessary instrument in this criterion is the appropriate rate of interest or rate of discount by which the net benefit at any point of time is weighted. It is commonly assumed that the correct rate of interest is that which reflects society's rate of time preference. (If, for example, society is taken to be indifferent between having $100 million today and $106 million next year, the *social* rate of time preference is 6 per cent per annum.) We shall, for the present, go along with this assumption, though later on it will be argued that it is correct only under special conditions. In a Crusoe economy, if 120 bushels of corn next year are deemed by Crusoe to be equivalent in satisfaction to 100 bushels of corn today – by which is meant that he is perfectly indifferent to having either 100 bushels of corn today or 120 bushels of corn in a year's time – Crusoe's rate of discount is 20 per cent per

annum. Until Man Friday arrives and has some say in the decision, Crusoe's individual rate of discount can also be thought of as the social rate of discount.

2   To be more accurate, however, Crusoe's reaction to the choice presented to him
gives us no more than the social rate of discount for the one year and, for that
matter, is strictly valid only for 100 bushels of corn this year, not for more or for
less. If, indeed, the same rate of discount did hold for successive years, then Crusoe
would be indifferent as between 100 today, 120 next year, 144 in the year following that, and so on. It is, however, quite possible that his discount rate rises with
the passage of time. Instead of being indifferent as between 100 today and 144 in
two years' time, he might specify 150 in two years' time. This would mean that for
the first year his rate of discount is 20 per cent, but for the second year he uses
a discount rate of roughly 25 per cent per annum.
   Again, even if we confine ourselves to the one year, it is not true that the same rate
of discount holds for *any* amount of corn. If Crusoe agrees, though only just, to postpone consumption of 100 bushels of corn this year in order to have an additional 120
bushels next year, it does not follow that he will be prepared to forgo another 100
bushels of corn this year in exchange for another additional 120 bushels next year. It
is more plausible to suppose that he should want more than an additional 120 bushels
next year to persuade him to forgo this year the consumption of yet another 100 bushels; say an additional 140 bushels next year. We could say that Crusoe's marginal willingness to sacrifice 100 today for 120 next year reflects a discount rate of 20 per cent
per annum, while his marginal willingness to sacrifice 200 today for 260 tomorrow
reflects a discount rate of 30 per cent overall. Put otherwise, we could say that for the
first 100 bushels the marginal discount rate was 20 per cent, and that the marginal
discount rate for another 100 bushels was 40 per cent.
   These possibilities are to be noted before passing on. For it is also the case in
society at large that, however the social rate of discount is determined, it is invari-
ant neither with respect to the magnitudes of the inter-temporal exchange of goods
nor to the length of time involved. If we have information about the variation in
the rate of discount with respect to either magnitude or time, however, there is no
difficulty, in principle, in adapting our chosen investment criterion accordingly. In
the meantime, our task will be simplified by assuming but a single social rate of
discount. Moreover, since we are to examine this concept in Chapter 25, we shall
also assume that this social rate of discount is known to us. If the reader prefers,
he can suppose, provisionally, that it has arisen from the interplay of market forces
plus, perhaps, some form of government intervention that has the object of ensuring that the resulting rate of interest in the economy correctly reveals society's preference as between present and future goods. If, for instance, the social rate of
discount is 10 per cent per annum, we shall take it that society as a whole is indifferent as between 100 today, 110 in a year's time, 121 in two years' time, and so
on. And that, therefore, the *present* value of 110 to be received in one year's time,
or 121 in two years' time, is exactly 100.

3   Having made these provisional simplifications, let us go on to consider the following propositions, all of them commonplace in the literature on the subject.
   The net present value[1] (or excess of present value over cost) of a particular
investment stream depends upon the rate of discount used. If, for instance, the

stream of net benefits is –100, 0, 150, the net present value of the stream would be a little less than 48 if the discount rate were 1 per cent, but would be $-33\frac{1}{3}$ if the discount rate were 50 per cent.

It follows that, which one of a number of alternative investment streams yields the largest net DPV must depend, in general, on the rate of discount that is employed. Only if there is one investment stream that is 'dominant' over all the others being contemplated, will it have a higher DPV irrespective of the discount rate. Thus, if there are but two investment streams, *A* having the stream –50, 20, 80, and *B* the stream –50, 20, 70, then stream *A*, being dominant, will have a higher present value irrespective of the discount rate. But if, instead, there is an *A* stream of –100, 0, 180, and a *B* stream of –100, 165, 0, a discount rate of 0.01, or 1 per cent, ranks *A*, with a net present value of about 76, above *B*, which has a net present value of about 63. If, however, the appropriate rate of discount is 0.5, or 50 per cent, the net present value of the *A* stream is –20 and is therefore ranked *below* the *B* stream, which has a net present value of 10. From these two examples, it should be manifest that there is a particular social rate of discount between 1 per cent and 50 per cent for which the two streams have exactly the same present value. Let us call this social rate of discount r^*. Then r^* is easily determined by equating the net present value formulae for the two streams, i.e. we set and solve for r^*, which turns out to be about 9 per cent.

$$-100 + \frac{180}{(1+r^*)^2} = -100 + \frac{165}{(1+r^*)}$$

In general, we can determine a net present value of a particular investment stream, say *A*, for each conceivable rate of discount. The resulting relationship can be plotted in Figure 23.1, where the vertical axis measures PV_r, or net present value of the investment stream in question, and the horizontal axis measures r, the social rate of discount. The net present value of the *A* stream becomes smaller, the larger the rate of discount r; hence the negative slope of the *A* curve. This is true for projects with an initial outlay followed by subsequent benefits. It will be noted that the negative slope crosses the horizontal axis and continues below it into the south-east quadrant. This indicates that, at discount rates above some critical rate of discount, the net

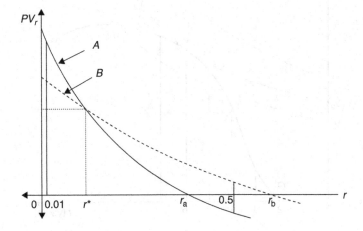

Figure 23.1

present value of the stream becomes negative (for example, at a 50 per cent discount rate, the stream –100, 0, 180, has a net present value of –20). A similar relationship can be plotted for the B investment stream.

If one of these two investment streams were dominant, it would lie above the other at all rates of discount. In the absence of dominance, the A and B curves will intersect, either in the positive quadrant, as in the figure, or else in the negative quadrant (not shown).

For all conceivable (positive) discount rates – save one, r^* – the present values of the two streams differ. At discount rates below r^*, the A stream has a higher net present value than the B stream, the reverse being true for discount rates above r^*. Only at r^* do both streams have the same net present value. It is obvious that if the rate of discount, from being a little above r^*, fell to a figure below r^*, the net present value of the A stream would change from being less than that of the B stream to being greater than it.

It may be observed finally, that there is a discount rate corresponding to each investment stream, r_a and r_b respectively, for which the net present values of the A and B streams are both zero. By definition, therefore, r_a and r_b are, respectively, the internal rates of return of the A and B investment streams.

4   If now, the annual net benefits that are generated by an initial outlay (eventually) become smaller over time and, also, instead of dividing the relevant time span into years or other unit periods, it is treated as a *continuum*, the resulting net benefit profile over time can be envisaged as a growth path, it being understood that no benefit is reaped at any date earlier than some given point of time, at which point the cumulative benefit may be discounted. Thus, rather than plot a profile of marginal net benefits over time, we can plot a profile over time of the *total* benefit, in effect a growth path as represented in Figure 23.2, where time is measured along the horizontal axis and the *total* undiscounted net benefit, or total value, reached at any point of time, is measured vertically. The vertical axis OV, which cuts the

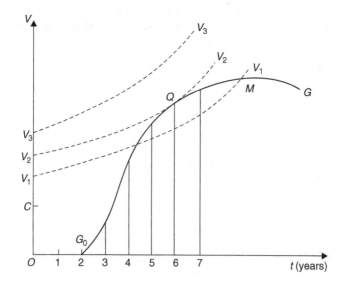

Figure 23.2

horizontal axis at time zero, can be used to measure the DPV reached at any point of time, given the rate of discount.

Common examples of such growth curves are those of trees or wine. Once a tree is planted, its value increases after a point in time, roughly in proportion to the increase in the volume of its timber (assuming a constant price of timber).

As for a barrel of wine, its value increases over time (up to a point) in consequence of the improvement in its flavour. Let us consider the timber example.

A continuous growth path is represented *by* G_0G in Figure 23.2. At time zero, total costs OC (measured above O along the vertical axis OV) are incurred in purchasing the sapling and in employing the labour to plant the tree. Although the sapling may begin to grow immediately after planting, its wood will be worth nothing until, say, the end of the second year, from which point of time it grows in value – at first more rapidly – to a maximum, after which it declines. Thus, the net value of the timber at any point in time is given by the vertical distance from that point of time.

In order to appreciate better the connection between this growth curve and the preceding Figure 23.1, along with its examples, we could split the time axis into discrete units, say years, and measure vertically the total value of the timber at the end of each successive year. Instead of a continuous growth path, we should then have a succession of vertical lines increasing in height up to point M. The heights of each of these vertical lines could then be regarded as the value of *alternative* investment streams. For instance, the vertical line above 4 on the horizontal axis could measure exactly 100. If OC measured an initial cost of 50, the investment option corresponding to $t = 4$ would be –50, 0, 0, 0, 100. The investment option corresponding to $t = 5$ could be –50, 0, 0, 0, 0, 112. The investment option corresponding to $t = 6$ could be –50, 0, 0, 0, 0, 0, 120, and so on for $t = 7, 8, 9, ..., n$.[2] Which of all the investment options would we choose? Bearing in mind the preceding proposition, we need have no hesitation in affirming that, in general, it will depend upon the social rate of discount.

For any given discount rate, we may construct a number of V curves over time, each corresponding to a different present value. For a social discount rate that is equal to 5 per cent, one such discount curve V_1V_1 would measure, say, 80 along the vertical axis at time zero. At a point directly above $t = 1$, the height of the curve would be 80 (1 + 0.05), or 84; at $t = 2$ the height of the curve would be 84 (1 + 0.05), or 88.2, and so on, the height at the end of each successive year being 5 per cent greater than that of the preceding year.

At a social discount rate that is supposed to be equal to the social rate of time preference of, say, 5 per cent, society is deemed indifferent to receiving timber worth, say, 100 as measured at some point in time by the height of the V_1V_1 curve, and receiving timber worth 105 a year later. Other 5 per cent discount curves such as V_2V_2, V_3V_3 and so on may be constructed on the same principle. The family of such 5 per cent VV curves is conceived as being 'infinitely dense', and optimization requires we select among them the highest VV curve that just touches the G_0G growth curve. In Figure 23.2 this is V_2V_2, which just touches G_0 G at Q. The optimal growth period, or gestation period, is then exactly six years. And the net present value of the timber that is cut down at the end of the sixth year is measured by the height OQ *less* the initial cost OC. It will be correctly surmised that point Q is one of mutual tangency between a VV discount rate curve and the growth curve.

It will be understood that, if the tree were not cut down at the end of the sixth year, it would continue to grow for a number of years. After point Q is reached at the end of the sixth year, however, the increase in its value falls below 5 per cent per annum. There is, therefore, more to be gained by cutting down the tree at the end of the sixth year, selling the timber and investing the proceeds at 5 per cent than the alternative of cutting the tree at a later date.

Notes

1 The term 'net present value' will be used occasionally as an abbreviation of 'net present discounted value' or 'net discounted present value'.
2 For expository convenience, we are ignoring the costs of tending the tree while it is growing. If these were constant at, say, 10 each year, the investment option correction to $t = 4$ would be $-50, -10, -10, -10, 100$.

24 The internal rate of return

1   The internal rate of return (IRR) is a more respectable form of the average rate of return mentioned in Chapter 22 in that, like the DPV method, it takes account of time.

A simple example will illustrate how the IRR is calculated. If we have a stream of net benefits –100, 50, 86.4, we can discount each of these net benefits to the present, $t = 0$, using a discount rate of 20 per cent. The present value of the net benefit of 50 in year 1, when discounted at 20 per cent, is 50/(1 + 0.2), or 41.67, while the present value of 86.4 in year 2, when discounted at 20 per cent, is 86.4/ $(1 + 0.2)^2$, or 60. The present value of both 50 in year 1 and 86.4 in year 2 is, therefore, 40 + 60, or 100, which is exactly equal to the initial *negative* net benefit, or net outlay, of 100. This 20 per cent discount, just because it equates the present value of the positive net benefits to the present value of the net outlay, is taken to be the internal rate of return of the above stream of net benefits.

The above example serves to illustrate a common definition of the IRR as being equal to that rate of discount, say λ, which when applied to a stream of net benefits, would make them equal to the initial outlay K; hence, the formula

$$K = \sum_{t=1}^{n} \frac{B_t}{(1+\lambda)^t} \text{ or, alternatively, } K - \sum_{t=1}^{n} \frac{B_t}{(1+\lambda)^t} = 0$$

in which we solve for λ.

2   There could, however, be additional outlays in future years. If, for example there were additional outlays, say K_2 and K_5 in years 2 and 5, respectively, these outlays have somehow to be discounted to the present and added to the initial outlay K in year 0. And if discounted, the relevant rate must also be λ which has, it may seem, yet to be determined.

Yet, on reflection, it will be understood that these later outlays can be left in place and, regarding them as negative net benefits to be discounted to the present along with the positive net benefits, so retaining the above formula. For example, given an initial outlay of 100 at time zero, a net benefit of 220 at the end of the first year and an *outlay* of 121 at the end of the second year – thus an investment stream equal to –100, 220, –121 – a discount rate equal to 10 per cent, reduces the present value of that stream to zero. The IRR is, therefore, equal to 10 per cent.

Inasmuch, then, as in conforming to the formula, both outlays and benefits are to be discounted to the present at the IRR, it will sometimes be neater to obviate mention of the initial outlay K and any subsequent outlays, treating them instead as negative net benefits in the year they occur. The formula then becomes

$$\sum_{t=0}^{n} \frac{B_t}{(1+\lambda)^t} = 0, \text{ in which } B_t \text{ can be positive, negative or zero}$$

It will be convenient, henceforth to continue using negative Bs for any *subsequent* outlays. Nonetheless, it should be understood that, although there can also be negative net benefits in future years that are in fact not cash outlays, being instead possible losses arising from environmental damage or compensatory payment, it makes no difference in the calculation of the IRR – or, for that matter, of the DPV, given the discount rate.[1]

3   The sense in which the internal rate of return, so defined, is an average over time is conveyed by the example of a man investing, say, 100 for five years. If the internal rate of return of some given investment stream were 25 per cent per annum, the man would have in mind *an equivalent*, though simpler, investment in which his 100 in the present grows by 25 per cent each year. He sees his 100 in the present becoming 125 by the end of the first year,156.25 by the end of the second year, and so on, to reach $100(1 + 0.25)^5$ by the end of the fifth year. More generally, if the investment stream in question were $-100, B_1, B_2, B_3, B_4, B_5$, where the Bs are any pattern of benefits, and the internal rate of return were known to be 25 per cent, then an *equivalent* investment stream would be $-100,0,0,0,0, 100[(1 + 0.25)^5]$, for this given investment stream, when discounted to its present value at 25 per cent, is, by assumption, equal to zero, and so also is the equivalent stream. Consequently, if a man is told that the internal rate of an investment stream over n years is equal to λ, he is justified in thinking of the investment as equivalent to one in which his initial outlay is compounded forward at the rate of λ per annum for n years.

Thinking of the IRR in this way, the man will want to compare any such investment with the opportunities for putting his money into other securities, either equities or government bonds. If the only alternative open to him, or the only alternative he will consider, is long-term government bonds, perpetuities say, yielding 6 per cent per annum,[2] an investment yielding a rate of return of more than 6 per cent (always assuming certainty or, at least, equal certainty) will be preferred to the purchase of these 6 per cent government bonds.

4   Let us now return briefly to the growth curve of the preceding chapter, depicted here in Figure 24.1. The reader will recall that using the tangency condition between the growth curve G_0G and the highest 5 per cent discount curve at Q determined the optimal gestation or investment period. Here, however, we have followed the convention of drawing the discount curve as straight lines by measuring the *logarithms* of the values along the vertical axis – thus successive x per cent differences appear along it as equal distances.

If the highest discounted present value OP, at the given social rate of discount (which we continue to suppose is 5 per cent) determines the optimal period OQ', do we obtain the same result using, instead, the IRR? We should hardly expect so, since this optimal OQ' period itself will vary with the particular magnitude of the rate of discount adopted, being longer the lower the rate of discount.

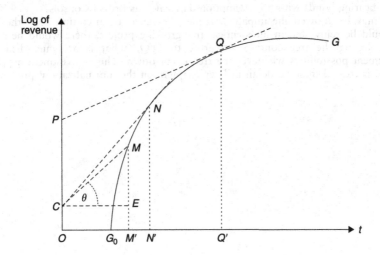

Figure 24.1

But first, how do we represent the IRR on this diagram? The answer is that it can be represented by the slope of a straight line from C to any point of the growth curve, say M. For this slope is determined by tan θ, which is equal to the *excess* benefit EM at time M' (that is, total benefit M'M *less* the cost OC at time zero) divided by time OM' in years. This ratio given by tan θ must be the IRR simply because, as required by definition, it is the rate of interest which reduces the *total* future benefit M'M to a present value that is equal to the initial cost OC.

Now the highest IRR possible is, on this construction, determined by the slope of the straight line from C that just touches the growth curve G_0G at point N, there being no straight lines from C steeper than CN that can also just touch this growth curve.

If the optimal investment period is now defined as that yielding the highest IRR, this will be a period equal to ON'. This *optimal* IRR period is clearly shorter than OQ, the optimal period on the net present value criterion with a given rate of discount. So which is it to be? Do we let the tree grow for a period OQ', or do we cut it down after ON' years? This is not the only sort of problem in which the results obtained using these two investment criteria differ. We shall defer the resolution of this apparent discrepancy,[3] however, until we have illustrated other discrepancies in the results obtained using IRR as compared with using DPV.

Notes

1 Later, when we come to introduce a normalization procedure in which net benefits, positive or negative, are to be compounded forward, the composition of each net benefit must be considered. In that case, a negative net benefit that is a cash outlay will, in general, be treated differently from a negative net benefit that is, say, a collective bad (such as the ambient pollution) that is inflicted on the community.

2 In the modern economy there is, of course, a wide diversity of government bonds even if we restrict ourselves to long-term issues. We simplify the treatment, for the time being, by

assuming there is only one type of long-term government bond, say 'perpetuities', i.e. interest-bearing bonds with no redemption date, such as British Consols.

3 A hint may be allowed the impatient reader, however. If, after time ON' the proceeds NN' could be reinvested in an identical tree-growing project, there would be a loss by, instead, letting the tree continue to grow to $Q'Q$. What is at issue, then, are the reinvestment possibilities whenever the tree is cut down. This reinvestment aspect of the problem is treated in some detail in later chapters on the 'normalization' procedure.

25 The alleged superiority of the discounted present value criterion compared with the internal rate of return criterion and the net benefit ratio

1   Consider the three alternative investment streams A, B and C, shown in Table 25.1. The *undiscounted* net benefit ratio $(B - K)/K$, in which B represents the net benefit in the first and only year in which benefits accrue, with K representing the initial capital outlay in year zero, will here serve as the criterion, one that will rank C above B, and B above A. Why the *undiscounted* net benefit ratio? For the simple reason that, whatever the rate of discount used, it will affect the net benefit at t_1 of A, B and C in exactly the same proportion. We may therefore infer that, irrespective of the discount rate used, the resulting *discounted* net benefit ratio would give the same *ranking* as the undiscounted net benefit ratio.

This conclusion is valid, however, only for a two-period investment in which the outlay appears in the first period and the benefit in the second. Add but one more period, and the ranking will, in general, depend upon the discount rate. For instance, a stream –100, 10, 100 cannot be ranked in relation to the stream –100, 90, 10 without knowing the discount rate. If this were 1 per cent, the first would clearly yield a larger net benefit ratio than the second. If, however, the discount rate were 50 per cent, the second would yield a larger net benefit ratio than the first.

The original two-period investment stream has another property: the internal rates of return of each of two-period streams A, B and C (as shown in Table 25.1) are equal to their corresponding net benefit ratios (also shown in the table), and therefore produce the same ranking, C, B, A. There is no mystery about this: for the net or excess benefit $(B - K)$ produced over the year, taken as a fraction of the capital cost K, is of course equivalent to one year's growth of the initial capital K. Thus the capital of 100 invested in A will have been perceived to grow by 5 per cent over the year, in B by 15 per cent, and in C by 25 per cent. A discount rate of 5 per cent for A, of 15 per cent for B and of 25 per cent for C will reduce the magnitudes of their respective benefits to their original outlays, 100 in each case – such discount rates being, therefore, by definition, the respective internal rates of return of A, B and C.

For such two-period investment streams, then, the ranking C, B, A is the same whether we use the IRR or the DPV method. Moreover, whatever the rate of discount that is employed, whether positive, zero or negative, the ranking remains unchanged.

2   This harmony between the net present value criterion and the IRR criterion will, however, as the reader probably suspects, break down if any of the investment streams being compared contains more than two periods. Indeed, this implication

Table 25.1

	t_0	t_1	(B – K)/K	Internal rate of return
A	−100	105	5/100	5%
B	−100	115	15/100	15%
C	−100	125	25/100	25%

accords with the proposition exemplified above: that, for investment streams in excess of two periods, the ranking will vary with the rate of discount used. The IRR ranking does not, however, at all depend on the adopted rate of discount, but is independently determined. If it then so happens that at the ruling discount rate a number of investment streams show the same ranking by the two criteria, an alteration of the discount rate, which changes the net present value ranking of the investment projects, will also produce a discrepancy between this new net present value ranking and the ranking by IRR.

We illustrate this latter statement using two different investment streams, A and B, as in Table 25.2. Both of these are ranked equally by the IRR criterion, being 10 per cent in each case. Not surprisingly then, if the discount rate employed also happened to be 10 per cent, the discounted net benefit ratio (B − K)/K would be zero for both A and B, as (B − K) would equal zero using a 10 per cent discount rate. Were the discount rate equal to only 1 per cent, the three-period B stream would show a (B − K)/K ratio of 19/100 and would rank above the (B − K)/K ratio for A, of 9/100, the reverse ranking being produced if the discount rate were doubled to become 20 per cent. In that case, B's discounted net benefit ratio would be equal to −16/100, which is therefore ranked below that of −8/100 for the A stream.

A diagrammatic representation of the variation in the discounted net present value, PV_r (B − K) with respect to the rate of discount for each of these investment streams, A and B, is displayed in Figure 25.1, where PV_r (B − K) is measured along the vertical axis and the rate of discount r along the horizontal axis. It can be seen at a glance that discounted net benefit PV_r (B − K) for each of the two streams of investment – indeed, for any investment stream – varies inversely with the rate of discount r.

It will be noticed that there is some rate of discount, here 10 per cent, at which the two investment streams will have exactly the same discounted net present

Table 25.2

	t_0	t_1	t_2	Internal rate of return	(B – K)/K at 1%	(B – K)/K at 20%	(B – K)/K at 10%
A	−100	110	0	10%	9/100	0	−8/100
B	−100	0	121	10%	19/100	0	− 16/100

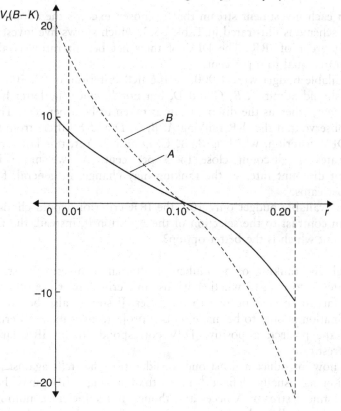

Figure 25.1

value. In this particular case, moreover, it so happens that this same discounted net present value is equal to zero; hence, the IRR for each will be 10 per cent. For discount rates below 10 per cent, B's $PV_r (B - K)$ exceeds that of A, the reverse being true for discount rates above 10 per cent.

3 In spite of this discrepancy between the two criteria, the IRR has been recommended in some circumstances, particularly as a method of allocating a given capital budget among a number of potential investment projects. Thus, one might select a number of public investment streams, subject to a budget, provided that

Table 25.3

	t_0	t_1	t_2	*Internal rate of return*	$PV_r(B - K)/K$ *(for r = 0.03)*
A	−100	110	0	10%	7/100
B	−100	0	115	7%	8/100
C	−100	106	0	6%	3/100
D	−50	52	0	4%	1/100
E	−200	2	208	2%	−2/100

the IRR on each investment stream that is chosen exceeds the adopted rate of discount. The scheme is illustrated in Table 25.3, which shows five investment streams in declining order of IRR. The DPV of their net benefit ratios is also given for a discount rate equal to 3 per cent.

If the available budget were 1,000, on the IRR criterion, only 350 of it would be spent. We should admit A, B, C and D, but not E, since the latter has an IRR of only 2 per cent, whereas the discount rate is taken to be 3 per cent. The reader will doubtless observe that the IRR ranking A, B, C, D and E differs from that resulting from the DPV criterion, which is B, A, C, D and E. Yet, this latter ranking holds only for rates of discount close to 3 per cent. As we move further from a 3 per cent discount rate, so the ranking may change, in general, for any set of investment streams.

Were the available budget only 100, the IRR criterion would choose investment option A, in contrast to the selection of the B option if, instead, the DPV criterion were used. But which is the better option?

4   Although the ranking of a number of alternative investment streams will, in general, differ according to whether we use one criterion or the other, we have no reason, so far, for preferring one to the other. It should also be noted that when the determination is only to be made on one project, investment criteria are consistent within the project; a positive DPV corresponds to an IRR larger than the chosen interest rate.

We may now introduce at least one consideration that tells against the use of the IRR criterion as usually defined:[1] more than a single IRR may be yielded by a given investment stream. A necessary, though not sufficient condition, for this to occur is that not all outlays (or negative net benefits) take place in the initial period. There have to be negative net benefits in later periods.

A simple example of such an investment stream, call it the H stream, could be –100, 420, –400. This stream is one that yields two IRRs, λ_1 of 46 per cent, and λ_2 of 174 per cent, since using either of these rates as a discount rate would reduce the discounted net present value of the H stream to zero.[2]

Figure 25.2 depicts the curve relating the net present value of the H stream to the rate of discount r. The curve will be seen to cut the horizontal axis, not once (as does each of the investment streams in Figure 25.3), but twice: once at the point where r is 0.46 and once where r is 1.74. Since either of these two discount rates reduces the present value of the H stream to zero, they are identified as the two IRRs λ_1 and λ_2.

Of course, the reader might think that, of these two IRRs, λ_1 (46 per cent) is the more reasonable. If he were obliged to adopt an IRR for such a stream, he would probably choose 46 per cent. But he would find it difficult to justify such a choice, if he were not allowed to draw on intuition. Moreover, even if the reader did feel confident about the 46 per cent IRR for the H stream, this example of two IRRs is only a special case. For one can devise investment streams to yield three, four or indeed any number of IRRs.[3] However open-minded the reader may wish to remain, he cannot deny that the case for preferring the present value criterion above the IRR criterion looks very strong.

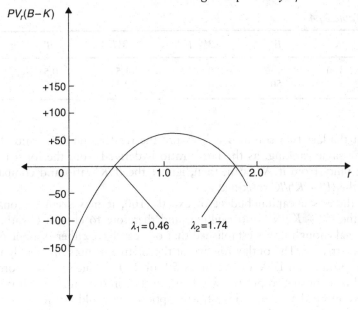

Figure 25.2

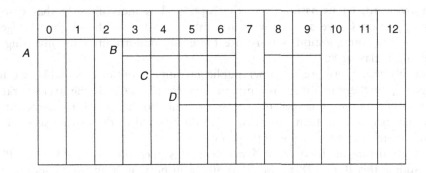

Figure 25.3

5 If, provisionally, we accept the DPV criterion, there remains the question of whether we are to rank (i) by excess benefit over cost $(B' - K')$, (ii) by the ratio of benefit to cost B'/K', or (iii) by the ratio of excess benefit to cost $(B' - K')/K'$. These alternative ranking methods are worked out in Table 25.4 for investment options A and C, where K' is taken to be the DPV of all outlays, initial and subsequent ones, if any, and B' is understood to be the DPV of all net benefits, the discount rate being given.

In the $(B' - K')$ column, A, which has excess benefit over cost of 50, is ranked above C, which has an excess benefit over cost of only 30. In the next, B'/K' column, however, C, with a ratio of benefit to cost of 2.5, is ranked above A, which has a ratio of benefit to cost of only 1.5. In the final column showing $(B' - K')/K'$, the ratio of *excess* benefit to cost continues to show C ranked above A.

Table 25.4

	K'	B'	$(B' - K')$	B'/K'	$(B' - K')/K'$
A	100	150	50	1.5	0.5
C	20	50	30	2.5	1.5

A glance at the last two columns will assure the reader that B'/K' and $(B' - K')/K'$ will give the same ranking, as the latter ratio is derived from the former simply by subtracting unity from it. We can, then, ignore the B'/K' ratio and compare the $(B' - K')$ with the $(B' - K')/K'$ ranking.

Now, if there is a capital budget of exactly 100, it may seem reasonable to be guided by the $(B' - K')/K'$ ratio ranking, and therefore to choose C rather than A. This is rational enough if it is established that one can have either A alone or, instead, five of the C streams. The outlay for five of the C streams uses up exactly the budget of 100, and produces a DPV of five times 50, or 250 – which is 100 more than can be obtained by choosing to put the whole of the 100 in option A. But if it is not possible to have more than one C investment option, we could be misled by using the ranking method $(B' - K')/K'$, for although this ratio is higher for C than it is for A, the excess net benefit for A, 50, is greater than that for C, which is only 30.

Let us, therefore, consider ranking by the $(B' - K')$ method and, to make things more awkward, let us assume also that option A is indivisible. In that case, by choosing option C, we are left with an outlay of 80 from the original budget of 100. The relevant question now is: are there any opportunities for investing this remaining outlay of 80?

Allowing that there are no other public investment options available, we must recognize that there is always the private investment sector. If the average rate of return over time in this private sector happens to be equal to perpetuity of 8 per cent per annum, then a sum equal to 80 invested in the private sector could be said to yield a return of 6.4 in perpetuity.

At a given rate of discount of 5 per cent, this perpetuity of 6.4 has a DPV of 128. Adding this B' of 128 to the B' of 50 (from putting 20 in the C option) gives a total B' of 178, which is more than can be obtained by investing the 100, instead, wholly in option A, which yields a B' of only 150, at least if we ignore further reinvesting possibilities.

Thus, if we do adopt the ranking method $(B' - K')/K'$, it is tacitly assumed that each of the investment options being considered may be multiplied in such a way as to ensure that the magnitude of the K' is the same for each of them. Where this cannot be assumed, we should be advised to use the $(B' - K')$ method of ranking and use the stratagem above in order that each option use a K' of the same magnitude. This can always be done, in the last resort if necessary, by investing the 'spare' funds of any option in the private investment sector.

In sum, for a valid ranking of alternative investment options, we must first make sure we have created for each option a K' of the same magnitude. Once this is done, we shall, in fact, obtain the same ranking, whichever of the three methods we use – $(B' - K')$, B'/K' or $(B' - K')/K'$.

6   Finally, a brief word about the treatment of a set of investment streams that have different life spans, some beginning earlier than others, some later.

A correct ranking of such streams requires, ideally, only one particular adjustment: that each of these investment streams be compounded forward to a common terminal year, this common terminal year clearly being that year in which the final net benefit (positive or negative) occurs in that investment stream stretching furthest into the future.

To illustrate, if we measure time in years along a horizontal axis, four investment streams to be compared can be represented as successive horizontal lines of different lengths, as in Figure 25.3.

It will be seen that investment stream A begins in year 0 and ends in year 7. Two successive and complementary streams are generated by project B, the first beginning in year 3 and ending in year 7, the second being from year 8 to year 10.

The C investment stream is from year 4 to year 8, while the D stream is from year 5 to year 12.

Year 12 is then to be accepted as the common terminal date for the four investment streams. In Chapter 28, where the normalization procedure is elaborated, we shall find that there is no difficulty in compounding the first three investment streams, A, B and C, to the terminal year 12.

Notes

1   A more accommodating definition is proposed in Chapter 28, following the critique of the DPV criterion.
2   From this definition of the IRR, say λ, we require a λ for which

$$-100 + \frac{420}{(1+\lambda)} - \frac{400}{(1+\lambda)^2} = 0$$

The reader will recognize the expression as a quadratic equation with two solutions, $\lambda = 0.46$ and $\lambda = 1.74$. A negative net benefit in the second period is not a sufficient condition for two IRRs, however. If it were small enough, there would still be a single IRR. An example would be the stream −100, 121, −1, which yields an IRR of a little over 20 per cent.
3   Determining the values of the IRRs corresponding to any investment stream implies solving for the roots of a polynomial. Any investment stream with n periods can be transformed into a polynomial with a maximum of $n-1$ different roots, each being a possible IRR. Only those that are positive will matter for investment criteria. Negative IRRs make sense, but are not usually of much importance. Complex roots do not appear to make sense in this context.

26 Investment criteria in an ideal capital market

1   Investment criteria, whether based on DPV or IRR, are devised so as to enable us to choose between alternative uses of investable funds. If there are two or more alternative investment options, each must be compared with the others.[1] If there is only one investment project under consideration, the alternatives are to use the funds either for private expenditure or for buying government securities. The latter course of action may be thought of as a financial transaction that does not of itself result in any new investment. Initially, it is but a purchase of government bonds on the open market: a transfer of cash from the individual to the government. For society as a whole, however, and certainly for public investment, we must transcend all financial transactions and, in the last resort, consider at least two alternatives: either consumption or else investment in this particular project.

Only in the absence of a progressive income tax would an ideal capital market be possible.[2] And, for the present, we shall also assume only one rate of interest which is to be used as the relevant rate of discount in the DPV criterion and which also reflects society's rate of time preference. A rate of interest of 5 per cent that reflects this society's time preference implies that such a society is wholly indifferent to having between $1 today and $1.05 in exactly a year's time. If, therefore, by reducing the consumption of $1 worth of goods today it becomes possible to gain $1.06 worth of goods next year, society is deemed to gain by the transaction.

If, instead, one returns $1.04 in a year's time, society is deemed to be worse off from having postponed consumption. Consequently, if a particular investment yields more than 5 per cent in a year's time, society is deemed better off from switching resources from the production of consumption goods to this particular investment good, and vice versa.

In circumstances where the only alternatives open to the use of present resources are either investment today or consumption today, an investment will be chosen if its rate of return exceeds the 5 per cent rate of time preference. If it does so, the DPV of its outlays and benefits over time will be positive, and the investment will be undertaken. Thus, given a rate of discount that is equal to the rate of time preference, a positive net present value indicates that the present value of a sum when invested exceeds its net present value if, instead, the sum is used to consume goods today. It follows that society is better off investing the sum today than using it to consume goods today.

2   In an ideal market economy, in which the only existing rate of return on investment is equal to society's rate of time preference, the economy is in equilibrium, at least with respect to the capital market. If, for example, the existing rate of interest

is 5 per cent, the marginal product of the existing capital stock is also equal to 5 per cent, as is also the rate of return on current investment or 'marginal efficiency of investment'. In such an ideal capital market, any new investment opportunity that has, with certainty, a net present value above zero (when its outlays and benefits are discounted at 5 per cent) must add to society's welfare and would therefore be undertaken. The consequent incentive to invest may be supposed to continue until equilibrium is restored, the rate of return being, once more, no greater than society's rate of time preference. In this ideal situation, there is apparently no problem about the appropriate rate of discount.[3]

However, once the yield on current investment tends to remain above society's rate of time preference, as it tends to do for a number of reasons, the choice of the appropriate discount rate is far from simple. In fact, the variety of proposals has engendered much controversy about the considerations that should enter into the devising of an appropriate rate of discount.[4] We shall examine the chief differences between these proposals in Chapter 28.

Notes

1 It is just possible that the reader may be wondering why we have continuously ignored mention of depreciation in the treatment of investment criteria. The short answer is that the principles which guide the rate of *amortization* are unrelated to those that arise in *selecting investments*. There is nothing mysterious about this. All investment criteria, whether based on DPV or IRR, implicitly make allowance for the maintenance of capital through the requirement that the outlays on the investment project be (more than) covered by the DPV of its expected future benefits.

2 Given the existence of a progressive income tax, a man who pays 40 per cent tax on his income will receive no more than 3 per cent net return on a market yield of 5 per cent whereas to the man who pays 20 per cent tax on his income, the 5 per cent market yield receives a net income of 4 per cent on his investment, and so on. It will be convenient, above, to assume zero income tax.

3 Even in this seemingly ideal economy, the prevalence of external economies in investment will result in a sub-optimal volume of capital formation which perhaps could be corrected only if the market rate of interest were appropriately reduced. This aspect was originally developed by Marglin (1963b), but it is not directly relevant to investment criteria for reasons given in note 4 following.

4 What may also seem to complicate the issue is that any long-run equilibrium rate of interest is, in any event, not uniquely determined by the interaction of individual time preference and investment opportunities. Such long-run rate of interest may be varied through monetary and fiscal policies.

   Such policies, however, are of macroeconomic interest. They are not directly pertinent to CBA. Stated briefly, the required data for the application of an investment criterion is (ought to be) the relevant opportunity yields of investment, on the one hand, and the social rate of time preference, on the other.

27 Calculation of rates of return and of time preference

1 We must now reconsider our supposition of a single rate of time preference for society, say r, and a single yield, say ρ, on private investment.

The latter task is simple in principle. On the assumption that risk-aversion among investors predominates, received doctrine has it that there is a tendency for private investment with a greater expected risk to carry a higher actuarial rate of return – that is, a higher average rate of return over a long-term period.[1]

Provided that classification of private investment according to actuarial rates of return is feasible, it might be thought that the highest actuarial rate of return (corresponding to the riskiest private investment) is the appropriate opportunity rate of return for public projects – on the argument that the outlay K raised to finance the public project could always have been invested in this type of private investment. Even if the argument were accepted, however, there may be relatively little of this riskiest private investment about, and it may therefore take too long to discover its actuarial rate of return. The economist might then choose for the appropriate opportunity rate ρ the rate of return on a less risky private investment, but one that is more common and more likely to be maintained over the future.

2 The reader is reminded, however, that, where the necessary funds for the public project are to be raised entirely by borrowing from the public, the relevant opportunity rate of return, which is to be used as the discount rate, has to be calculated, in general, not by reference simply to the rate paid by the government on the nominal value of the bonds issued. In so far as private investment is displaced – 'crowded out', in the jargon – the higher actuarial rate of return on private investment ρ is the appropriate rate.

Only in the limiting case in which the full amount of the initial outlay K that is borrowed by the government does not in fact displace any private investment – so that the aggregate volume of investment that would have taken place during the year is increased by the amount K – does the relevant rate of discount (which has to have reference to the opportunities forgone when the amount K is diverted from the use to which it would otherwise be put) equal society's rate of time preference, inasmuch as those who buy the K value of government bonds are reducing some part of their current consumption for some additional consumption over the future.

In the more general case where the amount borrowed by the government has the effect of displacing some part only of this amount of private investment, say $4 million of an outlay K of $10 million, the opportunity rate of this $4 million is equal to p, with society's rate of time preference r on the remaining $6 million. The appropriate discount rate in this general case is, therefore, a weighted average of r and p.

3   An estimate of the social rate of time preference is more elusive. We have already discussed an ideal capital market in which everybody's rate of time preference, whether or not he is a borrower or lender, is the same and exactly equal to the rate of interest prevailing on the market, and equal also to the rate of return on existing capital and new investment.

Although we can move a little in the direction of realism by envisaging a large number of loan markets, each differing from the other according to the terms of the loan, it is not possible to suppose that a person can borrow all he wishes at the going rate of interest. For if he could, he would also be able to renew the loan when it expired, so postponing repayment indefinitely. Yet, even if borrowers were all equally honest, unless we want also to suppose them equally wealthy, prudent and shrewd, they would not be equally creditworthy. For example, for an initial $100,000 loan to run for five years, the more creditworthy the borrower the lower, in general, will be the rate of interest charged.

In order to estimate a community's rate of time preference, however, it is not enough to take account of all the different loan markets, and within each such market the different categories of borrowers, for, as a result of rationing the amount of money lent to each borrower, the rate of interest he pays on the marginal dollar borrowed may be well below his rate of time preference. For more reliable estimates of people's time preferences, then, we must go beyond market data. We must use questionnaire surveys.

4   Following the basic maxim, it would seem that, if a person says he will defer consumption of 100 this year for no less than 105 next year, the implied rate of time preference of 5 per cent has to be accepted.[2] And if this 5 per cent holds over the entire time span, he will be indifferent as between consuming 100 this year, year 0, and consuming 100 $(1.05)^t$ in year t.

Can the rate of time preference r be higher than p, the average rate of return on private investment? Although virtually impossible for society as a whole, we must recognize the possibility that some individuals who perforce must, via taxation, reduce their consumption have very high rates of time preference. Let us take an extreme example of a man of 90 years of age, Mr A, who has to put a value on the amount of consumption he would require in ten years' time in order to compensate him for sacrificing the consumption today of an additional 200. His average rate of time preference over the next ten years may be inordinately high, and not unreasonably so. If he believes that his chances of surviving the next ten years are very low, he may truly claim to be indifferent as between consuming an additional 100 this year and an additional 20,000 in ten years' time. This average rate of time preference of about 70 per cent per annum is clearly expressive of his impatience to consume while he is still alive: it is the minimum incentive needed to persuade him to forgo present consumption in favour of consumption in the tenth year.

It would seem to follow that the age distribution of the beneficiaries and the losers in the different projects being compared would significantly affect the weighted average rate of time preference and, therefore might be a critical variable in determining their ranking. For example, a public investment whose beneficiaries were largely elderly people would certainly have a higher average rate of time preference and, in so far as it enters the discount rate, would reduce the present value of that project below that of a project whose beneficiaries were mainly young people.

5   It would seem reasonable to calculate society's rate of time preference as the weighted average of the several groups in the community that are affected, making society's rate of time preference R equal to $\Sigma^n w_i r_i$, where there are n different groups, r_i being the rate of time preference of group i, and w_i being the weight of group i, with $\Sigma^n w_i$ equal to unity.

It transpires, however, that the R so calculated is generally slightly smaller than an exact measure of society's rate of time preference as, if a sum x is compounded for a number of years at this rate R, it will compound to a sum that is slightly smaller than the sum compounded for each group separately and then added. Over the years, of course, the absolute difference between R and the true measure will grow. But save in exceptional circumstances the difference will remain relatively slight.[3] Where the range of the different rates of time preference for the community affected is not great, at least for the larger groups, the use of this weighted average R as society's rate of time preference is unlikely to make a significant difference to the calculation as compared with the use of the rate of time preference of each of the separate n groups.

Notes

1   Under a progressive income tax, the total tax paid over, say, a 20-year period is greater for a riskier investment with the same total gross return than for a less risky investment in as much as the gross return on the former is more unevenly spread than the same gross return on the latter. Thus, even in the absence of risk-aversion, the gross rate of return – which is what ρ measures – has to be higher for the riskier private investment simply in order to yield the same *net* return over time as for the safer private investment.

2   From the fact that a person is indifferent as between consuming an additional 100 this year and consuming an additional 105 next year, it is not to be inferred that he is 'myopic' or 'impatient'. As demonstrated in Appendix 10, in the complete absence of a loans market, a person may regard a given sum as being of equal worth whether he receives it today or some time in the future. Yet, once a loans market is introduced, this same person may adjust his pattern of consumption so that, indeed, he then becomes indifferent as between, say, 100 today and 105 in a year's time.

3   To illustrate with only two groups (group 1 with a weight of 0.7 and a rate of time preference of 10 per cent, the other group with a weight of 0.3 with a rate of time preference of 0.05): R would then be equal to $(0.7 \times 0.1) + (0.3 \times 0.05)$ equal, therefore, to 8.5 per cent. If x is \$1,000, then compounded at R for two years it becomes \$1000 $(1.085)2$ or \$1,177.25. For five years, it will be equal to \$1,503.65. If now we compound each group separately, after two years we have $\$700(1.1)2$ plus $\$300(1.05)^2$, a total of \$1,177.75 – a difference from compounding R of only 50 cents. After five years, the compounded sum of the two separate groups becomes $\$700(1, 1)$ plus $\$300(1.05)^5$, a total of \$1,510 – a difference now of less than \$7.

28 Critique of the discounted present value criterion (I)

1   All the well-known criteria proposed for evaluating public investment streams embody in one form or another a DPV procedure.[1] A distinction must be made, however, between (a) the older type of criterion, which simply applies what is thought to be an appropriate discount rate to the stream of benefits (positive or negative) in question, and (b) a newer type of criterion, in which provision is made for the allocation of the resulting benefits of a project as between consumption and further investment and within which category there can be differences between behavioural, institutional and political assumptions.

The differences within the (a) category are elucidated in a comparison of equations (28.1)–(28.4) which follow. Those within the (b) category are basically less controversial and may be represented by equation (28.5) alone. The latter differences, as we shall see, arise only from the degree of elaboration thought to be appropriate, and deserve only passing mention.

2   In order to economize on inessential elaboration of the analysis, the practice common in the literature of ignoring (initially at least) uncertainty in order to focus on a critical part of the logic of investment criteria is followed here.

Although, in general, there may be different rates of time preference for the different groups affected by the project and also different yields on private investment according to risk, an analysis conducted in terms of such generality adds only an elegant complexity to the exposition that is more likely than not to obscure the basic outlines of the argument. We shall, therefore, regard the rate of time preference r as a single figure (or weighted average of the rates of time preference of all groups affected by the project) and the yield ρ also as a single figure (or weighted average of the different rates of return on sums invested by the project).

If we write $PV(B)$ as a shorthand for the DPV of the stream of all the (net) benefits, B_0, B_1, B_2, ..., B_T, some of which may be negative, and K as the initial outlay, then under the older type of criteria (a) we may distinguish four alternatives:

$$PV_r(B) > K \tag{28.1}$$

$$PV_\rho(B) > K \tag{28.2}$$

$$PV_p(B) > K, where\ p = \sum_{n+1}^{n} w_i r_i \sum_{n+1}^{s} w_j \rho_j and \sum_{1}^{n} w_i + \sum_{n+1}^{s} w_j = 1 \tag{28.3}$$

$$PV_q(B) > K (\rho > q > r) \tag{28.4}$$

3   Criterion (28.1), the staple of textbook instruction, is superficially plausible enough. If r is rate of time preference, the community is indifferent between receiving the stream of benefits $(B) = B_1, ..., B_T$, and receiving its present value $PV_r(B)$. In particular, any project with a benefit stream that meets criterion (28.1) tells us that the present value of that stream of benefits exceeds the value of its initial outlay at time zero and, therefore, introducing the project realizes a potential Pareto improvement.

The rationale for criterion (28.2) is no less plausible. It suggests that, if funds equal to K are to be spent on a public project, the average yield from the project should be no less than the ρ per annum that the sum K could fetch if it were placed in the private investment sector instead. If, over the period, the benefit stream yields on average more than ρ, the $PV_p(B) > K$ criterion would be met, and there would be a net gain from adopting the investment project.

Clearly, criterion (28.3) is a generalization of (28.1) and (28.2) extended to cover all the different rs and ρs in the economy. Since the weights, the ws, are the fractions of K contributed by separable components of the reduced amount of consumption and of the reduced amounts of private investment, the resultant weighted rate of return represents society's actual opportunity yield per dollar of investing a sum K in a public project. In general, then, ρ will vary according to whether K is raised by tax finance, loan finance or as a mixture of both. Although (28.3) was originally proposed by Krutilla and Eckstein (1958), it was advanced again by Harberger (1968) in connection with a rise in interest rates in response to government borrowing,[2] which is supposed to check both private investment and consumption.[3] With such a weighted discount rate, Harberger (1968: 308) claimed (erroneously, as we shall see) that the 'so-called reinvestment problem disappears'.[4]

This criterion is also open to a more serious reservation. In essence, it is pre-Keynesian, ignoring as it does the stabilizing effect of 'liquidity preference' – the shape of the demand curve to hold the total stock of securities in the economy – on rates of interest. If, therefore, government borrowing for the public project has no effect or a negligible effect on interest rates, there may be no 'crowding out' of private investment and no reduction in current savings.

In so far as the economy is close to full employment, any government expenditure on a public project that is financed by borrowing – by an issue of bonds – must add to aggregate demand in the economy, and is therefore inflationary.[5]

If, in contrast, there is ample slack in the economy, the addition to aggregate demand arising from spending a sum K as initial outlay on a public project has no inflationary effect. In such circumstances, the cost of the public project could be negative, as argued in Chapter 13.

We turn finally to the well-known Arrow–Lind paper of 1970, which produced criterion (28.4) as a modification of the popular criterion (28.2), $PV_\rho(B) > K$. We shall accept without criticism their argument that the risks associated with public projects, when divided among a large population of taxpayers, are felt by each taxpayer to be negligible compared with the sense of risk apprehended by investors in private enterprise. A person can then be supposed to be indifferent between a rate of return p on private investment and the greater certainty of a somewhat lower rate of return q on his money when it is invested instead in a public project – a risk premium equal to $(p-q)$ being attributable to the greater risk entailed by investing in the private-investment sector. A potential Pareto improvement may then be realized if funds are removed from private investment, so forgoing yield p, and placed instead in a public investment at a yield greater than q. For then, everyone who invests in the public project will be made better off by a yield of a little more than q than by the higher yield p from private investment. Hence, the proposed criterion (28.4), $PV_q(B) > K$, for investments in the public sector.

This proposed criterion (28.4) is, however, no less vulnerable than the other three. Even though we assume that the government is not permitted to undertake any investments comparable with those undertaken in the private sector, adherence to this criterion might deprive the economy of worthwhile investments. If the sum K is raised wholly by taxation, it *may* involve a reduction in consumption only. The opportunity rate that is to be forgone on the sum K raised by taxation is then no more than society's rate of time preference r. It follows that a Pareto criterion would be met if the public project were to yield more than r, as in criterion (28.1).

In sum, although this (28.4) criterion is an interesting, though controversial variation of the (a) type of criteria, it is – apart from the above criticism – subject to a more fundamental critique along with the other three.

4 We turn briefly to the newer type (b) criterion, which recognizes that more care has to be taken of the reinvestment aspect of the returns on an investment project. Such criteria can be formulated as

$$PV_r(B) > AK \tag{28.5}$$

where A is the ratio of the social opportunity costs both of the public project itself and of the actual alternative use of the outlay K. Let us consider these two social opportunity costs.

Marglin's (1963a) treatment, in his classic article, assumes that the required sum K is raised from tax revenue and that, of every dollar so raised, a fraction θ_1 comes from an *initial* reduction in private investment with yield p, the remaining fraction $(1 - \theta_1)$ coming from a reduction in current consumption.[6] In addition, θ_2 is the fraction of each dollar of any return that is placed in the private investment sector. Under these conditions, an amount K left in the private sector of the economy would generate a stream of consumption over the future which, when discounted at r, would converge to aK, a being greater than unity.[7] This aK is the 'social opportunity cost' of a project requiring a nominal outlay of K.

However, the employment now of criterion $PV_r(B) > aK$ can be justified only if the streams of benefits are entirely consumed as they occur. If, instead, the fraction $(1 - \theta_2)$ of each of the benefits is consumed as it occurs, the remainder being invested in the private sector at ρ, and the returns to these investment components treated in the same way, the consumption stream so generated can be discounted at r to a present value of $aPV_r (B)$, with a greater than unity. The corrected criterion $aPV_r(B) > aK$ can then be written as[8]

$$PV_r(B) > AK \ where \left(A = \frac{a}{\alpha} \right)$$

Later contributions that explicitly recognized the reinvestment problem produced models which, though interesting in themselves, reproduced the same essential features of the Marglin model. Feldstein's three papers (1964a, 1964b, 1972), for instance, extend the formulation to cover other behavioural and institutional parameters. Bradford's (1975) paper is of the same family and, though he begins somewhat differently, his results conform to the same basic formula as Marglin's.[9] As there is no fundamental novelty of conception in the later papers adopting this approach, remarks on the Marglin model are applicable also to their analyses.

Without doubt, the introduction of the type (b) criteria, which face up to the reinvestment problem, is an important step forward in the art of project evaluation and goes far to remedy the defect inherent in the older DPV formulae. Yet, the insight that inspired the innovation was channelled into the conventional mould.

It is possible, however, to break out of this conventional DPV mould by adopting, instead, a normalization procedure with the singular feature that each of a stream of benefits is compounded forward to a terminal date rather than being discounted backward to the present, a procedure that is illustrated in the following chapter.

Notes

1 Mishan's proposed normalization procedure (1967c) is an exception, one that informs this and the following chapter.
2 Not surprisingly, Chicago School economists favour loan finance of public investments. Others favour tax finance, either on the grounds that it tends to reduce the volume of private investment less than does loan finance (see Musgrave, 1969) or else on the grounds that loan finance entails future tax levies in order to service the debt.
3 However, Dreze (1974: 60) asks whether government borrowing does affect the rate of interest and, if so, whether a higher rate of interest increases current saving. His answer is simply that 'there undoubtedly exist cases where government borrowing does not affect the rate of interest, but is simply offset by rationing of private investment'. Dreze compares his view with that of Arrow (1966), who argues that the divergence between 'the rate of interest implicit in consumption decisions and any market rate is so great that it must be accepted that savings are largely independent of the latter' and then goes on to say that the issue is 'to decide whether some consumers do react, at least, for some forms of consumption'.
4 Indeed, all formulae that assume a voluntary increase in savings in response to a rise in interest rates are suspect, for, in the absence of a well-functioning capital market – one in which interest rates move freely so as to bring the current flow of savings into equilibrium with the current flow of investment – an additional $1 million saved (although, by definition, entailing a reduction of current consumption by $1 million) may have no effect whatever on the current demand for investment.

5 Equilibrium mechanisms that are invoked by the inflation can act eventually to reduce aggregate consumption and/or investment. But there is no simple theory from which we may deduce reductions in the rate of inflation.

6 In fact, Marglin produces three models in this paper. His third model introduces alternative and less plausible behaviour assumptions, while his first model is little more than a stepping stone to the second model, which is treated above as *the* Marglin model.

7 In order for the infinite stream of consumption thus generated to converge, when discounted at r, to a finite sum, Marglin assumes that $\theta_2 p > r$.

8 In a limiting case, where $\theta_1 = \theta_2 = 0$, a will equal α, and $PV_r(B) > AK$ becomes equal to $PV_r > K$. (In Bradford, 1975 model, θ_1 and θ_2 are denoted, respectively, as α_t and α_{t+1} and, when these are equal, his criterion also reduces to $PV_r(B) > K$.)

9 Bradford's (1975) paper, in some ways a development of his earlier paper of 1970, constructs a model which closely resembles that of Marglin. This resemblance is easier to appreciate by comparing Marglin's equation (8), condensed and cast in discrete form, with Bradford's equation (15), using a common notation. Marglin's criterion then appears

as $\sum\limits_{t=0}^{\infty} ab_t\delta_t - aK_0 > 0$

while Bradford's takes the form

$\sum\limits_{t=0}^{T} ab_t\delta_t - \sum^{a_t} K_t\delta_t > 0$

where B_t is the tth benefit from the public project, K_t is the tth net outlay and a_t is the shadow price of a dollar of the tth net outlay. The discount factor to be applied to B_t, and K_t is δ_t. Bradford's public investment benefit stream is finite (and not infinite as is Marglin's), and his shadow prices a_t and α_t vary with t. For the special case $\alpha_t = a_t$, both reduce to the general form $PV_r(B - K) > 0$, which form includes the possibility also of a stream of net outlays.

29 Critique of the discounted present value criterion (II)

1 Since, for the purpose in hand, any one of the five criteria discussed in the preceding chapter will serve, we shall use criterion (28.2), $PV\rho(B) > K$, for demonstration.

Given, therefore, the initial outlay K in year zero, and the subsequent stream of (net) benefits, B_1, B_2, ...,B_T, we can re-write criterion (28.2) as

$$\sum_{t=1}^{T} \frac{B_t}{(1+\rho)^t} > K \tag{29.1}$$

By multiplying through by a scalar $(1 + \rho)^T$, we obtain the equivalent inequality

$$\sum_{t=1}^{T} B_t (1+\rho)^{T-t} > K(1+\rho)^T \tag{29.2}$$

which may be summarized as $TV \rho(B) > TV \rho(K)$, where $TV \rho(B)$ stands for the terminal value of the stream of benefits when each is compounded forward to terminal date T at rate ρ, and $TV \rho (K)$ stands for the terminal value of the outlay K when it also is compounded forward to terminal date T at rate ρ.

If and only if $PV \rho(B) > K$ is $TV \rho(B) > TV \rho(K)$; one form of the criterion, that is, entails the other. But the latter form is far more revealing: it makes clear that, for the criterion to be met, the aggregate of the benefits, B_1, B_2 ... B_T, when each benefit is wholly and continually reinvested to time T at this same weighted rate of return ρ, must exceed the sum which K amounts to when it also is wholly invested and reinvested to the terminal year T. Such a criterion would, of course, be applicable in the rare case when, in fact, both the benefits and the initial outlay of the project were to be used in exactly this way. It could be justified only if all benefits were encashed and wholly invested and reinvested at ρ, the return to private investment, until the terminal date, and similarly for the amount K.

In as much as this implicit requirement is seldom complied with, the use of a criterion that is valid only if such a requirement is, in fact, assured can be seriously misleading. Certainly, any of these four criteria is misleading when it is applied to a public project without information in the particular case about the disposal of the returns to the project and without information also about the sort of stream that would have been generated by the sum K had it not been taken from the economy.[1]

To illustrate, suppose that the outlay K required by a particular public investment is to be drawn entirely from the private investment sector, where it would otherwise have been reinvested continually at ρ to reach a terminal value at T of $TV_\rho(K)$. Suppose also that the project's benefits, in contrast, are expected to be wholly consumed as they occur over time. The value of such benefits therefore grows in value at the rate of time preference r to reach a terminal value at T of $TV_r(B)$. Now if $TV_r(B)$, as is likely, happens to be smaller than $TV_\rho(K)$, the terminal value of the sum K, the project has to be rejected on a Pareto criterion: society would be better off leaving the amount K in the private investment sector (there to be continually reinvested at ρ) rather than using it to finance a project whose benefits are consumed as they occur.

It should be evident that the use of criterion (28.1), $PV_r(B) > K$, would fail to reveal this possibility. Employing it could then sanction projects that would be rejected on a Pareto criterion. By reversing these suppositions in the above example, so that the outlay K is raised entirely through a reduction in present consumption so that it is to be compounded to the terminal year T at society's rate of time preference while, in contrast, all the returns over time to the project are to be wholly invested and reinvested at ρ to the terminal year, the employment of the $PV_r(B) > K$ criterion could reject projects that do, in fact, meet the Pareto criterion.

2   Thus transforming the criterion $PV_r(B) > K$ into its compounded terminal form $TV_r(B) > TV_r(K)$ enables us immediately to appreciate that, for its valid employment, all the returns from the project should be *wholly consumed* as they occur and that the sum K should be raised entirely from current consumption. Similarly, transforming the other limiting case $PV_\rho(B) > K$, into the form $TV_\rho(B) > TV_\rho(K)$ enables us also to appreciate at once that its Pareto validity is assured if, in fact, it is applied to a case in which the benefits, as they occur, are wholly invested and reinvested in the private investment sector at prevailing yield ρ, until the terminal date T, and if the sum K raised from the private sector is also wholly invested and reinvested at yield ρ until T.

In other words, the *correct* terminal value of a project's benefit stream and the *correct* terminal value of the opportunity cost of its outlay are both functions, in the simplest possible case, of three variables, r, ρ and c, where c is the fraction of any income or of any return on investment[2] that is consumed, the remainder $(1-c)$ being invested (unless otherwise determined) in the private sector at ρ.

In contrast, criterion (28.2), $PV_\rho(B) > K$, is valid only if both the initial outlay K and the stream of returns that it generates are all wholly invested and reinvested to the terminal year at ρ. And this condition is transparent once this criterion (28.2) is transformed into the more explicit form $TV_\rho(B) > TV_\rho(K)$.

By subtracting $TV(K)$ from $TV(B)$, we obtain the *net* terminal value of the project in question. Once this net terminal value is correctly calculated for a number of projects, all with an initial outlay K, the resultant ranking can be maintained whatever rate of discount is then used to discount them to the present.

3   In order to complete the critique, we need to re-examine the standard IRR criterion. Although, on the face of it, there should be an advantage in being able to calculate the IRR without reference to the prevailing interest rates or investment yields in the economy, it has fallen into disfavour among economists since,

as we have seen, we can derive more than one IRR for a given investment stream.[3]

The more important reason, however, is that, even in the more usual case in which all net benefits are positive, the standard IRR calculated for an investment stream does not accord with the true average rate of return of the net benefit stream. It transpires that, as conventionally defined, the IRR suffers from the same defect as common DPV criteria; namely, that the implied reinvestment rate of the net benefits has no necessary relation to the actual rates.

Given the standard definition of the IRR as that λ for which

$$\sum_{t=1}^{T} \frac{B_t}{(1+\rho)^t} = K$$

If we multiply through by the scalar $(1 + \lambda)^T$ we obtain

$$\sum_{t=1}^{T} B_t(1+\rho)^{T-t} = K(1+\lambda)^T$$

So explicated, the standard IRR is shown to be defined as that rate λ which, when it is used to compound each of the benefits B_t to the terminal year T, produces a terminal outlay that itself is equal to K compounded forward to year T also at λ. But this resulting λ has no necessary relation to the average rate at which the benefits B_t are being actually compounded forward to T.

Since in any given project it cannot be assumed that each of the benefits B_t is wholly invested at λ when it occurs, the standard definition is misleading. In fact, the disposal of each B_t as it occurs depends upon behavioural and institutional factors, in general on the values r, ρ and c. In order, then, to calculate the IRR as a uniquely determined average rate of growth of the initial outlay K over period T, we must first calculate the *actual* terminal value of each of the benefits that are generated by the outlay K.

A correct calculation of the IRR, consistent with the normalized procedure being proposed, must therefore be defined as that rate of discount λ which would reduce the actual terminal value of the sum of each of the benefits, so compounded, to equality with the initial outlay K. This can be formulated as that λ for which

$$\frac{TV(B)}{(1+\lambda)^T} = K$$

It follows that if, with a given outlay K, the terminal value of the benefit stream of project X exceeds that of project Y, which in turn exceeds that of project Z – which we can write as $X > Y > Z$ – then, by our definition above, their respective IRRs λ_x, λ_y and λ_z are those for which

$$\frac{X}{(1+\lambda_x)^T} = \frac{Y}{(1+\lambda_y)^T} = \frac{Z}{(1+\lambda_z)^T} = K$$

from which it follows that $\lambda_x > \lambda_y > \lambda z$.

However, for ranking purposes, at least, it would be pointless to calculate these normalized IRRs, as they will follow that of the terminal value of their respective benefit streams.

Notes

1   This critique, incidentally, applies as well to the usual DPV methods employed by private corporations for evaluating alternative investment streams – though in so far as the returns over time are likely to be treated more uniformly, the error may be less important.
2   For there may be public projects for which all or part of any of the expected returns over the future are required to be invested in designated public enterprises. Again, the amount K may be raised wholly or in part using the sums that are available simply in consequence of the non-renewal of existing public investments.
3   The reader is reminded that a necessary though not a sufficient condition for the standard IRR to have more than one value is that one or more of the net benefits be negative, a contingency not often encountered.

30 The normalized compounded terminal value criterion (I)

1   The normalized CTV procedure is designed to transform the stream of net benefits $B_1, B_2, \ldots, B_T$, arising from an initial outlay K into an equivalent stream, 0, 0, ..., $TV(B)$, this being shorthand for the terminal value of the stream of net benefits generated by the initial outlay K. From this $TV(B)$ we are to subtract $TV(K)$, or the terminal value of the outlay K, conceived as the terminal value of the opportunity cost of investing the sum K.

What we call normalization is the requirement that, in ranking two or more projects, they must not only have the same terminal date T, but also a common initial outlay K. This requirement is in no way restrictive.

If, for example, of two mutually exclusive projects, the initial outlay required for project Y is, say 80, this 80 being less than the outlay of the 100 that is required for project X, the outlay that is to be common to both projects must be the larger, being 100 in this example. If the project Y is to be undertaken, then an additional 20 of outlay must be spent. It may be possible to spend this 20 on an additional project that is a quarter the size of Y and yields benefits that are also a quarter the size of project Y. If, however, the project is not one that is divisible, the 20 to be spent can, at least, be returned to the private investment sector where, if returns are continually reinvested, it will produce a terminal value of $20(1 + \rho)^T$, which must be added to the terminal value of project Y that requires an outlay of only 80. If, however, this 20 is returned to the government, it will generate a terminal value that will depend upon how the government disposes of it.

Similarly, if the life span of project X is 20 years, and that of the alternative investment is only 16 years, the common terminal period is 20 years. The original terminal value of the benefits of the project that is reached in the sixteenth year must then be compounded forward to the twentieth year. This compounding for the additional four years must, however, follow the relevant pattern of behaviour.

To illustrate, consider first the simple case in which all the benefits, $B_1, B_2, \ldots, B_{16}$, are wholly consumed. If their terminal value in the sixteenth year amounts to, say, 250, this being the equivalent worth in the sixteenth year when all the preceding Bs are compounded to this sixteenth year at society's rate of time preferencer, then the terminal value of the Bs in the twentieth year will be $250(1 + r)^4$.

The other simple case is that in which all the annual returns are directed by the political decision maker to be invested and reinvested in the private sector at rate ρ until the sixteenth year. If the resulting terminal value in the sixteenth year comes to, say, 350 – this 350 being conceived as an increase in the capital stock – the terminal value in the twentieth year is equal to $350(1 + \rho)^4$.

In a more general case in which, of the *full* returns annually paid to subscribers, fraction c is consumed, the remaining $(1 - c)$ invested at ρ, the terminal value of the benefits in the sixteenth year may be divided into two parts:[1] (a) the equivalent terminal worth in the sixteenth year of all the amounts consumed, say 220, and (b) the increase in the capital stock in the sixteenth year that arises from the amounts each year that are invested in the private sector at the average yield ρ. We suppose this increase in the capital stock to be equal to 60.

Part (a) of the terminal value in the sixteenth year, equal to 220 will become equal to $220(1 + r)^4$ in the twentieth year. As for part (b), equal to 60, of the return to this additional capital in each of the additional years, the fraction c is consumed and the remaining fraction $(1 - c)$ invested. Therefore, at the end of four more years, we must add, first, the value of consumption (equal to the amounts consumed over the four years compounded forward at rate r), say this is equal to 20. Then, we must also add the further increase in the capital stock for four more years that results from the amounts invested in each of those years. We suppose this to equal 8.

Thus, using the figures we have adopted, the terminal value in the sixteenth year, equal to $220 + 60$, or 280, is extended to a terminal value in the twentieth year that is equal to $220(1 + r)^4 + 60 + 20 + 8$.

Needless to remark, similar principles must be used in extending for an additional four years the terminal value in the sixteenth year of the initial outlay K.

Finally, it should be noted, that this method of extending projects to a common terminal year where necessary is applicable also where the alternative to one or more projects is that of two (or several) successive projects that, usually, have relatively shorter lifespans: applicable also where one or more of the projects can be undertaken at a later date than the others.

2   The principle to be followed in compounding forward requires attention to the disposal of each of the benefits right through to the terminal year T. In the general case, the fraction c of the benefit in each year is consumed, the remaining fraction $(1 - c)$ being invested at ρ (unless otherwise directed). The terminal value of the amount consumed in year t being cB_t, it is compounded forward to become $cB_t(1 + r)^{T-t}$ in the terminal year T. The remaining part $(1 - c)B_t$ that is invested in year t is to be conceived as an addition to the capital stock. As such, it yields an annual return that is equal to $(1 - c)B_t(1 + \rho)$ in the following year and in *each* subsequent year to year T, of which annual returns, the fraction c is consumed and the remainder invested, and so on.

We may as well consider, first, the two simple cases mentioned earlier, (28.1) PV_r $(B) > K$ and (28.2)$PV_\rho(B) > K$, when each of these is transformed correctly into the CTV criterion. The first case, that in which c is equal to unity, requires that each of the benefits, being wholly consumed, is compounded to the terminal year at society's rate of time preference r. Their terminal value is therefore equal to $B_1(1 + r)^{T-1} + B_2$ $(1 + r)^{T-2} + \ldots B_T$, while the terminal value of the initial outlay is equal to $K(1 + r)^T$.

The second simple case is that in which c is equal to zero, as a result of which each of the benefits is invested and reinvested at rate ρ. The stream of benefits given by the project will then have a terminal value equal to $B_1(1 + \rho)^{T-1} + B_2(1 + \rho)^{T-2} + \ldots B_T$, this terminal value being conceived as the increase in the capital stock that is contributed by the project in question. As for the initial outlay K, its terminal value is equal to $K(1 + \rho)^T$.

In the more general case in which c is a positive fraction greater than zero but less than unity, we must treat the part of the benefit that is consumed differently from the part that is invested. The amount of the benefit B_t that is consumed has a terminal value of $B_t(1 + r)^{T-t}$. The terminal value of the remaining part $(1 - c)B_t$ that is invested is not so easy to calculate. Although this much is to be added to the terminal capital stock, this addition to the capital stock in year t also produces, in each of the following years until year T, an annual return equal to $(1 - c)B_t (1 + \rho)$ of which, again, fraction c is consumed each year and the remainder invested at rate, ρ. And so on.

3   The exact method of calculation will be easier to understand if we suppose that the project to be considered is one that generates a stream of benefits, B_1, B_2, ..., B_T, each annual benefit being equal to 10 million. In addition, we shall let $c = 0.8$, $r = 0.05$ and $\rho = 0.1$ and take T to equal 10.

(i) Of the B_1 of 10 million, therefore, 8 million will be consumed, the remaining 2 million being invested in the private sector at interest rate $r = 0.1$. The 8 million consumed has a terminal value, when compounded at the rate of time preference r, equal to 8 million $(1.05)^{T-t}$. As for the 2 million that is invested that year, it is far more prolific, as we shall see, for it adds that much to the private capital stock which is then a part of the terminal value.

(ii) This 2 million of additional capital yields an annual return of 200,000 beginning in the *second* year and ending in the terminal year, or tenth year. Of *each* of these nine annual returns of 200,000, 160,000 is consumed, its terminal value therefore requiring that it be compounded to the tenth year at a rate equal to 0.05. Altogether, they contribute to the terminal value a total of $160,000(1.05)^8 + 160,000(1.05)^7 + ... + 160,000$.The remaining 40,000 that is invested each year, from the *second* to the tenth year, must also be added to the capital stock.

(iii) Now each one of the successive annual investments of 40,000, beginning in the second year, will itself generate an annual return of 4,000, starting the year after the investment took place, and continuing until the tenth year. (Thus, the 40,000 invested in the second year will generate a return of 4,000 in year 3, 4,000 in year 4, and so on until year 10. The 40,000 invested in the third year will also generate a return of 4,000 in the fourth year, 4,000 in the fifth year, and so on until year 10, and similarly for each of the 40,000 in subsequent years).

(iv) Of each of these annual returns of 4,000, the amount 3,200 will be consumed, the remaining 800 invested, each 800 invested giving rise in the following year to an annual return until the tenth year of 80, and so we can continue.

Thus, we may reckon up the total number of additional returns so far that have been generated by the 2 million invested from the first benefit of 10 million, as follows: (ii) 9 of 200,000 plus (iii) 8 of 4,000 plus (iv) 7 of 80, and so on to the terminal year.

Having completed all these calculations, we now recognize that the amount we have added to the capital stock and the terminal value of all amounts consumed are those that flow only from B_1 – from the 10 million generated by the project in year 1. Clearly the same calculations must be undertaken for each of the subsequent benefits. B_2, B_3, ..., B_T that we have conveniently assumed to be also equal to 10 million. Clearly, the calculations required for each of the successive year's benefits will, as we approach closer to the terminal year, be smaller than the calculations required for the preceding year.

4 Turning to the calculation of the terminal value of the initial outlay K, the procedure is no different from that above. Thus, only in two simple cases mentioned in which the two criteria, $PV_r(B) > K$ and $PV_\rho(B) > K$ are correctly transformed into their corresponding CTV criteria, will the terminal values of K be, respectively, $K(1 + r)$ and $K(1 + \rho)^T$.

In all cases, the terminal value of K, so calculated, is conceived as the terminal value of the opportunity cost of any one of the public projects under consideration; that is the terminal value of K is calculated as what it would amount to if it were left in its current use or in some specifically designated alternative use.

5 The preliminary calculations above have been undertaken to show how the correct terminal value of the given ten-year stream of net benefits is to be determined on the simple but common assumption that, in ordinary circumstances, people generally save a proportion of their annual incomes. And since it follows that their incomes grow over time, so also does the amount being saved annually.

Wherever the actual behaviour pattern differs from this common assumption, the terminal value of any given stream of net benefits will, of course, also be different. In particular, it may be necessary to modify the simple assumption that people save a given proportion of each annual net benefit in two ways: (i) where only a proportion of the annual net benefits, say w, is paid out as income to subscribers to the project; and (ii) where, in addition, such income is subject to income tax.

In either case – often in both cases – the calculation of the terminal value will be yet more exacting. In case (ii), where each year a proportion of income received by the subscribers to the project is taxed, it is necessary to follow to the terminal year the disposal by the government of the additional revenues it receives in that year – at least if the government's annual disposal of the additional revenues takes a pattern that is different from that which would be taken if, instead, such revenues were left to be disposed of in the usual way by the subscribers to the project (since, if the patterns were the same, the terminal value would remain the same whether the annual income received by the subscribers were taxed or not).

6 Finally, a brief word about the possibility that some or all of the sum needed for the project is to be borrowed from abroad.

Clearly, the eventual repayment of the sum borrowed, say M, takes place in some future year or years. If the whole of M is repaid in the terminal year T, it will feature as a negative benefit in year T. In addition, each of the annual interest payments to the foreign country will appear as negative benefits. Consequently, there may be negative net benefits in some years.

There can, of course, be different arrangements for the payment of interest on the sum borrowed and also for the eventual repayment. But the above guidelines will suffice to determine their treatment.

Note

1 There can also be a general case with yet another behaviour pattern: namely, that in which each year only a part of the returns that year, say two-thirds, is paid out to subscribers, the remaining one-third being invested in the private sector at yield p (or else invested in some other designated public project). Of the amounts, received each year by the subscribers, fraction c is, again, consumed, the remainder being invested at yield p. Although the calculation required to extend the terminal value in the sixteenth year to that in the twentieth year is a bit more elaborate, no new principle is involved.

31 The normalized compounded terminal value criterion (II)

1   We should not be surprised if the student seeking to master the techniques of CBA demurs at the prospect of having to subject himself to so taxing and tedious a calculation, which is apparently unavoidable if a correct investment criterion is to be employed. For it must be admitted that, allowing for the magnitudes of the annual benefits and disbenefits to be reliable, the calculation of the project's exact terminal value of its stream of net benefits $TV(B)$ and of the exact terminal value of its outlay $TV(K)$ would be a daunting task: one that requires more time and concentration than even the most sophisticated DPV criteria discussed in Chapter 28. It must, nonetheless, be recognized that familiarity with the application or the principles necessary to calculate these normalized terminal values – which, alone, can determine whether or not implementation of the project meets a potential Pareto criterion – may be said at least to serve as a template by which the conscientious economist may judge the adequacy of the DPV criterion or of proposed proxies in the various textbooks.

Familiarity with the principles needed to calculate these normalized terminal values, however, is not to be regarded simply as a means by which to judge the adequacy of the more commonly used DPV criteria, for, on reflection surely the student will realize that modern sophisticated computers are quite capable of managing such calculations: one has only to 'feed in' the relatively simple instructions for compounding forward to the terminal year the annual net benefits or disbenefits at the appropriate rates r and ρ and, where necessary, the fractions w and c.

2   What is more, the possibility of contriving some preliminary approximations to the exact terminal values deserves consideration, in so far as in some cases they may eliminate the necessity of exact calculation.

In this connection, it should be evident that – in the absence of political constraints that would require returns over future years to be directed into public projects that have, on average, a yield greater than ρ, which we take to be the actuarial annual return on private investment – the correct terminal values of the project's net benefit stream and of its initial outlay $CV(B)$ and $CV(K)$, respectively, must lie between CV_r (B) and $CV_r(K)$, on the one hand, and $CV_\rho(B)$ and $CV_\rho(K)$, on the other; in other words, between the two terminal values when compounded forward to year T at rate r and their terminal values when compounded forward to year T at rate ρ.

The former, the lower limits, $CV_r(B)$ and $CV_r(K)$, are correctly used when c equals unity. The latter, the higher limits, $CV_\rho(B)$ and $CV_\rho(K)$, are correctly used when c is zero. In the unlikely case that r and ρ are not very different, then irrespective of the values of c, the terminal values $CV_r(B)$ and $CV_\rho(B)$ will not differ by much, at least for projects that have a short time span: similarly for CV_r (K) and $CV_\rho(K)$. In the usual case, however, in which ρ is significantly greater than r (say, at least one percentage point greater), the difference between compounding at r and compounding at ρ will (save for very short time spans) mean that neither alone will serve as an approximation for the terminal values of a project.

3   Useful approximations, for the general case, to the correct terminal values $CV(B)$ and $CV(K)$ may be contrived from three suppositions: (i) that the investment of a sum in any year remains entirely invested until the terminal year T at the yield ρ; (ii) either that income tax is negligible or that we may ignore the government's disposal of the revenues received from taxation in the belief that it is comparable with the ways in which beneficiaries of the project would themselves have disposed of them if not taxed; and (iii) that w is close to unity. Given these somewhat heroic suppositions, and provided that parameters r and ρ and also the overall propensity to consume c are maintained over the time span of the project, the *approximation*, App. $TV(B)$, to the correct terminal value of the net benefits $TV(B)$ becomes equal to

$$\sum_{t=1}^{T} cB_t(1+r)^{T-1} + \sum_{t=1}^{T}(1-c)B_t(1+\rho)^{T-1}, \quad \text{where } 1 \geq c \geq 0$$

In view of our supposition (i), the longer the time span of the project, the less reliable the approximation; that is, the greater *proportionally* will App. $TV(B)$ be above $TV(B)$.

Turning to the *approximation*, App. $TV(K)$, to the correct terminal value of the outlay $TV(K)$, let us first formulate the more general case, one in which fraction G of outlay K ($1 \geq G \geq 0$) is raised by taxation, the remainder $(1 - G)$ being raised by borrowing from the public. The App. $TV(K)$ becomes equal to

$$G\left[cK(1+r)^T + (1-c)K(1+\rho)^T\right] + \left[(1-G)K(1+\rho)^T\right]$$

Clearly, if the initial outlay K is raised entirely by taxation ($G = 1$) the App. $TV(K)$ reduces to

$$cK(1+r)^T + (1-c)K(1+\rho)^T$$

If, however, K is raised entirely by borrowing ($G = 0$), the App. $TV(K)$ is reduced to

$$K(1+\rho)^T$$

It transpires that, although these approximations to $TV(B)$ and to $TV(K)$ are sure to exceed those of their correct terminal values irrespective of how K is raised, the *proportion* by which App. $TV(K)$ in all cases exceeds $TV(K)$ will exceed the *proportion* by which App. *TV(B)* exceeds *TV(B)*. What this implies is that, whenever App. *T* (*B*) exceeds App. *TV(K)*, the Pareto criterion is met, indeed a fortiori met. On the other hand, where App. *TV(B)* is less than App. *TV(K)*, one cannot be sure that the Pareto criterion is not met: it is still possible, that is, when calculating the exact terminal values, *TV(B)* will exceed *TV(K)*.[1]

To be sure, if we chose to abide by these approximations, we may occasionally reject a project that, using exact terminal values, would indeed meet a Pareto criterion. Yet, it may be argued that this sort of error is tolerable because, if App. *TV(B)* does exceed App. *TV(K)*, we can be sure the exact measure of the excess of *TV(B)* over *TV(K)* is significant, if not substantial.

4 Once we turn our attention to special cases, however, even the exact calculations of the terminal values can be much easier. Among the more popular public projects are those that are undertaken to produce a collective good only: often environmental improvements such as a reduction of pollution or effluent. The collective benefits so generated over time are therefore to be deemed wholly consumed in each successive year. Moreover, inasmuch as such benefits are in kind – no part being paid out in cash – no tax is levied on the beneficiaries. The exact terminal value of a stream of such benefits is therefore simply equal to $\sum_{1}^{T} B_t(1+r)^{T-1}$. It would be too much, however, to expect the terminal value of the outlay K also to be simply equal to $K(1 + r)^T$ – which it would be only if K were raised solely by reducing consumption by this amount at time zero.

Another special case in which the calculation of the terminal value is much simplified is worth mentioning, even though it is less common. This is one in which all the benefits are cash returns – all goods being produced by the project being sold on the market – which cash returns each year are then wholly invested and reinvested until the terminal year T in the private investment sector at yield ρ. Were this to be the case, the exact terminal value would be equal to $\sum_{1}^{T} B_t(1+\rho)^{T-1}$. Again, corresponding to this simple calculation of the terminal value of the benefits, there can be an equally simple calculation of the terminal value of the outlay K. Were the sum K raised entirely by a loan and were the investors who subscribed to it to consume no part of the annual returns but continually reinvest returns until the terminal year T, the terminal value of the outlay K would then be equal to $K(1 + \rho)^T$.

Before ending this chapter, we must acknowledge the possibility that students who become familiar with the calculation of terminal values may wish to face the problem of selecting from a number of technically feasible projects that meet one or more given requirements, but subject to a stated budget. A procedure for the efficient selection of projects that meet the budget constraint is presented in Appendix 12.

Note

1 Moreover, for all cases in which App. *TV(B)* exceeds App. (*K*) and, which therefore do meet the Pareto criterion, the *ranking* of the projects accords with that of their respective *difference* – the difference, that is, between App. *TV(B)* and the corresponding App. *TV(K)*.

32 The Pareto criterion and generational time

1   The Pareto criterion on which a CBA is raised has regard also to the economist's basic maxim that the value to be attributed to a good or bad at any point in time is that value which is placed on it by the persons themselves at that point in time. Its application requires, in particular, that, if a person values a sum, say $400, expected to be received with equal certainty ten years from now as exactly equivalent in welfare to $60 received this year, the economist accepts this trade-off as part of his 'objective' data.

If, however, gainers or losers in the projects being ranked are expected not to be alive at the common terminal date of the projects or at the common commencement date, it is easily shown that a positive figure calculated by reducing all gains and losses to a single date – for instance, to a terminal value as proposed or the currently more popular present value – does *not* in fact meet the Pareto criterion.

Although not necessary for its demonstration, it will simplify the exposition if, for the time being, we conceive of a public project for which the finance is raised wholly by reducing current consumption. Further simplification is gained by assuming also the existence of institutions so accommodating as to produce a single rate of discount that is the rate of time preference common to all people affected by the project, this rate being exactly equal to the current yield on all investment.

With these highly convenient assumptions, it would follow in the usual way – that is, with the implicit proviso *that all persons affected are expected to remain alive over the investment period* – that the benefit–cost *ratio* would remain constant no matter what point of time was adopted in discounting and/or compounding gains and losses. Inasmuch as a benefit–cost ratio greater than unity entails an excess of benefits over costs, it also meets a Pareto criterion.

Thus, the problem addressed in this chapter is that which arises when the italicized proviso above is *not* met; that is, when gainers and losers come into being at some point of time later than the commencement of the project or else expire before its terminal date. To illustrate, suppose a benefit of $1,000 is to be received by person X in year 100. The common rate of discount r, which also corresponds to X's rate of time preference, is such, we shall suppose, as to discount this $1,000 to the sum $2 in year zero. But even though this r remains constant over his own lifetime, if person X is born in year 60, he cannot properly be said to be indifferent as between receiving $1,000 in year 100 and receiving $2 in year zero when he is in fact not alive in year zero, this being 60 years before he was born.

2 This difficulty has been circumvented up to now by assuming (implicitly) that each person affected by the project remains alive during the entire investment period, which assumption is incidentally too strict, as we shall see later. A popular alternative that simplifies matters wonderfully is to adopt a particular 'social' rate of discount, one the economist is to accept as a political datum and one to be used to cover any number of years, whether or not more than one generation is involved. Yet, as indicated earlier, the implications of introducing politically deter-mined valuations or parameters into what are putatively economic calculations are unacceptable. Such a device entails a rejection of the economist's basic maxim (that only the person himself is to determine the valuation of the effect on him of the good or bad) and therefore also of an economic or Pareto criterion. And in so far as the political authority in question is requiring the economist to come up with a strictly economic calculation, the economist's surrender to such a requirement not only prevents the economist from discharging his responsibility, but involves him in deception.

3 Let us first highlight the inter-generational problem by a simple three-person model, one that may also be interpreted as a three-generation model.

In Figure 32.1, chronological time is measured as t along the horizontal axis, and the logarithm of the net benefit for persons X and Y, and of the net loss for person Z, is measured as B along the vertical axis. The three sloping lines are to be con-ceived as 'time-indifference' curves for the three persons who alone are affected by a particular project, it being assumed that each person is indifferent between any two points. Although not essential to the analysis, it simplifies further to assume a common rate of time preference for the three persons r, say one that indicates indifference between having $1 at any time t and having $2 20 years later. All three indifference lines therefore slope upward from left to right at the same angle.

Consider first case (i), in which person Z, who lives from year 80 to year 140, is shown to be indifferent between losing consumption equal to $100 in year 80 and losing consumption equal to $200 in year 100. Person X, who lives from year 40 to year 100, is indifferent between consuming $120 in year 80 and consuming

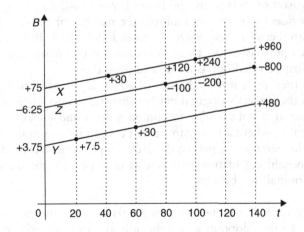

Figure 32.1

$240 in year 100. As there is an overlap of 20 years between the lifetimes of Z and X, extending from year 80 to year 100, a Pareto comparison can be made without violating the basic maxim. Whether year 80 is chosen or year 100 or any year between 80 and 100, the ratio of X's gain to Z's loss – 6/5 – remains valid. If, for instance, the year chosen is year 80, Z actually loses $100 of consumption in that year, whereas X, who actually gained $30 of consumption in year 40, would agree to accept, instead, $120 in year 80. Thus, whether or not X actually postpones consumption, his gain of $30 in year 40 is equivalent to a gain of 120 in year 80. Consequently, a potential Pareto improvement is realized in year 80, since X's gain of 120 in that year exceeds the loss of $100 by Z.[1]

The same exercise may be carried out for persons Y and X in as much as, between years 40 and 60, their lifetimes overlap. Y is indifferent between consumption of 7.5 in year 20 and 15 in year 40, whereas X actually receives 30 in year 40. In this case, both persons gain. But if, for argument's sake, we change Y's gain of 7.5 in year 20 into a loss of 7.5, equivalent to a loss of 15 in year 40, since it is then exceeded by X's actual gain of 30 in year 40, a potential Pareto improvement again exists.

Now consider case (ii) in which persons Y and Z alone comprise the community affected by the project. Since there is no point of time common to the two of them, a direct comparison between their actual or equivalent gains or losses is not possible. Y's gain of 7.5 in year 20 can be compounded forward as far as year 60 when he is still alive, but Z's loss of 100 is suffered in year 80, at the start of his life. Were it possible meaningfully to compound Y's gain forward beyond year 60 or to discount Z's loss backward from year 80, we should be able to talk of the project producing a potential Pareto loss for the Y–Z community – or, if the signs were reversed, a potential Pareto gain. But it is not possible, and therefore a valid comparison of gains and losses cannot be made for any single year.

For example, Y cannot be indifferent between receiving 7.5 in year 20 and receiving 60 in year 80, as he will not be alive in year 80. Nor can a valid comparison be made for year 60, as Z cannot be indifferent between losing 100 in year 80 and losing 50 in year 60, 20 years before he is born. Inasmuch as the basic maxim cannot be met in a case where no common point of time is shared by Y and Z, a Pareto comparison of their gains and losses is not possible.

It should be evident that we can multiply the number of persons and also reduce the time overlap between successive persons indefinitely. But once a time gap between any two persons exists, their comparison via compounding or discounting through time must be ruled out as an invalid procedure.

We conclude then that, in the absence of some dependable mechanism enabling us to transform the project's original net benefit stream into some new pattern over generational time, it is not possible to compare gains and losses on the Pareto criterion. In particular, where a time gap exists between two or more persons affected by the project in question, a potential Pareto improvement cannot be said to be met by a cost-benefit calculation that results in a positive discounted present (or compounded terminal) net benefit.

4   Among other facile but inoperative proposals to somehow circumvent the problem, in addition to the adoption of a politically determined social rate of discount, is that of recourse to the oft-touted economist's Nirvana, 'a well-defined social

welfare function'. However we imagine this abstraction to be created, it is even more far-fetched than the idea of a social rate of discount.[2]

It has also been proposed that projects that show modest benefits in the first years to be succeeded by heavy losses falling on future generations could be made acceptable if a state agency were established charged with appropriating a portion of the gains accruing in the early years, investing it at market rates of return. By the time the heavy losses occurred, the amount invested would have compounded to a sum that would fully compensate for the losses.[3] But until such an agency is indeed established, the economist cannot interpret the results of his CBA as if in fact it exists.

5 The question then naturally arises: when, over a period that covers two or more generations, the terminal years show an excess of benefits over costs which, as argued, cannot be said to result in a Pareto improvement, just what criterion can it be said to meet?

In fact, the answer is quite simple. Indeed, the answer is deducible from the proposal considered above, that a state agency be established to act in such ways as to ensure that, in implementing projects that show a positive net terminal benefit, no generation suffers a net loss. With such an investment project, it would be possible to make sure that each generation then enjoyed a potential Pareto improvement.

Since such an agency does not, in fact, exist, and a potential Pareto improvement in any period over the entire lifespan of the project could be assured only if such an agency did exist, the required potential Pareto improvement is hypothetical only – contingent, that is, on the actual establishment of the agency. In other words, the standard potential Pareto improvement, which rationalizes the economist's acceptance of projects that show an excess of net benefits, must itself be regarded as potential only so long as such an agency itself remains a potential, and not an actual, institution.

It must be concluded, therefore, that the excess net benefit criterion, when realized for a long-lived project does not in fact meet the standard economist's test of a potential Pareto improvement: the criterion confers no more than a *potential* Pareto improvement.

On reflection, moreover, it will transpire that a time span long enough to cover two or more generations is not necessary for interpreting a positive excess net benefit as no more than a *potential* Pareto improvement, for even for projects with short lifespans, say of five years or less, it will almost be impossible to avoid some generational overlap. In fact, it is enough for a person who contributes to the cost of the project to expire before receiving the later benefits to warrant regarding the net excess benefit criterion as fulfilling only a *potential* improvement.

6 It cannot be denied that a *potential* Pareto improvement is less compelling a sanction in warranting the economist's excess net benefit criterion than is the more generally accepted potential Pareto improvement. Certainly, for those who are apt to regard CBA, or allocative economics in general, as a normative study, at least in the sense that the economist's criterion would command a consensus or near-consensus, would be disconcerted to discover that the criterion involved no more than a *potential* improvement.

For those economists like ourselves, however, who regard CBA as an exercise in positive economics, there need be no heart searching. For the decision to sanction a proposed project is not the economist's responsibility. It is the responsibility of the political decision maker – in a liberal democracy, that of the community's representatives. Yet, in order for decisions to be taken in full awareness of the economic implications of cost-benefit calculations, the economist has a duty to explain its limitations. He is to emphasize in particular that the values he attributes to the goods and bads produced by the project are all derived, ultimately, from the subjective valuations of the persons affected by the project: also that the excess of net benefits over costs that is calculated must be interpreted not so much as a material improvement for the community as a whole, nor even as a potential improvement over the given time span, but as a *potential* improvement – with no account being taken of the distribution of gains or losses over time, whether progressive or regressive on balance.

Notes

1 Clearly, discounting these two sums in year 80 to present values, or else compounding them to terminal values, simply multiplies each sum by the same scalar, leaving the benefit–loss ratio unchanged at 6/5.
2 This 'well-defined social welfare function' may be visualized perhaps as emerging from a sort of conclave representative of present and future generations who, between them, will debate and eventually reach agreement about what is an equitable inter-generational distribution of real income and, possibly, other momentous issues. Yet, whatever that distribution of income agreed upon, even if it could somehow be brought about, it does not ensure that a positive DPV or CTV can be interpreted as realizing a potential Pareto improvement.
3 The reverse of a hypothetical investment stream – one that imposes costs on current generations from which future generations will reap great benefits – would seem to be more difficult for our state agency to handle. But although one cannot appropriate a portion of the gains of future generations so as to compensate losers in the present, as much may be achieved by compensating present generations for their losses by 'eating' into the existing stock of capital. In practice, this would translate into the state's taking action to increase current consumption through a reduction in income tax, the fall in revenue being met by a fall in public investment (or else by an issue of bonds that would 'crowd out' current commercial investment).

33 Cost-benefit analysis, weights and normative economics

1 There is a temptation for economists eager to advance the status of their discipline to argue that, irrespective of the results of distributional effects, a potential Pareto improvement may in fact lay claim to commanding a consensus within a Western society and, if so, be a component of virtual constitution. If so regarded, a potential Pareto improvement would have no less a constitutional legitimacy as a political decision within a democratic society. The grounds for such a claim are as follows.

2 First, there exist within Western societies economic institutions – such as progressive taxation and the system of welfare assistance – that act over time to translate the potential economic improvement into an actual Pareto improvement. Although it would be unreasonable to suppose that literally everybody in the community would actually be made better off by a change that met the Pareto criterion, it is not unreasonable to suppose that the bulk of the population affected by the change would be better off and that not many would be worse off.

Second, even though it may be the case that, for each change sanctioned by the Pareto criterion, a number of people will be made worse off, a succession of such changes is not likely to inflict losses on the same group. Over time, therefore, there can be a presumption that everyone or nearly everyone will be made better off by consistent application of the Pareto criterion.

Third, where the Pareto criterion countenances a change in which a group of people among the lower income brackets suffer a loss, political decision makers can generally be counted upon either to reject the scheme or else to arrange adequate compensation for the losers.

Persuasive though these arguments are, they are not conclusive. For lack of a better one, a majority may be willing to abide by the Pareto criterion, but others will continue to have reservations. One particular reservation has, in fact, no direct affinity with the above considerations. It arises, instead, from a scepticism about the basic maxim which accepts as the ultimate data for the economist the subjective valuations of the individuals comprising the population in question.

3 Within a modern growth economy in which the so-called 'Jones effect' is in evidence, in which personal attire is markedly exhibitionist, in which norms of taste are declining, and in which a growing proportion of its output is trivial if not regrettable, the valuations of individuals in forming a collective decision have less to recommend them. Certainly, there is greater reluctance today among segments of the public to accept the judgement of the market in the face of substantial

expenditures on commercial advertising designed to influence the valuations placed on goods by individuals. One can bring to mind consumption activities that flourish in the atmosphere of the 'new permissiveness' that are held by a large proportion of the population to be degrading at the same time that they are believed by others to be innocuous or liberating.

In addition to such instances of an incipient fragmentation of a consensus about the propriety of consumer goods and activity, there is another reason for doubting the worth of individual valuations. The untoward consequences of consumer innovations – one thinks in this connection of food additives, chemical drugs and pesticides, synthetic materials and a variety of novel gadgets – tend to unfold slowly over time. Their valuation by the buying public at any point in time may therefore bear no relation to the welfare anticipated. Indeed, the very pace of change today – the rapidity with which new models appear year after year – makes it virtually impossible for the public to learn from its experience. In sum, society can have little confidence that the valuations people place on goods have a close correspondence to their subjective wants – at any rate, close enough to justify their use, on the standard argument, as indicators of claims on society's resources.

In these circumstances, a promotion of the claim that the Pareto criterion commands a consensus is unwarrantable. The welfare economist must settle for a criterion that – although quite meaningful and occasionally commendable – cannot be sure of advancing social welfare or of meeting a consensus. The Pareto criterion continues to serve, albeit in a more humble capacity. It is seen to require simply that the sum of the valuations be positive, a requirement which need have no normative connotations.

Thus, the figure which the cost-benefit economist offers to the decision makers is no more than a summation of all individual valuations of a particular project or change, calculated at a point in time. This time is usually the present time, to which the value of expected benefits over future periods is reduced by a discounting procedure. Simply by providing ΣV (where the Vs may be interpreted as compensating variations) for the specified projects and ranking them accordingly and as required by the decision makers, the economist may regard himself as quite neutral in any official debate on the respective merits of the projects. He has, that is, no warrant for asserting a social ranking or preference for any of the projects arising from his findings.

This is a modest but useful task. And, as we are learning, not an easy one to discharge conscientiously. The findings of a cost-benefit study are properly regarded as a contribution to the political decision-making process, a contribution, incidentally, that governments and their public continually demand and whose significance they perhaps tend to overrate.

4 In this section, we shall examine those proposals which, if adopted in a cost-benefit calculation, would entail a departure from a potential Pareto criterion as represented by $\Sigma V > 0$ (aggregate money valuation). These proposals arise in connection with equity and distribution and also in the treatment of so-called merit goods, of intangibles and of the social rate of discount.

5 The impact of large investment projects on the *distribution* of welfare has recently attracted some attention.

One form of response to this concern has been an attempt to incorporate distributional effects into a cost-benefit calculation by effectively expressing gains and losses in terms of utility rather than in terms of money. For each dollar of gain or loss to a specified income group, there corresponds a particular marginal utility: the higher the income group, the lower the marginal utility of a dollar gain or loss.

Having transformed all the Vs into utility terms into Us, the resulting cost-benefit criterion is met when the aggregate gains in terms of utility exceed aggregate losses, i.e. when $\Sigma U > 0$. Clearly, a cost-benefit criterion in money valuation terms, $\Sigma V > 0$, may be met which, however, fails the valuation in utility terms, $\Sigma U > 0$, and vice versa. The particular weighting systems that have been proposed are of necessity somewhat arbitrary, and all assume diminishing marginal utility of income.

One method is that of positing a particular form of the utility-income relation. If, for example, one adopts a function that results in a constant elasticity of *minus* 2 with respect to income, a 1 per cent increase in income is to be associated with a fall of 2 per cent in the level of the utility indicator.

Another method of weighting, that of calculating a set of weights from the marginal rates of income tax, derives from the premise that the object of a progressive income tax is to share the 'real' burden of any increment of tax equally among all income groups. Thus, if on the marginal dollar of income, the 'rich' (say those in the $100,000 to $500,000 bracket) pay 80 cents, and the 'not so rich' (say those in the $10,000 to $25,000 bracket) pay 10 cents, it may be inferred that 80 cents for the rich has a utility that is equal to 10 cents for the not-so-rich or that an additional dollar to the rich is worth only $\frac{1}{8}$ as much as an additional dollar is worth to the not-so-rich.

A third method of weighting would be to calculate the set of weights as a result of the ratio between the income of the different income groups and that of the average national income. Thus, assuming the average national income is $50,000, the weight for the rich (income of $200,000) would be $50,000/$200,000 which equals $\frac{1}{4}$ and that of the poor (income of $10,000) would be $50,000/$10,000 which equals 5. It can be seen that there is an inverse relationship between the weight and income, and this is so reflected.

Alternatively, the weighting system can be made dependent upon political decisions taken in the recent past. One way of doing this, first proposed by Weisbrod (1968), rests on the assumption that all public projects that were adopted, notwithstanding their failure to meet cost-benefit criteria, were adopted as a result of an implicit set of utility weights attaching to the earnings of different groups. By comparing a number of such projects, these utility weights can be made explicit and, perhaps, become incorporated into the economist's cost-benefit criterion.

Again, although they differ from the actual techniques used by Weisbrod, the proposals made by Dasgupta *et al.* (1972) also defer to prevailing political agenda in giving expression to distributional, regional or merit priorities and in deriving particular prices such as the social rate of discount. Such proposals amount to the employment of what we may call politico-weights, their purpose being to reflect – and therefore unavoidably to promote – the government's planning objectives or political priorities.

Finally, we can use sensitivity testing to work out a range of alternatives weights. If a change in the weights results in an insignificant change in the CBA, we can deduce that the model used is robust. What this implies is that the CBA is relatively reliable and that the imposition of weights to account for income distribution is not a serious issue. Conversely, if a small change in the set of weights greatly alters the result of the CBA, this becomes a serious issue, as the final result is very sensitive to the change of weight, especially when the reliability of the set of weights is unknown.

6 It cannot be emphasized too often, however, that CBA as generally practised is to be regarded as no more than economically informative calculations in the service of those having to make social or political decisions. It is then clearly understood that the outcome of a cost-benefit calculation is, of itself, not socially decisive. It does not meet even conventional welfare economics criteria for an improvement in social welfare, in as much as these criteria also have regard to distributional considerations. It is certainly not to be thought of as an alternative to the government's economic policy or as overriding it – although it may properly be seen as a corrective to economic policy or, at least, as an aid in reaching political decisions. A CBA as understood here, and quite generally, is conducted solely in terms of economic valuation and therefore, by definition, excludes distributional effects or existing social predilections in favour of certain groups or regions or types of goods. It may have to ignore intangible spillovers simply because, for some, they defy measurement – although in such instances the economist must make this omission explicit and, in addition, provide whatever information is available.

Of the occasional influence of a project on broad social goals, CBA can only draw public attention to the fact. In sum, a well-conducted cost-benefit study can be only a part, though an important part, of the data necessary for informed collective decisions.

Attempts to work more into the technique of CBA, to endow it with greater self-sufficiency for policy purposes, by recourse to distributional weights or national parameters formulated by reference to political decisions or, at any rate, by reference to non-economic considerations, are to be resisted by economists in that they entail the following disadvantages.

First, there is the obvious difficulty of securing widespread acceptance of a given set of distributional weights or of any other weights.

If the weights are chosen through the political process or from political priorities, they may vary from one year to the next and from one country to another, according to the composition of legislators, political fashions or the exigencies of bureaucrats.

Whether and to what extent such politico-weights do, in fact, vary over time, it has to be acknowledged that they are selected or deduced so as effectively to vindicate the policies or projects favoured by the government in question.[1] Such a 'politically massaged' CBA may help ensure political consistency in the government's selection of projects, yet it does so only by jettisoning the economic rationale of the basic cost–benefit criterion, $\Sigma V > 0$.

If, however, the weights are to be chosen by the economist, they are perforce arbitrary. They will vary with the social climate and are also likely to encounter squabbles among economists, or between social groups and economists. And since some projects will be sanctioned on one set of weights and rejected using another set, one can anticipate some political in-fighting over the weights to be adopted. In this way, a continuing search by economists for an ideal set of weights may result in the public's discrediting the employment of cost-benefit techniques or, indeed, of economic measurement generally.

Second, the proposed utility-weighted criteria are at variance with the allocative principles by which the perfectly competitive economy is vindicated. It is sometimes argued that conventional CBA carries an implicit weighting system, namely, that one dollar is equal to one 'util', irrespective of who gains or loses the dollar, or that a dollar gained or lost has the same value for both poor and rich. But the rationale of the conventional CBA is not to be interpreted as having any affinity with a social goal of maximizing or increasing aggregate utility. No interpersonal comparisons of utility are to be invoked. As frequently indicated, cost-benefit methods derive their rationale from the concept of a potential Pareto improvement – the social value of output being so increased that (by costless redistributions of net gains) everyone *can* be made better off by the change in question.

This much being granted, a traditional CBA can be properly regarded as an extension of an efficient price system; certainly it enables the economist to select projects and programmes that are estimated to produce an excess of social benefit over resource cost and, indeed, of opportunity cost. If, however, the economist elects to use a contrived cost-benefit criterion, using a system of weights and possibly also politically directed valuations, so departing from the traditional $\Sigma V > 0$ criterion, then clearly projects and programmes may be sanctioned even though the value of the benefits they confer fall short of the costs incurred – so that their introduction implies that everyone, via costless redistribution, can be made worse off. Such contrived cost-benefit criteria therefore entail a departure from the norms of allocative efficiency.

Third, no matter how accurate or acceptable are the set of utility-weights proposed, their incorporation into a CBA does not, in general, serve the purpose for which they are presumably designed – to promote equity, or at least to guard against projects that are distributionally regressive. For whatever the set of weights employed, the resulting utility-weighted cost-benefit criterion could still admit projects that make the rich richer and the poor poorer, especially if the rich persons affected by the project are numerous or are made very much richer.

Although the device of incorporating utility weights into a CBA as a means of enforcing the claims of equity or distribution is evidently unsatisfactory, distributional and other social goals must be respected by the economist who offers advice to society. The least he should do is to point up the distributional implications wherever they appear significant. And since he need not affect to be so unworldly as to be in ignorance of society's commitment to greater equality, or to its declared aversion to measures that harden the lot of the poor, the economist can afford, on occasion, to be more emphatic. In particular, wherever an investment project that appears to be advantageous by ordinary cost-benefit criteria causes particular hardship to some groups, the economist should consider the practical possibilities of adequate compensation.

7   It is frequently alleged that a CBA or, for that matter, a competitive economy, ignores considerations of the social merit of certain goods, services or activities, an allegation that no perceptive economist would deny.

To some extent, their omission in a particular cost-benefit calculation may be ascribed to seemingly insuperable difficulties in their evaluation (although, as indicated earlier, all available information about them should be made explicit). Wherever the range of benefits of such good things as better health, improved education or expanded recreational facilities can be satisfactorily measured, wholly or in part, they will, of course, be included in the calculation, and what cannot be included will be described.

On the other hand, merit goods or merit benefits, such as national pride, more civic participation, better community relations or the alleviation of poverty, though they might notionally be brought 'into relation with the measuring rod of money' are likely to elude all economists' attempts to translate them into unequivocal money valuations.

Socially desirable goods of this latter sort are sometimes measured by what have come to be known as social indicators, the units proposed varying from one good to another. Health, for instance, might include longevity, infant mortality, reduction in diseases, improved weight control and so on. The measurement of poverty might include the proportion of families living below some index of 'real' income, existing on a sub-standard diet or occupying sub-standard low-cost housing.

Wherever programmes are expected to have significant welfare effects that cannot realistically be evaluated, the measurements of the appropriate social indicators should be drawn to the attention of the decision makers in addition, therefore, to the calculated benefits.

There can be yet other intangible welfare effects on the community for which no social indicators are feasible: they may serve to augment civic pride or to promote self-confidence, objectives deemed desirable by society and therefore, if necessary, to be drawn to the attention of the public body that commissions the CBA.

There is, finally, the proposal that the economic valuation of some goods or of the benefits to particular groups or regions be raised or lowered in order to reflect the declared or the inferred national objectives. Thus, if for broad policy objectives the government looks more favourably on benefits accruing to area A residents than on benefits accruing to area B residents, a dollar of benefits to the residents of area A will carry a greater weight than a dollar of benefits to the residents of area B. In addition to some doubts about the implications of this practice aired in endnote 1, it is unsatisfactory on other grounds.

Wherever a public body commissions a CBA, it presumably expects an independent economic assessment which it treats as an important input in arriving at a political decision that also takes into account other desiderata. And in this regard only a wholly independent economic assessment will serve, one that is raised on a single criterion, a potential Pareto improvement, formalized here as $\Sigma V > 0$.

Were an estimation of the relevant ΣV to reveal a net loss, it would be properly regarded as telling against the introduction of the project. Yet, such an economic assessment is, of itself, not decisive. There may be countervailing considerations turning on equity or other social merits to set against it.

If, however, instead of a wholly economic assessment based on ΣV, the proposed evaluation of the project or programme is one in which the valuations of benefits and losses are transformed by a weighting scheme putatively designed to express the government's national objectives and priorities, then in so far as it is successful in expressing them, all government-proposed programmes will be approved. Were it otherwise, were government proposed programmes to be rejected by this contrived criterion, the only conclusion that could reasonably be drawn would be that the weights initially assigned were faulty, or that the government's priorities are inconsistent.

Therefore, any government or any decision maker prepared to sanction the use of a cost-benefit assessment built on politico-weights should be made aware that such an assessment acts as little more than a mirror which reflects its own political priorities and biases. Consequently, such an assessment can no longer act as a check to political ambition. On the contrary, it acts only to reinforce, indeed, to vindicate it.

8   As we have discovered, there are substantial difficulties in discovering an acceptable rate at which society as a whole can be deemed to discount the future. The difficulties arise not because society is too large a group, or because of large differences between them of income and wealth. Such differences do not prevent the economist from calculating the valuation of other goods and bads.

The difficulties arise for a number of related reasons: capital markets tend to be imperfect; in advanced economies, rates of return vary widely according to risk and length of investment; and then there is the existence of progressive income tax. Concerning the latter, even supposing that everyone in the community had the same rate of time preference, say 6 per cent per annum, the introduction of a progressive income tax system would alter the requirements of different income groups. Imposing a 40 per cent income tax on the marginal incomes of the wealthy would result in their requiring a 10 per cent premium in order to induce them to postpone $x consumption until next year. Those paying 20 per cent income tax on their marginal incomes, in contrast, would require only a 7.5 per cent premium to induce them to postpone $x for a year, and so on. Again, for any given rate of return on investment, a portion may be paid out, part of which may be consumed and part invested, the remainder of the investment return being reinvested either in the same project or in some others.

Notwithstanding such difficulties, the economist must endeavour to calculate appropriate rates of discount, based ultimately on individual valuations only, if he is to offer an independent economic assessment to the political decision maker – an injunction that is consistent with our arguments for disallowing into our economic criterion all social or political weights or valuation. It follows that any arbitrary or politically inspired rate of discount proposed as being appropriate for public projects or programmes has to be rejected, for its employment could well sanction projects that would fail the economist's $\Sigma V > 0$ criterion, and vice versa.

Moreover, where the *de facto* decision maker is virtually a dictator or a powerful bureaucrat, though perhaps a humane bureaucrat, the idea of empowering him to set crucial prices or, specifically, the social rate of discount has even less social warrant. In poor countries, for instance, the bureaucrat is likely to be one among the group imbued with 'Western ideas' of the desirability of rapid economic growth. He is likely to think of himself as the custodian of future generations, charged with the sacred task of transforming a 'backward' economy into a 'modern' economy in the face of the resentment, inertia and 'superstition' of the masses. In the endeavour to achieve a faster rate of economic growth than that which would accord with existing behaviour patterns in the mass of people, the 'policy maker' will be prone to adopt a social rate of discount for the guidance of economic decisions that is appreciably lower than that which is in realistic relation to people's actual time preference, or to the rates of return that would emerge under ideal economic institutions. Too low a discount rate may also arguably affect efficiency in the use of scarce money resources in terms of foregone opportunities. It may also encourage too much public investment over private investment.

9   While eschewing politically determined weights or parameters in any criterion of economic efficiency (based, as it is, wholly on individuals' valuations) we can hardly avoid the incidence of political constraints in any cost-benefit calculation. As such constraints do not entail arbitrary or non-economic valuations, they act only to circumscribe the range of calculations and are to be construed as information on how the government, as decision maker, proposes to act or is expected to act. To be sure, the government may not act wisely in as much as it violates mainstream economic norms. In undertaking a CBA, however, the economist is in no way endorsing government policies or the particular constraints proposed in the designated project. Indeed, he may go on record as opposing them, notwithstanding which he is obliged to accept them. For he is seeking to discover whether, within the proposed constraints, the introduction of the project or programme in question will yet realize a potential Pareto improvement.

Political constraints may include the location of the project, the level of operation of one or more plants over a given period, restrictions on exports of the product or even the sort of workers to be employed. In addition, they may include restrictions on the distribution of the goods produced by the project and, in respect of any money portion of the returns over time to the investment, the proportions to be either reinvested in the project or invested in other enterprises.

Thus the economist, in evaluating a project, does not claim to be achieving optimal results. He is not claiming that nothing better can be done. On the contrary, he will readily agree that better can be done (for the economy at large as well as for the outcome of the project he is concerned with) if certain political or administrative constraints were to be modified or removed. But by making provision in his cost-benefit calculations for the constraints that are expected to prevail over the project's lifetime, the economist is addressing himself specifically to the question: what difference does it make to the economy if, under the constraints likely to be operative over the relevant time period, this specific investment project is introduced? In particular, does the project, under these conditions, bring about a potential Pareto improvement?

10   A question that often arises is that of how to treat the various ways in which the project or programme can be financed. After all, the $500 million, say, that is required for the project can be provided by raising that sum on the open market or by borrowing it from the Treasury or by a reduction in government expenditures on health, education, pensions, etc., or else from additional taxes, whether excise or income taxes – or, of course, any combination of these.

The ways in which the necessary funds are to be raised also come under the category of political constraints which the economist perforce has to accept. And inasmuch as any designated way of raising the required funds entails the foregoing of some existing stream of benefits (one that would have been generated if, instead, the sum in question had not been withdrawn to finance the project), these foregone streams of benefits are to be thought of as opportunity costs.

A calculation of these opportunity costs is not, however, included in the economist's brief – not unless he is directed otherwise by the decision maker. He need confine himself only to estimating the $\Sigma V > 0$ of the project under consideration, in order to determine whether the aggregate is positive.

Although the above remarks may seem self-evident to some students, they can bear emphasis in as much as the notion, and proposed measurement, of what is sometimes referred to as the 'excess burden' or 'deadweight burden' on society incurred when the necessary funds are raised by an (increase in) income tax or by an excise tax continues to appear in some currently used cost-benefit textbooks. This rather old-fashioned but persistent concept is something of 'a green mare's nest' notwithstanding that the analytic errors involved have been treated at length in the more fastidious literature on welfare economics.[2]

Finally, although the treatment of all aspects of the subject in this volume is related to a cost–benefit criterion based on the concept of a potential Pareto improvement, we cannot stress too often that such a criterion might well conflict with the law or with popular opinion. The law might well forbid the undertaking of certain enterprises that can realize a potential or even an actual Pareto improvement. For example, gladiatorial contests, public exhibitions of obscenity, the sale of hallucinatory drugs might be forbidden by laws expressive of public opinion, even though every person directly affected might freely choose to participate.

The reverse is no less likely: the law may enact measures that do not realize a potential Pareto improvement. Issues over which feelings run high – for example, the choice within a country between several regions which are to receive government subsidies in order to encourage industrial or environmental development – can sometimes be more satisfactorily resolved through the political process. In addition, it has to be borne in mind that political decisions can modify the legal framework within which economic behaviour is circumscribed and, consequently, economic valuations also. In particular, they can determine which of the two groups representing opposing interests – as occurs in any development that creates adverse spillover effects – has the legal obligation to compensate the other. As we shall see, such a decision can make a significant difference to the valuation of such spillovers.

Notes

1 Once political valuations are believed pertinent for some items, there is no clear case for limiting the extent of political intervention for that purpose. If decision makers can attach weights to merit goods, why not to ordinary goods also on the argument that, as among ordinary goods, some have smaller social merit than others? If they can attach a valuation to accidents or loss of life, why not also to a wide range of spillover effects? And if so much can be justified, there seems to be no logical reason against going further and having political decisions override all market prices and subjective valuations. Indeed,

there is no reason why each and every investment project should not be approved or rejected directly by the political process, democratic or otherwise. With such a dispensation, the economist could entertain the public by cleverly explicating the implicit prices or weights that could justify any particular investment decision so that it could compare them with those corresponding to some other investment decisions.

2 See in particular Chapters 31–34 in Mishan (1981), also Appendix 3 on the Second-Best Theorem.

Part VI
Uncertainty

34 Risk and certainty equivalence

1 The treatment in this section of the methods for dealing with uncertainty in project evaluation is, inevitably perhaps, the least satisfactory feature of this introductory volume. In the evaluation of any project, there is sure to be some guesswork about the magnitudes of future costs and benefits, arising mainly from technological innovations and shifts in demand and supply which may affect the prices of the inputs and outputs. In this consequence, economists making use of the methods discussed in this section cannot be sure of arriving at a common figure or set of figures for a specific project. The problem of how to make decisions in any situation where the past affords little, if any, guidance is not one that can be satisfactorily resolved by either logic or empiricism, and what rules have been formulated are either of limited application or of no practical value. We shall, however, consider briefly and in a simple-minded way the various methods that have been proposed to deal with this problem of uncertainty, beginning with the device of reducing an uncertain prospect to an equivalent certainty.

2 Suppose that I am uncertain of the price my house will fetch on the market when I come to sell it in five years' time. Though uncertain of the exact price, I will surely entertain some ideas of what the price is likely to be. With luck, I think it could be $60,000, possibly even more. Allowing for this, that and the other, it is, however, more likely to be $50,000. Yet, it could well be as low as $40,000, and one cannot altogether exclude the possibility of it fetching a sum lower even than this.

I should be glad to be free of the anxiety caused by this uncertainty about the sale price of my house for a guaranteed price of $50,000 five years hence. Indeed, I could be induced to agree to a smaller sum than $50,000. The question naturally arises: what is the lowest guaranteed sum I would be prepared to accept in five years' time to be rid of the uncertainty? If it were $45,000, then $45,000 is said to represent the certainty equivalent that corresponds to the range of my uncertain prospects.

If, conversely, I contemplated buying a particular house in five years' time for a sum which can be as low as $72,000 but might be as high as $100,000, I might be induced to agree to pay, in five years' time as much as (but no more than) $86,000. If so, $86,000 becomes the certainty equivalent corresponding to the uncertain purchase price.[1,2]

In general, it is asserted that to any *uncertain* future sum of money to be paid or to be received there corresponds a *guaranteed* sum between which and the uncertain sum in question the individual is indifferent, this guaranteed sum being the certainty equivalent.

On the more common assumption of risk-aversion for transactions of some importance, a person is prepared to pay some premium for safety. If, therefore, the expected figure for the sale of his house appears to be $50,000, by accepting a guaranteed price of $45,000 he can be said to be paying a risk premium of $5,000. If, conversely, he is concerned with the problem of buying a particular house in five years' time, and the most likely price is $80,000, by accepting a guaranteed future price of $86,000, he can be said to be paying a risk premium of $6,000. It goes without saying that the higher the degree of uncertainty about the future price, the greater the risk premium a person will be willing to pay.

3   This notion of certainty equivalence is, perhaps, a useful ploy in working through abstract economic constructs where the troublesome fact of uncertainty can be formally accommodated, without any amendment to the theory, simply by attributing a certainty equivalent to every uncertain magnitude. But it provides little guidance to the economist engaged in evaluating a project. If he cannot be sure of a figure at any time in the future, he will have to guess at it and, if he is at all sensible, he will choose to err on the conservative side. There is no way of insuring himself. The knowledge that some rational being, when faced with the problem of placing a value on some future magnitude, might well choose a value very different from that chosen by another equally rational individual may be of some consolation to him in his perplexity. But it cannot provide him with a clear decision rule.

4   Further theoretical elaboration is of interest but of small practical value. For example, by measuring expected value (or arithmetic mean) along the horizontal axis and variance on the vertical axis, a 'gambler's indifference map' can be constructed. The indifference curves will slope upward from left to right indicating that increasing uncertainty (as measured by variance) must be compensated by an increase in expected value. If we now have a number of alternative future benefits to choose from, all incurring the same cost, and each identified by a particular expected value and variance, that touching the highest indifference curve is chosen.

Such a construction enables us formally to rank a number of alternative uncertain benefits without first reducing each to a certainty equivalent. But though, formally speaking, the method is more direct, exception can be taken to the idea of being able to measure mean and variance in situations of genuine uncertainty. For uncertainty, strictly interpreted, implies ignorance of the probability distribution. Moreover, in the absence of a *community* indifference map and in the absence of agreement on the characteristics of the data, the method provides no more guidance in the face of uncertainty than does the method of uncertainty equivalents; which is to say it provides practically no guidance at all.

5   Finally, a word on the notion of risk. Although there is no universal agreement on the definition of 'risk', the common usage of the term is often associated with

the notion of a possibility of loss, injury or other adverse consequences of an event. The driver of a car bears the risk of injury or loss of life to himself or to others when an accident happens. What is uncertain is whether he will be involved in a car crash within the year. A risky event has a number of possible outcomes, but the actual outcome is not known in advance. For instance, storing waste materials in landfills is a risky event, as the groundwater under the landfill may be contaminated by accidental leakage.

Risk can be distinguished between objective and subjective risk. The former refers to the situation when the probability of occurrence of a chance event is objectively known, for example, death from stroke. Such deaths do occur frequently, so that the probability of this event can be determined objectively from the available statistics. If the probability of a random event is not objectively determined, it becomes a subjective probability or an uncertainty. This usually arises when the event happens very infrequently, such as an explosion from a nuclear power plant. Assessing subjective probabilities can be difficult and is much affected by the individual's perception or attitude towards the event.

Nonetheless, the dichotomy between objective and subjective risk is becoming less clear, especially when more data and experiences become available.

It is often the case in practice that the objective and subjective risk estimates of the same event are different. A classic example pertains to nuclear power plants. The subjective risk estimate of nuclear power by the general public is usually greater than the objective risk estimate by the experts. The difference is partly due to the differences in the availability of information to both parties. Nonetheless, such conflicting risk assessments between the experts and lay opinions have been a source of frustration as well as challenge to public policy makers in making the appropriate decisions with respect to such facilities.

Notes

1 If there were only two possible outcomes, $100,000, expected with a probability of $\frac{1}{4}$ and $72,000 expected with a probability of $\frac{3}{4}$, the certainty equivalent might be thought equal to $\left(\frac{1}{4} \times \$100,000\right) + \left(\frac{3}{4} \times \$72,000\right)$, or $79,000. In 'normal' cases, it would be less than $79,000, as explained in Chapter 38. In the present chapter, we do not, however, assume that probabilities can be attached to each of a range of possible outcomes.

2 The higher degree of uncertainty might be measured by a higher degree of variance if it were possible to talk of likelihood in a probabilistic sense, one arising from repeated experiment in an unchanged universe – which is not, however, the case for uncertainty.

35 Decision rules and heuristics (I)

1   As decision rules and heuristics can be used as a technique for dealing with cases of complete ignorance of the initial probabilities of possible outcomes, the reader might be inclined to pitch his hopes for useful guidance a little higher. Again, I think he will be disappointed. But before pronouncing judgement, we shall illustrate with one or two simple examples represented as payoff matrices, where the choice of the projects is to be made given the payoffs that are dependent on varying states of events.

2   Consider first a reservoir which is full at the beginning of the season and can be used both for irrigation and for flood control. Without any prior knowledge of whether or not a flood will occur, a decision is required on the amount of water to be released. If a little water is released now, it will be good for the harvest, but it will be ineffectual as a contribution to preventing future flood damage. If, instead, a lot of water is released now, it will make flood damage virtually impossible, but it will damage the harvest to some extent.

   Now, the amount of water that can be released from the reservoir can range, in general, from nothing at all to the whole lot. As for the flood, if it occurs, it can be either negligible or highly destructive. In order to illustrate the principle, however, we can restrict ourselves to two possible outcomes: full flood (b_1) and no flood (b_2). The options open to the decision maker are also to be restricted for simplicity of exposition: they will release one-third of the water in the reservoir (a_1), release two-thirds of the water in the reservoir (a_2) and release all the water in the reservoir (a_3).[1] In addition to the possible states of nature, b_1 and b_2 and the options open to the decision maker, a_1, a_2 and a_3, we are also assumed to have a clear idea of the quantitative result corresponding to the particular outcome and the option adopted. If, for example, a decision is taken to release two-thirds of the reservoir, which is option a_2, and a full flood, b_1, happens to occur, the net benefit – that is the value of the harvest *less* the value of the damage done by the flood – is assumed to be known. In this example, we shall assume it is equal to $140,000. Again, if instead we choose the a_3 option, that of releasing all the water, the net benefit that arises if the full flood b_1 occurs is assumed equal to $80,000. Since there are three options or strategies and two possible occurrences or states of nature, there will be six possible outcomes altogether, each identified by a net benefit figure. The scheme is depicted in Table 35.1.

   A glance at Table 35.1 will convince the reader that, provided the six figures are all accepted as correct estimates of net benefits, option a_3 – requiring the release of

Table 35.1

	b_1 Flood ($)	b_2 No flood ($)
a_1	130,000	400,000
a_2	140,000	260,000
a_3	80,000	90,000

all the water in the reservoir – will never be adopted. Whether b_1 or b_2 occurs, the net benefits of adopting the a_3 option will be lower than those of either a_1 or a_2. In the jargon, option a_3 *is dominated by* the other options, a fact that is revealed by the figures in the a_1 row (130,000 and 400,000) and those in the a_2 row (140,000 and 260,000), both sets of figures being larger than the a_3 row figures (80,000 and 90,000). We could then save some unnecessary calculation by eliminating the dominated option a_3, since there are no circumstances in which it would pay to adopt it. Nevertheless, we shall retain it in this simplified example, as the additional exercise will be useful, while the additional calculation will be slight.

Given no information other than in Table 35.1, we could employ either of two standard methods to produce a decision: a *maximin* procedure and a *minimax* procedure. We shall illustrate the former in the remainder of the present chapter, and the latter in the following chapter.

3   *The maximin procedure*: If he looks along the first row of Table 35.1 showing the net revenues, $130,000 and $400,000, corresponding to each of the two possible alternative states of nature, b_1 and b_2, when the decision maker chooses option a_1, it will be realized that the worst that can happen is the occurrence of b_1, yielding a revenue of only $130,000. Assuming that the decision maker is a conservative person, he will want to compare this worst result, or minimal net revenue, that he can obtain from choosing a_1, with those minima he might obtain if instead he adopts the a_2 or a_3 option. Now the choice of a_2 can realize a net yield of either 140,000 or 260,000 according to whether b_1 or b_2 occurs, respectively. He can then be sure of at least 140,000. Similarly, if he chooses option a_3 he can be sure of obtaining at least 80,000. These three row minima, 130,000 for a_1, 140,000 for a_2 and 80,000 for a_3, are all shown in the third column of Table 35.2 (which is the same as Table 35.1 except for the addition of two columns).

Down this third column he reads off the worst possible outcome corresponding to each option. If he chooses a_1, he can be sure of not getting less than 130,000. If

Table 35.2

	b_1 ($)	b_1 ($)	Row minima ($)	Maximum (maximum of row minima) ($)
a_1	130,000	400,000	130,000	
a_2	140,000	260,000	140,000	140,000
a_3	80,000	90,000	80,000	

he chooses a_2, he can be sure of not getting less than 140,000. If he chooses a_3, he can be sure of not getting less than 80,000. It will then occur to him that, if he chooses any option *other than* a_2, he might get less than 140,000; for example, if having chosen a_1, b_1 occurs, he will receive only 130,000, whereas, if he chooses a_3, he will receive only 80,000 or 90,000 according to whether event b_1 or event b_2 occurs. The largest net revenue he can be *sure* of obtaining is, then, $140,000. The maximin principle therefore requires that he choose option a_2 (releasing two-thirds of the reservoir) and assure himself of no less than 140,000.

The guiding idea has been to pick out the maximum figure from column three, which column contains the minimum possible net revenues corresponding to each option. Hence the figure chosen – 140,000 in column four of Table 35.2 – is spoken of as the *maximin*.

4   One feature of the above example is that capital costs are taken to be constant for each of the alternative options. This enables us to compare directly the net revenues – annual revenues *less* annual loss – in each of the first two columns. If we assume instead that revenues are fixed and that costs alone vary according to the decision made and the event that takes place, we can go through the same sort of exercise.

An example would be the installation of a boiler in a works.[2] Again, we can suppose three options: a_1, installing a coal-fired boiler, a_2, installing an oil-fired boiler or a_3, installing a dual boiler, one that could be switched from using coal to using oil, and vice versa, at negligible cost. Three possible occurrences are to be considered: b_1, coal prices rise relative to oil prices over the next 20 years by an average of 25 per cent; b_2, the reverse of this; and b_3, the relative prices of the two fuels remain, on average, unchanged.

The outcomes of the relevant calculations are summarized in Table 35.3, the figures being the DPV (in thousands of dollars) of the streams of future costs associated with each option for each of the three possible outcomes.

By convention, costs are to be regarded as *negative* revenues, so the figures in Table 35.3 are all negative. Looking along row a_1, the worst outcome is –13.0. If a_1 is chosen and b_1 should occur, the cost would be 13. (13 is the highest absolute figure in the row but, seen as a negative revenue and considered algebraically, –13 is less than –12; thus –13 is the lowest figure in the row.) The largest costs, or the smallest gains, corresponding to options a_2 and a_3 are, respectively, –12.5 and –12.8, which figures are entered in the fourth column. Of these row minima, the maximum (or least cost) is –12.5, corresponding to option a_2 which, on the maximum principle, would be the one to be chosen. Having chosen a_2, we can be sure that the cost to which the firm can

Table 35.3

	b_1	b_2	b_3	Row minima	Maximim (maximum of row minima)
a_1	−13.0	−12.0	−12.0	−13.0	
a_2	−11.3	−12.5	−11.3	−12.5	−12.5
a_3	−12.8	−12.8	−12.8	−12.8	

be subjected cannot exceed 12.5; this cost would be incurred if event b_2 took place. If, however, event b_1 or b_3 occurred the cost would be only 11.3.

Notes

1 This example is taken from Dorfman (1962: 130ff).
2 This example has been adapted from that given in Moore (1968).

36 Decision rules and heuristics (II)

1 There is one implication of this maximin principle that is obviously unsatisfactory. It seeks security above all and is therefore highly conservative. In Table 35.2, for instance, we are led by it to choose a_2 rather than a_1, simply because, in choosing a_2, we can be sure of obtaining at least \$140,000 whereas, if we choose a_1, we can be sure of obtaining at least \$130,000. If we feel pretty certain of getting the least in all cases, we should indeed be wise to choose that least which is largest. And the least for a_2 is \$10,000 larger than that for a_1. But if it so happens that the event b_2 does take place, our choice of a_2 yields us only \$260,000 whereas, had we instead chosen option a_1, event b_2 would yield as much as \$400,000. In other words, if b_2 takes place after all, we shall forgo an extra gain of \$140,000 (\$400,000 minus \$260,000). The cost of playing safe – of ensuring \$10,000 more if the worst should happen – is that of losing the opportunity of gaining \$140,000 more if the best should happen.

2 We can 'cook up' another set of figures for this example, those in Table 36.1, in order to bring out this defect even more sharply.

The row minima for options a_1 and a_2 are shown in the third column to be 13 and 14, respectively. On the maximin principle, the a_2 option is to be chosen as that which guarantees a net receipt of no less than 14 – but it is clear that the most that can be gained from choosing option a_2 is only 15. By comparing this choice with the rejected option a_1 we cannot but realize that we are sacrificing the chance of gaining 5,000 in order to increase our guaranteed minimum receipts from 13 to 14. With outcomes such as those in the columns of Table 36.1 it is hard to think of anyone employing the maximin method and choosing a_2, for he will be aware that, if event b_2 turns up, he will receive 15 only whereas, if he had instead chosen a_1, he would receive 5,000: he becomes aware, then, that by choosing a_2 (so as to ensure that if the worst happens he will receive one more than if, instead, he chooses a_1) he lays himself open to a potential loss of 4,985 (5,000 *minus* 15) should the event, b_2, occur.

Table 36.1

	b_1	b_2	Row minimum	Maximin
a_1	13	5000	13	14
a_2	14	15	14	

A less conservative person would not want to guide his choice by the maximin principle even if the figures were less enticing than those in Table 36.1. Indeed, if he were at all enterprising, and had an eye open for the larger gains that are possible, he would adopt something like the reverse of the maximin principle. What he would want to avoid is the possibility of an outcome that will make him regret his choice. Since his regret will increase with the size of the loss of possible gain – 4,985, in the above example, if he chooses a_2 – he will adopt the principle of minimizing his regret. Hence, the alternative *minimax regret* procedure suggested by economists.

3 *The minimax procedure*: We can illustrate this procedure by constructing Table 36.2 using the primary data given in Table 35.1. Suppose a flood occurs, which is to say that the b_1 event takes place, the initial choice of option a_2 would have secured for the b_1 event the largest net revenue of 140,000. If, on the other hand, a_1 had been chosen, the net revenue would have been 130,000, or 10,000 less than could have been obtained had we chosen a_2. We therefore put 10,000 in the cell opposite a_1 and below b_1 in Table 36.2. This 10,000 entry is to be interpreted as follows: if b_1 occurs, the prior choice of option a_2 yields the largest receipt, 140,000. By choosing some other option, say a_1, we receive only 130,000, a *potential loss of 10,000*. Below b_1 and opposite a_3, however, we place the figure 60,000 because, if b_1 occurs, our prior choice of a_3 would yield 80,000 – a potential loss of 60,000 (140,000 *minus* 80,000) compared with the largest yield of 140,000 that would come from having chosen a_2. Opposite a_2 itself, we obviously put a zero, as there is no potential loss from having chosen a_2 if event b_1 occurs.

We now fill the cells down the second column. The highest net revenue if event b_2 occurs is 400,000, corresponding to the choice of option a_1: hence, a zero opposite a_1 and below b_2. If a_2 is chosen instead, only 260,000 can be collected – a potential loss of 140,000 (400,000 *minus* 260,000) is involved. Below b_2 and opposite a_2, therefore, we place the figure 140,000. If, finally, a_3 is chosen, only 90,000 can be collected, involving a potential loss of 310,000 (400,000 *minus* 90,000). Below b_2 and opposite a_3 we therefore place the figure 310,000.

Since the derived figures in the first two columns are now to be regarded as potential losses, row a_3 is again dominated by the other rows. Its potential losses for either event b_1 or b_2 are larger than those of any other row. The standard computational procedure would be to eliminate a_3 before calculating the figures for the row maxima column. But, again, in so simple an example, it adds to the interest while causing no difficulty.

As it is regret-at-potential-losses we now seek to minimize, we glance along the rows and pick out the largest potential loss that could arise from each option in turn. The largest figure along row a_1 is 10,000. It is therefore placed opposite a_1 under the third column containing the row maxima. For row a_2, the largest

Table 36.2

	b_1	b_2	Row maxima (of potential losses)	Minimax (minimum of row maxima)
a_1	10,000	0	10,000	10,000
a_2	0	140,000	140,000	
a_3	60,000	310,000	310,000	

potential loss figure is 140,000, and it is entered accordingly opposite a_2 and in the third column. For row a_3, the largest potential loss figure is 310,000, and this is shown opposite a_3 in the third column.

Of these largest potential losses from choosing a_1, a_2 or a_3, the decision maker chooses the smallest, which is 10,000, corresponding to option a_1. Accordingly, the figure of 10,000 is entered in the fourth column of Table 36.2. By choosing option a_1, he can be sure of one thing: that whichever event occurs, his potential loss – that is, the additional gain he might, in that event, have obtained had he instead selected one of the other options – can be no greater than 10,000. For clearly, if instead he chooses a_2, the potential loss he may suffer is 140,000. While if he chooses a_3, the potential loss he may suffer is 310,000.[1]

As a further illustration of the minimax-regret method, Table 36.3 is constructed from the primary data given in Table 35.3. For the first column, below b_1 the best choice is a_2, as it would entail the least cost 11.3. If option a_1 were chosen instead, the cost would be 13, and therefore the loss of potential savings would be 1.7 (13 *minus* 11.3). Similarly, if a_3 were chosen, the cost would be 12.8, and the loss of potential savings would be 1.5 (12.8 *minus* 11.3). The figures in the next two columns are obtained in the same way. In the fourth column, we put the row maxima. From these, the smallest potential loss, 0.5 corresponding to option a_2, is chosen and entered in the fifth column.

4   Not surprisingly, perhaps, the more obvious shortcoming of this minimax method is the opposite of that found in the maximin. The conservatism of the maximin, it will be recalled, is such that cases can arise in which large potential gains are sacrificed for very little extra security. In order to skirt this contingency, the so-called minimax-regret method courts the opposite danger, for cases can arise in which the application of this more enterprising minimax method will effectively jettison the chance of a good gain for the hope of getting a bit more.

The net revenue figures in Table 36.4 are chosen to illustrate this shortcoming of the minimax regret procedure.

Application of the maxim, in principle would select option a_1, so ensuring a receipt of 300. Table 36.5, however, uses the data in Table 36.4 to derive corresponding figures in each cell for potential losses.

Table 36.3

	b_1	b_2	b_3	Row maxima	Minimax
a_1	1.7	0	0.7	1.7	
a_2	0	0.5	0	0.5	0.5
a_3	1.5	0.8	1.5	1.5	

Table 36.4

	b_1	b_2	b_3	b_4
a_1	300	300	300	300
a_2	120	500	120	120

Table 36.5

	b_1	b_2	b_3	b_4	Row maxima	Minimax
a_1	0	200	0	0	200	
a_2	180	0	180	180	180	180

In the concern (should event b_2 occur) not to regret the loss of 200, the person employing the minimax-regret principle incurs instead the risk of the somewhat smaller potential loss of 180 should any of the other three events, b_1, b_3, b_4, occur. Put more directly, his choice of a_2 ensures that, if event b_2 occurs, he will obtain 500 rather than the 300 he would obtain by choosing a_1. (If, however, b_1, b_2 or b_4 occurs, he will collect only 120 rather than the 300 he would obtain by choosing a_1.)

5   A minor characteristic, sometimes regarded as a defect, arising from the use of the minimax method is that, if one of the rejected options is withdrawn, that option which had been chosen before its withdrawal might not be the option chosen by this method in the new circumstances. This possibility is illustrated using the figures in Table 36.6, which happen to be the same as those used in Table 35.1 except for the last line.

On the maximin method, a_3 would be chosen. Using the minimax procedure, however, we first derive from Table 36.6 the potential loss figures which appear in Table 36.7, and, from the row maxima column, we choose the lowest figure, namely 160,000, corresponding to option a_2.

Now if option a_1 in Table 36.6 were withdrawn, the resulting potential loss figures for the remaining options, a_2 and a_3, would be those given in Table 36.8. The

Table 36.6

	b_1	b_2
a_1	130,000	400,000
a_2	140,000	260,000
a_3	300,000	200,000

Table 36.7

	b_1	b_2	Row maxima	Minimax
a_1	170,000	0	170,000	
a_2	160,000	140,000	160,000	160,000
a_3	0	200,000	200,000	

Table 36.8

	b_1	b_2	Row maxima	Minimax
a_2	160,000	0	160,000	
a_3	0	60,000	60,000	60,000

row maxima are now 160,000 and 60,000 for a_2 and a_3, respectively. Therefore, on the minimax procedure, a_3 becomes the chosen option.

If, on the other hand, option a_3 were to be withdrawn from Table 36.6, the potential loss figures for the remaining options, a_1 and a_2, would be those given in Table 36.9. The row maxima corresponding to a_1 and a_2 are now 10,000 and 140,000, so that, on this principle, a_1 is chosen.

There is, however, nothing paradoxical about such results. From the standpoint of the minimax-regret principle, the initially rejected options that are removed are indeed relevant to the decision. Thus, in withdrawing option a_1 the yield of 40,000 if event b_2 occurs (in Table 36.6) is no longer available to us. Thus, when a_1 is no longer available, the potential loss from choosing a_3 falls from 200,000 (when a_1 was available) to only 60,000, as shown in Table 36.8.

Similarly, if option a_3 alone is withdrawn, leaving us with a_1 and a_2, the 300,000 outcome if b_1 occurs is no longer available to us. The potential loss from choosing option a_1 if b_1 occurs falls, therefore, from 170,000 (when a_3 was available) to only 10,000 (when a_3 is no longer available) as a result of which, the a_1 option is then chosen, as indicated in Table 36.9.

We need not therefore regard this feature of the minimax procedure as a defect of the method. Rather, we should confine our criticism to that already indicated in the preceding section as illustrated by Tables 36.4 and 36.5, in which the chance of some minimum gain is put at risk in the hope of securing a bit more.

6   In sum, it would appear that the choice of maximin or minimax regret would not be adopted in advance and independently of the primary data by any person unless he was cautious to a fault (in which case he would always apply the maximin principle) or being recklessly opportunistic or, more precisely, fearful of losing potential gains (in which case he would always apply the minimax-regret principle).

There are, in addition, more decision rules similar to the maximin and minimax criteria to be briefly mentioned. The maximax criterion is one that takes an even more optimistic and risk-taking stance, where the maximum is selected across the maximum payoffs within each strategy. Therefore, possible losses are entirely ignored, and the strategy yielding the largest possible outcome is chosen.

The Laplace criterion assigns equal probabilities to all possible payoffs, and selects the strategy that gives the largest equally weighted payoffs. This is conditional on insufficient information on the probabilities of the various outcomes. Otherwise, deriving the expected value would be preferred (see Chapter 38). The Hurwicz criterion is one other alternative, in which the goal is to balance the optimism and pessimism. A coefficient of pessimism, α, is assigned to the worst possible outcome within each project, and the counterpart $(1 - \alpha)$ is assigned to the best possible outcome within each project. As such, the decision maker expresses an arbitrary risk preference when determining α. It should also be noted that this

Table 36.9

	b_1	b_2	Row maxima	Minimax
a_1	10,000	0	10,000	10,000
a_2	0	140,000	140,000	

method is dissimilar to finding expected values, in that only two outcomes, the best and the worst, of the possibly many outcomes are taken into consideration.

One must conclude that, even where conditions are such that these methods can be applied, the fact alone that the choice of whether to use maximin- or minimax-regret will depend upon the person and upon the data makes the application of decision rules somewhat unsatisfactory. Since subjective judgement enters into the choice of whether to use maximin- or minimax-regret, competent economists inspecting the same data can come up with different decisions.

Note

1 This 'minimax-regret' or 'minimax-risk' (of loss) principle, as it is sometimes called, is really a misnomer. The figures for losses in Table 36.2 are given without sign. But if we follow the convention of treating losses as negative signs, we should write all the figures in Table 36.2 with a minus sign. For instance, if a_3 is chosen and b_1 occurs, the potential gain is 80,000 minus 140,000 or – 60,000.

The largest potential loss in each row of Table 36.2 should then really be expressed as a *negative* figure: –10,000 for a_1, –140,000 for a_2 and –310,000 for a_3. These negative figures can then be regarded as the lowest or minimal row gains. Of these (algebraic) row minima, we choose the (algebraic) maximum, namely, 10,000, corresponding to option a_1.

The formal procedure is in fact no different from that used in connection with Table 35.3, where the negative items happen to refer to costs.

In effect, then, the same maximin procedure as before is employed, with the important difference that the row minima figures we are now maximizing refer to (negative) *potential* gains (compared with other options) instead of *actual* gains.

However, we shall here follow the convention of using positive figures to refer to potential losses, and of describing the procedure as 'minimaxing-regret'.

37 How practical are decision rules and heuristics?

1   The final stage of a typical cost-benefit study requires that we evaluate a stream of net benefits

$$(B_1 - K_1), (B_2 - K_2), \ldots, (B_n - K_n)$$

in which the Bs or benefits and the Ks or costs are uncertain and, indeed, increase in uncertainty the further they are from the present.

The difficulties we encounter in the attempt to apply decision rules and heuristics may be illustrated by recourse to a simple example in which the net benefits of a project are spread over four years as follows: –100, 30, 80 and 50. The –100 figure indicates a net capital outlay of 100 in the first year, and the remaining figures are net benefits in successive years. The penumbra of uncertainty surrounding each of these figures might suggest, for example, that for the –100 figure we substitute a *range* –95 to –105: for the figure of 30, a range 25 to 35, and so on. For practical purposes, however, we would not use a continuous range, only discrete figures. The range –95 to –105 could, for instance, be split into three possible outcomes –95, –100 and –105. The range 25 to 35 could also be split into three outcomes or perhaps five, say, 25, 28, 30, 32 and 35. Similarly for the other two figures. If we take these arbitrarily chosen figures from the range of net benefits in any period to be independent of the arbitrarily chosen figures from the range of any other period's net benefits, a combination that included one of the possible net-benefit outcomes from each of the four periods – say –95 from the first period, 32 from the second, 75 from the third, and 50 from the fourth – would add up to the outcome of a single event. There are obviously as many events as there are combinations of such possible outcomes for the four-year period.[1]

2   The uncertainty about the net-benefit figures in each period can, however, be attributed instead to the uncertainty about future *price* movements of both the inputs and outputs associated with the project. It is true that the price movements themselves depend upon a number of future possible events, such as technical conditions of demand and supply. But for each combination of such possible innovations, changes in domestic and foreign policies, and alterations in the events, there will be a corresponding range of possible prices for both the inputs and outputs in question. We may therefore express the uncertainty about all future events in each period by reference to some price range of each of the inputs and outputs.

Suppose that in the A_1 investment project, giving rise to a four-year stream of net benefits (including the initial year's capital outlay), there are the prices of only four items to be anticipated: that of homogeneous labour; that of homogeneous material; that of homogeneous machinery; and that of homogeneous output. Since prices do become more uncertain as we move into the future, the range of possible prices becomes wider and, as it becomes wider, it may be split into a larger number of possible prices. In token of this consideration, we shall divide the price range of each item into three alternative prices for the first period, but into five alternative prices for the second, third and fourth periods. In each of the four periods, there will be a larger number of possible net benefits, each possible net benefit corresponding to a different combination of the prices of each of the above-mentioned four items. Thus, for the first period, the three alternative prices for each of these four items will generate 3^4, or 81, possible outcomes, each of such outcomes being an alternative net benefit in the first period. For the second period, the five different prices for each of the four items will generate 5^4, or 625, possible outcomes, each being an alternative net benefit. Similarly, there will be 625 possible net benefits for each of the two remaining periods.

Matching any one of the 81 alternative net benefits in the first period with any one of the 625 possible benefits from each of the other three periods so as to produce a particular permutation of four successive benefits, provides us with a single event, b_1. Since there are 81 different net-benefit outcomes in the first period and 625 different net-benefit outcomes in each of the three remaining periods, the total number of different events that are possible is given by 81×625^3, or close to 20 billion different events.

3   If we now introduce another investment option A_2, which also yields a stream of possible net benefits over four years *and uses the same inputs and outputs*, we must calculate figures for roughly another 20 billion events. If, however, the A_2 stream covers more periods than the A_1 stream, or if there are additional inputs or outputs to contend with, we shall have to increase the number of events. Each of these additional events will carry a net-benefit figure for A_2, positive, zero or negative. Corresponding to these additional events for A_2, there will be zeros for A_1. There may, however, be inputs or outputs in the A_2 investment option that replace those in the A_1 option; for example, steel may be the only material used in the A_1 investment option, and aluminium the only material used in the A_2 option. In that case, there will be a number of events that are strictly relevant only to A_1 and a number that are strictly relevant only to A_2. Corresponding to those events that are strictly relevant to A_1, there will be net revenues (positive, zero or negative) for the A_1 option, and zeros for the A_2 option, and vice versa.

One has but to reflect (a) that the price-range of any important item can be split into more than three or five possible prices, (b) that the number of important items to be bought or sold over the lifetime of a project can easily exceed four, (c) that the number of periods of any of the investment streams under comparison can exceed four and, indeed, is often likely to exceed ten, and (d) that there are frequently more than two investment options to compare, to realize that the number of possible events, or outcomes, can run into billions of billions. Attempts to deal with the uncertainty aspects of cost-benefit studies in this fashion is, therefore, hardly a practical proposition even with the most advanced computers.

When it is further recalled that, as distinct from simple decision rules, not only is the number of distinct events *not* given to us exogenously (as indicated above, it is generated from alternative prices chosen arbitrarily from guesses about the likely range), but also that not all events are equally likely, inasmuch as not all the alternative prices are equally likely, it is not surprising that, in any practical evaluation of investment projects no recourse is had to the formal apparatus of decision rules.

Note

1 It is hardly necessary to say that, in adding these four figures, those for the second, third and fourth periods must be compounded or discounted at the relevant rates.

38 Simple probability in decision making

1   The techniques illustrated in decision rules are based on the assumption that there is no knowledge at all available that could throw any light on the likelihood of each of the alternative events, b_1, b_2, b_3, occurring over the period in question. In the complete absence of such knowledge, we can no more suppose that b_1 is as likely to occur as b_2 than we can suppose that b_2 is more (or less) likely to occur. We can say no more of the events in question than that each is possible. Once a suspicion about the greater likelihood of one or more of the possible events occurring begins to form, the simple decision rules method may require modification. In general, the more information about likelihoods we can obtain, the more agreement about the best decision we can hope to secure. If, from years of keeping records about floods, we could attach probabilities to each of two possible outcomes b_1 and b_2 in Table 35.1, our procedure would be to include those probabilities as weights in working out a solution.

2   Suppose that event b_1 (flood) can be expected with a probability of p_1, say 3/5, and event b_2 (no flood) therefore with a probability p_2 of $(1 - p_1)$, or 2/5, we make our calculations in a way illustrated by Table 38.1.

   If option a_1 is chosen, each of the outcomes, 130,000 and 400,000, corresponding to the possible events, b_1 and b_2 respectively, is multiplied by the probability of the occurrence of the event, 3/5 and 2/5. The weighted average, or mathematical expectation, of the gains from choosing a_1 is entered in the third column, as also is the weighted average of gains from choosing a_2 and $a3$. The largest weighted average is obviously 238,000, arising from the choice of option a_1, which can be regarded in the circumstances as the proper decision.

   Now if this figure of 238,000 could be regarded as the anticipated value of net revenue from choosing a_1, in the sense that there is a stronger likelihood of a net revenue of 238,000 occurring when a_1 is chosen than of any other single value, we might have less hesitation in opting for a_1 rather than a_2 or a_3. But this figure of 238,000 for a_1 can be regarded as the expected value only in the conventional statistical sense; that is to say, if it were possible to repeat this experiment year after year for, say, the next 100 years or so, then – provided that the relevant climatic conditions remain unaltered – the *average* net revenue from choosing a_1, taken over the 100 years, would be close to 238,000. For roughly 3/5 of the century, or for roughly 60 out of the 100 years, event b_1 would occur, and for the remaining years event b_2 would occur.

   It is clear, then, that if we are thinking in terms of many years ahead, on the one hand, we can (if relevant conditions are not expected to change very much) expect to come close to the (undiscounted) average of 238,000 by repeatedly opting for

Table 38.1

	$b_1(p_1 = 3/5)$	$b_2(p_2 = 2/5)$	Weighted average	Largest weighted average
a_1	130,000 × 3/5	400,000 × 2/5	238,000	238,000
a_2	140,000 × 3/5	260,000 × 2/5	188,000	
a_3	80,000 × 3/5	90,000 × 2/5	84,000	

a_1. If, on the other hand, we are interested in the outcome next year alone, we obviously cannot expect a net revenue of 238,000 from choosing a_1. For in one year, only one event will occur. If b_1 occurs, the net revenue will be 130,000. If, instead, b_2 occurs, the net revenue will be 400,000. All we can say is that, based on past evidence, there is more chance of b_1 occurring than b_2. And the higher the probability of b_1's occurring, the more we are disposed to expect it and to have our decision governed by the thought of its occurrence.

If, to take more extreme probabilities, we discovered from the records that floods occur, on the average, in nine years out of ten, we should be justified in expecting a flood next year, and in being surprised if it did not occur. The net revenue we can most reasonably expect if we choose a_1 is therefore 130,000. By the same logic, the net revenue we should be inclined to expect by choosing option a_2 is 140,000. This being so, we might conclude that the rational thing is to choose a_2. But once we have probabilities attached to the various events it would not be very sensible to focus our expectations on the event with the highest probability and ignore the possibility of the other events occurring. Thus, whether the probability of event b_1 occurring is 3/5 or 9/10, the decision maker is not completely indifferent to the outcome arising from event b_2 – unless that outcome is the same, say 200,000, whatever option is chosen. The greater the gain in choosing a_1 (given that b_2 occurs) compared with that in choosing a_2, the more weight he will give to the a_1 option. To illustrate with extreme figures, if choice of a_1 would entail an outcome of 1,000,000 if event b_2 occurred whereas the choice of a_2 entailed an outcome of zero for the same event, the nine chances out of ten that b_1 would occur – conferring an additional 10,000 if a_2 were chosen rather than a_1 – would hardly be likely to prevail against the thought that if, despite its slim chance, b_2 did occur a net gain of 1,000,000 would be collected.

3 We may conclude tentatively that dependable probabilities will be taken into account by the decision maker in such cases; moreover, that the use of these probabilities as weights in the method indicated above (by reference to Table 38.1), would be acceptable to many as a rough general rule. By choosing an option based on a weighted average of events, rather than on the basis of a single most likely event, we are in effect refusing to neglect the possible impact of the less likely event(s) on our decision, and doing so in a systematic and conventional manner.

39 Mixed strategies in decision making

1 Records covering many years can provide information *additional* to the probability of each of a number of alternative events occurring, such as b_1 and b_2. For instance, in addition to discovering that over, say, 100 years event b_1 (flood) occurred in 60 out of 100 years, that is, with a frequency of 3/5, and event b_2 (no flood) therefore with a frequency of 2/5, the records may reveal the following information: (i) prior to event b_1, a period of several weeks of cloudy weather – a condition we refer to as z_1 – was observed in half the number of b_1 events; (ii) prior to event b_1, a period of several weeks of mixed weather – referred to as z_2 – was observed in one-third of the number of b_1 events; (iii) prior to event b_1, a period of several weeks of clear weather – say z_3 – was observed in one-sixth of the number of b_1 events.

The same sort of information will be available for event b_2 which, it is assumed, is completely independent of b_1. Let us suppose, therefore, that z_1 (several weeks of cloudy weather) was observed prior to one-sixth of the number of b_2 (no flood) events; that z_2 (several weeks of mixed weather) was observed prior to one-third of the number of b_2 events; and that z_3 (several weeks of clear weather) was observed prior to one-half of the number of b_2 events. If we can assume that basic climatic and other relevant conditions will remain much the same, we can treat these frequencies as probabilities. And if so, we can get better results than those reached by adopting what are called 'pure' strategies; that is, by adopting *one* of options a_1 or a_2 or a_3. These better results are attained by recourse to 'mixed' strategies, which are no more than a combination of pure options – adopting a_1, a fraction of the time, a_2, another fraction of the time and a_3, the remainder of the time.

2 Thus, instead of the choice between the three simple options, a_1, a_2 and a_3, let the reader think of a larger number of quite arbitrary mixed strategies; call them $s_1, s_2, s_3, ..., s_n$. For example, strategy s_1 might require that, if z_1 is observed, a_1 is to be chosen; if z_2 occurs, a_1 is to be chosen; if z_3 occurs, a_3 is to be chosen. Strategy s_2 might be as follows: if z_1 occurs, choose a_1; if z_2 occurs, choose a_2, while if z_3 occurs, choose a_2 again. Strategy s_3 might be, if z_1 or z_2 or z_3 occurs, choose a_2, and so on.

Now suppose event b_1 were to take place, we should, as indicated above, expect to observe weather condition z_1 with a probability of 1/2, z_2 with a probability of 1/3 and z_3 with a probability of 1/6. The expected or average outcome over a period of time from adopting, say, strategy s_1 (in the event that b_1 occurs) is obtained by weighting each of the net revenues attaching to the options designated by strategy s_1

by the probabilities of the zs. Thus, strategy s_1 prescribes that we select option a_1 (with outcome 130 in case of event b_1) should z_1 occur, which it does with a probability of 1/2. The first component of strategy s_1, in that event, is $1/2 \times 130$. The second component of strategy s_1 requires that we select a_2(with outcome 140 for event b_1) should z_2 occur, which it does with a probability of 1/3. Consequently, the second component of strategy s_1 is equal to $1/3 \times 140$. Similarly, the third component of strategy s_1 prescribes option a_3 (with an outcome of 80 for b_1) should z_3 occur, which it does with a probability of 1/6. Hence, it is equal to $1/6 \times 80$.

Given event b_1 then, the expected value of revenue from employing strategy s_1 is equal to

$$(1/2 \times 130)(1/3 \times 140) + (1/6 \times 80) = 125$$

Given the same b_1 event, we could work out the expected value of the revenue from employing strategy s_2. The same steps in the calculation give it as

$$(1/2 \times 130)(1/3 \times 140) + (1/6 \times 140) = 136$$

Given the same b_1 event again, the employment of strategy s_3 will realize an expected value equal to

$$(1/2 \times 140)(1/3 \times 140) + (1/6 \times 140) = 140$$

And so we could go on calculating expected revenues, in the event b_1 takes place, for all the other strategies.

If, instead, event b_2 occurred, the relevant probabilities of z_1, z_2 and z_3 would be 1/6, 1/3 and 1/2, respectively, and employing the original s_1 strategy would, therefore, yield an expected value of revenue equal to

$$(1/6 \times 400) + (1/3 \times 200) + (1/2 \times 90) = 199$$

Employing strategy s_2, however, would yield an expected value of net revenue equal to

$$(1/6 \times 400) + (1/3 \times 260) + (1/2 \times 260) = 284$$

while recourse to strategy s would yield an expected value of revenue equal to

$$(1/6 \times 260) + (1/3 \times 260) + (1/2 \times 260) = 260$$

These results can be displayed in Table 39.1 for all n possible strategies, though only the first three strategies and the last strategy are represented there. Some strategies are likely to be dominated by others and would not stay in the table. After eliminating all the dominated strategies, we are left with a choice of mixed strategies which we could re-number $S_1, S_3, ..., S_m$.

Table 39.1 (In thousand dollars per annum)

	b_1	b_2
s_1	125	199
s_2	136	284
s_3	140	260
–	–	–
–	–	–
s_n	140	160

3   What is the advantage of all this? On the surface, it would appear to offer a larger range of choices.[1] Granted that the use of these strategies offers us more choice, how do we go about selecting the best strategy?

In fact, we are 'back to square one' – *except* that there are apparently many more choices of strategy than the initial three options. With the data given in Table 39.1, that is, we could employ the maximin method, or the minimax-regret method, or some other method in order to select one of these new strategies. Indeed, where we can attach probabilities also to events b_1 and b_2, we can employ the method outlined in the preceding chapter: we can, that is, calculate the weighted average net revenue for each of the listed strategies and choose that yielding the highest revenue.

Again, however, if we are concerned with the outcome over the next one or two years only, the method outlined is of much less use than if, instead, we can adopt the strategy for a largish number of years. Consider, for instance, the calculated net revenue of 125 that arises from employing strategy s_1 in the event that b_1 takes place. True, if b_1 is to occur, we shall observe z_1 with a probability of 1/2, z_2 with a probability of 1/3 and z_3 with a probability of 1/6. But in responding to the zs according to the adopted strategy, here s_1, we cannot hope to realize in this same year a revenue of 125. For in the one year one of z_1 or z_2 or z_3 is observed and, therefore, according to the strategy chosen, one of a_1 or a_2 or a_3 is adopted. The net revenue in that event is one of 130 or 140 or 80 – not 125, however, which is but an average figure to which the revenues will converge only if, whenever b_1 occurs (which is about 3/5 of the total number of years), we continue to use strategy s_1. Similar remarks apply to the figure of 199. It follows that if, say, over the next 100 years event b_1 could be expected to occur 3/5 of the time and event b_2 the remaining 2/5 of the time, the repeated use of strategy s_1 could be expected to give a series of (undiscounted) revenues that would average about (3/5 × 125) + (2/5 × 199), or 155. If, over the same period, s_2 instead were repeatedly employed, the average (undiscounted) revenue to expect would be (3/5 × 136) + (2/5 × 284), or 196. We could work out the (undiscounted) average revenues for all the mixed strategies listed, and expect, in general, that at least one such strategy would produce a weighted average above the highest (238), for the pure strategy makes no use of the zs.[2]

4 We may conclude that the information about such indicators as the zs can be of use in improving the decision process through mixed strategies only when events over a large number of years, or over a large number of similar projects, are anticipated. If, for example, a reservoir is to be used under the same environmental conditions for many years to come, or if a large number of similar reservoirs are to be constructed, there can be advantages in using information provided by the zs in order to produce a variety of mixed strategies. Having chosen the maximum-yielding strategy, it must be employed repeatedly over the future in the first case, or applied to each of the many reservoirs in the second case. If, however, what matters is the revenue for only one or two years and/or for only one or two reservoirs – or if, alternatively, environmental conditions cannot be expected to remain unchanged – (so that one cannot reasonably attach probabilities to events b_1, b_2 or to the indicators z_1, z_2, z_3), the method of contingent probabilities outlined above is of little practical use.

Notes

1 We can, of course, include the pure strategies (the choice of option a_1 alone, a_2 alone or a_3 alone) among these mixed strategies. The choice of a_1 alone might be numbered strategy s_8, with a_1 being chosen irrespective of the occurrence of z_1, z_2 and z_3, so yielding 130 for b_1 and 400 for b_2 as in Table 38.1. The choice of a_2 alone would enter, say, as strategy S_9, with a_2 being chosen regardless of the occurrence of z_1, z_2 and z_3, so yielding 140 for b_1 and 260 for b_2 as in Table 38.1, assuming as before that all the figures are in thousands of dollars.
2 Given an appropriate rate of discount, we could, of course, calculate the DPV of any future net revenue and produce a strategy that would yield a highest weighted average *discounted* net revenue.

40 Four additional strategems for coping with uncertainty

1   If decision rules, as a useful method for dealing with future uncertainty, is something of a forlorn hope, the certainty equivalence perhaps too crude, and the more sophisticated conditional probability approach (of the earlier chapter on Mixed strategies) rather cumbersome, there yet remain a number of proposals that may be employed. In this penultimate chapter, we outline four of these proposals:

  (i) tampering with the discount rate of interest
 (ii) the setting of upper and lower limits to the calculated annual net benefit figures
(iii) the construction of a normal distribution of possible net benefit figures when allowance is made for future price movements
(iv) recourse to yields on commercial investment.

2   The commonly used device (i) consists simply of adding one or two percentage points to the Pareto-determined rate of interest – that used in conditions of certainty and discussed at length in Part V – which, for brevity, we can refer to as the pure rate of discount (or compounding). Bearing in mind the possibility of future losses, it may be thought advisable to add, say, two percentage points to the pure rate of 6 per cent, so that 8 per cent would be used in calculating the net benefit figure of the project before presenting the result to the political decision makers.

There are, of course, some obvious objections to this common device. First, the choice of percentage points to be added to the pure rate is quite arbitrary. Second, the proportional reduction in the initial annual net benefit figures (those calculated with the pure rate) not only increases with the number of years, but does so at an exponential rate, so adding to the arbitrariness of the procedure.

Moreover, the device implicitly assumes that, although the magnitude of the future net benefits is uncertain, they must certainly decline, a built-in pessimism about the movement of prices or valuation over the future that is generally unwarranted.

3   When device (ii) is used, it is implicitly acknowledged that it is no less possible for the annual net benefits to rise over the future as to fall. Thus, if we restricted ourselves to tampering with the discount rate, we should present to the policy makers both a pessimistic net benefit figure for the project from adding some percentage points to the pure rate and also an optimistic net benefit figure from subtracting some percentage points. Although more even-handed, such a proposal

would still be subject to the objection that the successive resulting magnitudes of the annual net benefit figures increase or decrease at an exponential rate.

It may, therefore, be better to eschew any tampering with the discount rate and, instead, attempt to make allowance for the future uncertainty by setting an upper and lower limit to the net benefit figure for each successive year, such limits becoming wider as we move further from the present. For example, in a first period comprising, say, two or three years, the upper and lower limits could be set, respectively, at 1.5 per cent above and 1.5 per cent below the initial net benefit figure for those years (as calculated with the pure rate of interest). For the second such period, the respective limits could be widened to 2.5 percentage points: the third period to 4 percentage points, and so on.

Although this ruse would obviate the exponential feature entailed in a resort to tampering with the discount rate, the determination of an upper and lower limit to the successive annual net benefit figures is unavoidably arbitrary. Yet it is, on balance, preferable to tampering with the discount rate; not only does it avoid the unwarranted exponential feature, economists with some experience in the application of cost-benefit methods will have some judgement about the extent of upper and lower limits for future annual net benefits.

4   Allowing that we cannot be sure whether future net benefits will rise or fall below those initially calculated, we may resort to (iii), constructing something like a normal distribution of possible net benefit figures for the investment project (whether DPV or CTV), each net benefit figure depending on forecasts of the more relevant input and output prices. One begins with the estimates, or rather 'guesstimates', by one or several experts (if they can be found) of the movement in the prices of these relevant materials over future years. And it is from an average of these informed guesstimates of price movements over the future that the required probability distribution of possible net benefit figures for the project is to be constructed.

The method can be illustrated by supposing, say, four chief inputs, K_1, K_2, K_3 and K_4 – or K_i inputs (where i = 1, 2, 3, 4) – the 'guesstimated' prices for each successive period t, where t = 1, 2, ..., 10, to be set respectively at p^t_1, p^t_2, p^t_3 and p^t_4 for each of the four inputs, and allowing a 20-year project to be divided into ten periods of two years each.

Each of our experts is required to offer three alternative prices for each of the inputs in any one period: a most likely figure along with its likelihood of occurring (in percentage terms); and both an upper-limit figure and a lower-limit figure, along with their respective likelihoods. So as not to encumber the exposition we shall suppose that the annual benefits produced by the project are wholly in kind and are enjoyed by a fixed population, as a result of which it may be further assumed that the real value of each of the annual *benefits* remains unchanged over the time span of the project.

For our first two-year period, that is for t = 1, our experts are to choose three alternative prices for input K_1, say coke; that is, three alternative prices for p_1 along with their respective probabilities.[1] We then use the average of each of these three prices, along with an average of their corresponding probabilities. We treat the remaining three inputs in the same way for this first period so that, for this one period, there are altogether 12 possible future prices to consider. These 12 possible future prices must then be guesstimated for each of the subsequent nine periods.

5 We now illustrate the procedure, beginning with the three guesstimated p_1^1 prices of the first input, coke, in the *first period*. Let us suppose that the actual price of coke in the immediate present (p_1^0 at time zero) is \$20, the most likely price in the first period *averaging* \$22 with probability 60 per cent, the upper-limit price averaging \$25 with probability 30 per cent, and the lower limit price averaging \$18 with a 10 per cent probability.

Given this most likely price of p_1^1 is \$22, which is \$2 more than the actual p_1^0 price of \$20, and the probability attributed to its occurring is 60 per cent, its *weighted* P_1^1 price is calculated as equal to p_1^0 plus 60 per cent of \$2, or \$21.20. Or, put formally, $P_1^1 = p_1^0 + \Delta p_1^0 \, (pr.)$, where Δp_1^0 is the difference above the original price of coke of \$20 at time zero, and *pr.* is the probability of its occurrence.

The weighted *upper-limit* price P_1^1 is, in this formula, equal to \$20 + \$5(0.3), or \$21.50, and the weighted *lower-limit* price p_1^1 equal to \$20 − \$2(0.1), or \$19.80. The three weighted prices for the K_2 input in this first period are calculated in the same way, as are also the three weighted prices for the remaining two inputs, K_3 and K_4.

Again, if in the *second period*, the most likely price of the K_1 input, coke, comes to \$24 with a 50 per cent probability, the weighted most likely price of P_1^2 is equal to \$20 + \$4(0.5) or \$22. Similarly, a \$27 *upper* limit for p_1^2 with a 30 per cent probability, and a p_1^2 *lower* limit of \$17 with a 10 per cent probability, will result in a P_1^2 of \$22.10 and a P_1^2 of \$19.70, respectively. The most likely weighted prices for each of the other inputs, K_2, K_3 and K_4, are calculated in the same way.

Performing the same operation for the three alternative weighted guesstimate prices of each of the four inputs for the remaining eight periods, we end up with a total of, say, *m*, permutations of 40 such prices for each of the ten periods. In consequence, we can calculate *m* distinct net benefit figures for the project in question (although all of these *m* net benefit figures need not be different).

It transpires, however, that the number *m* in our simple example, is very large indeed.

If, for ease of exposition, we refer to these weighted guesstimated future input prices simply as future prices, this total number of permutations *m* can be calculated as follows: for the first period, any one of the three future prices of input K_1 can be combined with any one of the three future prices of input K_2, which two chosen prices can then be combined with one of the three future prices of input K_3, which resulting three prices can then be combined with any one of the three future prices of input K_4. Hence the number of permutations of the four chosen input prices in the first period come to 3^4, or 89, permutations of a set of four input prices.

Each one of these 89 permutations of four prices in the first period, however, can be combined with any one of the 89 permutations of four input prices in the second period. For these first two periods, then, the total number of permutations of a set of eight input prices amount to 89^2. Continuing in this way for each successive period, the total number of permutations of the resulting set of 40 input prices amounts to 89^{10}. The number *m*, therefore, runs into trillions.[2]

6 Not much imagination is required to enable us to realize that we need not spend the best years of our lives in attempting to calculate the net benefit figures

for each of these m permutations. A relatively small sample of two or three hundred of such permutations chosen at random should suffice for producing a normal distribution of net benefit figures that is not very different from the normal distribution of the m net benefit figures.

Such a sample, it should be evident, is generated as follows: one chooses at random – or set the computer to choose at random – only one of the three alternative future prices of input K_1 in the first period and only one of the three alternative future prices of each of the remaining three inputs, K_2, K_3, K_4, in that period. We continue doing the same for each of the nine remaining periods, so choosing at random a set of 40 different prices in all. From each of the set of 40 input prices, a particular net benefit figure is calculated.

When this operation is repeated two or three hundred times, the resulting two or three hundred calculated net benefit figures, when ranked according to magnitude, should reveal a normal distribution with many of the same characteristics as those in the distribution of the whole population of m net benefit figures. Should there be any doubt about this, one continues drawing random samples. If after, say, another hundred or so such samples are taken, no significant change in the distribution can be observed, we may conclude that the sample distribution is satisfactory.

7   It cannot be gainsaid that this ingenious stratagem for dealing with future uncertainty has an appeal to the theoretical mind. The problem, however, is that of securing plausible guesstimates of the price movement of the relevant materials over a longish time span. Quite apart from having to make allowance for inflation over future years, the prices of some materials that may be used as inputs for the project might well be quite volatile over time. Yet, even for the less volatile input prices, forecasts of their future movements are not likely to be held with any confidence beyond a decade or so.

It must be concluded that this stratagem for dealing with future uncertainty can be useful only under limited circumstances: where, for instance, the time span of the project is relatively short and where, in addition, it is reasonable to expect little variation in the relevant input and output prices over the allocated time span of the project. Moreover, even if the resultant range of cost-benefit figures is held with a fair degree of confidence, it would be acceptable, or more acceptable, only if the demand for each of the *goods* produced by the project was unlikely to deviate much from its anticipated growth path.

8   In Western economies with a large private investment sector and a well-organized capital market, the economist may plausibly adopt the return on private investment (stratagem iv) as the appropriate opportunity yield for the returns on investments in the public sector.

Assuming that the risk run by each type of private investment can be arranged as a probability distribution, some average of the range of expected or actuarial rates of return on private investments may be adopted as the opportunity yield in evaluating each of the anticipated annual returns of a public project at some common point of time, either present or future.

9   It has been argued, however, that, where the funds for investing in a public project are raised wholly from tax revenues, this yield in the private investment sector may be replaced as the appropriate opportunity yield for public investment purposes only if

the (subjective) cost of risk-bearing is the same for the taxpayer as it is for the individual private investor. The argument[3] is that, if the benefits and costs are to be measured, as they should be in terms of compensation variations – willingness to pay a maximum sum for benefits received, willingness to accept a minimal sum for losses incurred – the (subjective) costs of risk-bearing must be subtracted from the net benefits of the investment project in order to obtain a correct measure of its value to the recipient. According to this analysis, where the number of taxpayers is large, the risk borne by each one in respect of any particular public investment project becomes negligible. In contrast, the risk-bearing costs of a similar project to a limited number of private investors can be appreciable. Hence, it is concluded, it is not so much the government's pooling of investment risks from its undertaking of a large number of investment projects that justifies the ignoring of the risks – or not only such investment pooling – but rather the fact of spreading the risk of any single investment over a very large number of taxpayers.[4] As a corollary, it follows that a public investment with an expected rate of return below that of a private investment may yet be economically superior, for what is relevant in the comparison is not the expected rates of return *per se* but the expected rates of return net of the (subjective) costs of risk-bearing.[5]

10   Obviously, the riskier the type of private investment, the higher the expected rate of return – a consequence both of risk-aversion and the tax disadvantages of investing in projects that yield highly variable returns.[6] But whatever the reasons for the higher gross rates of return expected on riskier private investments, the conclusion remains unaffected. If the placing of public funds in the riskier type of private investment can, in fact, realise higher gross returns over time, then – in the absence of the Arrow–Lind conditions – no public investment ought to be undertaken that is expected to yield gross returns that are any lower.

To illustrate, if the A-type of private investment has an expected yield of 10 per cent before tax and the B-type of investment, which is riskier, has an expected yield of 14 per cent before tax, then, for society as a whole, continued investment only in the A-type investment produces a return of 10 per cent, whereas continued investment only in the B-type investment produces a return of 14 per cent.[7] If a succession of specific public projects is expected to yield, say, 12 per cent, then, in undertaking them, the agency is indeed foregoing the opportunity of earning an additional 2 per cent by investing instead in the B-type investment

Of course, one might do better yet if more information could be secured at low cost. If it were possible to know in advance the actual return to be realized on each particular B-type investment that the government could undertake as an alternative to a given public project, then such actual private yields – which would vary over time from one B-type of investment to another – could properly be used as the appropriate opportunity yield rather than the overall actuarial rate of return on all risky B-type investments. Such information, alas, is just not available at low cost: if it were, there would be no problem of uncertainty. The information we can more reasonably hope for is an average rate of return for the B-type investment when a fair number of such investments have been undertaken. And, under given conditions, we might reasonably anticipate that this average rate, say 14 per cent, will continue over the near future. Only if this 14 per cent can reasonably be expected to continue up to the terminal year of the public project in question, however, can it be regarded as the appropriate opportunity yield in any public investment criterion? If the return on this B-type investment is expected to rise or fall over that period, modifications have to be made accordingly.

11   Care must be taken in the use of this highest actuarial rate of return, say, ρ, that is to be adopted as the basis of the social opportunity yield in public investment criteria. Only where the political constraint is such that the public agency has the option of wholly reinvesting at ρ all the returns of any project, is ρ to be used as the appropriate reinvestment rate (in the absence of superior public reinvestment opportunities). The reader will recall from our treatment of investment criteria in Part V that, in some cases, the public agency is constrained to distribute the benefits in cash or kind direct to the public, i.e. it is not permitted wholly to reinvest these returns in the private investment sector. Since, in these other cases, the usual behaviour assumption that is adopted has it that the public saves only a fraction of the cash return paid out to the recipients, which fraction saved may be supposed to be added to investment in the private sector.

12   We must remind ourselves, however, that we have assumed that a Western country has a large private investment sector. The larger this sector, the more appropriate it is to use the highest actuarial rate of return that may confidently be expected from private investments as the opportunity yield for public investment projects, at least in the absence of political constraints bearing on the alternative uses of public funds.

In countries where the private investment sector is not large, the employment of some average of yields on private investments (as the opportunity yield for public investment projects) is not appropriate, and we must seek further information to enable us to make plausible assessments of expected rates of return on alternative uses of the funds available for public projects. If such an assessment is not possible, we may have to fall back on using the community's rate of time preference as the opportunity yield in evaluating public investments. But if we do take this step, we must concede that we have lost sight of the uncertainty problem.

13   Thus, although this last of the four stratagems – the employment of some average of the actuarial yields on private investment as the opportunity yield on public investments – is the simplest way of coping with future uncertainty, it can hardly be recommended as an effective stratagem.

An average of the actuarial rates of return on a chosen set of private investments may make allowance for the future variability of this chosen average *only* if the range of the future variability is not much different from the past. But, of course, there can be no presumption that this will tend to be the case. The private investor knows this or, if he does not, he ought to. And in tacitly accepting this unavoidable future uncertainty, he is, in effect, a gambler.

In contrast, the economist entrusted with advising the political decision makers by producing net-benefit estimates of particular public investments cannot be so cavalier in this respect. He is obliged to deal explicitly with the unavoidable uncertainty of the relevant variables over the future. He must select some stratagem that places limits on the possible movement of the range of annual net-benefit estimates over the future. And, wherever possible, he must also consider the costs of using any method that might possibly reduce the incidence of uncertainty over the future.

Notes

1 We could, of course, distinguish these three alternative prices by adding to p_1^1 a suffix, say M, L and U, to indicate the *most* likely price, and the *lower* and *upper* prices, respectively, of the input coke in this first, second and subsequent periods. But we have avoided cluttering up the notation unnecessarily.

2 Even if there were only two input prices to consider in each period, and only two guesstimates for each input price, the total number of permutations of the resulting 20-price set would come to over one million.

3 Assuming that increased investment in the public sector entails reduced expenditure in the private sector, the above argument is valid wherever funds are raised by tax revenues (not by selling government securities), and wherever the public agency is restricted in the use of its investable funds to specified projects.

4 If the assumptions of rationality and full information are relaxed, we can justify neglecting the risk-costs of public investment in so far as the taxpayer experiences no anxiety about possible losses simply because he overlooks any connection between a loss incurred by a public investment and a possible increase in his tax payments.

5 An amendment to the Arrow–Lind thesis was made by Fisher (1973). He points out that, in so far as the risks involved are external diseconomies, or 'public bads', the damage experienced by each person does not diminish with the increase in the number of people who, also, will be the beneficiaries of the public investment.

6 The individual investor in risky projects may, however, be able to overcome the tax disadvantages to some extent by spreading his investment over a number of such projects.

7 Ignoring the tendency for the return to decline as more B-type investment is undertaken.

Part VII

Topics frequently encountered in cost-benefit analysis

41 Valuation issues and methods

1   All decisions involve certain trade-offs. Policies are no exception. Where the trade-offs can be easily and accurately measured, it is easy to decide on courses of action that maximize welfare. However, there are instances where the trade-off involves items for which there are no existing values to refer to. Consider the following cases:

1   The Copenhagen summit was widely perceived to be unconstructive as not many countries readily embraced the emissions targets. Among others, a common argument against steep emissions reduction was that it would hamper growth and the alleviation of poverty.
2   The Singapore government launched a bid to hold the inaugural Youth Olympic Games (YOG) in 2010. One of the cases made in favour of submitting the bid in 2008, despite the costs involved, was that it would increase national pride.
3   Residents of Penang, Malaysia commonly lament the loss of heritage sites as the state develops, and urban infrastructure replaces old buildings.

The three cases highlighted are similar, in that the trade-offs involve non-market goods (environmental conservation, national pride and heritage). This poses a problem, because the lack of defined markets means that we cannot use the pricing mechanism to ascertain the value of these goods in conducting CBA.

While the idea of monetizing the environment and feelings such as national pride may be offensive to some, one should consider the relative merits of such practice against the alternatives.

2   First, not specifically taking the loss of these goods into account is equivalent to assigning a value of zero to them. This is very likely to cause over-consumption of such goods that diminish their value – a phenomenon observed countless times throughout humanity's history.

Second, practices that take into account the impact on such non-market goods without placing a specific value on them may be socially inefficient. To illustrate, one may employ the political system of one-person-one-vote referendums to collectively decide whether to undertake projects that damage the environment. However, a major drawback of this method is that it does not take into account the intensity of preferences. Under such a system, it is possible that certain projects that the majority have a marginal preference for and the minority have strong preferences against would be carried out, although they have deleterious effects on social welfare.

Having delineated the rationale for putting money values on non-market goods, the three most common economic valuation techniques are discussed.

Economic valuation techniques

3   In the CBA literature, valuation techniques typically revolve around deriving a demand curve for the good in question in order to compute its value. The three most commonly used techniques are the contingent valuation method (CVM), hedonic pricing and the travel cost method.

Contingent valuation method

4   The CVM is, by far, the most direct and intuitive method to derive values for nonmarket goods. Essentially, it involves eliciting the maximum amount that people are willing to pay for welfare improvements and the minimum that they are willing to accept as compensation for welfare loss, to derive a demand curve for the good in question.

To do so, one designs a survey that measures people's responses to a hypothetical change in an attribute or amenity in terms of the maximum they would be willing to pay to enjoy a benefit, or the minimum they would be willing to accept to forgo it. The amount that they are willing to pay or accept would logically be the monetary sum that leaves them at the same level of welfare as before (see Chapter 7). The process may involve simply asking respondents to state a single value or more sophisticated methods like bidding, where respondents are asked whether they would be willing to pay (or accept) successively lower (or higher) amounts to derive the maximum (or minimum) willingness-to-pay (or acceptance). The willingness to pay (WTP) or willingness to accept (WTA) of the survey sample (whichever the case may be) is then extrapolated for the whole population and adjusted where necessary. The values are totaled to provide an estimate of the area under the demand curve for the hypothetical change in that variable, which may be interpreted as the value of the good.

We illustrate one CVM approach with a hypothetical example. Suppose we wanted to measure the value of an increase in green cover for a particular city in conducting a CBA for a citywide greening project. For simplicity's sake, let us assume that pretests have revealed that survey participants can effectively separate the benefits of increased green cover from other environmental goods. Instead of eliciting WTP values, we may ask participants whether they would approve the project if it cost $5, $10, $20, $50 or $100 respectively. Each value is presented to only 20 per cent of the participants. Let us imagine the survey reveals the approval rates in Table 41.1.

If the population of the city is one million, the estimated aggregate number of approvals for each cost will be as shown in Table 41.2 and can be plotted as a demand curve as illustrated in Figure 41.1.

The area under the demand curve is the total WTP for the project, which may be interpreted as the value for increased green cover. In this case, it can be approximated by taking the sum of the area of the four trapezoids, which would yield the value of $34,750,000.

Table 41.1 Approval rates for hypothetical greening project

Project cost $	Approval rate %
5	95
10	85
20	65
50	30
100	5

Table 41.2 Aggregate approvals for hypothetical greening project

Cost $	Aggregate approvals Approval % × 1,000,000
5	950,000
10	850,000
20	650,000
50	300,000
100	50,000

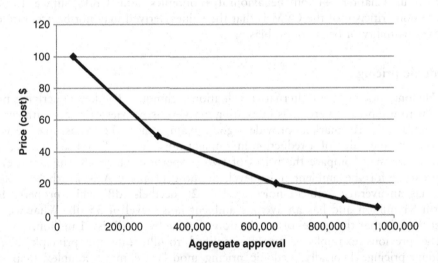

Figure 41.1 Demand curve for hypothetical greening project

An important caveat has to be made here. That is, for most non-market goods, especially environmental goods, apart from the usual use demand, option demand, as first put forward by Weisbrod (1964), and existence demand are likely to be significant and ought to be accounted for in the CVM. The two concepts are similar but not equal. Option demand is the willingness of consumers to pay to keep a good available for future use while existence demand is the willingness-to-pay to keep a good in existence even if one never has any intention to use it. The applicability to environmental goods is obvious; most people would be willing to pay to preserve a natural area so that they can visit it in the future and a great number would do so simply for the sake of knowing that they have done some good. Hence, in conducting CVM, option and existence values should be measured.

While the CVM is highly intuitive and straightforward, it has two key weaknesses. The first is the susceptibility to survey bias; the other is the susceptibility to behavioural bias.

Most survey bias may be corrected by proper survey design. However, strategic bias is one major source of bias that may not be easily dealt with. This is the case when survey respondents over- or understate their WTP or WTA for strategic reasons. This is illustrated clearly by the following scenario. Imagine a surveyor asks a participant to state his/her WTP for a natural park's usage to ascertain the park's value. If the participant thinks that his/her WTP amount will be used to formulate charges for using the park, he/she will have an incentive to understate his/her true WTP. Similarly, if a participant thinks that his/her WTA amount will be used to formulate compensation, he/she will have an incentive to overstate the amount. To minimize strategic bias, great care has to be taken in the survey design to avoid giving participants the impression that charging and compensation are in any way related to the survey.

Apart from survey bias, CVM, being reliant on surveys, are also susceptible to behavioural biases. The exact behavioural effects on valuation will be expanded further in Chapter 44 on behavioural economics and CBA. Suffice to say, a common criticism of the CVM is that the values derived may not be accurate due to the possibility of behavioural bias.

Hedonic pricing

5   Hedonic pricing is an alternative valuation technique. The key underlying principle is to use price differentials in existing markets as proxies of prices with certain attributes. Property markets provide a good example here. Let us assume we want to compute the value of a reduction in ambient noise levels. To do so with hedonic pricing, we may compare the prices of two properties, which are similar in every way except for the ambient noise level. Suppose property A is worth $2 million and has an average ambient noise level of 20 decibels (dB) while property B is worth $1 million and has an average ambient noise level of 35 dB. What we can infer then, is that the 'price' of a reduction of noise by 15 dB is $1 million.

The previous example is overly simplified to illustrate the principle behind hedonic pricing. Typically, hedonic pricing models are more complex than that even though the reasoning that underpins the method is the same. In actual hedonic pricing models, it is common to apply multiple regression techniques to find out the marginal effect of a particular attribute on price. This can then be used to find out the value of that attribute. We illustrate this with a simple example. Suppose data on property prices reveals that prices were well-estimated by the following function:

$$p = \sum_{i=1}^{n} b_i x_i$$

where p represents the price of the property, x_i represents the attributes (e.g. x_1 is the distance from a train station, x_2 is the noise level, etc), b_i measures the effect of the attribute on house prices and n is the total number of attributes.

Let us imagine that in the above specification x_2 is the ambient noise level as measured in decibels and its corresponding coefficient b_2 is equal to -10. In such a scenario, the value of a reduction in ambient noise level by 10 dB would be $100.

The key criticism of hedonic pricing is that it requires the strict assumption of perfect markets to yield accurate estimates. If people wish to move but cannot due to some reason or another, the market for property will be imperfect and property price differentials will not reflect the true 'price' of various attributes. In addition, other factors may distort market prices such as imperfectly competitive market structures and government intervention in the form of taxes and subsidies.

To overcome these problems, an alternative method of examining the prices of goods that yield the desired outcomes known as the Defensive Expenditure approach has been proposed (European Commission, 2000). For example, to find out the value of noise reduction, one can simply look at the cost of soundproofing one's home. If the cost of soundproofing one's home is $1,000 then we may infer that the value of noise reduction is $1,000. However, this method is not without its flaws either. The main problem with this method is the difficulty in separating the multiple uses of certain goods. For example, thicker windowpanes contribute to lowering a home's noise penetration as well as providing increased thermal insulation. The price of thicker windowpanes thus reflects the value of noise reduction as well as increased warmth. Hence, using the price of thicker windowpanes, as an estimate of the value of noise reduction, results in an overestimation of its value. Such limitations should be kept in mind when hedonic price models are employed.

Travel cost method

6 The travel cost method is a more recent development in valuation techniques. It is also known as the Hotelling–Clawson–Knetsch technique and is most often applied to estimate the value of recreational sites such as marine parks, mountain resorts and wilderness areas in North America. The main idea is to derive a demand curve by using the cost of travel as a proxy for price. First, a sample of the user-population is stratified according to the distance from the target site. The stratification involves separating the surrounding areas into concentric zones with the target site in the centre. For each zone, an average zonal participation rate is then computed. The average zonal participation rate is then plotted against the travel cost. This graph will allow us to estimate the change in total visitation for any change in the travel cost by estimating the change in the average zonal participation and multiplying it by the zonal population before totalling. The demand curve is then derived by postulating that people will respond to a dollar increase in the price in the same way that they would respond to a dollar increase in travel costs.

As this method is more complex, we will illustrate its workings via the use of a numerical example. Imagine we wanted to estimate the annual value of a hypothetical park. The user populations come from cities A, B and C with certain characteristics where all flow variables are measured on a per annum basis (see Table 41.3).

Using the data on the number of trips per million and the travel cost for the three cities, we may then use linear extrapolation (or any other form) to estimate the relation between trips and cost. The relation is plotted in Figure 41.2.

We hypothesise that if entrance fees were introduced, each dollar increase in entrance fees would have the same effect as a dollar increase in travel costs. Hence, from Figure 41.2, we can estimate the number of trips made per thousand of population for each city if there were an entrance fee of $0, $5, $10, $15 and $20. Figure 41.3 shows the process for a $5 entrance fee. A, B and C mark out the estimated trips per thousand population for each town when a $5 entrance fee is imposed. Table 41.4 shows the estimated trips per thousand of population for all three cities when differing entrance fees are imposed.

The trips per thousand of population can then be multiplied by the respective populations of each city and summed up to get the total visits (trips) for each entrance fee (price). The process is illustrated by Table 41.5.

Finally, a demand curve can be estimated by plotting the price against the total number of trips, as exhibited in Figure 41.4.

As with CVM, the value of the park may be estimated as the area under the demand curve. For this particular example, the value of the park is approximately $73,000 per annum.

Table 41.3 Hypothetical data on park use, population and travel costs of three cities

City	Trips (annual)	Population	Trips per 1,000 population	Miles (round trip)	Travel cost (total $)
A	1,600	2,000	800	50	5.00
B	6,000	10,000	600	100	10.00
C	2,400	6,000	400	150	15.00

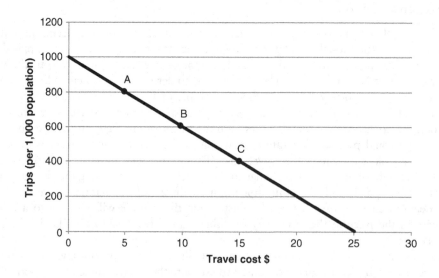

Figure 41.2 Relationship between trips per thousand of population and travel cost

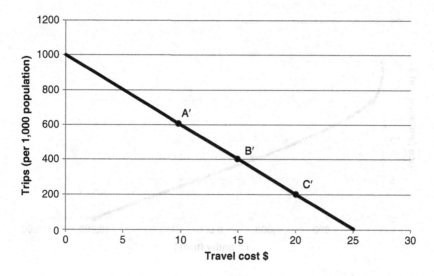

Figure 41.3 Estimated trips per thousand of population with a $5 entrance fee

Table 41.4 Estimated trips per thousand of population for various entrance fees

Price (entrance fee) $	Trips per thousand of population		
	A	B	C
0	800	600	400
5	600	400	200
10	400	200	0
15	200	0	0
20	0	0	

As with other valuation methods, the travel cost method is not ideal. First, the method implicitly ignores option demand (people's WTP to maintain the site even though they currently do not use it) as the final demand is derived from an inter-polation of actual trips made which only reflects use demand. Second, as people spend both time and money in visiting recreational sites, the travel cost method, which only takes into account monetary expenditure, tends to understate the true value. Third, the value derived is only accurate to the degree by which visitors' travels are directed to the particular site only. However, when people go sightsee-ing, they tend to visit a few places in one trip and it is difficult to separate the value of each site from the rest. Fourth, visitors need to be spread out geographic-ally at sufficient distance in order to have travel costs that vary adequately. This restricts the application of the method. Finally, the travel cost method makes the

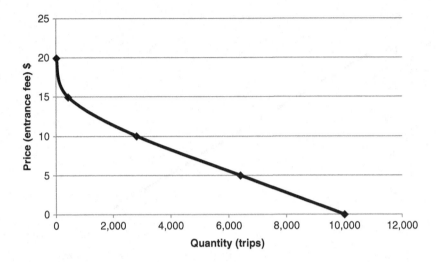

Figure 41.4 Demand curve for hypothetical park

Table 41.5 Total visits made for various entrance fees

Price (entrance fee) $	Total visits Trips per 1,000 of population × 1,000 of population			
	A	*B*	*C*	*Total*
0	1,600	6,000	2,400	10,000
5	1,200	4,000	1,200	6,400
10	800	2,000	0	2,800
15	400	0	0	400
20	0	0	0	0

implausible assumption that whole populations, from which the visitors are drawn, have similar preferences.

Having explained how each technique is conducted and the weaknesses of each method, we now present examples of actual valuation studies that have made use of the methods mentioned. The valuation method, author/s, year, valuation item and the estimated value of the item in the studies are all presented in Table 41.6.

Non-economic valuation techniques

7   The valuation techniques and examples discussed thus far (CVM, hedonic pricing and the travel cost method) are all economic valuation techniques because they involve estimations of demand curves. However, there are times when policy makers rely on non-economic methods for efficiency reasons. These techniques include the dose–response function, where a relationship between a stressor and a receptor is identified to determine both safe and hazardous levels for the stressor, the defensive

Table 41.6 Examples of valuation studies using differing valuation techniques

Valuation method	Author (year)	Valuation item	Estimated item value
Contingent valuation method (CVM)	Quah and Tan (1999b)	Scenic view of East Coast Park (Singapore)	Present value of Singapore dollars S$2.1–7.2 billion
	Amirnejah et al. (2006)	Existence value of North Forests (Iran)	US$30.12 per household per annum
	Aabø (2005)	Public libraries (Norway)	400–2,000 Kr per household per annum
	Hammitt and Zhou (2006)	Air-pollution-related health risk (China)	Prevention of a cold episode: US$3–6 per episode Prevention of chronic bronchitis: US$500–1,000 per case
	Yu and Abler (2010)	Air pollution in Beijing (China)	120.15 to 128.60 Yuan for blue skies
	Xie and Zhao (2018)	Green electricity in Tianjin (China)	32.63 Yuan per month per household
Hedonic pricing	Dewenter et al. (2007)	Mobile phone brand name Premiums (Germany)	Brand premium in the range $57–172
	Day et al. (2007)	Noise avoidance in Birmingham (UK)	Road noise reduction (ldB)[1]: £31.49–201.16 per annum (1997 value) Rail noise reduction (1 dB)[1]: £83.61–1,488.88 per annum (1997 value)
	Kong et al. (2007)	Percentage of urban green landscape within 0.3 km radius in Jinan City (China)	63.55 yuan per percentage point increase
	Jiao and Liu (2010)	Recreational spaces of the Changjiang River and the East Lake in Wuhan, and city-level parks (China)	Up to 4109.2 Yuan/m^2
	Gibbs et al. (2017)	Airbnb price listings based on physical and host characteristics, and location (Canada)	Varying for different characteristics and locations
Travel cost method	Shrestha et al. (2007)	Nature-based recreation in public natural areas of Apalachicola River, Florida (US)	US$74.18 per visit day US$484.56 million per annum
	Fleming and Cook (2008)	Lake McKenzie (Australia)	AU $ 13.7–31.8 million per annum AU$104.30–242.84 per person per visit
	Gürlük and Rehber (2008)	Recreational value for bird-watching at Lake Manyas (Turkey)	US$103.23 million per annum
	Jeuland et al. (2010)	Private benefits of 'free' cholera vaccine in Beira (Mozambique)	US$0.85 per complete treatment (of two doses)
	Mayer and Woltering (2018)	Recreational ecosystem services of national parks (Germany)	€385.3 million to €2.751 billion

1 Value depends on original noise level

expenditure approach, which takes the value of an item as the amount people are observed to spend in order to protect themselves from a decline in the availability of the good, and the replacement cost method where the value of an item is estimated as the cost of replacing it. As these are closer to heuristic rules-of-thumb that have little economic basis than proper estimation procedures, we shall not elaborate further on each method. In general, the CBA practitioner is advised to use economic methods to yield more accurate and reliable estimates to aid optimal decision making.

Conclusion

8   In conclusion, we summarize the various valuation techniques with Figure 41.5.

The continual development and refinement of valuation techniques provide little excuse for the practitioner not to explicitly take into account monetary values of externalities and non-market goods. The development of the paired-comparison approach (see Chapter 43) is a good example. However, in utilizing any valuation technique, the practitioner should bear in mind the possible limitations and constraints. The choice of valuation method ought not to be arbitrary. For any item, the optimal valuation tool depends on the context of the CBA. Should the markets within the CBA frame prove to be close to perfect, hedonic pricing may produce the most accurate estimations. Otherwise, CVM or the travel cost method may be preferable.

Further, where time and cost impose impossible constraints, the practitioner may turn to the use of non-economic valuation techniques. That said, it is recommended that a superior alternative known as the benefit transfer method is applied instead. As benefit transfer is the subject of the next chapter, we shall not elaborate here.

Lastly, in the unlikely scenario where all valuation techniques fail to work, the practitioner always has the option of falling back on the familiar recourse of presenting the item separately from the rest of the CBA and letting the policy maker decide whether the trade-off is worth it. This approach is, however, greatly discouraged and should be avoided as far as possible.

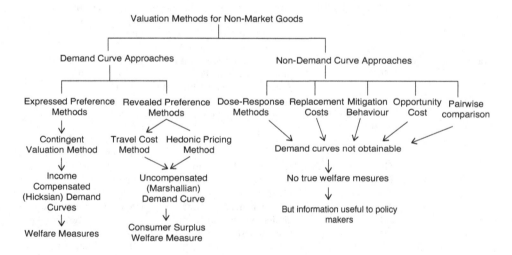

Figure 41.5 Valuation methods for non-market goods

42 Benefit transfers[1]

1   In eliciting monetary values for benefits and costs, benefit transfers is a useful valuation approach that involves the adaptation and generalization of information from existing research to different settings.

Existing primary research and studies are referred to as study cases/sites, while the setting in which the information is adapted is referred to as the policy case/site. The policy site could be different from the study sites in terms of economic, biophysical, temporal and/or spatial situation.

2   Benefit transfer could be the choice of method because it has been deemed that primary valuation is not warranted, primary valuation is too costly to conduct, there is a lack of expertise to conduct primary data collection, and/or there is immediate urgency to make a policy decision.

To conduct a benefit transfer, a thorough literature review of relevant studies is crucial. Only with a sufficient number of studies would the adaptation of information be able to give precise and robust estimates. Since benefit transfer essentially draws from other valuation studies, it faces the same potential problem of measurement errors. On top of that, benefit transfers is also subjected to transfer errors (errors when generalizing across different contexts), especially when adapting information to a setting which is notably different.

3   Benefit transfers can be broadly categorized into two types: value transfer and function transfer (Rosenberger and Loomis, 2003) (see Figure 42.1).

Value transfer involves a direct application of summary statistics from study cases to the policy case, making adjustments when necessary. The summary statistic could be Willingness-To-Pay or Willingness-To-Accept measures, or even demand elasticities. Adjustments to be made include the difference in impact between study and policy cases, the different affected population, currencies, inflation, and so on.

Function transfer involves the application of a statistical function instead of directly using the summary statistic. Compared to the former, function transfer requires more extensive adjustments to be made through statistical functions to reflect the characteristics of the policy case, but yields more precise and robust estimates as the differences in site characteristics are better accounted for.

4   Value transfer can be further separated into three types: transfer of point estimates, transfer of measures of central tendency, or transfer of administratively-approved estimates.

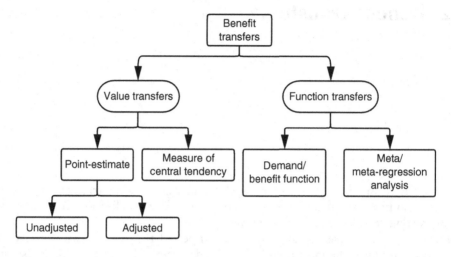

Figure 42.1 A classification of benefit transfer methods.

A transfer of point estimates typically uses a range of point values from various existing study cases. The shortcoming of this method is that the study sites and policy site should ideally be similar in terms of characteristics, including the geographical location, the baseline state, the degree of change, the composition of the population, as well as other market, institutional and cultural characteristics. It is, however, common that these assumptions are often not satisfied. In such instances, the value to be transferred will have to be adjusted. Among other factors, such adjustments can take the form of adjusting the value for income, the stock of the good available in the region, differences in project impacts and differences in time. Apart from scaling to adjust for the factors mentioned, expert judgement may also be employed for the adjustment, as was the fashion in the 1970s and 1980s. Alternatively, the practitioner may choose to only transfer values of subsamples of the original study that have similar characteristics to the policy site. Such transference, however, is subject to the availability of data from the original study. The current preferred method is to systemically adjust the values for differences in site characteristics or survey method differences by looking at how both factors affect the estimated values (i.e. the role of the factors in the value's function). This transfer method, however, falls under the classification of function transfers, which will be explained in later paragraphs.

For adjusted point-estimate value transfers, the steps involved are to search through the existing valuation studies, identify a completed valuation study for the item in question (preferably for a site similar to the policy site to reduce the amount of adjustment required), decide in what way the selected value needs adjusting, make the necessary adjustments and then use the result as the value of the item for the policy site.

Transfers of measures of central tendency use the mean or the medium of estimates in, or the confidence interval of, study cases. The choice of using a median over mean is especially so if study cases have outlier estimates which could skew the mean. To carry out a measure of central-tendency value transfer, the practitioner searches for all relevant valuation studies for the item in question, computes a measure of central- tendency of the values (i.e. mean, median, etc.) and uses the result as the value of the item for the policy site. Unlike point-estimate value transfers, transfers of measures of central-tendency do not lend themselves well to adjustments. The reason is relatively straightforward. Values of measures of central-tendency do not accrue to any particular study site and hence do not have comparable site characteristics to adjust for.

In addition, an alternative and simple approach is the transfer of administratively-approved estimates. However, these study cases' estimates have often, if not always, undergone the government's evaluation and approval, of which the process in which these estimates have been endorsed and published might not be entirely objective, and thus is not recommended.

Table 42.1 is a list of the steps to conduct a transfer of point estimates. The logic of conducting a transfer of measure of central tendency and a transfer of administratively-approved estimates is the same.

5   Function transfer can also be further classified into benefit function transfer and meta-analysis function transfer.

Benefit function transfer is straightforward. It applies the regression coefficients from an existing benefit function (from a single study case) to the summary statistic of the policy case. The explanatory variables are the characteristics which affect the value estimate in both the study and policy sites, and this is a judgement to be made by the researcher. Using the same regression coefficients also implicitly assumes that both populations react in the same way towards the value of the goods and services, which might not be empirically true.

For example, if regression analysis of an original study shows that the WTP is a linear function of income and male–female ratio with coefficients of 0.5 and 0.4 respectively (i.e. WTP = 0.5 (Income) + 0.4 (Male:Female)), then the WTP of the policy site can be estimated by plugging the income level and male–female ratio into the expression.

Table 42.1

Conducting a Point Estimate Transfer

Step 1	*The context of the policy site is to be defined. Information on site characteristics includes the type of goods and services, the presence of complements and substitutes, the location of the site, the affected users and non-users and their sociodemographic information, the magnitude and timing of the change in the goods and services brought about by the policy vis-a-vis the status quo.*
Step 2	*A thorough literature review is to be conducted, detailing the year of the studies, the valuation technique employed, the type of goods and services in question, the location in which the studies are conducted, the assumptions made, and the overall quality of the studies.*
Step 3	*From the literature review, select the relevant studies which correspond to the policy context as defined in Step 1. Note has to be taken in the point estimates, where they might not be in the desired units/denomination, and should be adjusted accordingly to account for inflation, income elasticities and currencies.*
Step 4	*To reach the final point estimate for the policy case, the values from the literature are to be aggregated across the goods and services, the affected user and non-users, and the project lifetime.*

To conduct a benefit function transfer, the practitioner must first search through the existing valuation studies to select a completed valuation study for the desired item (a study on a site similar to the policy site is preferred for higher accuracy). Here, we assume data on the affected populations at both sites is available. If not, in the selection of the original study, the practitioner must limit the choices to studies in which the affected population's profile is documented and also collect data on the profile of the policy site's affected population. The next step is to decide what the selected value needs to be adjusted for and regress the study site value on the study site parameters to obtain the value function. The final step is to plug the policy site parameters into the value function to compute the value of the item for the policy site.

The drawback of this method is that the practitioner still has to collect data on the policy site, albeit a different type compared to indigenous value elicitations. Where such data is readily available, benefit function transfers are efficient both in terms of cost and time. Where they are not, it might be better to employ some other transfer method or conduct an original study. Another failing of this method is its inability to account for differences in physical site characteristics and valuation methods. For example, open-ended value elicitation typically leads to lower valuations than dichotomous choices. However, such discrepancies cannot be adjusted for if benefit function transfer is used.

On the other hand, meta-regression analysis function transfers are similar to benefit function transfers in that a function is transferred. However, in demand function transfers, the function is transferred from only one original study, which necessarily restricts the independent variables to only site characteristics related to the respondents. In meta-regression analysis function transfers, the function is derived from more than one study, which allows for variations in the study site's physical characteristics, the value-elicitation approach and the survey methodology. This allows these cross-study differences to be included as independent variables.

To illustrate, dummy variables may be used to code for the type of item being valued (e.g. 'old forest'=1 versus 'young forest'=0), the value-elicitation method (e.g. 'stated preference'=1 versus 'revealed preference'=0), the survey method (e.g. 'by phone'=1 versus 'by mail'=0) and others. As in benefit function transfers, once the relationship between the value and the independent variables is established, the practitioner only has to plug in the values of the independent variable of the policy site to compute the desired valuation of the item.

The steps in a meta-regression analysis function transfer are largely similar to those of a benefit function transfer. First, the practitioner must search through the existing valuation studies and make a database of all relevant studies. Here, each study should be meticulously coded for differences in the valuation item, aspects of the methodology and other facets of the affected population's profile. Second, the practitioner establishes the relation between the value of the item and all of the previously mentioned parameters (or a selection based on the practitioner's judgement) by running a regression of the value on the independent variables. A value function is thus obtained. Finally, the practitioner plugs the policy site parameters into the value function to compute the value of the item for the policy site.

There is a clear advantage of not being restricted to one study site. The meta-analysis function transfer approach explicitly includes methodological explanatory variables, such as the method of valuation specific to each study, into the regression model, which allows for control of a large number of possible confounding variables. The number of studies to be included is, however, a trade-off between relevance and amount of information.

Table 42.2 identifies examples of valuation studies in which the various benefit transfer methods have been applied. For each case, the study details, transfer source, transfer method, as well as the original and estimated values of the item are presented.

Having explained the rationale behind benefit transfers and the different benefit transfer techniques, we will now answer the two questions that are most relevant to practitioners – what are the limitations of benefit transfer and, in general, which transfer technique performs best?

Limitations of benefit transfers

6   The literature on the criticisms and limitations of benefit transfer is rich. We can, however, summarize them along the lines of five fundamental limitations.

First, benefit transfer relies on extracting values from existing studies. Any inaccuracy in the original valuation is carried over during the transfer. Hence, the accuracy of the transferred value is necessarily constrained by the accuracy of the original study. Where the quality of the original study is poor, the results of the benefit transfer will be poor.

Related to the above, the second limitation of the benefit transfer method, stemming from its dependence on primary studies, is that the (lack of) availability of relevant studies constrains the potential use of this method. If no relevant primary study can be sourced, there can be no value to be transferred. This limitation is especially relevant for value transfers. For function transfers, however, in particular meta-regression analysis function transfers, even physical site characteristics and original valuation methodology may be adjusted for. Hence, in theory, we could pool *all* valuation studies into a database and the values of *any* item may be obtained via meta-regression significantly increase the potential pool of studies a practitioner may draw from. While that is so, it must also be noted that this argument is purely theoretical and is based solely on the perspective of wanting to have the largest number of studies from which values can be transferred. In practice, such actions would result in a huge loss of accuracy.

Apart from the issue of whether the above limitation more strongly applies to value or function transfers, we note that this limitation is likely to be less relevant over time as the stock of valuation studies increases. The continued development of valuation study databases (e.g. EVRI, Envalue, ValueBaseSWE) will further add to the ease of finding relevant studies to transfer required values from.

The third limitation lies in the degree of similitude between the policy and study sites. Although there are mechanisms to adjust for most differences, each adjustment invariably causes some loss of accuracy. As such, the greater the difference between the policy and study site, the less accurate the transferred values and hence, the less efficient the benefit transfer.

The subjectivity involved in benefit transfers constitutes the fourth limitation. In the process of transferring benefits, the practitioner must make any number of value judgements. For instance, in function transfers, the choice of independent variables that enter the demand function depends on the assumptions of the model,

Table 42.2 Cases of benefit transfers

Study		Source		Benefit transfer methodology		Values		
Year	Title of study (author/s)	Year	Title of study (author/s)	Transfer type	Adjusted for	Item	Original	Transferred
2007	The Economic Value of Iowa's Natural Resources (Otto et al., 2007)	2005	Updated Outdoor Recreation Use Values on National Forests and Other Public Lands (Loomis et al., 1991)	Unadjusted point-estimate value transfer	Nil	Value per activity day for recreational activities in Iowan parks	(2007 US$): Camping: 33.11 Fishing: 32.91 Hunting: 47.45 Trail use (general recreation): 16.88 Wild-life viewing: 31.29 General use: 16.88	Exactly the same
2003	The Economic Cost of Particulate Air Pollution on Health in Singapore (Quah and Tan, 1999b)	1995	Assessing the Health Costs of Particulate Air Pollution in the UK (Pearce and Crowards, 1995)	Adjusted point-estimate value transfer	Income	Value of statistical life in Singapore	(1999 US$) 2.98 million	(1999 US$) 3 million
2007	Introducing Willingness-to-pay for Noise Changes into a Transport Appraisal: An Application of Benefit Transfer (Nellthorp et al., 2007)	2004	The Valuation of Transport-Related Noise in Birmingham (Bateman et al., 2004)	Adjusted point-Estimate value transfer	Income Time Household tenure	Mean value of noise reduction by 1 dB in the interval of 45–50dB per household per annum in the United Kingdom	(1997 £) 10.2	(2002 £) 13.7

Year	Study	Period	Source studies	Method	Variables	Description	Value (transferred)	Value (observed)
2004	The Economic Value of Marine Recreational Fishing: Applying Benefit Transfer to Marine Recreational Fisheries Statistics Survey (MRFSS) (Jeong and Haab, 2004)	1994–1997	The Economic Value of New England and Mid-Atlantic Sportfishing in 1994 (*Hicks et al.*, 1999) The Economic Value of Marine Recreational Fishing in the Southeast United States: 1997 Southeast Economic Data Analysis (Haab *et al.*, 2000)	Benefit function transfer	Travel cost Travel time (where wage rate is not available) No. of intercept sites Historic harvest rate Species distribution	Mean access value per fishing trip for states along the northeast and southeast of the United States	(Only selected states shown) (1994 US$) Connecticut: 5.31 Delaware: 2.42 (1997 US$) Georgia: 3.41 North Carolina: 37.19	(Only selected states shown) (1994 US$) Connecticut: 5.90 Delaware: 3.40 (1997 US$) Georgia: 2.19 North Carolina: 25.44
2007	Meta-functional Benefit Transfer for Wetland Valuation: Making the Most of Small Samples (Moeltner and Woodward, 2009)	1991–2004	Nine primary studies on the economic valuation of wetlands in the United States[1]	Meta-analysis function transfer	Wetland type Wetland acreage Household income Percentage of active users Policy scenario	Mean and total value of wetlands in eastern Nevada to Nevadan residents only	Varies between the nine studies	(US$, base year unavailable) 4.749 per household 3,567,616 in total
2018	Valuing Coastal Beaches and Closures Using Benefit Transfer: An Application to Barnstable, Massachusetts (Lyon *et al.*, 2018)	1975–2013	98 observations from 25 studies on the economic value of public beaches in the United States	Meta-analysis function transfer	Study characteristics (e.g. type of water), people characteristics (e.g. length of visits), site quality characteristics (e.g. water quality).	Value of a beach day and the lost value of a beach closure; Consumer surplus value of a beach visit	Varies across the 25 studies	(2018 US$) 22 per visit

1 Loomis *et al.*, 1991; Hanemann *et al.*, 1991; Writehead and Blomquist, 1991; Mullarkey, 1997; Roberts and Leitch, 1997; Blomquist and Whitehead, 1998; Poor, 1999; Tkac, 2002; Klocek, 2004.

which in turn, are based on the value judgement of the practitioner. Similarly, in value transfers, what the original value ought to be adjusted for is also at the practitioner's discretion. However, logically, as in ideal CBA practices, items that enter a CBA ought to be valued from the viewpoint of the affected parties. Following this line of reasoning, the fact that benefit transfers increase the role of the practitioner while diminishing the influence of the affected parties would very likely result in a greater loss of accuracy.

The final limitation concerns the methodological bias in primary studies. Apart from the issue of the quality of the original study constraining the quality of the transferred value, methodological bias also creates other problems in benefit transfers. For value transfers and benefit function transfers, it presents a problem as such bias cannot be accounted for and corrected in the transfer process. These transfers that do not explicitly account for the methodological bias in the original studies implicitly accept them in their valuations. For meta-regression analysis function transfers, there is the issue of what a practitioner is supposed to do if or when it is discovered that different methods consistently produced different value estimates (e.g. CVM consistently yielding higher/lower estimates than hedonic pricing, CVM by phone producing higher/lower estimates than by face-to-face surveys, etc.). There are no absolute guidelines with regard to what should be done about the above. Clearly, if a particular method can be shown to consistently produce more accurate value estimates than others, then adjustments should always be made to correct the methodological bias caused by other methods. However, the evidence on the superiority of indigenous valuation techniques is mixed at best. Besides, if one method can be shown to consistently produce better estimates than the rest, there would not be such an array of varying methods used in primary studies in the first place. The lack of best practice in indigenous valuation techniques demands that practitioners exercise their value judgements, adding to the subjectivity of the transferred value.

Comparison of benefit transfer methods

7   In terms of broad comparisons, there seems to be some consensus that on average, function transfers provide more accurate estimates than value transfers. Rosenberger and Loomis (2003) reached this conclusion by observing the percentage difference between the transferred and actual values across 13 sites in which both benefit transfer and indigenous value elicitation were employed. They go on to state that meta-regression function transfers provided better estimates than benefit function transfers. Groothuis (2005) reached a similar conclusion and further showed that the degree of error caused by benefit function transfers were significantly less than value transfers when the original study employed CVM. However, Rosenberger and Loomis (2003) also acknowledged that misapplications of function transfers could result in very significant errors.

The evidence largely supports the idea that function transfers, especially meta-regression analysis transfers, outperform value transfers. However, accuracy of transfer is only one facet of efficiency; application limitations are another. With regard to application limitations, there is, first, the issue of degree of applicability. Function transfers require a minimum amount of information for the regression analysis to be robust. Value transfers, on the other hand, may be carried out as long as one original study may be found. The continued increase in the stock of valuation studies will work in favour of function transfers. However, the stricter requirement of a minimum number of studies will always render function transfers less applicable, even if only slightly.

Second, there is the issue of time. Both methods require exhaustive searches of the literature. However, in function transfers, additional time has to be spent on coding the various aspects of the original studies while this step is not necessary for value transfer. In this light, value transfer may be more time-efficient than function transfers.

In summary, while function transfers provide more accurate value estimates, value transfers are more time- (and hence cost-) effective. As such, there is not a constant optimal method and the practitioner has to exercise judgement as to which method best suits the CBA purposes, taking into account accuracy issues, as well as time and cost constraints.

Conclusion

8   To conclude, we take note of a few caveats in conducting benefit transfers. First, while benefit transfers may be relatively more efficient in both costs and time, it should never be the first option. Benefit transfers only provide recourse when indigenous valuation methods are not possible; it is not an alternative. Where possible, practitioners should always opt for indigenous valuation methods. Second, practitioners should always be aware of the limitations of benefit transfers and the ensuing accuracy issues. Third, related to the issues of accuracy, benefit transfers typically provide a range of transferable values. Hence, it is only when the CBA criteria are met for the whole range of values (i.e. when sensitivity analysis yields consistent results) that the practitioner may comfortably provide a recommendation.

Note

1   Adapted from Soh, C. (Quah and Toh, 2011).

43 Pair-wise comparison[1]

1   The recognition of flaws generally inspires improvement. In the same vein, the recognition of the limitations of stated and revealed preference approaches in valuation methods has spurred the development of novel techniques. The pair-wise comparison method is one such example. While the method is not entirely new, being first thought up by Thurstone in 1927 (Thurstone, 1927) to measure attitudes in psychological studies, its introduction into the valuation of non-market goods literature is considered rather novel. Peterson and Brown (1998) were the first to employ the method to compare the preferences of individuals concerning six different public goods.

In this chapter, we first review the main weaknesses of stated and revealed preference approaches. This is followed by an illustration of how the pair-wise comparison method may be carried out and how it avoids the problems inherent in both stated and revealed preference approaches. Finally, we conclude by summarizing the main points and present cases in which the method has been applied in valuation studies.

2   Stated preference approaches are methods that require individuals to state explicitly what a particular item is worth to them. Revealed preference approaches, on the other hand, are methods that derive the value of items implicitly through observing the effects that the item in question has on related markets. To give examples of each approach, the contingent valuation method (CVM), discussed in Chapter 41, is a stated preference approach while hedonic pricing and the travel cost method are revealed preference approaches. Detailed explanations and evaluations of each specific method are provided in Chapter 41 on valuation issues and techniques. Nonetheless, a brief review of the main weaknesses of stated and revealed preference approaches is presented here for ease of reading.

Limitations of the stated preference approach

3   The key problem with stated preference approaches is that it is highly susceptible to survey and behavioural bias (see Chapter 44). This is because any method that requires individuals to state explicit amounts that they are willing to pay or accept must necessarily involve a survey of some sort. While survey bias may be eliminated or at least kept to a minimum by improving the survey technique and providing proper training for surveyors, behavioural biases prove to be difficult to eradicate.

Limitations of the revealed preference approach

4   The problems with revealed preference approaches are no less thorny, the principal weakness being the assumptions regarding the market that it requires. This is because the approach generally relies on price differentials within a market (usually housing or labour) to calculate the value of certain items (e.g. measuring the value of a life through observing the wage differentials between a job that carries some mortality risk and one that does not). Hence, the accuracy of the valuations will be constrained by the degree to which price differentials reflect people's differing preferences.

Immediately, the associated problems become obvious. In order for price differentials to reflect the true marginal value of an item, the approach has to assume that, at the equilibrium set of prices, individuals are indifferent between their situation and any other alternative. This, in turn, requires rationality and perfect information on the part of individuals, such that at any set of prices, if a better alternative exists, rational individuals with perfect information would know of it and immediately switch to it. This then causes a change in relative prices, until eventually equilibrium can be reached in which price differentials reflect the values of differing characteristics between goods and no individual can be made better off by switching to an alternative. To enable the smooth switching between alternatives, individuals would also have to be perfectly mobile – a situation that is hardly realized in the real world. Additionally, other common market distortions such as those caused by taxes or subsidies also reduce the effectiveness of the method by altering the price signals.

As can be seen, the assumptions that have to be fulfilled before revealed preference approaches produce reliable estimates, limit the efficiency of the method.

Carrying out a pair-wise comparison study

5   At times when we might not be as confident of the final monetary values derived, the pair-wise comparison approach, or the damage schedules approach, is preferred. This non-monetary method has received limited attention and is able to measure whether one good is worth more than another. It values goods in relative terms rather than absolute nominal terms. The approach aims to develop an interval ranking of relative importance for a set of policy options, derived from respondents' preferences. Since it is only an indicator of relative social preferences, it does not face the problem of WTP and WTA non-equivalence and of loss aversion (Champ and Loomis, 1998; Knetsch, 1990; Loomis et al., 1998).

To understand how it does so, we must first understand how the method is carried out. We will illustrate the method via a hypothetical example.

Suppose a practitioner is tasked to find out the relative ranking of four items:

1   preventing the loss of 1 ha of rainforest in the Amazon rainforest;
2   a 1 per cent decrease in unemployment from 5 per cent to 4 per cent;
3   a reduction in global carbon emissions by 5 per cent;
4   a 2 per cent decrease in infant mortality rates.

The items presented are purposefully kept short for ease of presentation. However, when employing the pair-wise comparison method, it is better to describe the items in as much detail as possible to minimize the need for respondents' imagination.

The first step is to conduct a survey into which the items are presented as binary choices to individuals who have to select the option that they deem more important or valuable. If the number of combinations is not too many, all possible combinations of binary choices should be shown to every respondent. The possible combinations for our example are shown in Table 43.1. Only one pair would be presented at one time for the respondent to choose.

As can be seen from Table 43.1, for any of the four items, the maximum number of times it can be chosen over other items by a single individual would be three. The number of times the item is actually chosen is also known as a preference score. For an individual in our sample, the preference scores might then be as shown in Table 43.2.

The variance stable rank method may then be employed to summarize the preferences of the entire sample. This is done by summing up the preference scores of each item across all respondents in the sample and then dividing it by the maximum number of times it could have been selected. The resulting figures can then be multiplied by one hundred to place them on a scale of zero to one hundred.

Going back to our example, suppose that the sample consisted of 100 individuals. After summing up the preference scores of each item, we may get values as in the first column of Table 43.3. We may then derive the variance stable rank as shown in the last column of Table 43.3.

Table 43.1 Combination of items as binary choice sets

Option			Option	
1	Preventing the loss of 1 ha of rainforest in the Amazon rainforest		2	A 1% decrease in unemployment from 5% to 4%
1	Preventing the loss of 1 ha of rainforest in the Amazon rainforest		3	A reduction in global carbon emissions by 5%
1	Preventing the loss of 1 ha of rainforest in the Amazon rainforest	versus	4	A 2% decrease in infant mortality rates
2	A 1% decrease in unemployment from 5% to 4%		3	A reduction in global carbon emissions by 5%
2	A 1% decrease in unemployment from 5% to 4%		4	A 2% decrease in infant mortality rates
3	A reduction in global carbon emissions by 5%		4	A 2% decrease in infant mortality rates

Table 43.2 Sample of an individual's preference score

Items		Preference score
1	Preventing the loss of 1 ha of rainforest in the Amazon rainforest	1
2	A 1% decrease in unemployment from 5% to 4%	3
3	A reduction in global carbon emissions by 5%	0
4	A 2% decrease in infant mortality rates	2

Table 43.3 Variance stable rank of items

Items	Sum of preference scores (x)	Maximum sum of preference scores (y), (n – 1) × 100	Variance stable rank scale, (x/y) × 100
1 Preventing the loss of 1 ha of rain-forest in the Amazon rainforest	110	300	36.7
2 A 1% point decrease in unemploy-ment from 5% to 4%	284	300	94.7
3 A reduction in global carbon emissions by 5%	67	300	22.3
4 A 2% decrease in infant mortality rates	139	300	46.3

The values obtained from the method are scale values since the figure reflects the proportion of times the item is preferred. This allows for measurements of intensity of preferences. In addition, some degree of indifference is allowed since scores of different items may be the same. In the example used above, it can be seen that individuals had a strong preference for the decrease in unemployment.

At this point, one might ponder the relevance of the above exercise with regard to deriving monetary valuations of non-market goods. The issue is easily resolved. To derive monetary valuations as opposed to simply finding out the intensity of preferences between various items, as shown in the example, one simply substitutes (or inserts) two or more of the items with monetary gains (e.g. a two percentage point decrease in infant mortality rates versus a gain of S$300). The remaining steps are the same. The ranking derived may then provide estimates for the values of the items. For example, if the ranking of a reduction in infant mortality is bracketed between that of a gain of S$300 and S$350, then the value of the reduction in infant mortality must lie somewhere between the two. Quah *et al.* (2006) provide a good example of how this may be carried out.

Strengths and limitations of the pair-wise comparison method

6   The advantage of the pair-wise comparison lies in how it avoids the major limitations of stated and revealed preference approaches. In using surveys like the stated preference approaches, the pair-wise comparison method easily avoids the strict assumptions mandated by the revealed preference approaches.

At the same time, through providing a third viewpoint of that of a selector, the method also circumvents the endowment effect that causes a positive divergence of WTA from WTP which plagues stated preference approaches. This is because the WTA is obtained from the viewpoint of a seller while the WTP is obtained from that of a buyer. Knetsch and Sinden (1984) observed it is the difference in the reference points that gives rise to the discrepancy. The selector's reference point that the paired comparison uses thus side steps the effect by eliminating the loss aversion caused by perceived losses when one takes the viewpoint of the seller as opposed to that of the buyer (Kahneman et al., 1999). As it is the loss aversion that leads to the endowment effect in the first place, the endowment effect is avoided.

Apart from working around the major limitations of the stated and revealed preference approaches, the pair-wise comparison method has also been shown to be relatively easy and cost-effective to implement (Rutherford *et al.*, 1994; Peterson and Brown, 1998; Chuenpagdee *et al.*, 2001; Quah *et al.*, 2006; Ong *et al.*, 2008).

As with all other techniques, the pair-wise comparison method is not perfect. The key problem a practitioner may run into when employing this method is that of survey participants having intransitive preferences (i.e. A is preferred to B; B is preferred to C; and C is preferred to A). The only two possibilities that could give rise to this observation are indifference between certain choices (the method requires participants to make a choice between two options even if they are indifferent which could give rise to seemingly intransitive preferences) and truly intransitive preferences. It is not difficult to find out which case it is. One

Table 43.4 Studies using the pair-wise comparison approach

Author	Year of study	Items of study
Peterson and Brown	1998	Comparisons between: • 6 public goods (2 environmental, 4 non-environmental) • 4 private goods • 11 monetary sums
Rutherford et al.	1994	Comparisons between: • 4 non-pecuniary environmental losses resulting from oil spills
Chuenpagdee et al.	2001	(Part 1) Comparisons between: • 8 losses of economic resources (Part 2) Comparisons between: • 8 increases in economic activity
Quah et al.	2006	(Part 1) Comparisons between: • 8 losses related to the environment (Part 2) Comparisons between: • 10 monetary gains • 4 environmental improvements
Ong et al.	2008	(Part 1) Comparisons between: • 2 improvements pertaining to education • 2 reductions in losses pertaining to education (Part 2) Comparisons between: • 2 improvements pertaining to transportation • 2 reductions in losses pertaining to transportation (Part 3) Comparisons between: • 2 improvements pertaining to the environment • 2 reductions in losses pertaining to the environment
Ibarra et al.	2010	Comparisons between: • 7 losses of environmental livelihood resources

simply has to re-present the upsetting choice to the survey respondent. If the respondent switches choices, it is probably a case of the former and the issue is resolved. If not, it is possible that the individual in question truly has intransitive preferences and the practitioner may then choose to subtract that individual from the survey sample.

Conclusion

7 The growing understanding of the limitations of current valuation approaches has resulted in efforts to either refine the existing methods or to explore new (and possibly superior) techniques. Motivated by relatively recent findings from behavioural economics that highlight the weaknesses of the CVM, the pair-wise comparison method is an illustration of the latter.

The strengths of the method lie in its not requiring the strict assumptions of the revealed preference approach and in its avoidance of the behavioural bias inherent in stated preference approaches.

While still comparatively uncommon, there are a small but growing number of valuation studies that have made use of the technique. Each study illustrates the simplicity and cost effectiveness of the method. In concluding this chapter, we present a summary of these studies in Table 43.4. For each study, the author, the year of publication and the items of comparison are presented to illustrate the variety of items that the pair-wise comparison method may be applied to.

Note

1 Adapted from Quah and Toh (2011).

44 Cost-benefit analysis and behavioural economics[1]

1   In the previous chapter, some of the behavioural biases inherent in stated preference approaches are briefly mentioned. The relevance of behavioural economics in CBA is further illustrated in this chapter.

2   Three groups of people – international transportation experts attending a professional conference, senior Singaporean public servants and university students – were asked which of two transportation projects they would recommend should be built or if they saw them as equally valuable and therefore expressed no preference. One project would shorten the road distance between two destinations; the other would replace a bridge and eliminate a detour made necessary by the failure of the original bridge. The two projects would cost the same and would save equal numbers of motorists the same amount of travel time and expense. Only one could be built. The choice of people in each of the groups was, interestingly given their diverse backgrounds, nearly the same. A solid majority, of about two-thirds, in each group favoured the second project that eliminated the detour, with the remaining third nearly evenly split between favouring the road improvement and expressing no preference (Chin and Knetsch, 2008).
   Most people would probably not find these results particularly surprising – in large part, because they too feel it is better to return or restore something that was enjoyed and then lost, than it is to provide a gain of something new. What would probably be a big surprise to most people, however, is that nearly all economists and policy analysts in and out of government agencies throughout the world, who evaluate and recommend possible projects and policies, along with the people who write the textbooks and manuals on which their valuations and recommendations are based, would find the choices made by the participants in this transport study completely contrary to their assumptions about people's preferences. To economic and policy analysts, whether a project provides a gain or reduces or eliminates a loss should be totally irrelevant, and therefore analysts should have no preference for either project as they cost the same and provide identical savings of time and costs to equal numbers of travellers.
   The main reason the views of analysts would differ from those of other people on this choice of project, and in so many other real cases, is that their analyses and predictions of likely consequences of alternative actions are based largely on the traditional assumptions of what has become known as standard economic theory. Indeed, analysts are often reminded that 'any measurement ... should be consistent with standard economic theory of individual preferences' (Freeman, 1993). By and

large, such admonishments are well taken as far too many 'analyses' and popular discourses on the economic justification for projects and policies often reflect little more than self-serving assertions that lack much in the way of a reasonable claim as guidance to further social well-being. When employed as intended, the standard tools of traditional economic and policy analyses have, with little doubt, provided useful guidance that has led to improved policies, regulatory reform, provision of infrastructure and design of institutions in countries throughout the world. There is wide agreement that people would generally be much better served by far greater use of such analyses and more attention to the results, in coming up with proposals to deal with problems and to take advantage of opportunities.

However, what has also become increasingly clear in recent years, as a result of research by psychologists, a growing number of economists and other decision-making scientists, is that some of the assumptions of standard economics often fail to reflect how individuals and groups actually make decisions, and value and choose among alternatives. The findings suggest, for example, that contrary to the strong assumptions of standard theory, people commonly value losses more than gains, spend or save money received from some sources differently from money received from others, have regard for the well-being of others and adhere to norms of fairness even at the expense of maximizing their own wealth.

Testing the assumptions of standard economics against people's observed actual valuations and choices does not have a long tradition in economics. Such research has been common only in the past couple of decades, giving rise to what has become known as the sub-field of behavioural economics or economic psychology. The findings are not only providing evidence of systematic departures of actual behaviour from behaviour assumed in standard economics, but also they are bringing attention to other factors that influence people's behaviour and choices beyond those taken into account in standard economics. These behavioural findings have direct implications for public as well as private decisions. Behavioural economics is not in any way a substitute for standard economics, but is instead an increasingly useful supplement to economic analyses that can greatly improve the usefulness of economics in many areas, including applications to improve the design of policies and regulatory reform dealing with environmental matters to make them more consistent with people's real preferences.

The insights from behavioural economic findings can be applied to an extremely wide range of subject areas and problems – essentially to all of economics, decision making and policy analysis, including environmental concerns. Specific applications are continually being made in all areas – some, such as behavioural finance, at a far faster rate than others – making it impractical to attempt a complete cataloguing in any. However, a few illustrative examples can show how behavioural findings might be used to improve how CBA, and in particular, environmental problems are dealt with.

Mental accounting

3 A standard assertion of standard theory is that individuals treat money gained from whatever source – wages from their labours, returns from investments, inheritances, gifts or whatever – as all the same. It is all figuratively put into the same big account from which they make payments for the vast array of goods and

services they want – an assumption economists refer to as fungibility. People are assumed to make choices and decisions over incomes and expenditures as if they are completely substitutable regardless of source or purpose.

Common observations, as well as the evidence from careful empirical studies, however, suggests that people treat money quite differently depending on how it is obtained and the reason for spending or saving it (an excellent review is provided by Thaler (1999)). Most people, for example, spend differently on food while on holiday than at home, they treat windfalls differently from earned cash, they increase the tax withheld from their pay-cheques to ensure a refund at the end of the year rather than a requirement to pay more, and they are willing to spend time to save money on a small purchase but not to save the same sum on a large one. Overall, they tend to organize information and make many decisions based not on one overall account of income and expenditure, but instead on smaller mental sub-accounts.

A fairly transparent example of mental accounting is the discounting of capital gains relative to dividends, particularly by retired people drawing on their invest-ment accounts for living expenses. Corporations can presumably choose to transfer their earnings to shareholders by paying dividends, by buying up shares to increase the value of the remaining shares, or by retaining the earnings and have them accrue as an increase in the value of the corporation and corresponding increase in the value of individual shares. Despite often more favourable tax treatment of cap-ital gains in many countries, retired investors generally greatly prefer to receive the return in dividend cheques that they can spend rather than accumulate equivalent sums by periodically selling their increasingly valuable shares. Even though the bal-ance on their account remains the same with any of the three options, having to sell portions of their holdings to capture their returns conveys an adverse feeling of 'dipping into their capital' that is absent from receiving and spending their dividend capital (Thaler, 1999). The sums may be equivalent, but the mental accounts, and choices, differ.

Forgone gains versus losses

4   A generally useful approach to using behavioural findings to improve outcomes can be demonstrated by the instructive example of how they were used in framing workers' decisions as to how much they would contribute to their own retirement fund (Thaler and Benartzi, 2004). While not an environmental case, it is one of the best known and most successful applications of behavioural findings that has been reported, and is also one that clearly illustrates how behavioural findings might be used in any area – environmental included.

It is a usual practice in most countries to inform new workers of not only their pay level, but of any deductions that will be made from this pay for taxes and pos-sibly outlays for various benefits. It is common to also ask employees at that time how much the employee would like deducted as their contribution to a retirement plan (to be matched or added to by the employer in accord with the employment contract), with greater contributions resulting in higher pensions. Unfortunately, posing the contribution choice in this way has resulted in employees choosing, and keeping, very low retirement savings rates, in many cases, which are unlikely to provide a suitable or expected living standard on their retirement – a problem that has been brought to public attention particularly in the United States and Europe.

In response to a request to use behavioural economics findings to modify the information and pension contribution choice format used by a particular company, Richard Thaler and Shlomol Benartzi first noted three aspects of current procedures that actively discouraged employees from contributing more to their retirement savings (Thaler and Benartzi, 2004). The first is the well-known finding that losses are far more aversive to people than forgone gains, and contributions were in this instance framed as subtractions from their reference income. The second is that people commonly exhibit declining discount rates for things further in the future, that is, payments required at present or in the near term are much more important, and therefore aversive, than similar contributions made sometime beyond the immediate future. The third is the related finding that people find it much easier to commit to doing something in the future than to agree to doing it now.

After determining that these three characteristics of the process were probably inhibiting the choice of higher retirement contributions, Thaler and Benartzi focused their attention on the means of mitigating the impact. The result was the suggestion that instead of asking employees how much they want deducted from their present pay packet, they ask how much of future wage increases they would want to contribute. Thus, rather than the very aversive idea of giving back a portion of their present pay, the modification asked for a much less painful foregoing of a gain. It also asked for a commitment to do something in the future rather than make a sacrifice now.

The result of implementing this suggestion was very dramatic and favourably so. The average retirement savings rate was 3.4 per cent before the change and 11.6 per cent after, well over a threefold increase. Further, the higher rate has not decreased over subsequent years, as the wage increases over time better ensure that the contributed sums also increase. This basic change in format has now been incorporated into the retirement programmes of hundreds of firms with many thousands of employees, and the results have been similar in essentially every case. Employees were, of course, free to continue choosing low savings rates under the modified procedure, but being relieved of the inhibiting framing of the choice, most did not choose to do so.

As seemingly obvious as the contribution inhibiting factors would appear to most people once they are pointed out, it is worth noting that none would be given any weight in standard economic analyses and, consequently, no change in contribution levels resulting from the modification of procedures would be anticipated by standard economics. It was only with the additional insights provided by behavioural findings that the problem could be better understood and, therefore, effective changes suggested.

Sunk cost effect

5   Another implication of mental accounts, and one somewhat more closely related to environmental matters, stems from the so-called fixed or sunk cost effect. The dictates of standard theory explain that once an expenditure is made, it is sunk and irretrievable and therefore decisions should be based only on gains and losses from that point on – the expenditure is equally gone whether the activity is continued or

abandoned. For example, if a person pays a non-refundable deposit of US$100 towards the purchase of an automobile or household appliance, and then finds the identical model available from another dealer for US$200 less, it would make no financial sense to go through with the original purchase because of the US$100 that had already been paid. The individual may regret having paid the deposit to the first dealer, but it is now gone, sunk, and it is only comparisons with the remaining balance that determines the cheapest alternative.

The evidence of people's actual behaviour, however, suggests that most of them often take some account of their previous outlays or commitments when considering future moves. They are more likely to endure a blizzard in going to a sporting event if they have already purchased a ticket than if they have not (Thaler, 1999), and the more people have paid for a season ticket to performances of a theatre group, the more likely they are to go to every event (Arkes and Blumer, 1985). Attention to sunk costs can also give rise to more tragic consequences, as in cases when continuations of armed conflicts are supported with the persuasive emotional appeal that cessation of hostilities would mean that people killed earlier 'would have died in vain'.

The use of cars is, in most places, a major environmental issue as greater use has a direct detrimental impact on, for example, air quality, congestion and greenhouse gas emissions. Moreover, people's inclinations not to ignore sunk costs can have an impact on their use.

Many countries and cities attempt to discourage the purchase and use of cars by imposing high purchase and operating taxes, and other charges. The use of very high purchases taxes or other fixed costs – sometimes reaching levels equalling or even greatly exceeding the purchase price of the car – can, however, because of the sunk cost effect, have an impact opposite to the one of curtailing use that is intended. Having paid the high purchase costs, many people then feel that they need to drive more to justify this high outlay and rationalize their greater use by telling themselves and others that, 'I paid a lot to be able to have a car, so I am going to use it and spread this cost out over more trips'.

The opposite, and usually more socially desirable, incentive is created by imposing a high tax, not on the purchase of a car, but on its use. People would then be more transparently faced with an added cost on each trip. This might be made even more the case, and therefore more effective, if the user charges or fees are more transparently tied to the actual social costs that added use imposes on others by adding to congestion and pollution. This would not only face car owners with the costs of driving, but would also be likely to make it easier for them to self-justify using alternative transit arrangements.

Given the opposite likely impacts of purchase and user taxes or charges, if the aim is to discourage car use, especially at certain times and in particular areas, this might be best supported by reducing fixed cost taxes and increasing variable taxes or charges. The latter might be done with a fuel tax, but this would be largely insensitive to the important differing impacts of where and when the car was driven – driving late at night in remote areas generates less congestion, pollution and other external costs than driving in business districts during rush hours. A system of tolls, for example, can be made more sensitive to the actual distance travelled at particular times and places, though they too are not without problems.

Decoupling

6   In the normal model of a purchase transaction, a buyer pays the stated price to a seller and takes away the good. The buyer is then presumably keenly aware of the price, and sensitive to it, and makes decisions accordingly. Arrangements that 'decouple' payment from consumption usually cause potential buyers to be less sensitive to the terms of the purchase. A fixed charge for multiple items, for example, often results in consumers paying for and consuming items they would not have purchased if priced separately – a strategy often used by resorts charging an all-inclusive tariff. Credit cards are perhaps the most common decoupling device. While offering great convenience, they are also a very effective means of separating purchase from payment, thereby lessening the restraint provided by the necessity of paying cash to the seller.

Road tolls can be an effective means of facing motorists with the real costs of their driving on particular roads at particular times, and thereby promote socially efficient use of roads and other transportation options. However, their effectiveness is at least in part, and likely in large part, dependent on motorists being sensitive to the charges imposed by alternative routings and times. This is likely to be greater with the need to make a cash outlay when passing a toll point.

The desired sensitivity to the collection of tolls and their resulting effectiveness is, however, likely to be a great deal less with the use of automatic toll collection devices. A probable serious consequence of the use of such automatic collection devices is to largely decouple use of the roadways from payment, by having the toll payments almost completely unknowingly deducted from bank accounts or cash cards or by monthly billings posted to owners long after the contribution to congestion and pollution has taken place. Whatever the convenience and other benefits of automatic toll collection, they seem likely to come at a cost of reducing awareness of the link between payment and road use, and consequently of the effectiveness of the tolls.

The appeal of dedicated funds (ear-marking)

7   A firm principle of standard economics and of public finance is that monies collected for the use of public facilities should be put into the general public revenue accounts of the government, where they can be used for whatever purposes are deemed to be socially most desired, and not dedicated, or ear-marked, for use by agencies collecting the money or used for purposes related to the provision of the service for which the sums were collected. The reason for this policy directive is straightforward. If the money is left with the agency collecting the money, its necessarily narrower focus may well result in using it for a purpose that is less valued than if it could be allocated to some other public use. Money collected for the use of a park, for example, might be better used in providing healthcare than in expanding parks. In addition, funds from road tolls might be better used to hire more food inspectors than to build more roads. Better then to put the monies into the general fund and allocate it to healthcare and food inspectors.

Although the rationale for the standard economics principle of putting all collected sums into the most general of accounts may be clear, people's reactions have, in many cases, been found to be seriously at variance with it. Money paid in fees that are returned in some form related to the use for which the money is collected, appears to often mitigate the feeling of loss. For example, users of public parks and campsites have been found, not surprisingly, to be much more accepting of an increase in entrance or user fees if the money collected is used to maintain or improve the facilities in the area they are using rather than put into general government revenues.

The lesson for the use of money collected in pollution charges or allocation of pollution rights in a cap-and-trade scheme may be closely parallel. Using the funds for a purpose related to the reason for the payment of fees may well make the collection scheme acceptable to a large portion of the individuals affected by the requirement. An instructive example is provided by the way the government in Columbia overcame the strong resistance to a proposed financial disincentive scheme to control pollution. The objection to the proposal persisted until the government changed its policy and announced that the monies collected from the pollution charge programme would not be put in general revenue accounts, but would instead be used to fund sewage treatment plants throughout the country. Again, the more limited view of standard economics missed the real opportunity to advance environmental provision that became evident with the wider view of preferences that were more apparent with the insights provided by behavioural findings.

Valuations of gains and valuation of losses

8   Probably the most extensively studied of all behavioural findings – and probably, the most important – is the evidence that people frequently value losses much more than gains. This very unexpected result was first reported in 1974, in a study of people's valuation of duck habitat (Hammack and Brown, 1974). It has been replicated in a very wide array of survey studies and real exchange laboratory and natural experiments conducted over the years since (reviewed in, for example, Kahneman et al. (1990) and Rabin (1998), and with particular reference to environmental values in Horowitz and McConnell (2002).

There is near-universal agreement that economic values are correctly measured by the sacrifice that people are willing to make. In the case of a gain, this measure is the maximum sacrifice that an individual is willing to make to obtain it. In practice this is taken to be the maximum amount of money that the person is willing to pay for it (commonly abbreviated as WTP). In the case of a loss, it is the minimum sacrifice the individual is willing to take to accept it – in practice the minimum sum of money to accept the loss (or WTA). While there are then these two different measures for gains and for losses, the dictates of standard economics are quite clear that there should be little or no difference between them, and consequently little or no difference in the valuations of gains and losses. That is, the amount a person is willing to pay to gain a good should be equivalent to the sum the individual will accept to give it up – 'we shall normally expect the results to be so close together that it would not matter which we choose' (Henderson, 1941).

The assumption of equivalence between valuations using either the WTP or WTA measure has long been used to justify the overwhelming current practice of using whichever measure is most convenient. As WTP values are usually easier to estimate than WTA values, nearly all valuations are made with this measure in spite of the clear principle that losses are to be assessed in terms of people's WTA valuations – 'In practice, the WTP is generally used to value benefits because it is often easier to measure and estimate' (US Environmental Protection Agency, 2000). The practice of estimating essentially all environmental values with the WTP measure – losses as well as gains – continues in spite of the mounting empirical evidence demonstrating that WTA values are typically much larger than WTP valuations. In their review of 45 environmental valuation studies, Horowitz and McConnell found that the median WTA/WTP ratio among them was 2.6 (the mean ratio was approximately 7).

An example of the many experimental studies that have shown the significant disparity between the measures, and one of many that was carried out with real money exchanges to help motivate the participants to give more seriously considered responses and with questions that revealed real preferences and precluded strategic behaviour, involved valuations of a 50 per cent chance to win US$20 (Kachelmeier and Shehata, 1992). One half of the individuals in a large group of people were asked the maximum sum they would pay for a ticket that gave them this chance to win US$20. The other half were given a ticket that gave them the identical chance to win the same prize and were then asked the smallest amount they would accept to give up their ticket. Then the roles of people in the two groups were reversed and the alternative valuations were obtained from each, so that in the end everyone valued the ticket two ways: by the maximum amount they would pay to get one (their WTP valuation) and by the minimum sum they would accept to give one up (their WTA valuation). Note that the item being valued – a 50 per cent chance to win US$20 – is exactly the same for both valuations, giving no reason to expect people to value the ticket differently when buying it or selling it. Indeed, this is what standard economics says, and consequently what analysts assume when they assess alternatives and make recommendations. The valuations of people in this experimental demonstration, like those in dozens of others, were sharply different from these expectations. The buy and sell valuations were not equal as standard economics assumes, they were far from it. When asked the maximum amount they would pay for a ticket, the average for all of the participants was US$5.60; when asked the minimum sum they would require to give up a ticket, these *same* people valued it at US$11.02.

The results from a series of studies of people making common choices in non-experimental settings have also been reported over the years and show similar and consistent results. For example, shoppers making routine purchases of eggs showed a much greater sensitivity to price increases, which impose losses (a price elasticity of –1.10) than to price decreases, which provide gains (elasticity of only –0.45) – here too losses were taken to be more important than gains (Putler, 1992). Similar behaviour has been observed among investors in securities who often do not sell shares that have gone down in price because they are reluctant to realize they have made a loss, a reluctance that does not influence their sell decisions on shares that have gone up in price (Odean, 1998). Consistent behaviour has also been reported among sellers of houses of the influence feelings of gain or loss have on them when selling above or below their original purchase price (Einio *et al.*, 2008).

Given the evidence of pervasive and large disparities between people's valuations of gains and losses, a failure to take this into account can lead to bad choices that can compromise public welfare and to economically unwarranted deterioration of the environment. This might be illustrated with the case of a decision to preserve an important bird habitat in the United States, or to allow it to be developed for some alternative purpose. In the study noted above, people who benefited from the natural habitat were willing to pay an average of US$247 to preserve it, but the average amount they demanded to agree to its demise was over four times larger – US$1,044 (Hammack and Brown, 1974). The valuation that should be used in this case is the latter, as the change at issue is the loss of the habitat, but the usual current practice all over the world is to use the lesser amount of what people would pay to preserve it. Consequently, alternative developments that would result in the destruction of the habitat that are worth more than the equivalent of the US$247 would be seen to be economically justified and worth doing even if they are worth less than the actual value of the loss of the equivalent of US$1,044.

The choice of measure to value changes

9 When there was the secure belief that there was little or no difference between people's valuations of gains and valuations of losses, the issue of which measure of value was most appropriate to use in specific cases seemed to be of little practical importance – the circumstance that has led to current practice of WTP use for all changes. The now widely observed and reported disparities between the measures change this; the choice of measure is now an issue of substantial consequence.

The major focus of the concern over the appropriate measure is whether a negative change is best regarded as a loss, which would call for the WTA measure, or a reduction of a gain, which is best assessed with the WTP measure; and whether a positive change should be considered a gain, calling for the WTP measure or a reduction of a loss, which is most accurately assessed with the WTA measure. Current practice, to the extent that this is taken into any account, is to regard all positive changes as improvements or gains, and to consider all negative changes as losses. This is, however, unlikely to lead to a useful distinction.

A more useful discrimination might be suggested with a simple thought experiment involving a hypothetical environmental change of an oil spill. Most people seem likely to regard such a spill as imposing a loss from what would be considered the normal or expected condition of their surroundings free from the spilt oil washing up on foreshores. Given the presumption of it being a loss, the appropriate measure of its value is then the WTA of people to accept it. The value of cleaning up the spill turns on whether people regard this mitigation as being a gain or a reduction of a loss. Here it seems most likely that most people would consider the clean-up activity as a restoration of the norm of an environment free of the spilt oil – much as they would probably regard clearing a road of spilt lorry cargo to allow normal traffic to resume. To the extent that this is the case, the proper measure of the value of the clean-up is the minimum sum people would accept to forgo this action and remain with the consequences of the spill (the WTA measure), and not how much they would be willing to pay to have the clean-up proceed as is now overwhelmingly the choice in environmental (and other) valuation efforts.

While usually a less frequent issue, a similar discrimination is applicable to negative changes. The WTP to avoid a loss is only applicable to changes that would change things back to a normal or expected condition. Other negative changes are best regarded as losses from this neutral reference and are therefore more appropriately assessed with the WTA measure.

While the choice remains an empirical issue in particular cases, it is at least arguable that most environmental changes, and particularly the ones that most people are concerned with, are most likely to be best considered as losses, prevention of losses, mitigation or eliminations of losses, and are therefore in all of these cases best assessed with the WTA measure.

To the extent that valuations of losses exceed those of gains, the current practice of using the WTP measure, rather than the appropriate WTA measure, for losses and reductions of losses will in most cases give rise to systematic understatements of their value. This will likely lead to undue encouragement of activities with negative impacts, such as pollution and risks to health and safety, as such losses will be under-weighted. Similarly, compensation and damage awards will be too small to provide proper restitution and deterrence, and inappropriately lax pollution and other environmental standards against further degradation will be set because assessments of added costs of further harm will be heavily biased. Too few resources will be devoted to avoiding environmental deterioration because the determinants of allocation efficiencies will be biased against avoiding losses, and full accounting of resource values and appropriate pricing of resource services, such as environmental amenities, will be frustrated.

Opting in versus opting out and the power of the default

10 Recognition of the disparity between people's valuations of gains and losses also helps in explaining the difference in outcomes due to default designation of options – people are reluctant to give up an entitlement for an alternative, as the loss looms larger than the potential gain. This was quite evident in the results of an experiment in which people in one group were given a decorated mug and others in another group a 400 gram Swiss chocolate bar, and then all were given the chance of a costless exchange of whichever good they were initially randomly given, for the alternative. People in both groups had a presumably equal opportunity to end up with the good they preferred, and as there is no reason to expect more people favouring either good to be in one group or the other, the strong prediction of standard economics is that the proportions ultimately going home with each good should be about the same in both groups. The result was quite different. Ninety per cent of those given a mug kept it rather than exchange it for a chocolate bar and 89 per cent of those initially given a chocolate bar kept it (Knetsch, 1989). For most participants, whichever good they were initially given, and had in their possession at the time of deciding whether or not to exchange it for the other, was more valuable to them when facing its loss than the one they could acquire as a gain. For everyone, the good they had was the default and it mattered in terms of their final choices.

A similar influence of default positions is observed in non-experimental circumstances of people making everyday decisions. For example, car owners in two US states, New Jersey and Pennsylvania, were offered a choice of two insurance options: one was considerably less expensive but restricted recovery in the event of an accident; the other was more expensive but had fewer restrictions. Both options were nearly identical in the two states, but the default option differed. Even though the transaction costs of changing from the default to the other alternative were essentially zero and the cost differences substantial, only 20 per cent of the car owners in New Jersey and 25 per cent in Pennsylvania changed from the default. As a result of the different defaults, the more expensive but less restrictive policy was chosen by motorists in Pennsylvania, where it was the default, and 20 per cent in New Jersey, where the cheaper alternative was the default – a 55 per cent difference (Johnson *et al.*, 1993).

In countries where organ donations, usually from people killed in accidents, are made only in cases in which the donor has given *ex ante* consent, donations are typically around 20 per cent and lead to perpetual shortages of needed transplants. The default for donations differs in many European countries, Singapore and others, where people are assumed to have given consent to the taking of their organs after death unless they have made an explicit declaration to the contrary. In these countries, the rates of donation are commonly above 80 per cent, which is more in line with the proportions of survey respondents who indicate they favour the taking of organs for this purpose.

Default positions exert a strong influence over choices in all areas, including environmental. This is evident, for example, in people's attachment to what they consider as normal conditions – often the present ones – that are free of oil spills, pollution, extinction of favoured species and the like. It is also specifically apparent in environmental impact assessments, which many countries require before permitting certain types of development or activity. The focus of such appraisals is overwhelmingly on implications of changes from the status quo, or other neutral reference, that might result from the development or change being assessed.

Mitigation versus compensation

11   There are two general forms of remedy that people causing injury or harm to others may be required to provide. One is to undertake mitigation measures to reduce or eliminate the harm that was caused by the person responsible. The other is to pay compensation to the victims for the harm they suffered.

Conventional economic analysis suggests that, all else being equal, compensation will normally be a more efficient and preferred means to deal with losses. Mitigation restricts the remedy to dealing only with whatever has been injured whereas compensation payments permit recipients to use the funds for whatever good or service is of most value to them – which may well be something totally unrelated to the thing that was harmed. Thus, if a negligent action causes an accident that severely damages an older car, the owner should be less satisfied with having the car repaired than with a monetary payment that can be used to either repair the car, as part payment for a newer car, or to underwrite a family holiday.

The evidence of the disparity between people's valuations of gains and losses suggests an alternative view of people's preferences over the remedies. They may well view the compensation remedy as really very much two separate issues, one that provides the gain of money, which is discounted for being a gain, and the other as leaving them with the injury, which is valued more highly for being a loss. The mitigation measure, on the other hand, will be viewed as reducing the loss and valued more because of this.

The strength of this distinction has been borne out in survey and experimental studies, as well as in the observations of reactions of injured parties. For example, upwards of 70 per cent of respondents favoured spending large sums of money on only very partially effective efforts to mitigate a minor environmental problem rather than spend the same sums on 'whatever use is decided on by local residents in a referendum' (Knetsch, 1990).

Fairness and other regarding behaviour

12 The standard model of behaviour used in most analyses of issues also suggests that people seek to maximize their personal welfare, with little regard for others outside of their immediate household. Here too, the empirical evidence suggests that regard for others and feelings of what is and is not fair does in fact influence the actions and choices of most people. While standard analysis has long taken account of issues of vertical equity, that is the treatment of and consequences for the poor relative to the rich, there has been much less explicit regard for issues of horizontal equity, that is the like treatment of people in like circumstances. The empirical evidence that is available, however, indicates, among other things, that people do appear to care and change behaviours to accommodate others, and that some simple rules seem to dictate much of what people regard as fair dealings (Kahneman *et al.*, 1986).

For example, one rule seems to be that it is generally unfair for one party to gain at the direct expense of another party. In a random household survey of Canadians, and confirmed by later studies in other countries, a large majority of respondents judged a department store holding an auction to secure the highest profit from the sale of one remaining toy doll to be unfair, as the store would benefit at the expense of the customer. However, when the added profit went to a charity, the auction was then judged to be fair – the store was then seen not to benefit at the expense of others.

It also appears to be unfair for one party to exploit circumstances to increase profits. Very large majorities of respondents judged it very unfair for a greater than intended increase in rent to be imposed when the landlord learned that the tenant had taken a job nearby and was therefore unlikely to move.

People did feel, however, that it was fair for landlords and others to pass on cost increases. They also said it was fair to share losses with employees by cutting their wages, though this was very unfair if the firm was making profits.

While fairness motivations and regard for others are not generally considered, at least very explicitly, in policy analyses, there is considerable evidence that they influence a wide range of people's behaviours. There is also surprisingly consistent regard for fairness in judgements in common law jurisdictions, as rulings closely mirror the findings of fairness studies as to what is and is not fair (Cohen and Knetsch, 1992). Prices generally more closely reflect changes in costs than they do shifts in demand, as it is almost unquestionably fair to pass on these costs along with a fair profit. Many markets, such as resorts during holiday periods, fail to clear the fairness standards because taking too great an advantage of opportunities is regarded as unfair 'gouging'.

The evidence suggests that a greater sensitivity to fairness concerns would increase the success of policy design and result in greater support and socially useful change. For example, fees that transparently reflect costs of provision or charges that reflect recognizable environmental damages are likely to be far more acceptable than levies that are less so.

It seems also likely that the responsibility–cost link might usefully be exploited in the design of measures to deal with environmental externality costs, to the extent that if people can be explicitly shown the costs they impose on others by, for example, driving their cars at peak traffic times, there may be greater acceptance of paying this full cost for doing so and of making greater effort to use alternative transit modes or times in order to lower these costs.

Conclusion

13 Although there is yet much more to be done in this area, it seems already clear that the level of debate and decisions about environmental policies and regulations, like so many other areas, could be markedly improved with more attention to behavioural findings. Establishing priorities more in keeping with people's feelings of the seriousness of problems would be easier, and improved means to resolve or mitigate them might be possible.

The results from behavioural economics research have not, however, with a few notable exceptions, yet reached the mainstream of environmental economics textbooks or been used in any appreciable way in environmental decisions, despite publication of findings in *every* leading professional journal in economics, psychology and related fields, the degree to which they conform to the common sense of most people, Daniel Kahneman sharing the 2002 Nobel Prize for Economics for his work that led to the development of the field and a literature pointing to applications extending well over two decades. Analysts continue to show 'restraint' in giving up their present assumptions and procedures. There may be various reasons for this lack of more serious attention, but career incentives that reward going with the tried and tested, and censure results that depart from the norm, may well be among them (Knetsch, 2000). While care must be taken with environmental applications, as with all analyses, the case for continued lack of attention to these findings seems to lack an easy justification.

Note

1 Reproduced and adapted from Knetsch, J (Quah and Toh, 2011).

45 Cost-benefit analysis in developing countries[1]

1   The differing circumstances under which developed and developing economies operate have no bearing on the fundamental principles underlying CBA. However, in applying the principles, certain valuation techniques commonly used in developed countries are not as appropriate for developing countries. To shed light on this, this chapter examines how labour, goods and financial markets differ between developing and developed economies, and how these differences may result in erroneous CBA if certain valuation techniques are used. The chapter further discusses behavioural aspects, and the relative advantages and disadvantages of employing various valuation techniques specifically in conducting CBA in developing countries.

Differences between developing and developed nations, and the implications on CBA: labour markets

2   There are three differences between developed and developing economies pertaining to labour markets that could significantly influence the results of CBA. The first is the higher level of disguised unemployment in developing economies, the second is the higher level of household production, and the third is the incompleteness of labour markets in developing nations.

Unlike in developed nations, the majority of the workforce in developing nations is employed in agriculture. In India, for example, 44 per cent of the labour force is employed in the agricultural sector (World Bank, 2018). This in itself will not necessarily distort a CBA. However, a significant portion of these agricultural workers are actually only employed in name and paid a token wage despite making no marginal contribution to the production process. This practice of disguised employment is not uncommon in developing nations, where farm owners routinely hire family members and pay them a token wage, even when there are clearly no additional productive gains to be made from their employment apart from familial goodwill.

This phenomenon has serious implications for CBA, which requires that items be valued at their opportunity cost. The opportunity cost to reallocate a disguised unemployed labourer to a new position is zero. However, conventional CBA values the cost of labour using the wage rate. If a government project resulted in a labourer moving from disguised unemployment to a new, productive position paying the same wage, that old wage would count as a cost for a project (see Chapter 12). But in reality, there is no opportunity cost associated with that labourer's prior position – the prior employer loses no productivity when the worker leaves, and just saves the wage. In this instance, the cost is overestimated.

The challenges posed by disguised unemployment are illustrated in the following scenario. Imagine a communal farm that currently produces $9,000 worth of output every year. The farm is co-owned by the whole village that has a population of 30 people. All the villagers who work on the farm received an equal share of the total output's value, i.e. $300 per year. Because there are more than enough farmyards, ten of the workers do not actually contribute to the total farm output. That is, even if they stopped working, the farm output would remain exactly the same. Therefore, the marginal output of the last ten farmhands working in the village is zero.

Now, imagine that the government proposed to start a project in this particular village that would generate $1,000 in benefits. To carry out this project, the government will have to hire ten local workers, at a total cost of $3,000, which is the exact amount those ten villagers would have earned working at the farm for the year. A typical practice in CBA is to enter the prior wages of the workers who switch jobs as a cost item, because it is assumed that their prior wages represent their productivity at their past jobs. Since the project reallocates their labour, the opportunity cost is the work they would have otherwise been doing.

Using this calculus, the hypothetical project yields net costs, because the wages of $3,000 are greater than the benefits of $1,000. However, in truth, the opportunity cost for the ten farmhands giving up their previous employment should be zero, since their marginal productivity was zero. When they quit working at the farm, it continues to generate $9,000 worth of output. The average output per farmhand increased from $300 to $450, because ten of the original workers no longer draw income from the farm. Those ten workers, in their new positions, together generate $1,000 worth of value. Adding together the farm and new government project, the total productivity for the village is now $10,000. Indeed, the government could pay for the project by taxing the 20 villagers that remain as farmhands, and everyone could be made better off by the new project's additional benefits.

Therefore, it is especially important that developing countries pay attention to this limitation, and that low-skilled labour is reduced by a shadow wage rate factor, if available, to adjust for the overestimation.

There still is a caveat. Although hiring the disguised unemployed is said to carry zero opportunity cost based on productivity, this does not account for the value of foregone leisure or household production, including childcare and household work and maintenance. Such items may be significant if leisure is highly valued by individuals or if a large portion of the disguised employed are indeed actually employed in valuable household production.

This leads us to our next point: there are higher levels of household production in developing nations than in developed nations. Household production is defined as the production of goods and services by members of a household for their own consumption, using their own capital and their own unpaid labour[2]. This value is difficult to measure. Valuation methods generally fall into two categories: the opportunity cost method, where household production is valued at the foregone wage rate, and the replacement cost method, where the value is the cost of employing other people to do the work (Quah, 1993).

In developed economies, household production can be priced because labour markets are generally efficient and reflect opportunity costs, and because demand for hired help exists. The same cannot be said for developing economies, where labour markets are largely incomplete, and households undertake most household production. The households do not pay themselves for their household production, and therefore, such production cannot be easily priced. The same problem can be seen in the production that occurs in the underground economy, where illicit transactions of goods and services are not captured.

The valuation problem is twofold. First, there is the methodological issue that techniques relying on market behaviours to measure preferences will be inadequate because markets for hired help either do not exist or are significantly incomplete in developing countries. Second, the higher levels of production undertaken by households mean that CBA, which does not incorporate this production, is biased and inaccurate. While developed nations may sometimes face similar problems in conducting CBA, the scale of the impact is much smaller. Accordingly, the accuracy of CBA is much higher because of the existence and relative efficiency of the market for hired help, and much lower levels of household production.

The third difference between labour markets in developed and developing economies is their relative incompleteness and hence, inefficiency of the latter when compared to the former. This arises for a variety of reasons, including the extent of information failure and the ability of employers in developing countries to exercise monopsonistic power in the labour market.

The implication of the above differences is that wages in developing countries rarely reflect an individual's valuation of job attributes. In an efficient labour market, by contrast, undesirable job attributes are compensated with wage premiums, which may then be used to place a value on the job attributes. The wage premiums represent individuals' willingness to accept the disutility arising from the undesirable job attribute. The implication for CBA in developing countries is that intangible job characteristics, such as status and location, cannot be valued using hedonic pricing. A specific implication is the potential error in estimating the value of statistical life (VOSL) (see Chapter 50), which is conventionally calculated by studying the wage premiums associated with the increased level of risk of losing one's life on the job, and then extrapolating to estimate the theoretical amount required to compensate someone for the loss of life. Using wage premiums that do not accurately reflect the compensation required for the differing levels of risk results in an erroneous VOSL. This has severe implications for all other CBA that will be used to evaluate projects that impact health and safety, since the values of many costs and benefits are derived from the VOSL.

Goods markets

3   Another major difference between developing and developed economies is that the goods markets in developing economies are likely to be less efficient than those of developed economies because of information asymmetry. The disparity is even more apparent since the advent of the Internet, which has, by and large, been more accessible to and more effectively utilized by the developed world. This point is best illustrated by the growth of online shopping, which has driven down prices in the developed world but has not had the same impact in the developing world.

Additionally, unlike in developed economies, the goods markets of developing countries are more likely to be distorted by taxation, subsidies, or other forms of governmental interventions (Dinwiddy and Teal, 1996).

The inefficiencies and distortions of the goods markets mean that in developing countries, prices may not reflect the true values of goods. Therefore, using prices to value input items, as is usually done in developed countries, would likely result in an inaccurate CBA in a developing country.

An indirect issue that arises from the inefficiencies and distortions of the goods markets is the valuation of intangibles and externalities. Typically, in developed economies, where the goods markets are considered efficient, intangibles and externalities are valued in relation to consumption through a revealed preference approach. For example, in estimating the value of national parks and related recreation in the United States, the travel cost approach is commonly used. This approach obtains a demand curve by examining the price of recreation in a national park, which is the cost visitors are willing to pay to travel to visit the park (Beal, 1995; Fix and Loomis, 1997). However, the credibility of such revealed preferences breaks down when a goods market does not produce prices that reflect the true value of a good. In the example of the national park, if fuel were distributed through a rationing system, then the private cost of travelling would be very hard to determine, and the demand curve obtained through typical techniques would be inaccurate. Rations and other forms of price distortions are prevalent in many countries in the developing world. The consensus is that where there are market distortions, shadow prices – the estimated prices of a good or service for which no accurate market price exists – should be used.[3]

The calculation of shadow prices is also subject to complications and much debate. Tradable goods in developing economies are an example of a class of goods for which it is difficult to obtain shadow prices. The problem arises due to the fact that exchange rates are required in the calculation of shadow prices for tradable goods. Unlike developed economies, the exchange rates of developing economies may fluctuate wildly and may not be reflective of the appropriate exchange rates. This exacerbates the issue of accuracy when using CBA, especially the technique of shadow price calculation.

Financial markets

4   Like the labour and goods markets, the financial markets in developing economies are also weaker than those in developed economies. Private banks in developing countries usually wield considerable monopolistic power, which they may exploit by charging interest rates above what a free market would produce (Yildirim and Philippatos, 2007). This bears on the issue of discounting, as the social discount rate takes into account both the opportunity cost of capital and a society's time preference (see Chapter 40). In developed economies, the opportunity cost of capital is usually estimated by the market interest rate, coupled with sensitivity analysis, especially where social time preference rate is not well studied. This is reasonable because financial markets in developed economies are generally mature enough to generate sufficient competition to drive down the market interest rate so that it truly reflects the opportunity cost of capital. Thus, it is less contentious to use the market interest rate to represent the opportunity cost of capital in calculating the social discount rate in developed economies. Unfortunately, the same cannot be said for developing economies.

Interest rates in developing economies are likely to be higher than the true opportunity cost of capital, because of profiteering by private banks. If the social discount rate for developing economies is calculated using the market interest rate as the opportunity cost of capital, the result is a higher social discount rate than is appropriate for measurement. Consequently, both future benefits and costs are more heavily discounted, and CBA is biased in favour of projects that yield short-term benefits and long-term costs. Thus, both the opportunity cost rate and the social time preference rate used as discount rates in most cost-benefit studies need adjustment downwards.

The market power exercised by private banks is different from the way time preferences in developing and developed societies are influenced by other social and economic factors. Populations in developing economies have shorter lifespans and lower incomes. Thus, these populations often have a higher preference for current, rather than future, consumption when compared to the preferences of populations in developed countries. Developing societies are likely to have shorter time preferences, and *ceteris paribus*, their social discount rate will therefore be higher. This difference in preference further raises social discount rates, albeit not as a result of some inefficiency in the market, but more reflective of genuine differences in individual preferences.

5   Overall, the nature of the labour, goods, and financial markets in developing economies clearly differs from those in developed economies. These differences can significantly affect the result and accuracy of a CBA if certain valuation or discounting techniques are used. These distinctions between developed and developing economies should be kept in mind by analysts seeking to develop accurate measures of the costs and benefits of social policies in developing countries.

Behavioural economics and cost-benefit analysis in developing countries

6   In addition to fundamental differences between developed and developing countries with regards to discount rates, differences in behaviours also affect experimental design and results. This difference in behaviour detracts from traditional CBA, suggesting that both gains and losses have to account for psychological as well as physical attributes.

Loss aversion

7   In practice, the study of loss aversion is the most common example which alters measurement values in CBA. Theoretically, gains and losses should be identical in nature and hold the same valuation when it comes to measurement. In the case of gains, it is the maximum amount that a person is willing to pay while losses account for the maximum payment that a person is willing to accept for the loss. Results of CBA should then be a summation of the respective valuations of gains and losses, with the end results being similar (Henderson, 1941).

Yet, there is a significant disparity when measured, with values that accounted for a person's willingness to accept being far larger than his willingness to pay (see Chapter 44). Knowing that differences do arise when considering people's valuations of losses and gains, failing to account for this will create inefficient and often biased decision making. This is especially the case when analysing developing countries where the majority of the population is often poor, making them more risk averse since their margin for error is lower as compared to individuals in developed countries.

The choice of measurement

8   Another debate would be the use of appropriate methods of measurement. Due to loss aversion, the use of the WTP criterion, a method of measurement in CBA, may sometimes not be appropriate for situations where WTA measures should have been implemented instead, leading to systematic undervaluation of the actual costs (Knetsch, 2003).

This presents a danger in policy making in developing countries as policies that aim to counter actions that have negative externalities, such as pollution, are likely to be under-weighted, and there may be an undue encouragement of activities that have negative consequences. This explains lax environmental standards, especially since the benefits of economic growth are quantitative while the costs are subject to measurement bias.

Sunk costs

9   Another behavioural oddity is that of sunk costs. Behavioural economics shows that many people consider sunk costs when making decisions, leading to suboptimal choices. This has serious implications for the evaluation of infrastructure expansion. For example, would an old ferry's capital cost be considered when deciding a new ferry or alternative transport mode? Behavioural economics, in considering sunk costs, tells us that economic agents often fall prey to this fallacy.

In developed economies, this may not pose a major problem with a larger budget but, in poorer developing countries, it makes a big difference as to whether the old ferry is kept or scrapped. The correct decision based on CBA is that as long as the old ferry can still cover its operating cost, the decision to have the new ferry should not be affected by this. In other words, CBA does not consider sunk costs.

Challenges of various valuation techniques in developing economies

10   As illustrated, incomplete accounting in the labour, goods and financial markets in developing economies make the assumptions required by revealed preference approaches untenable. Stated preference approaches may not be entirely suitable for developing economies either. The behavioural effects may be even more pronounced in developing economies because of the relative rarity of people's experiences in survey participation. List (2003) shows that behavioural effects are, at least in part, brought about by a lack of experience with the decision-making circumstances. Therefore, the magnitude of behavioural biases in stated preference approaches is likely to be much more significant in developing nations. Methodological biases in stated preference approaches also tend to be larger in developing nations because of the lack of trained interviewers (Hanley and Barbier, 2009). One common problem is the inability of both interviewers and interviewees to

differentiate between willingness to pay and ability to pay. Such misunderstandings are further exacerbated by cultural and linguistic differences. Additionally, surveys typically carry significant costs that cash-strapped governments will be hard-pressed to cover. Thus, particularly for developing nations, these two valuation techniques have obvious pitfalls which may render results dubious.

11   While neither revealed nor stated preference approaches are entirely suitable for developing nations, a pair-wise comparison approach may prove to be a valid and useful option (see Chapter 43). Nonetheless, in conducting CBA, governments of developing economies will have to exercise caution in choosing the most appropriate valuation method for their purposes in order to avoid distortions.

Conclusion

12   CBA can and should be used by the developing world. CBA is a very useful tool for policy makers. Conducting the analysis requires asking important questions, including what costs and benefits should be measured and how to measure them; what communities and stakeholders will receive the benefits and pay the costs; how uncertainties and equity issues will be addressed; what the appropriate investment decision criteria are; and whether there are constraints on the results. Systematic decision making that uses consistent and transparent methodologies is valuable in formulating public policy in both developed and developing countries.

Notes

1 Adapted from Quah (2017b); Quah (2013).
2 For a more detailed definition, see Ironmonger (2001).
3 This issue is not a new one, and there is an abundance of literature dealing with the matter. Boardman *et al.* (2006) provides a good summary of the literature and methods.

46 The value of time

1   Transport projects are designed chiefly either to accommodate an increasing number of travellers or to reduce journey time. Less frequently, they are designed to increase comfort or convenience of travel.

It is hardly necessary to remark that, if a project does save journey time, the required compensating variation is equal to the largest sum a person is willing to pay in order to save that amount of time. And, indeed, there have been a few interesting but unsophisticated attempts to estimate this willingness-to-pay figure for travel time saved for different income groups. Although further refinements would take account of the element of comfort and reliability, it will be argued in this chapter that, notwithstanding frequent recourse in CBA to arbitrary calculations based on hourly earnings, the value of time saved (or spent) necessarily varies with the context in which time is saved (or spent).

2   It is possible also to put a value on the time saved from improvements in industrial technology. If, for example, the introduction of a new method of producing good x turns out to increase productivity by 50 per cent, which enables a given output to be produced in one-third less than the previous time, the valuation of the time that is saved will depend on the output of the good x that is subsequently produced.

Following the above, if, to take one extreme, the workforce employed in producing x is constrained to work the same number of hours for the same pay, output will rise by 50 per cent, and the supply curve of x will fall by one-third. In a competitive economy, the resulting increase in consumer surplus – which will then be the chief measure of social gain – is likely to be less than it would be if the output of x that was produced were such that price is equal to marginal cost.

At the other extreme, the whole of the gain from increased productivity is appropriated by the workers employed in producing x by a rise of 50 per cent in their wages. In consequence, the supply curve of x remains unchanged and (ignoring any additional demand for x resulting from the increased income of the x workers, which is apt to be negligible) also the demand curve for x.

Although, more generally, the outcome will be somewhere between these two extremes, we need not trouble to elaborate further because, in CBA, the need to value time saved, when it arises, is almost invariably in connection with improvements in transport or travel, whether by land, sea or air.

3   In the attempts to measure the value of time saved, at least under the assumption that there are no changes in comfort, etc., a once-common method was to

value an hour saved by a given person as equal to the social value of his (marginal) product.[1] Thus, if an improvement in public transport had no other effect than that of enabling a man to save exactly one hour from his journey to work each day, this method of valuing time saved would be valid only if (i) our man would accept an offer, if it was made, of working an additional hour at the existing rate of pay, and (ii) the social marginal product of the additional hour worked were a valid measure of the additional social benefit.

While (i) is far from certain, (ii) is certainly not true. For one thing, a part (generally the greater part) of the measured value of the additional hour's output will be some minimal compensation to our man for the additional work undertaken – which, by definition, does not increase his welfare. This method of valuing time saved cannot, therefore, be accepted as a proxy for the true value of time saved, namely, the amount a man is willing to pay for the time saved, ignoring any externalities.

4   Although it is indeed correct to value the amount of time saved by the most a person is willing to pay for it, which will, therefore, vary widely between one person and another, we are not to suppose that the saving of time is always a good thing. The tacit assumption that travelling is but an unavoidable disutility, simply a means to reach a destination, is not generally valid.

There can be situations when reducing time is far from being a good thing. Indeed, when a person is willing to pay for additional time, whether in travelling or in some other activity – a prime example being that of the plea of the lover in the once-popular song, 'Give me five minutes more, only five minutes more ... in your arms'. Apart from the joys of a prolonged embrace, however, there can be many familiar instances when the saving of time is a negative benefit or, put more positively, the availability of *more* time is a positive benefit.

If a person is on a train bound for a seaside holiday, some delay at a small railway station that allows him to detrain, to stretch his legs and enjoy the views, might be much welcomed. A summer holiday along the coast of the Costa del Sol that is unexpectedly prolonged for a couple of days is a delay that is more likely to be thought of as a bit of good luck than otherwise. Again, a representative of a firm who is on a business trip may not mind a delay in congenial surroundings, as it is in the firm's time anyway. He may well enjoy travelling much more than spending time in the office and will always prefer say, crossing the Atlantic by ship rather than by plane. So far as he is concerned, any shortening of his travel time is regarded as a loss.[2]

5   Turning to those cases which the cost-benefit economist more frequently addresses, those in which any time saved is unambiguously a good, the valuation of time saved will obviously vary according to the circumstances. A young man desperate to be on time for his first date would be willing to pay a large sum to avoid delay if his car were stuck in a traffic jam.

In more ordinary circumstances, a reduction by, say, a half hour of his daily commuting time would be valued by a person according to the anticipated use to which he would put the spare half hour. He might use some of the extra time available at the gym or jogging. He might stay longer at home in the mornings, extending his breakfast time, reading the newspaper or watching television. The satisfaction he obtains from the way he chooses to spend the additional half hour will, of course, determine the most he is willing to pay for it. (It is not impossible, however, that he preferred the original journey if he travelled by train, there being just about enough time to relax, read the newspaper and perhaps finish the cross-word puzzle).[3]

A more interesting case would be that in which there are enough people, each willing to pay an additional $3,000 several times a year to fly the Atlantic in no more than an hour if the opportunity arose. If this were known, it might prove worthwhile to construct and operate such an aero-engineering phenomenon. Were it to be so, were such flights to take place, we should be able to make a rough calculation of the worth (on average) of the saving of five hours of flying time to those who choose regularly to fly on the new supersonic plane.

6   Finally, in considering any reduction in an existing delay, the extent of the delay is important. There is obviously some *minimum sensible* level below which any delay has no perceptible value for society. An investment that would save about ten seconds' time on a daily journey is not worth having, even if many millions of people 'benefit' from it. No one would really care much. Indeed, in a journey that currently takes, say, six hours, a ten-minute saving of time is hardly likely to have a perceptible effect on people's welfare, and there would be a case for ignoring it, irrespective of the number of people involved. In general, it is the proportion of time saved that counts as much as the absolute amount of time saved.[4]

Notes

1   For a good review of the literature on the value of travel time savings in project evaluation, see Abelson (2003).
2   To the corporation who employs him, however, the saving in time might be a gain, but only if the time saved were large enough to enable his presence in the office to add something to profits. Obviously, a few hours' saving would be useless in this connection, and it is uncertain whether even a few days would make a difference. Furthermore, even though a saving of the executive's time can be counted on to increase the corporation's profit somewhat, the economist engaged in *social* CBA does not necessarily equate the increased profit with increased social benefit. The increase in profit may well be at the expense of the profits of competitors. Only if the saving in the executive's time resulted in some additional value of output to the economy as a whole (*net* of external effects) would it rate as a social benefit. In contrast, the owner of a small business, say a retail shop, who can travel only by closing his shop, or by suffering a reduction in sales, would benefit by the saving of a few daylight hours of travelling.
3   One of our colleagues enjoys reading journal papers by deliberately choosing public transportation over private cars!
4   As stated earlier, there are other fairly obvious factors such as comfort to be considered also. Many people will prefer a journey during which they can sit and read quietly to a shorter journey during which they can do neither, or to a shorter journey during which they have to make one or more changes. They may also prefer a means of transport *A* which arrives punctually to a means of transport *B* which, although it *averages less* on the journey, sometimes takes longer than the *A* transport. Greater frequency of public transport or a more convenient timetable may be rated more highly than some perceptible saving in existing journey time. Although it appeared some time ago, an excellent article by Tipping (1968) discusses such factors in more detail. For a study that relates the value of automobile travel time with implications, and for congestion and public policy, see Small *et al.* (2003). Here, the authors use a variant of stated preference models to estimate the value that commuters are willing to pay to save travel time.

47 Measuring the benefits of recreational areas

1   Increases in population, in income per capita, in leisure opportunities, in health consciousness and improvement in transport infrastructure have, to a large extent, accounted for much of the growth of recreational activities. This, in turn, has led to the increasing importance given to issues of public planning and managing of land and water resources.

2   In most discussions on the value of facilities for recreation, there is some mention of 'non-economic' considerations. Recreational activity may be seen, for instance, as promoting creativity or individual freedom, or as encouraging democratic participation or inculcating a healthy outlook. Whether such values or attitudes can, or should, be brought into the calculus is an open question. There is certainly a repugnance at the idea of attempting to bring humane and perhaps transcendental considerations 'into relation with the measuring rod of money', and though we are in sympathy with it, we are uncertain just where the line should be drawn. For that reason, we shall steer away from this controversy, at least until the close of the following chapter, and confine ourselves to the concepts of the direct benefits that the economist should certainly attempt to measure.

3   Let us restrict the analysis to parks, particularly large national parks, as an interesting exercise in the application of cost-benefit principles. Clearly the economic justification for introducing a park of any size whatever is that its total social benefits will exceed its total opportunity costs. As for the *optimal* size of the park under consideration, it is required, in addition, that the marginal social benefit be equal to the marginal cost.

4   Now consider in more detail the long-run determination of the *size* of a park within some given location. The information we should need from each potential visitor to the park is as follows: for any x acres of a park in a given location, what is the incremental value he places on the number of separate trips per annum? To illustrate, for a specific kind of park of one acre, the value the ith person places on each of a number of successive trips per annum can be plotted in Figure 47.1. As he is not constrained to take more trips to the park each year than he chooses, we shall count only trips with positive values. The figure reveals that he will choose to make four separate trips each year, the fifth trip having a zero or negative value for him. The total area of these four rectangles represents the maximum sum he is willing to pay per annum for this specific kind of park of one acre.

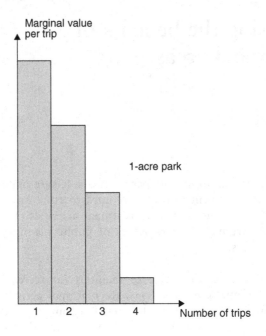

Figure 47.1

For a park in the same location of two acres, his marginal valuation of successive trips will be somewhat larger. In consequence, he would choose to make more trips as depicted in Figure 47.2; in our example, six trips per annum.

We could then repeat the exercise for parks of three, four, five acres and so on to some maximum acreage possible.

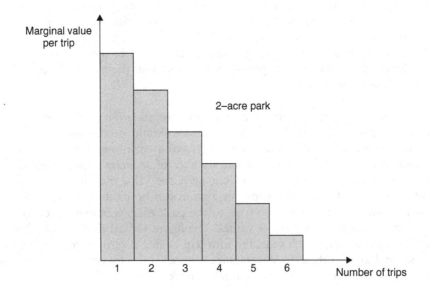

Figure 47.2

For the *i*th individual visitor, we now plot the *differences* in, or increments to, his *total* valuation for successively larger parks as in Figure 47.3. The total valuation of a park with only one acre is given by the area of that first rectangle in Figure 47.3, which area is, of course, equal to the total area of the four trips he would choose to make each year to a one-acre park, as already shown in Figure 47.1. The size of the second rectangle in Figure 47.3 is equal to the difference between the total area of Figure 47.2 and that of Figure 47.1, this difference being the additional amount of money he would pay for a park that is of two acres – one acre larger than the original park. Clearly, the size of the third rectangle in our Figure 47.3 must be equal to the additional money the individual is willing to pay for a park of three acres, and so on until the increment he is willing to pay for the park of an additional acre is shown to be just a little above zero when the eight-acre park is contemplated.

It should be evident that these successive increments of value for successive one-acre increments of parkland (assumed to be declining) would become more like a smoothly declining marginal valuation curve as the increments became smaller.

If, for convenience, we assume continuity in the construction of this individual marginal valuation curve, and also for marginal valuation curves of all prospective visitors, they must now be added together to construct a marginal valuation curve for all the prospective visitors taken together. As a park is a collective good inasmuch as, in the absence of congestion costs, the costs of creating and maintaining the park are not attributable to any one person (the benefits being simultaneously enjoyed by all the visitors) their marginal valuation curves are to be aggregated vertically, whereby, we end up with a *collective* marginal valuation curve with respect to the size of the park, each increment of valuation being equal to the sum of the valuations of all the individuals for that increment.

The intersection of this collective marginal valuation curve with that of the long-run marginal cost of extending the size of the park determines the optimal size of the park to be built.

Formally speaking, then, the necessary (marginal) conditions to be met for determining the optimal size of the park are given by

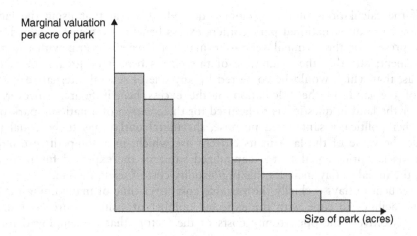

Figure 47.3

$$\sum_{i}^{n} V_i \geq k$$

where V_i is the ith person's marginal valuation with respect to park size, and k is the long-run marginal cost. (Since the park is an optional collective good, all the V_i are positive.[1])

The necessary total condition that has to be met is that $\sum^{n} V_i \geq K$, where Vi is the total valuation of the chosen park by the ith person, and K is equal to the total long-period opportunity cost of the park.[2]

5   Two issues must now be faced: the implications of the *ceteris paribus* clause relevant to the problem, and the treatment of costs and benefits over time.

The calculation of the benefits by the above method is designed for the introduction of an additional park and for the determination of its size, given the existing spread of population, the existing resource endowments and the existing product and factor prices, in particular, the existing number of parks and recreational facilities provided either free or at some set of prices. Clearly, if there are already a number of such parks available in the community, the *apparent* aggregate benefit of all these parks, if obtained simply by aggregating the areas under the marginal benefit curves of the community obtained on the above principle, will overstate the *true* social benefit – the difference between the apparent and the true benefit being larger the closer can the parks be regarded as substitutes for one another. A correct method of calculating the aggregate social benefit of a number of parks is outlined in Chapter 5. In principle, the method would require that the parks be introduced in hypothetical sequence: to the total benefit of introducing only a single park in the community, there is then added the total benefit of introducing a second park on the assumption that the first park is, indeed, already in existence, and so on. A correct calculation of the total social benefit is, of course, important whenever the economist is concerned with the total contribution to society's welfare of an existing number or a proposed number of parks.

6   If the calculations of the economist do indeed reveal that using the land in question to create a national park confers excess benefits over cost – valued either in the present or the terminal year – he may yet have to reckon with a political requirement; one that the magnitude of this excess benefit be greater than, or as great as, that which would be conferred by any one of several alternative specified uses of the land. In the calculation of the excess benefit figure, however, and whether the land in question is to be used for the creation of a national park or for any other politically sanctioned purpose, the initial outlay has to be equal to or include the value of the land in its current use which, in a competitive economy, has a market price equal to the capitalized value of the expected future returns. Thus, the initial outlay includes this opportunity cost of using the land.

Subsequent outlays – chiefly the variable costs over time of maintaining the park and its facilities to cope with the expected number of visitors – are, as indicated earlier, effectively the opportunity costs of the factors that are employed for this purpose.[3]

Turning, to the calculation of the terminal (or present) value of the net benefit stream, since the annual benefits enjoyed by the visitors are, so to speak, in kind – conceived as being consumed as they occur – they may be compounded forward to the terminal year (or discounted to the present) using society's rate of time preference r.

7   Finally, we remind the reader that an excess of benefits over cost – whether calculated as a terminal value or a present value – may be interpreted as conferring on the community a potential Pareto improvement only if all who are affected by the project remain alive over the period. If, as is likely, generations overlap during the life of the project, the inter-generational difficulty broached earlier has to be faced. The excess benefit over cost that is calculated must then be understood as conferring only a potential *potential* Pareto improvement.

Notes

1 Fora park of x acres, $V_i = \delta V_i/\delta x$ and $k = \delta K/\delta x$, where K is the total cost.
2 The reader might think that, if such information were readily available, he could perhaps use linear programming methods to determine the number, size, location and other specific features of parks serving the community. But in as much as the parks are substitutes, the value people attach to any one of them depends, *inter alia*, on the existing number of parks, their size, location, etc. The objective function to be maximized cannot therefore be calculated. In order to devise some optimal system of parks, we should have to use a sequential procedure; finding, say, the highest discounted benefit–cost ratio for the location of some minimal size park, followed by the next highest benefit–cost ratio for some minimal additional park area, either attached to the first or located elsewhere – and so on down to a point where the budget is exhausted, or where the benefit–cost ratio of the marginal park acreage is no higher than that of investment projects generally.
3 Should the number of visitors prove to be greater than the number anticipated, and congestion costs are incurred, we conclude that we have underestimated the number of visitors and, therefore, also the excess benefit.

48 Travel cost method

1 Although we are primarily concerned in this volume with the validity of the concepts and techniques used in CBA, and with particular attention to what exactly it is that we should be seeking to measure, we cannot in this instance resist some brief discussion and comments on the ingenious attempt made as far back as 1959 by Marion Clawson to derive a demand curve for recreational activity, in particular for national parks, under a number of simplifying assumptions.[1]

The Clawson concept is that of an already existing park of given acreage and facilities, so the question of determining the optimal size of the park does not arise in his paper. In principle, and considering only direct benefits for the present, one could discover for each person the maximum sum he would be willing to pay (over and above the costs of the journey) for the privilege of one trip a year to this particular park, for two trips a year and so on, until he would pay nothing for an additional annual trip. The aggregate over all persons of such maximum sums constitutes a measure of the total direct social benefit per annum.

The first relationship estimated by Clawson could be looked at as a sort of gravity model, inasmuch as the traffic from any particular area to the park is inversely related to the distance and directly to the population of the area. From areas of varying distance to Yosemite National Park (the park example he used), Clawson estimated the total dollar cost per one-day visit in the year 1953 on the basis of time and mileage, using a number of assumptions of varying degrees of plausibility, such as four persons per car travelling 400 miles a day and, more restrictive, that the main purpose of the journey was to visit Yosemite and there being then no entrance charge to the park.

2 The elements of his method can be brought quickly into focus by inventing figures for only three hypothetical areas *A*, *B* and *C*, situated at varying distances from Yosemite, rather than by introducing his more elaborate estimates. The hypothetical data required are given in Table 48.1

The corresponding figures of the last two columns enable us to plot three points, *A*, *B* and *C*, in Figure 48.1.

If we now make the strong assumption that the population of each of these areas is a perfect sample with respect to all relevant variables of the population of all three areas taken together, a curve fitted through points *A*, *B* and *C*, can be interpreted as a relation between the proportion of the total population visiting Yosemite and the cost per visit. Thus, if, as stated, 50 per cent of the population of area *A* is willing to make the trip when the cost is \$20, we may infer that this sum is the *least* any person from area *A* is willing to pay for the trip – the marginal trip,

Table 48.1

Area	Population	Distance from Yosemite	Number of visits to Yosemite as percentage of population[a]	Journey cost per visit[b]
A	10,000	100 miles	50%	$20
B	20,000	300 miles	15%	$40
C	30,000	800 miles	5%	$100

Note

a There is, of course, nothing to prevent the number of visits per annum exceeding 100 per cent of that area's population, though in fact, this was not the case caused by Clawson.

b If it can be assumed that expenditure on food etc. once in the park is little different from what it is at home, we could add together for the visitors coming from any one area, say the sea area, two-day, three-day and n-day stays in the park along with the one-day stays there. Since the journey costs are the same for the marginal n-day visitors, the total benefit enjoyed by this n-day visitor can also be taken to be just equal to the total travelling costs. If these assumptions are implausible, it would be necessary to separate the demand curves for one-day, two-day, and up to n-day visitors.

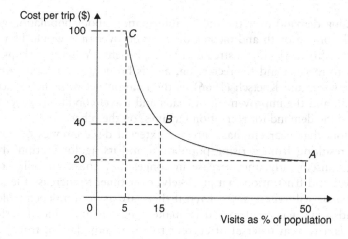

Figure 48.1

that is, is worth just $20, and the intramarginal trips are worth more. This means that a sort of marginal valuation curve passes through point A and – inasmuch as the population samples of areas B and C are identical with that of A – it also passes through points B and C.[2]

3 Having made the assumption that the inhabitants of A, B and C may be regarded as identical with respect to the value they place on Yosemite National Park, the percentages along the horizontal axis of Figure 35.1 can be translated into actual numbers of visits from a total population of 60,000, this being the combined populations of areas A, B and C. Corresponding to the cost per visit of $20, $40 and $100 along the vertical axis of the figure, the annual numbers of visits are 30,000, 9,000 and 3,000, respectively.[3]

This resulting curve, referred to by Clawson as a demand curve, can properly be interpreted as a WTP or marginal valuation curve. Thus, if we imagined that all the 60,000 inhabitants lived so close to Yosemite that the cost of the trip itself is virtually zero, the dollar cost per trip measured along the vertical axis of the figure can be translated into the price charged for entry into the park; the lower the price, the greater the number of annual visits to the park.

On the one hand, a monopolist contemplating this demand curve would, of course, set a price or entrance fee that would maximize his net revenue, as a result of which the number of visits would be fewer than the optimal number. On the other hand, although a perfectly discriminating monopolist would vary the entrance fee so as to attract the optimal number of visits, he would, by definition, appropriate to himself the whole of the consumer surplus that would otherwise be enjoyed by the visitors.

The effect of congestion or crowding at recreational sites may have a significant negative impact on the demand for park recreation. Congestion can be estimated directly by eliciting users' willingness to pay for its reduction.

4   In predicting demand over the future, information about population growth, per capita 'real' income growth and income distribution over time would be required for all types of investment yielding a stream of future benefits. What is perhaps of particular relevance to the demand for recreation, and is brought out in some of the charts drawn by Clawson and Knetsch (1966), is the relation between the reduction in the working week, and the improvement in roads and travel conditions generally, on the one hand, and the demand for recreation facilities, on the other.

Other factors that bear emphasis are the external diseconomies or adverse spill-over effects resulting from a rising population and its agglomeration about urban centres and, consequently, the increase in congestion, noise, air pollution and the resulting stress and frustration that are likely, over time, to increase the demand for national parks or wilderness areas. Even if there are as yet no dependable estimates of such trends, one may be disposed to make generous allowance for them. Thus, unless there is a radical reversal of current trends in population, traffic and industrialization, the world inhabited by our grandchildren will be more crowded and built-up than the world today. The average person at some time in the future is then sure to be willing to pay more for recreation facilities, for natural beauty and wilderness areas, than is the average person today with the same 'real' income. In other words, if the trends associated with sustained economic growth persist into the future, the terms of trade between manufactured goods and natural goods will tend to move increasingly in favour of the latter.

5   Two other factors should be entered into the benefits of such reserved areas of natural beauty which, though they appear related, are in fact quite distinct. First, there is the 'option demand' arising from a willingness to pay by all those people who do not anticipate making specific use in the foreseeable future of the particular area, notwithstanding which they are aware of the possibility that their customary sources of recreation might be reduced or withdrawn. They therefore have an interest in supporting the preservation of the area. For instance, they may, at some future date, have to move to another area of the country and, as a form of insurance, they would be willing to make some contribution to a number of reserved areas that they cannot use today but may be able make use of later.[4]

Second, there is a 'non-participant' (or 'disinterested') demand (sometimes called 'existence' demand) arising from the willingness to pay by all those people who are concerned simply that such goods be available to the nation or to humanity at large. They may not be concerned in the least with insuring themselves against future contingencies, and they may well believe that they will never have occasion to enjoy the good in question, but it gives them satisfaction to know it exists. There are, for instance, a large number of people who do indeed care that wilderness areas be left on Earth, that Venice should not sink beneath the waters, that whales and other species should be preserved, and yet will readily admit that they will never visit a wilderness area or travel through Venice or behold a whale. Their welfare would be reduced if they were to know that such things had disappeared from the Earth.

Such non-participant demand might indeed be thought of as translating into money values, at least, some of those 'non-economic' considerations referred to at the beginning of the preceding chapter. If people's feelings about what is 'right and proper' are sufficiently strong to induce them to contribute something in order to have their aspirations realized, there is no good reason for excluding them in principle from a cost-benefit calculation – always provided that the ends sought are not such as to be precluded by an ethical consensus.

6 Finally, we should remind ourselves that WTP used as a measure of the valuation of a benefit is the appropriate CV^{12} measure for the introduction of a good. If, however, the situation is one where some public good is already in existence and the issue is to decide whether it should be demolished in order, say, to erect an industrial estate, the CV^{12} measure of the loss endured is the minimum sum necessary to compensate people for the loss of the park. And this loss will have to include that suffered by those people who do not use the park or even expect to use it yet derive satisfaction from the knowledge that it exists.

As indicated earlier, the use of the CV^{12} measure in cases of environmental destruction – which, in effect, confers property rights, on the beneficiaries of recreational areas – will favour preservation of the environment.

Notes

1 Also see the seminal work on recreational valuation and parks by Clawson and Knetsch (1966). More recent work on comparing benefits and costs in recreation economic decision can be found in Walsh (1986) and Loomis and Walsh (1997).
2 If it were assumed, instead, that some benefit arises from the journey itself, the curve passing through points *A*, *B* and *C* in Figure 35.1 would be closer to the horizontal axis, for the 'true' cost of the journey requires that any incidental benefits are to be subtracted from the calculated time and resource costs of the journey.
3 It may be remarked that the curve in Figure 35.1 bears resemblance to a rectangular hyperbole. This just happens to be the curve that emerges from our postulated data, however, and is unlikely to be the case in any empirically constructed demand curve for recreational areas.
4 A more common example of an optional demand for some facility is that of the willingness of a veteran motorist to pay something toward the upkeep of a bus or rail service that he would not normally make use of but to which he may have recourse if his car should break down.

49 Cost-benefit analysis and public health

1   A major problem in public health studies is on how to give value to changes in health status. Changes in health status may be caused directly by new medical interventions, public health programmes or indirectly by policy interventions improving public safety or environment. Economic evaluations in public health studies are not very common and only recently attracted more attention because of stricter budgetary constraints and higher awareness of costs and benefits not captured by prices and market mechanism. For example, palliative care provided does create costs and benefits beyond direct hospice costs and improvements in quality of life for patients. Palliative care affects family members by changing their quality of life (mental health expenditures), productivity at work, school performance. Moreover, society is also affected through changes in tax incidence, shift of health expenditures across healthcare categories and productivity among members of society whose families are not involved in palliative care directly. Before its application in Public Health studies, CBA was already set as a decision-making framework incorporating health costs and benefits in environmental and public economics that has a long tradition of use of economic valuation techniques.

2   Hence, CBA is especially preferred when there is a need to evaluate large-scale projects with potential long-term effects on public health. These projects include environmental and public health programmes, the effect of new technologies and medications and other more conventional health expenditures and investments such as new hospitals, biomedical research institutes, hospices and vaccines. Carefully executed and complete CBA provides the most transparent framework for decision making. Most of the methodological challenges of CBA evaluation in public health arise from programme effects that could characterize them as 'public goods' that caused positive externalities. Such examples include nation-wide or community level lifestyle interventions to prevent or delay Type 2 diabetes in the US. Though the benefits of delayed/prevented Type 2 diabetes are huge, most of these benefits and savings could be seen only in the long-term horizon (Zhuo et al., 2012). Another example is the construction of walking and cycling tracks that may seem not beneficial from the standpoint of improved road safety due to high costs but certainly beneficial if long-term health benefits of local communities are to be included in CBA (Salensminde, 2004).

To many non-economists working in the area of health and medical care, making a formal evaluation of treatment programmes and health expenditures seem less necessary. It is always worth the money and effort as they would often conclude since healthcare is an absolute necessity and the expenses are unavoidable.

However, public funds are scarce and there are choices that need to be made. Benefits from healthcare expenditures are often not evenly distributed in society and every dollar of sub-optimally used funds poses opportunity costs for society as a whole. The primary question is whether society is willing to pay the costs for such health changes. More costs do not mean more benefits, more expenditures do not mean more gains if we take a stance of a wider public.

3   Are healthcare issues economic issues? And if so, then to what extent can we make use of our economics tools to deal with these issues? Economic evaluation has been developed to provide a useful framework for helping to make the necessary choices faced in the field of healthcare. Only by making an economic evaluation can one be sure that all other ways of making people better off have been considered and, at the same time, all scarce resources have been allocated efficiently.

CBA is more attractive than other valuation frameworks such as cost effectiveness analysis (CEA), cost utility analysis (CUA) because it takes into account both tangible and intangible costs and benefits expressed in the same monetary units. Hence, it allows for easier comparison between policy options and clearly outlines the distribution of costs and benefits for various groups of society. CEA is more widely used in health evaluations because of its relative simplicity and avoidance of 'problematic' valuation of benefits in monetary terms. However, CBA and CEA are not mutually exclusive and they rather complement each other across different cases of health intervention in terms of scale, consequences, externalities etc. For example, CEA could compare different policy options only if they cause non-monetary consequences such as life-years gained and saved years of life. It also omits externalities and neglects non-health benefits. On the other hand, CBA provides a more consistent framework for deciding when government intervention is desirable or not when the wider public is taken into account. There are fewer assumptions imposed behind CBA if you compare it to CEA and CUA though costs and benefits are much more difficult to calculate as they need to be expressed in monetary terms.

4   Common criticisms of CBA's valuation techniques used in public health studies are the same as for CBA used to assess other projects affecting the wider public. Namely, they are the problem of which benefits and costs to include (which outcomes and externalities), what is the time frame for benefits to occur, behavioural biases, etc. These are not very critical and can be successfully addressed if CBA's guidelines are carried out thoroughly. Therefore, complete CBA is an essential tool for decision making, prioritizing expenditures and policy evaluation.

5   Most often, CBA involves the evaluation of a wide range of health, transportation and environmental public projects that impose costs on society in exchange for the reduction in fatality risk. Therefore, a comparison between the costs of reducing risk and the benefits of such reduction is necessary. However, such a comparison between costs and benefits is challenging because it often requires an estimate of the economic value of a statistical life (VoSL). The economic approach of valuing life or, more specifically, valuing the risks of death, is quite different and more appealing than an accounting procedure based on one's

income where the value of an individual's life is calculated as the present value of future earnings. The economic approach of valuing the risks of death requires estimating the rate at which an individual would trade monetary wealth for a small change to the chance of dying within a specified time-period. VoSL, in economics, is a technical term used to evaluate the trade-off between risks of death and monetary wealth. It is neither commonly attached to individual's lives nor used to compare the value of one person's life relative to another's. The word 'statistical' implies that the valuation of a statistical life is concerned with the valuation of changes in the level of risk exposure rather than valuation of the life of a specific individual. When one expends wealth to avoid potentially fatal risks (i.e. WTP) or accepts wealth to take such risks (i.e. WTA), the trade-off between wealth and the probability of death is implicitly defined.

In VoSL literature, the concept can be measured by a person's WTP or WTA. WTP is the maximum monetary amount an individual is willing to sacrifice for a reduction in the risks of death, while WTA stands, in contrast, for the minimum amount an individual is willing to accept for an increase in the risks of death. WTP and WTA values are individual trade-offs in terms of the expenditure needed for improving safety and reducing risks versus alternative types of consumption. These values are explicitly intended to reflect preferences, perceptions and attitudes toward risk of those affected. Totalling such a measure across individuals can provide an estimated VoSL.

6   Another analytic technique widely used in health economics valuations is quality-adjusted life years (QALY). It was designed as a measurement unit to be used in CUA and CBA of healthcare interventions by various healthcare economists in the 1960s and 1970s. The concept of QALY is meant to include the dimension of quality into quantity measured of life since longer life does not mean a better life. Methodologically, it is a ranking of the health status from 0 (dead, 0 QALY) to 1 (perfect, 1 QALY) multiplied by a number of years saved. QALY allows more accurate comparisons between the outcomes of different health interventions. It is further possible to get WTP per QALY using valuation techniques. Obviously, the concept of QALY and its valuation in monetary terms are not without methodological controversy. As pointed out by Pinto-Prades *et al.* (2009), estimation of universal monetary value for QALY is faced with considerable challenges due to differences in severity, duration and risk reductions across diseases and medical interventions.

Nevertheless, these issues are fundamental to any techniques used to value health benefits. Regardless of its limitations, QALY and other valuation techniques do pave the way to better informed decision making. When QALY is included in CBA, it could drastically change the benefit–cost ratio of which intervention is preferred. For instance, CBA of dual-dispatch defibrillation in Sweden revealed that benefits far exceed costs when QALY is applied. It contrasts with the results of cost-effectiveness analysis since it demonstrated efficiency below threshold levels used in Sweden for health interventions (Sund *et al.*, 2012) . In another study, CBA of cataract surgeries using self-reported health status has shown that long-term benefits are well above costs of operation calibrating effects of poor eyesight on quality of life. Researchers have used value per QALY as provided by the National Institute of Clinical Excellence (UK) which was estimated in the range £30,000–70,000 (Weale, 2011).

7   The valuation methods such as Stated-preference and Revealed-preference are subject to methodological and behavioural biases. VoSL, QALY and other measures of health gains are hard to estimate and subject to methodological controversies. Moreover, usually valuations done in the context of healthcare face criticism from the standpoint of ethics as they attach monetary values to seemingly priceless necessities. Nonetheless, CBA remains to be an essential framework that contributes to informed decision making in a real world where resources are scarce and technologies and policies could harm and benefit society in unpredictable ways. Even if complete CBAs are not carried out, it is at least important to carry out valuation studies of non-market goods and externalities to estimate damages. What is important in CBA is the systematic process towards deriving an answer to a proposal and not the final answer itself.

50 The value of statistical life

1 The question to be faced by economists interested in CBA is how to calculate the loss or gain that arises from changes in the incidence of death as in fatalities or disablement during the construction or operation of a project.

Since the analysis of saving a life is symmetrical with that of losing it, we may concentrate initially on the loss of life, bearing in mind also that the analysis applies equally to loss of limb or health, to disablement or disease.

Consistency with the basic axiom of mainstream economics, that the only acceptable valuation of a good or bad is that placed on it by the individual affected, requires that the loss of a person's life has to be determined also by reference only to his own valuation,[1] more precisely by his compensating variation. Choosing the CV^{12} measure, the value of life to person A is the minimal sum he is prepared to accept for its surrender.[2] In ordinary circumstance, his value would be infinite: no sum would be large enough to persuade a person to part with his life. So valued, it might seem that no project, no matter how worthy, could be undertaken on the Pareto criterion if, during its construction and operation over time, one person at least can be expected to meet with a fatal accident. This would be true, however, if a specific person A were known in advance as the person destined to expire, which is never the case in fact. All that can be known in this connection is that a number of persons engaged in a project can be expected to be killed or disabled over a given period. Each person engaged in working for that project is faced with a known risk. And if the risk is known to him, it will be costed as the minimum sum acceptable to him for taking the risk, given the wage available for the same work in a riskless enterprise or project.

Assuming risk-aversion in such cases, the relevant sum to be subtracted from the estimated benefits of a project is simply the aggregate of these minimal payments required annually by the workers to compensate them for the risk they undertake in working for that enterprise or project. Thus, if there are n workers employed in the risky project, the additional labour cost for the risk of death and disablement will be measured as $\sum_{i=1}^{n} CV_i^{12}$.

2 In general, of course, every activity will incur some degree of risk (even staying at home in bed bears some risk of mishaps: the bed might collapse; the wind might blow the roof off; a marauder might enter). A change from one environment to another, from one style of living to another, may alter the balance of risk, imperceptibly or substantially. Only the dead opt out of all risk. However, the actual risk attaching to some activity may be so small that only the hypersensitive would

take account of it. In common with all changes in economic arrangements, there is some *sensible minimum* beyond which some slight change in risk will not register or matter.

Again, since it is a change in risk – a reduction or increase in risk – that is often at issue, what is important is the person's response to the change that matters. It will be useful, therefore, to use the standard indifference diagram in Figure 50.1 to bring out the characteristic response of the individual to changes in risk.

Thus, the sum of money is measured along the vertical axis of the figure – here as a capital sum, although it could also be measured as a period payment – and the degree of risk of death is measured along the horizontal axis increasing by equal increments from right to left (from left to right, therefore, one can measure the increasing probability of survival). Point r_0 is virtually riskless, while point r^* is the critical or highest risk along the horizontal axis – that beyond which no sum of money will compensate the individual.

The indifference curves are ordered in the usual way, I_2 having a higher welfare level than I_1, the locus of each indifference curve being a continuum of alternative combinations of money and risk, between which our individual is indifferent. The assumption of risk-aversion over the operative range requires the curves to slope downward from left to right, while the concavity of the curves indicates that successively larger sums are needed to compensate the individual for assuming successive increments of risk. For instance, movement along the I_1 curve from Q_2 to Q_3 shows that the individual would require $150,000 to increase his risk from r_2 to r_3. For a further equal increment of risk, however, that from r_3 to r_4, the movement along the curve from Q_3 to Q_4 reveals that the minimal compensation required is now $300,000.

It will be noticed that, although the indifference curves are asymptotic to the vertical dotted line passing through point r^*, they will all touch the horizontal axis at r_0, where the risk is zero, or may also be drawn to touch the horizontal axis for a short distance to the left of r_0, so indicating that although there is some discernable risk, it is too slight to warrant attention by the individual.

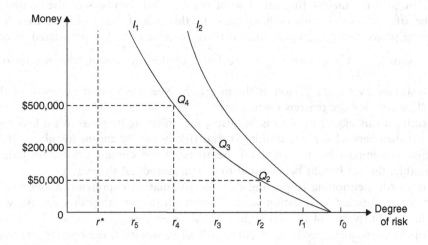

Figure 50.1

3   It may be thought that a cost-benefit calculation must take account not only of the cost of risks incurred in the production process but also in the consumption process: the costs, that is, of risks run by those who use the goods produced by the projects.

Although the larger the risk associated with the use of a good, the smaller is the amount the buyer is willing to pay for it, no adjustment is necessary to the economist's calculation of willingness to pay, since the consumer himself may be supposed to have made the adjustment. When a new car is bought, the buyer who is to drive the car is assumed to know the risks over time to which he will be exposed in driving the car. The most he is willing to pay for it is adjusted accordingly. Allowing that he is risk-averse, the higher the risk, the larger the deduction from his willingness to pay.[3]

4   In order to formulate a more general expression of the social cost of a given risk, that is of society's valuation of the loss suffered by having to bear with a given risk, a little taxonomy will be useful.

For the introduction of a known risk of death r, affecting equally each of m persons in a community, the cost of only the direct physical danger to all of them can be written as $\sum_{j=1}^{m} c_j$, where the letter c_j is shorthand for the CV^{12} measure of the jth person.

To this direct cost of the risk must be added the indirect cost arising from the possible impact on the welfare of any of the other remaining $(n - m)$ members of the community who are not themselves exposed to the risk in question. Thus, it may be that a person A who is not exposed to the risk, being fond of person B who is so exposed, or expecting to lose financially from B's demise, suffers a reduction in his welfare, the measure of his loss being a negative CV^{12} (the minimum sum acceptable to A for having to bear with the risk imposed on B). *Per contra*, if person A hates person B, or if he stands to gain from B's demise, his increase in welfare can be measured by his positive CV^{12} (the most A is willing to pay to maintain the risk of B's death).

Although it is unlikely that any one of the $(n - m)$ members of the community will be affected, emotionally or financially, by this risk of death of more than a few of the m persons, the aggregate sum of these reactions can be formulated as equal to the sum $\sum_{i=m+1}^{n} \sum_{j=1}^{m} c_{ij}$, where c_{ij} is the CV^{12} of the ith person who reacts to the risk sustained by the jth person in the m group. Needless to remark, most of these c_{ij} will be zero for the reasons given above.[4]

Clearly, if this aggregate sum is negative, the dollar figure measures a loss to the $(n - m)$ members of the community of the risk borne by the m members. If it is positive, the impact on the $(n - m)$ members of the community is, on balance, favourable, the net benefit being equal to the magnitude of the sum.

It is worth mentioning in passing that the summation expression above remains unaltered if the risk in question is that arising from an infectious disease which may be caught by any of the remaining $(n - m)$ members. The relevant CV^{12} measures of the consequent decline in welfare will all be negative, the resulting aggregate being a net loss.

5   Two developments arising from the proposed measurement of risk in CBA deserve comment: (i) a proposed extension of this measure of risk to the value of life, and (ii) a recognition of the seeming irrationality of those people placing a value on risk or chance.

(i) The proposed extension of a calculated risk premium to the value of a person's life can be illustrated by a simple example, one in which the individual at risk is concerned only with his own safety – not, that is, the effect of him having an accident on the welfare of anyone else.

Suppose that for a large group of men engaged in the same sort of work, the compensatory sum required for a risk of a fatal accident of 1 in 1,000 is, on average, equal to $800 then, for every 1,000 workmen, one workman may be expected to be killed each year. Since the aggregate sum that has to be paid to 1,000 such men each year comes to $800,000, this sum may be regarded as an agreed payment for the life lost.

Put generally, if the risk of a fatality, or an increase in the risk of a fatality, is equal to $1/n$, and the appropriate compensatory sum is, on average, equal to C, the value of a life is calculated to be equal to Cn.

But some caveats are necessary here. Although, in the simple example below, it may be convenient for the employer, who can expect such fatalities to occur over the years, to reckon the cost of each life lost as equal to $800,000, it does not follow that he or anyone else actually believes that the life of any particular person who dies in an accident is worth $800,000. Certainly, the person who died would not have agreed to surrender his life for $800,000.

It may be prudent to call this $800,000 the value of a *statistical* life. Even so, we should have to recognize that any such derived statistical life is pertinent only for that particular occupation in a particular region at a particular time: it is also applicable only for the existing degree of risk from which the increment of risk is to be calculated. By reference to Figure 50.1, if the existing degree of risk was taken to be equal to r_0, or about equal to zero risk, a small increment of risk may warrant an average compensatory sum of no more than $5 per annum, yielding a statistical life equal to $5,000. If, however, the existing risk of a fatality were r_1, an equal increment of risk would require a much larger average compensatory sum, say, $50, yielding the value of $50,000 for a statistical life. And if, instead, the existing risk of a fatality in that work were already as great as r_3, the same increment of risk would not be borne for less than an average sum of, say, $2,000, the resulting value of a statistical life being then equal to $2 million.

Obviously, any calculated statistical life has no claim to generality and no relation whatever to the value a person places on their own life – which, as indicated earlier, is likely to be infinite. It may, of course, continue to be regarded as an alternative to the calculation of the compensatory sum for a specific risk or increment of risk. But it is an alternative that is unnecessary and misleading.

Although the VOSL literature began to be established in economics in the late 1970s and early 1980s, policy makers viewed the idea of placing a value on human life as being immoral. As a result, in early government studies particularly in the United States, the human capital measure given by the average present value of the lost earnings of those affected by a policy was presented as the measure of the economic benefits of reducing fatality risks. This measure, which is often used in court cases to compensate for wrongful death, is easy to calculate. However, for many reasons, this human capital measure is no longer well accepted. One main reason is that people with low income would be attributed very low values of human capital, making this measure ethically debatable. Besides, such a measure only takes into account material losses such as an individual's productive capacity without appraising the intangible aspects such as joy of life, health and the prevention of sorrow, pain and distress.

6   Turning to (ii), although the method proposed in this chapter for measuring the valuation of any specific risk by reference to the compensating variation cannot be faulted, it transpires that, when it comes to the individual valuations of risks, they are far from being consistent. This apparent inconsistency may be attributed to the difficulty people have in apprehending the import of significant differences in very large numbers and very small fractions. For instance the risk of, loss of, say, 1 in 100,000 – or, alternatively, the chance of a gain of 1 in 100,000 – is not apprehended as being much smaller than a risk or chance of 1 in 10,000, or much smaller even than 1 in 1,000.[5]

This would be the case in an experiment in which a person is willing to pay as much as \$50 for the reduction of an existing risk by 1/1,000, yet willing to pay the same sum also for a reduction in that risk by 1/10,000 and, indeed, willing to pay this same \$50 for a reduction of the risk of 1/100,000.

Yet, something like this sort of reaction has been shown to exist in papers written some time ago, for when we take this same compensatory sum of \$50 for a reduction in risk of 10^{-3}, 10^{-4} and 10^{-5}, in that order, the resulting statistical value of life itself works out to be equal to \$50,000, \$500,000 and \$5 million, respectively.

These figures are, in fact, not that different from the findings of Mulligan (1977). For corresponding to these alternative reductions in risk of 10^{-3}, 10^{-4} and 10^{-5}, he comes up with a statistical value of life equal to \$62,000, \$428,000 and \$3,756,000, respectively.[6] Clearly, this difficulty in apprehending the numerical significance of differences in very small fractions must be taken seriously – as it presumably is by insurers and lottery promoters.

Although this fact of life is admittedly disquieting, the economist engaged in cost-benefit calculations may not allow himself to become overwrought for, in most cases, the increase or reduction in risk he has to evaluate is likely to be much larger than, say, 10^{-3}. He may therefore be justified in expecting a reasonable degree of consistency.

Therefore, although it is a matter of conscience to enter the above caveat before concluding, it is also as well to recognize that, for the usual order of change in risk that he meets within cost-benefit studies, the expressed compensating variations may be accepted as valid estimates for calculating the loss of incurring a risk or the benefit of reducing risk.

7   A word on the deficiencies in the information available to each person concerning the degree of risk involved. These deficiencies of information necessarily contribute to the discrepancies experienced by people between anticipated and realized satisfactions. For all that, in determining whether a potential Pareto improvement has been met, economists are generally agreed – as a canon of faith, as a political tenet, or as an act of expediency – to accept the dictum that each person knows his own interest best. If, therefore, the economist is told that a person A is indifferent between not assuming a particular risk and assuming it along with a sum of money

V, then, on the Pareto principle, the sum V has to be accepted as the relevant cost of him being exposed to that risk. It may well be the case that, owing to either deficient information or congenital optimism, person A consistently overestimates his chances of survival. But once the dictum is accepted, as indeed it is in economists' appraisals of allocative efficiency, CBA must accept V as the only relevant magnitude – this being the sum chosen by A in awareness of his relative ignorance.[7] Certainly, all the rest of the economic data used in a CBA, or any other allocative study, whether derived from market prices and quantities or by other methods of enquiry, is based on this principle of accepting as final only the individual's estimate of what a thing is worth to him at the time the decision is to be made. The thing in question may, of course, also have a direct worth, positive or negative, for persons other than the buyer or seller of it, a possibility which requires a consideration of external effects. Yet, again, on the above dictum, it is the values placed on this thing by these other persons that are to count. Thus, while it is scarcely necessary to urge that more economical ways of refining and disseminating information be explored, the economist engaged in allocative studies traditionally follows the practice of evaluating all social gains and losses solely on the basis of individuals' own evaluations of the relevant effects on their welfare, given the information they have at the time the decision is taken.

8   To sum up and conclude, given the common set of relevant economic characteristics of any group, the benefit of a given reduction in the existing risk (or the cost of an increment in that risk) as calculated from the valuations of people who are directly or indirectly affected by the change will vary (i) according to the existing degree of risk and to the magnitude of the change in risk, (ii) according to the kind of casualty associated with the change of risk, and (iii) according to the way that the risk translates itself into casualties. A quick word about each of these.

(i) A project that is expected to save each year no more than about one life in 10 million is likely to yield (in the absence of any other benefit) a zero contribution *by direct reference to individual valuations*. However, the installation of a plant that is expected to increase the death rate by 10 per cent within a certain area may inflict an average loss per person of several thousand dollars. Needless to say, it would be as absurd to derive a social value for human life from the former instance as from the latter – and quite arbitrary to use any other instance for the purpose.

(ii) The particular kind of death envisaged also plays a part. For exactly the same increase in the risk of death, say 5 per cent, beginning from exactly the same existing risk, the individual valuation of loss may be much higher if the kind of death being risked is that by nuclear radiation than if it is that by drowning or by influenza.

(iii) Again, even the same risk of the same kind of death may be valued differently according to whether (a) expected deaths take the form of a probability distribution, so that the number tends to vary from one year to the next: the smaller the variance, the less bearable is the given risk; (b) the expected number of deaths – irrespective of the variance of the probability distribution – occurs within a particular community located *within* a larger population, rather than the same number of deaths being dispersed throughout the larger population.

9   There can therefore be no question of the economist engaged in a cost-benefit calculation having recourse to some all-purpose value of human life, however ingeniously calculated. In a CBA, the economist is to attend directly only to the observable data that lends itself to valuation: thus he is to value an increased or reduced risk of death, or of other misfortunes, as simply one among the several goods or bads associated with the construction or operation of a specific project. And, as argued in the chapter, the valuation of the given change of risk is correctly measured only by the compensating variations of those who are directly or indirectly affected by it.

To be sure, the general economic literature offers occasional examples of economic models putatively designed to produce formulae for calculating the monetary value of a human life, models that again, though with greater sophistication, draw on the expectations of a person's economic activities over the duration of his life, and their effect on himself and others.

In practice, one method to estimate the *value of statistical life* is to directly survey respondents and elicit their WTP for a reduced health risk, or WTA for the opposite, subjected to their budget constraints in reality. If an average respondent is willing to pay $10,000 for a 1 per cent reduction in the risk of death within the current time period, the VOSL can be computed to be $10,000/1 per cent = $1 million. The same logic applies to non-fatal risks, which uses the *value of statistical life year* (VSLY): the value society places on reducing risk of premature mortality or to prolong life. If the average respondent is willing to pay $10,000 when the expected gain in longevity from reduced pollution is 1 month, then it can be concluded that the WTP for one full year of life would be $10,000*(12/1) = $120,000.

In practice, estimating VOSL can be time consuming and costly, while the bulk of studies have been conducted in many developed countries, particularly the United States and Western Europe. Therefore, it has been common practice to use a benefit transfer approach to transfer such values, with adjustments, for income differentials across countries. That is, from countries where these values have been made available (usually based on US or European studies) to countries where these values have not been estimated. Generally, the transferred value is scaled by the ratio of per capita income of the country in which the value does not exist, to the per capita income of the country of which the value is adapted, to correct for the income differential between the two countries. The adapted value is then adjusted using the elasticity of WTP with respect to income, which measures the responsiveness of WTP for a small percentage change in income.

The benefit transfer approach (see Chapter 42), even though widely used, seems to introduce some unique issues and challenges making this practice subject to controversy and scrutiny. These issues include how to convert values from one currency to another, how to account for differences in quantifiable characteristics between countries such as income and how to account for differences in non-quantifiable characteristics such as cultural differences. One of the authors of this book has conducted the first study deriving indigenous values of a statistical life for Singapore. It is a contingent valuation survey conducted to elicit Singaporeans' WTP to reduce the baseline risk of death by 5 in 10,000 and 1 in 10,000. From a sample size of 800, aged 40 to 75 years, the mean of WTP translates into values of a statistical life of S$850,000 (US$615,950) and S$2.05 million (US$1.49 million), respectively. They found that refining VOSLs for the specific characteristics of the affected population at risk remains an important priority for government agencies in the conduct of economic analyses. Improving the applications of VOSLs in this way can result in more informed government interventions to address market failures related to environmental, health and safety mortality risks (Quah and Toh, 2011).

10   Another way to measure the inherent trade-off one makes between risk of death (or illness), with the consumption of other goods and services, is to look at the exchange one makes between income earnings and the risk of job-related death (or illness). To illustrate, a job with a 0.2 per cent risk of death might warrant a wage premium of $1,000 over another job with a 0.1 per cent risk of death, *ceteris paribus*. This implies that the employee has to be compensated $1,000 for taking on the additional 0.1 per cent fatality risk. If this is representative of the average employee, and if labour markets are perfect, then the value of statistical life can be calculated to be $1,000/0.1 per cent = $1 million. Viscusi and Aldy (2003) provide a comprehensive review of this approach.

Alternatively, one could choose to use medical expenditures (direct costs) and ill-ness-associated lost productivity (indirect costs) as a proxy for the value of life. This is also known as the cost of illness approach, where the human capital value of health – the productivity returns – is directly accounted for. Also, money spent on healthcare could otherwise be spent on other goods and services. These are costs which are averted in good health. Dividing the cost of illness by mortality rate then gives the cost of life lost. The main shortcoming of this approach, as opposed to the two methods before, is that it gives an underestimation as we omit the intrinsic value of life. In reality, we expect people to value life per se, as living life generates happiness and meaningful experiences. We also expect that patients would not completely return to their initial healthy state with medical treatments, and would to be willing to pay even more to avoid the pain and sufferings from illnesses, and to stay at a healthy state instead of being cured at an unhealthy state. Note that healthcare subsidies, which distort prices, or health insurance coverage, which leads to moral hazard problems, further complicate the measurement.

There are other similar approaches to value a statistical life, such as observing revealed behaviours and WTP in insurance markets. One may also look at prevent-ive expenditures instead of medical or insurance expenditures, e.g. price premium for residential housing with lesser pollution, or WTP for helmets to reduce motor-cyclists' injury risks. Discounted lifetime wages could also be indicative of a life's worth, at least in terms of its contribution to society from the provision of labour and human capital. Note that instead of using WTP to measure the trade-off between health-risk reductions and the consumption of other goods and services, one may instead measure the trade-off between different health states of varying durations (Hammitt and Zhou, 2006). This is the underlying principle of the non-monetary measures of disability-adjusted life-years (DALY) and quality-adjusted life-years (QALY), where weights are assigned to life years of different health qual-ity. For example, a year lived in illness might be worth half of that in good health. In extension, using the various valuation methods, DALY and QALY can be accordingly monetized as well (Lvovsky *et al.*, 2000).

Whatever one's reaction to such models, there is no way of testing their validity. As indicated earlier, in ordinary circumstances, the value of a person's life to himself is unlikely to be finite; no sum of money, no matter how large, will induce him to surrender his life. As for checking the monetary value produced by such models by reference to some chosen statistical value of life, the exercise would be pointless for, even were the model's calculated value of life 'confirmed' by the statistical value of life, the model's calculated valuation would be worse than superfluous; it would be a case of 'love's labour lost', as it would be far simpler to derive the statistical value of life directly from the relevant compensatory sum for the risk in question.

At all events, since such models, however regarded, have nothing to contribute to CBA, what brief comments we have on their character are relegated to Appendix 10.

Notes

1 Earlier attempts by economists to calculate the value of human life depart from that axiom, They include (a) those based on the expected lifetime earnings and or consumption of the individual, (b) those held to be implicit in the policy decisions of society, and (c) those deriving from insurance premiums. They are examined and revealed as inadequate in Mishan's (1971a) and Mishan's (1971c) articles. Also see Viscusi and Aldy (2003).
2 The alternative measure, CV^{21}, which would be finite, is the most a person is willing and able to pay to avoid being put to death. Where the prevailing ethos is one that believes that each person has a right to life, the CV^{12} measure is the appropriate one to use.
3 The same may be said of the consumption of tobacco products where the damages of smoking are widely advertised, but there is evidence to support the belief that awareness of the dangers of smoking attracts young people to take it up; at least to be seen by their peers to be smoking, in which case the risks add to the sum they are willing to pay.
4 If we wish to allow that some of the m group who are directly at risk are themselves affected by some of those in that m group, we should re-write the above expression as $\sum_{i=1}^{n} \sum_{j=1}^{m} c_{ij}$ (where, again, a number of the c_{ij} are equal to zero).
5 Mishan's (1971a) paper suggested, *inter alia*, that this interesting fact of life also explains why people both gamble and insure without invoking the ingenious hypothesis about the shape of the utility curve advanced by Friedman and Savage (1948). Also see Mishan (1971b).
6 If the relevant segment of the indifference curve is linear, these empirical findings by Mulligan can be expressed as equal to a compensatory sum of \$62 for a reduction of risk by 10^{-3}, of about \$43 for a reduction of risk of 10^{-4} and about \$37 for a reduction of risk of 10^{-5}.
7 Person A, for example, may find himself disabled for life and rue his decision to take the risk. But this example is only a more painful one of the fact that people come to regret a great many of the choices they make, notwithstanding which they would resent any interference with their future choices.

51 Estimating the economic cost of air pollution on health[1]

1 A number of developing countries around the world face the dual challenge of sustaining their rapid pace of development while simultaneously ensuring that this development occurs in a sustainable manner. Industrialization, coupled with surging populations, has resulted in severe environmental degradation, a key aspect being air pollution. Pollutants such as sulphur dioxide, nitrogen oxide, lead, ozone and particulate matter have primarily caused the most significant and obvious damage to air quality in cities worldwide. In such a scenario, it becomes imperative for governments and industries to have a useful and accurate method to estimate the economic cost of air pollution, for policy making, regulation, surveillance and innovation. This chapter closely examines one such method of estimating the economic cost of air pollution with case studies to examine its use.

Particulate matter in the atmosphere refers to any dust, dirt, smoke and liquid droplets emitted into the atmosphere through industrial activity, vehicles, construction, fires and windblown dust. Particulate matter may also originate through the condensation of emitted gases into tiny droplets. Particulate matter is not only found to be widespread, but is also considered to be the most damaging, and measures relating to particulate matter in the air are used to create a useful measure of the economic cost of air pollution.

Concentration of particulate matter in the air is expressed in micrograms of particles per cubic metre of air sampled ($\mu g/m^3$). The particulate size measure is known as PM_{10} and includes all particles with an aerodynamic diameter of 10 μm or less. These particles are a health concern as they can penetrate deep into the sensitive lower regions of the respiratory tract and are known as inhalable particles.

Studies examining the effects of exposure to air pollution identify PM_{10} as the pollutant most responsible for the life-shortening effect of dirty air. The biggest concerns with respect to human health include adverse effects on breathing, aggravation of existing respiratory and cardiovascular disease, change to the body's immunity against foreign materials, lung tissue damage, carcinogenesis and premature death. The reduction in immunity and increased susceptibility to respiratory infections also lead to an increase in the incidence of pneumonia in more vulnerable sections of the general population.

2 Establishing the link between increased emissions and human health is more straightforward. The next step entails establishing a link between the predicted health effects and the corresponding economic cost. For the health effects, the monetarization approach determines such values according to individuals' stated preferences or WTP. The argument for this approach is that the basis for most

judgements regarding changes in human well-being are people's preferences. Similarly, changes in human mortality and morbidity, which are vital aspects of human well-being, should also be valued, based on what individuals are willing to pay for better health or the compensations they are willing to accept to forego an improvement in health. A vital moral and ethical issue arises when this economic analysis is undertaken. Conflicts arise between the ethical validity of assigning a value to a human life and the need for economic analysis. To clarify, the VOSL is unrelated to the value of a human life.

The VOSL can be defined as the value of a small change in the risks associated with an unnamed member of a large group dying (Dixon et al., 1994). It represents an individual's WTP for a marginal reduction in the risk of being dead. The calculation of VOSL should be achieved by several approaches – hedonic value methods: property-value approach, compensating wage differential approach, preventive expenditures approach and contingent valuation method (CVM).

The valuation of reduced morbidity can also be calculated through measures of an individual's WTP or by using cost of illness (COI) approaches. COI measures the total COI that is imposed on society including the value of lost productivity (loss in earnings) due to illness, medical costs such as hospital care, medicine, the services of doctors and nurses and other out-of-pocket expenditure.

Several studies have been conducted to determine the economic costs of air pollution damage to human health from PM_{10}. The economic cost of health damage per capita in developing countries appears to be fairly consistent in the range of US\$15 to US\$247. Most of these studies conducted use consensus dose–response functions (DRFs) in the estimation of the economic cost of air pollution. This implies that the costs of particulate air pollution in terms of its impact on human health is largely determined by the size of the population at risk and the unit economic values used to value the increase in mortality and morbidity.

3   Estimating the economic cost of particulate air pollution on health in a particular city or region involves using the damage function/dose–response approach. This approach measures the effects of premature death (mortality effects) and the effects of health deterioration (morbidity effects) of particulate air pollution. Subsequently, the economic values of these health impacts are calculated in terms of the statistical lives that could be saved and the COI incurred.

The procedure can be adopted through three steps:

1   Determine the ambient concentration of the pollutant, PM_{10}, in the city or region being analysed for pollution costs.
2   Apply the damage function approach using dose–response relationships to estimate the health impact of this PM_{10} pollution (where the health impacts considered are the increase in mortality and morbidity). This is one of the most accepted methodologies of doing so.
3   Assign an economic/monetary value to the increase in mortality and morbidity.

Examining the second step in detail, the damage–response functions are adopted from Ostro (1994) and Rowe *et al.* (1995) and are used to estimate the health effects of air pollution, specifically of PM_{10}. The strength of this approach is its simplicity and its easy interpretation. For this stage, we need to determine a few factors.

First, we need to develop estimates of the effects of air pollution on various health outcomes, as DRFs link variations in ambient levels of pollutants to certain health effects. For this we calculate the partial derivate of slope of the DRF to provide an estimate of the change in a given health effect associated with a change in air quality.

Second, we multiply this partial derivative (slope of the DRF) by the population at risk of the air pollutant under consideration. For some pollution related health effects, this might include the entire population exposed to air pollution, whereas for other effects, there may be particularly sensitive subgroups such as the children, the elderly or asthmatics to account for.

Third, we look at the change in air quality under consideration. This is calculated as the deviation between the actual ambient levels of air pollutant and the acceptable average concentration of air pollutant. As a result, the change in air pollution is dependent on both the policy under consideration (to determine the acceptable concentration) and the available data (to determine the actual ambient level of air pollutants). Usually, the relevant change in air pollution can be calculated by using either the change from current air pollution levels to some ambient air quality standard or a given percentage of reduction, such as 5 or 10 per cent.

The estimated health impact can be calculated by the relationship

$$\Delta H_{ij} = a_{ij} \times \text{POP}_i \times \Delta A_j \tag{51.1}$$

where ΔH_{ij} is the change in the population's risk of health impact i due to pollutant j, a_{ij} is the slope from the dose-response curve for health impact i due to pollutant j, POP_i is the population at risk of health effect i and ΔA_j is the change in ambient concentration of air pollutant j.

4   DRFs relate information on changes in the ambient air quality of different pollutants for different health outcomes. The changes in ambient air pollution levels of different types of pollutants can then be statistically related to any observed changes in morbidity and mortality in a population. However, different studies estimate different coefficients for such an effect. So, we can use three alternative assumptions about health estimates, giving the central estimate the most weight. The high and low end estimates are calculated by increasing and decreasing the coefficient by one estimated standard deviation respectively. According to a paper by Ostro (1994), the suggestion is to use 0.062, 0.096 and 0.13 as the lower, central and upper coefficient, respectively, for the estimator of percentage change in mortality.

Using the DRF in Equation (51.1), the number of cases of premature mortality due to PM_{10} can be expressed as

$$\Delta \text{Mortality} = b \times \Delta PM_{10} \times \text{crude mortality rate} \times \text{pop} \tag{51.2}$$

where b is the mortality coefficient determined above (0.062, 0.096 and 0.13 for lower, central and higher estimate, respectively) and POP is the population exposed to risk.

To complete the estimation of health effects, it is possible to calculate the economic valuation of this effect. This can be developed from estimates of the WTP for reducing risk, to attach values to the expected changes in premature mortality or a modified COI approach to value changes in morbidity. Thus, the change in value (ΔT_i) of the health effects due to change in air pollution under consideration is the summation of all effects and can be presented by

$$\Delta T = \sum V_i \Delta H_i \qquad (51.3)$$

where T is the economic value of the health effects, V_i is the WTP to reduce a particular type of health risk and H_i is the reduction in a particular health risk.

Due to the substantial uncertainty about much of the research on which these estimates are based, upper and lower boundary estimates are provided to indicate the ranges within which the actual health effects are likely to fall.

Although the valuation of mortality and morbidity is important to CBA of air pollution programmes, relevant studies are fairly limited in scope. Using the benefit transfer approach (BTA, as described earlier, in Chapter 42), it is assumed that the stated preferences of people in the developed countries will be similar to those of people in any developed region being analysed, for the economic cost of air pollution. Transfer of these values may neglect factors that would cause people to value health differently, yet despite these drawbacks, these are cost advantages in terms of time and resources.

In the third step, for the estimation of the monetary valuation of premature mortality due to PM_{10}, the VOSL in the United States is adjusted to derive the VOSL for the region or city in question. This adjustment to the $VOSL_{US}$ is done using purchasing power parity (PPP) estimates of GDP per capita of the United States and the region being analysed. Thus, $VOSL_{Region}$ can be computed based on the following expression:

$$VOSL_{Region} = VOSL_{US} \times \left(\frac{GDP_{Region}}{GDP_{US}}\right)^e \qquad (51.4)$$

where $VOSL_{Region}$ is the value of a statistical life for the region in question in a particular year, $VOSL_{US}$ is the value of a statistical life for the United States in the same year's prices, GDP_{Region} is the GDP of the region in question, GDP_{US} is the GDP of the United States and e is the elasticity of WTP with respect to income.

5   A similar approach can also been used to estimate the effects of changes in air quality on air pollution-related illnesses (morbidity). Again, to determine morbidity coefficients of the morbidity effect of PM_{10} concentration we turn to Rowe *et al.* (1995). The coefficients relate to the effect of the increase in the number of morbidity cases due to:

1   respiratory health admissions (RHA);
2   emergency room visits (ERV);
3   restricted activity days (RAD);

4   lower respiratory illness in children (LRI);
5   asthma attacks;
6   respiratory symptoms; or
7   chronic bronchitis.

The increase in the number of morbidity cases can be estimated using the equation

$$\Delta Morbidity = c_i \times POP \times \Delta PM_{10} \qquad (51.5)$$

where c_i is the morbidity coefficient for each measure of morbidity effect (extrapolated from Rowe *et al.* (1995) and POP is the population exposed to risk.
   For the estimation of the monetary valuation of PM_{10}-related morbidity we use predetermined unit values for each morbidity effect estimated in the United States (adapted from Rowe *et al.* (1995); see Table 51.1) with various adjustments. The morbidity unit value for the region in question is expressed using the equation

$$MUV_{Region} = MUV_{US} \times \left(\frac{GDP_{Region}}{GDP_{US}} \right)^e \qquad (51.6)$$

where MUV_{Region} is the morbidity unit value for the region in question in a - particular year, MUV_{US} is the morbidity unit value for the United States in the same year's prices, GDP_{Region} is the GDP of the region in question, GDP_{US} is the GDP of the United States and e is the elasticity of WTP with respect to income.
   Note that under the BTA we transfer not only the DRFs from established work, but also the economic unit values of the effects of mortality and morbidity.

6   When estimating the cost of air pollution, we require a number of pieces of information: population at risk of air pollution; the level of ambient concentration of the air pollutant in question; the crude mortality rate (to estimate mortality effects of the pollutant); coefficients (relating to mortality and morbidity) of the DRFs; and the unit economic values of the effects of mortality and morbidity.
   Unfortunately, we do not have the indigenous DRFs and unit values for most regions that we would like to examine for the costs of air pollution. As a result, it remains necessary to use DRFs and unit economic values for mortality and morbidity

Table 51.1 Mortality and morbidity effects of a 1 $\mu g/m^3$ change in PM_{10} using benefit transfer

Mortality and morbidity	Lower estimate	Central estimate	Upper estimate
Mortality	0.062	0.096	0.13
RHA/100,000	0.657	1.2	1.73
ERV/100,000	11.6	23.7	35.4
RAD	0.029	0.058	0.078
LRI	0.001	0.0017	0.0024
Asthma attacks	0.033	0.058	0.196
Respiratory symptoms	0.08	0.168	0.256
Chronic bronchitis/100,000	3	6.12	9.3

Source: Rowe *et al.* (1995).

effects estimated in the developed countries to derive the cost of particulate air pollution in other developed regions being analysed.

There are a variety of approaches to making a benefit transfer. However, the existing approach to benefit transfer outperforms the others and was developed by Alberini *et al.* (1997). The BTA involves the use of the estimates from a particular environmental impact valuation study in one area to estimate the economic value of environmental impact of a similar study in another area. The underlying assumption is that the latter project will have a similar impact (Pearce *et al.*, 1994). The process of data collection to establish indigenous DRFs and values can be extremely costly and time consuming, making the above-mentioned approach all the more desirable (Krupnick *et al.*, 1993).

It remains necessary, however, to make sure that the implicit assumption behind such a transfer of DRFs from developed countries should be fulfilled. This implicit assumption is that the relationship between the levels of air pollution and the consequent health effects in the developed countries can be extrapolated to estimate the health impact of particulate air pollution in the region being analysed. This restricts any possible estimation of the economic costs of air pollution using this approach just to developed cities. Similarly, for the transfer of unit economic values of the mortality and morbidity, it is implicitly assumed that the stated preferences of people in the developed countries are similar to those of the people residing in the region being analysed.

Besides restricting the number of countries or regions that can be analysed using such an approach, extrapolation DRFs and unit economic values from developed countries do have their drawbacks:

1   Transfer of DRFs may not be valid if the local context contains factors that would affect their function. For example, differences in baseline health or nutrition, access to healthcare, demographics and occupational exposure may cause a level of pollution to cause more damage.
2   Transfer of values may also neglect factors that would cause people to value health differently. For example, the concept of what constitutes full health may differ with culture and not only with income.
3   There are other environmental factors specific to location and culture, and the interplay of these factors limits the reliability of the BTA in assessing environmental impacts.

Despite these limitations, the cost advantages in terms of time and resources of benefit transfer continue to encourage its use for the economic cost analysis of developed regions. Furthermore, for the case of particulate matter, there appears to be a consensus in the DRFs and many related studies converge (as observed by Pearce, 1996). Finally, a brief review by Khatun (1997) has shown that the available studies for developing countries suggest a dose–response coefficient similar to those estimated for developed economies.

7   By using the method described above, we can estimate the economic cost of air pollution in Singapore. The mortality and morbidity effects of the ambient concentration of PM_{10} in Singapore are estimated by using Singapore-specific data on the ambient concentration of PM_{10}, the crude mortality rate and the population at risk

of air pollution, combined with the coefficients of the DRFs obtained from Ostro (1994) and Rowe *et al.* (1995).

Following the DRF in Equation (51.2), the level of premature mortality due to PM_{10} can be expressed as

$$\Delta\text{Mortality} = b \times \Delta PM_{10} \times 1{,}100 \times \text{crude mortality rate} \times POP \qquad (51.7)$$

where b is the mortality coefficient determined above (0.062, 0.096 and 0.13 for lower, central and higher estimate, respectively) and POP is the population exposed to risk.

First, for Singapore, since the annual level of PM_{10} in 2009 was higher than the WHO air quality guidelines (WHO-AQG) of 20 $\mu g/m^3$ by 15 $\mu g/m^3$, we determined a change of 15 $\mu g/m^3$ and took ΔPM_{10} to be 15. The population exposed to particulate air pollution is equal to the total population in Singapore. This assumption can be justified by its small geographical area. According to the Singstat Time Series Online, the crude mortality rate in Singapore is 4.3 per 1,000 and the size of its population (POP) was 4,987,000 in 2009.

Based on this information, the mortality effect of PM_{10} in Singapore can be estimated, by the relationship above, to be

$$\Delta\text{Mortality} = 0.096 \times 15 \times 1{,}100 \times 0.0043 \times 4{,}987{,}600 = 309 \qquad (51.8)$$

This figure is obtained using the central estimate of 0.096. Similarly, the upper and lower estimates of the total number of mortalities are 418 and 199, respectively.

Table 51.2 presents the results of the estimation of the morbidity effects of particulate air pollution for Singapore using Equation (51.5) and the morbidity coefficients. Note that for the estimation of the number of RADs due to PM10, only the adult population is considered since they are the main participants in the work force, and for the estimation of the number of LRI in children, only the population under the age of 15 is considered. All other estimates are computed using the entire population figure of 4,987,000.

Table 51.2 Mortality and morbidity effects (number of cases) of a 15 $\mu g/m^3$ change in PM_{10} using benefit transfer

	Lower estimate	Central estimate	Upper estimate
Mortality	199	309	418
Morbidity			
RHA	492	898	1,294
ERV	8,678	17,731	26,484
RAD (1,000)	1,190	2,380	3,201
LRI	10,019	17,031	24,044
Asthma attacks (1,000)	2,469	4,339	14,664
Respiratory symptoms (1,000)	5,985	12,569	19,152
Chronic bronchitis	2,244	4,579	6,958

Source: Author's calculation.

Second, to estimate the mortality costs, we transferred the estimates from countries where WTP studies have been conducted to Singapore's case using Equation (51.4).

1   The $VOSL_{US}$ in 2009 prices is calculated as US$7.0725 million.
2   Per capita GDP at PPP for Singapore was $50,523(in international dollars) and for the United States was $46,381(in international dollars) for the year 2009. Hence, the ratio of Singapore's GDP per capital to the United States GDP per capital is 1.0893.
3   For the elasticity of WTP with respect to income, e, we assume a value of 0.32. It is argued that environmental amenities such as clean air are not luxury goods and hence the income elasticity of WTP to avoid illness is less than 1. Empirical evidence from some studies also supports this argument. For example, the Alberini *et al.* (1997) study in Taiwan estimated an income elasticity of WTP of about 0.32, while the Loehman *et al.* (1979) study estimated that the income elasticity is between 0.26 and 0.6. These empirical studies all suggest that WTP is lower in a low income country than in a higher income country, but less than proportionally to the income differential. Thus, for the estimation of the $VOSL_{Singapore}$, the income elasticity is assumed to be equal to that in Taiwan, which is 0.32.
4   This gives us a $VOSL_{Singapore}$ of US$7.27 million.

Similarly, in estimating the morbidity cost, we transfer estimates from countries where morbidity unit values have been computed to the Singapore case using Equation (51.6). Note that in estimating the cost of RAD, 20 per cent of RAD results in lost workdays and the remaining 80 per cent of the RAD values at one-third of the daily average wages. Taking an exchange rate of US$1=S$1.4034, the monthly average wages in Singapore for 2009 is approximately US$2,964. Making an additional assumption that people work for 20 days every month, the daily wage rate in 2009 is US$148. As a central estimate we obtain the cost of RAD in Singapore as US$164.61 million. All the findings of the unit values of morbidity are summarized in Table 51.3.

Finally, based on Equation (51.3), we compute the economic costs due to changes in levels of PM_{10}. For the central estimate of the mortality cost, we multiply the number of cases of mortality by the estimate for $VOSL_{Singapore}$ in 2009 using the BTA. This is calculated as 309 × US$7,072,500 = US$2,244.72 million. The estimated morbidity costs are summarized in Table 51.4, along with the total health damage cost due to particulate air pollution in Singapore.

Table 51.3 Unit values for morbidity effects in 2009 (US$) using benefit transfer

	Lower estimate	*Central estimate*	*Upper estimate*
Morbidity			
RHA	9,820.9	19,641.6	29,462.5
ERV	370.8	741.5	1,112.3
RAD (1,000)	NA	69.2	NA
LRI	NA	NA	NA
Asthma attacks (1,000)	18.0	50.2	80.2
Respiratory symptoms (1,000)	8.0	14.0	20.1
Chronic bronchitis	NA	193,739.1	NA

Source: Author's calculation.

The total estimated economic cost of health damage attributable to PM_{10} in Singapore is US$3,745.26 million (central estimate), which is about 2.04 per cent of the total GDP of Singapore in 2009. Based on these estimates, premature mortality accounts for about 60 per cent of health costs and other illnesses account for 40 per cent as shown in Table 51.4.

8   Dose–response relationships are mostly based on data from the United States, Canada and the United Kingdom, relating to information on changes in the air quality and pollution levels for different pollutants and health outcomes. Through an approach similar to the one described above, Ostro (1994) applies previous work from Europe and the United States to Jakarta.

When coefficients listed in Table 51.5 are applied to Jakarta, Ostro estimates the health impacts associated with decreasing particulate levels to Indonesian standards (from current levels to 90 $\mu g/m^3$) and WHO standards (from current pollution levels to 75 $\mu g/m^3$). Many parts of Jakarta city had PM_{10} levels ranging between 100 and 200, with certain 'hot spots' having readings of 300 or 350. Table 51.6 shows the derived health benefits of reducing particulate matter to the Indonesian standard of 90 $\mu g/m^3$.

Table 51.4 Costs of mortality and morbidity due to a 15 $\mu g/m^3$ change in PM_{10} in 2009 (US$ million)

	Lower estimate	Central estimate	Upper estimate
Mortality	1,449.71	2,244.72	3,039.72
Morbidity			
RHA	4.8	13.1	29.5
ERV	3.2	13.1	29.5
RAD	82.3	164.6	221.4
LRI	NA	NA	NA
Asthma attacks	44.5	217.7	1,176.4
Respiratory symptoms	48.1	175.9	384.8
Chronic bronchitis	NA	911.6	NA

Source: Author's calculation.

Table 51.5 Morbidity effects of 10 $\mu g/m^3$ change in PM_{10}

Morbidity	Central estimate	High estimate
RHA/100,000	12.0	15.6
ERV/100,000	235.4	342.5
RAD/person	0.575	0.903
LRI/child/per asthmatic	0.0169	0.0238
Asthma attacks/per asthmatic[1]	0.326	2.73
Respiratory symptoms/person	1.83	2.74
Chronic bronchitis/100,000	61.2	91.8

Source: Ostro (1994).
1 Applies to the 8.25 per cent of the Indonesian population that is assumed to be asthmatic.

Table 51.6 Health effects of reducing PM_{10} levels to Indonesian standards of 90 $\mu g/m^3$ for Jakarta

Health effect	Central estimate
Premature mortality	1,200
Hospital admissions	2,000
ERV	40,600
RAD	6,330,000
LRI	104,000
Asthma attacks	464,000
Respiratory symptoms	31,000,000
Chronic bronchitis	9,600

Source: Ostro (1994).

Under the central estimate of the dose–response relationships, Ostro estimated that each year the benefits of reducing the PM_{10} levels to Indonesian standards for a population of 8.2 million people in the Indonesian capital include a reduction of 1,200 premature deaths, 2,000 fewer hospital admissions, 40,600 fewer emergency room visits and more than 6 million fewer RADs, among many other benefits.

However, to estimate the right investments and control options to be undertaken, any policy maker would like to compare the benefits to the costs. The economic benefits, as noted below, are largely due to the health costs avoided and reduced premature deaths. In this case, monetary values were not placed on the health outcomes. Yet, presenting the impact of particulate air pollution as in Tables 51.5 and 51.6 can be a powerful message for policy makers.

9   This methodology is limited in two respects. First, this methodology uses DRFs and unit economic values for mortality and morbidity effects estimated in developed countries for the estimation of the cost of particulate air pollution. In a strict sense, these adopted values do not apply to the region being analysed (in this case, Singapore). Second, as Pearce (1996) noted, a major weakness of air pollution-damage literature has been the focus on outdoor pollution. In terms of human person hours, 89 per cent of all developed-country person hours are spent indoors, leaving only 11 per cent of time spent outdoors. In developing countries, the percentage of time spent indoors and outdoors are 70 per cent and 30 per cent, respectively. In other words, in developed countries the major part of an individual's time is spent indoors, away from the direct effect of particulate air pollution, not outdoors. However, given the paucity of data on indoor air quality, only outdoor air quality is considered in this analysis. In view of these limitations, the findings of this methodology are to be treated as indicative rather than conclusive.

This discussion also highlights the uncertainties involved in economic valuations of environmental amenities like clean air. These uncertainties include doubts about the authenticity of the impacts on health, possible statistical invalidities and a lack of consensus regarding the monetary valuation of various types of benefits. To reduce such uncertainties, the best approach is to establish dose–response relationships of local and regional PM_{10} and conduct studies investigating the value that residents actually place on clean air. Such data collection to establish DRFs and values will not be easy or cheap, but these efforts could then provide the impetus for more in-depth analysis of environmental impacts.

10   Air pollution does not stop at national or provincial borders. Particulate matter and other pollutants brought by winds could originate from dust storms, forest fires occurring in other countries that they are sometimes located regionally very far from. Examples include Asian Dust caused by deforestation in Northern China that transports industrial pollutants to Japan and Korea, Winter Haze created by coal heating in North China which ends up all over East Asia and Transboundary Haze in South-East Asia. We will focus on the latter case of regional transboundary pollution.

Large-scale forest fires caused mainly by the fires set as part of the slash-and-burn agriculture in Indonesia have occurred since 1960s, choking not only parts of the country but also its neighbouring Singapore and Malaysia. The frequency and intensity of burning has, unfortunately, increased during the last few years. In some bad episodes that occurred in 1997, 2013 and 2015, affected countries had their respective air pollution index readings for some areas go far beyond hazardous to human health.

11   Forest fires bring about not only huge devastation of ecosystems but also harm public health. Millions were kept indoors as air pollution rose to hazardous levels and tens of thousands of people in search of treatment for respiratory, eye and skin ailments overwhelmed medical clinics and hospital. It also disturbs air and sea transportation in countries affected. Overall, haze pollution generated from such forest fires exacted a heavy economic toll on society. With the emergence and development of reliable quantitative methods and techniques in economics and statistics, the exercise of calculating the dollar losses to society from haze pollution has been undertaken. These methods and techniques have developed from very crude calculations, used at the beginning of the twentieth century, to the more sophisticated approaches better grounded in economic theory, which are now widely used.

12   For the more severe 2015 episode, a study by the World Bank in 2016 shows that more than 2.6 million hectares of forest, peat and other land were burned in 2015, accounting for an area that is close to 4.5 times the size of Bali. This study shows the estimated losses and damages of eight burned areas including Jambi, Riau, South Sumatra and West, South, East and Central Kalimantan as well as Papua. According to this study, the cost of the 2015 fires is estimated at US$16.1 billion, which is approximately 2 per cent of the Indonesian GDP in 2015. These costs include short-term effect of haze exposure on health and also school closures. Other costs cover fire-fighting costs and costs to the environment. While the World Bank's study has comprehensively estimated the cost of Indonesia's fires and haze on Indonesia, the study has yet to capture regional or global losses of the haze.

Indeed, the haze episode reported in 2015 was one of the most prolonged in Singapore's environmental history with air quality deteriorating into the 'Unhealthy' range for 40 days, 'Very Unhealthy' range for five days and 'Hazardous' range for one day. The bad haze episodes impacted Singapore adversely in various sectors which include school closure on 25 September 2015, cancellation of multiple large-scale outdoor public events such as charity runs, and more than 40,000 Singaporeans claiming medical subsidies for haze-related illness as of 19 October 2015. In 2018, our team estimated the cost of the 2015 episode on Singapore, hoping that our findings could provide added information about the magnitude of the problem and hence contribute to informed decisions about various policy alternatives that could be used to prevent forest fires in Indonesia. We quantified and estimated the economic impact of transboundary haze pollution in 2015 on Singapore using reliable quantitative methods and techniques developed in CBA. We included in the estimation both tangible and intangible costs associated to haze pollution. Tangible costs are those for which a market value can be calculated. When reduced, tangible costs yield resources that become available to the society for consumption and investment purposes. Such tangible costs can usually be quantified with readily available data and survey. Intangible costs, on the other hand, are difficult to measure but nonetheless have a real impact on society. Unlike the tangible costs, when reduced, the intangible costs do not release resources for alternative uses.

13   Specifically, in the estimation of the tangible costs of haze, our study included (1) health cost, (2) loss in tourism, (3) loss in business as an indirect effect from loss of tourist receipts, (4) productivity loss due to RADs and (5) cost of mitigation and adaptation by government agencies and households. For the estimation of the intangible costs, the value was derived from the contingent valuation study conducted by us in 2018 to estimate Singapore residents' willingness to pay for a pro-environment collaboration project that could effectively stop 'slash and burn' practices and hence solve the annual haze pollution issue. The survey was conducted on 793 Singapore citizens and permanent residents aged 21 and above.

The total tangible cost, total intangible cost and total cost of the 2015 haze episode are summarized in Tables 51.7–51.9. Some key findings from the study are also highlighted and discussed.

14   The total cost of the 2015 haze episode on Singapore which lasted for two months was estimated at S$1.83 billion, amounting to 0.45 per cent of the country's gross domestic product. This economic burden was equivalent to a per capita (resident population) cost of S$468. Accordingly, the total tangible cost was

Table 51.7 Tangible cost of haze: total tangible cost and its percentage of GDP

Cost component	S$	Percentage
Health cost	810,089,768	55.31
Loss in tourism	163,729,280	11.18
Loss in business	158,817,402	10.84
Productivity loss	264,862,654	18.08
Cost of mitigation and adaptation	67,064,491	4.58
Total tangible cost	1,464,563,595	100.00

Note: The health cost is estimated based on a threshold PSI of 70.

Table 51.8 Total cost of haze: total cost and its percentage of GDP

	S$	Percentage of GDP
Total tangible cost	1,464,563,595	0.36
Total intangible cost	363,583,440	0.09
Total cost of 2015 haze episode	1,828,147,035	0.45

Table 51.9 Economic burden of haze: per capita cost

	S$
Per capita cost (resident population)	468

estimated at S$1.46 billion (0.36 per cent of GDP) while the total intangible cost stood at S$363.58 million (0.09 per cent of GDP).

15 The largest item within the total tangible cost of haze was health cost. Exposure to haze has an impact on health, both on morbidity and premature mortality. For morbidity, symptoms of ill-health include sore throat, coughing, difficulty breathing, nasal congestion, painful and watery eyes, running nose, sensitive skin and chest pain. Besides ill-health, severe pollution could also lead to premature mortality. The total health cost was estimated at S$810.09 million which accounted for close to 55 per cent of the total tangible cost of haze.

16 The next largest cost was the loss in productivity. Affected countries suffered a loss in productivity due to haze-related illness. This is commonly known as RADs which is formally defined as days in which an individual spends over half of the day in bed, away from work or school, or cutting down on usual activities because of illness or injury. Specifically, RADs focus on workdays among gainfully employed adults or schooldays lost among children due to physical illness, injury, a mental or emotional problem or even caring for a family member with health problems. RADs provide an indication of the burden of illness in the workplace and in school. Such losses can be significant because smoke haze pollution leads not only to ill-health but also to school closure in Singapore and Malaysia. Our study reported a total cost of S$264.86 million or 18 per cent of the total tangible cost.

17 Loss in tourism and loss in businesses were pretty much the same. We found that the international tourist arrivals in Singapore were adversely affected by haze. Haze in 2015 resulted in a decrease of 57,248 tourist arrivals per month in the month of haze for Singapore. Loss in tourism and loss in businesses together accounted for a total of S$322.55 million or 22 per cent of the total tangible cost.

18 In addition to all these losses, both households and government also incurred aversive expenditure which includes face masks, air purifiers, provision of information by the government, fire-fighting and cloud-seeding. Singapore Civil Defence

Force (SCDF) spent S$46,530 to battle forest fires in Sumatra. The total cost incurred for the Singapore Air Force (SAF) during the haze deployment in 2015 was reported at S$839,508. Demand for N95 face masks and air purifiers at retailers increased significantly during the 2015 haze episode. Anecdotal evidence suggested that demand for air purifiers increased by several fold, comparing the period of haze with no haze. From our survey, average spending by households on masks and air purifiers was around S$54.01 per household. With 1,225,300 resident households in Singapore, total spending by households was estimated at S$66.178 million.

19   As for the intangible cost of haze, we estimated that an average Singapore resident is willing to pay up to S$118.04 from their annual income for haze-free air if the duration of haze was expected to last for two months. This result suggested that Singapore residents experienced sufficiently negative impact of air pollution on their day-to-day life during the haze periods that they are willing to trade-off personal wealth for better air quality. The estimate of total WTP, based on our survey was S$363.58 million.

20   From our study we found that if haze is here to stay, for a one-month haze episode, Singapore citizens and permanent residents were actually willing to pay approximately S$51.31 (S$102.62 for two months) from their annual income on measures that can reduce the local impacts of haze through timely dissemination of information on air quality, provision of face masks and subsidized healthcare for haze related illnesses during any haze period and programmes that encourage work-from-home and study-from-home during the haze period.

Based on the findings in the study, we provide a few suggestions:

21   The estimate of S$1.40 billion (excluding the cost of mitigation and adaptation of S$67.06 million) for a two months haze episode suggests that any measures that require the country to invest a few hundred million dollars in averting a bad haze year or a billion or so in permanently mitigating haze are deemed feasible.

22   In the event that haze is here to stay, our study suggests that a clear response from the government which includes timely dissemination of information to the public and provision of face masks and subsidized healthcare for haze related illness is highly applaudable. The Singapore government can take even a more active role in encouraging programmes that allow for work-from-home and study-from-home. Besides, the government can also consider imposing a mandatory shutdown of outdoor sports facilities when PSI levels reach very unhealthy or hazardous levels. Compensation schemes should be carefully designed for affected businesses.

23   In the event that haze turns out to be a regular occurrence in the long run, the government should educate the public to accept that the haze is here to stay, and come up with adaptation strategies which could be more effective in mitigating the ill effects of haze in order to live with it.

Note

1 Reproduced and adapted from Chia, Wai-Mun (Quah and Toh, 2012) and opinion article by Quah and Chia (2019, September 17) in *Straits Times* with additions.

52 Economic cost of diseases

1 CBA is most commonly applied by government or regulatory bodies, both national and international, to evaluate whether certain policies are worth undertaking. Further, of the policies brought under the domain of CBA, a significant proportion are related to reducing the incidence of particular diseases. As such, this chapter discusses how the economic cost of disease, and hence the benefits from reducing the incidence of the disease, is typically measured. The steps involved in the measurement are then illustrated through a study of the economic cost of dengue, an infectious tropical disease, in Singapore.

2 If an individual were to compile a list of all the costs involved in falling ill, he/she would most likely state items such as 'medical costs', 'loss of wages' and the 'general misery of being sick'. Similarly, the costs of any disease may be broadly classified into:

1   the expenditure on medical care;
2   the loss of current production; and
3   the pain and discomfort associated with the disease.

The expenditure on medical care would include the costs of the services provided by all medical personnel, the cost of drugs prescribed and the equipment and facilities required. Also, it makes sense to distinguish medical costs of the patient and medical costs of the patient's family. Disease incidence affects the quality of life and mental health of the patient's family members which may incur additional medical costs because of this. Aside from the patient and his/her family-specific costs, there are also additional direct medical costs for society as a whole due to the administrative costs of healthcare and increased tax incidence. Direct medical cost is probably the easiest to measure and usually constitutes a bigger part of the total disease burden. The benefit of preventing direct healthcare costs alone may justify policy intervention. For example, a community-based lifestyle changes programme in the US could delay and prevent Type 2 Diabetes and generate $5.7 billion in direct medical savings in a span of 25 years (Zhuo et al., 2012). Diabetes is extremely costly for US Health Care, accounting for one-tenth of its expenditures in 2007.[1] Nonetheless, due to the high cost of policy intervention, the benefits can be seen only in the long term, within 25 years of implementation.

The loss of current production has two components. First, there is the loss of earnings from having to take time off due to treatment and convalescence. Second, the loss of earnings from reduced productivity due to having been weakened by the disease. What is more, the patient's family members' productivity and school performance may also be compromised which will only increase the total cost of disease for society. Non-family workers may also be affected due to the illness of their colleagues and experience reduced productivity.

The third category, the pain and associated discomfort, is the hardest to measure. While it is undoubtedly a cost, a standardized and reliable measure has yet to be developed. Most current procedures are arbitrary in nature. Most common methods include contingent valuation studies through stated preference, given the obvious methodological difficulties in capturing the intangible costs and benefits. Nonetheless, well-being losses caused by diseases should not be omitted in full CBA as they may constitute a sensible proportion of the total costs of disease. Indirect evidence of high intangible costs may be drawn from a study done on well-being losses from informal care provision by female caregivers in Germany (Schmitz and Westphal, 2015). Informal care by family members is an essentially non-market service that is hidden from direct healthcare costs. These intangible costs may magnify the total burden of disease for society to such a degree that omission of these costs can lead to misguided decision making and as a result to non-efficient use of public funds.

Although the above classification provides a useful framework for calculating the economic costs of diseases, a common criticism levelled at it is the absence of explicit links to economic principles. However, the criticisms are of a more theoretical nature and we will not discuss it in detail here.

Instead, we present an actual study of the cost of dengue in Singapore, to illustrate the method discussed above.

3   Recent reports on dengue, a mosquito-borne disease, have documented a sobering increase in the number of incidences and deaths. The disease without doubt is currently one of the most common arthropod-borne diseases worldwide, representing a major health and economic burden to many tropical and subtropical countries. Cases of dengue fever (DF) were described more than 200 years ago and histories of dengue and dengue epidemics were documented (Ehrenkranz *et al.*, 1971; Halstead, 1980; Pinheiro, 1989; Gubler, 1991; Halstead, 1992; Gubler and Trent, 1994). After the Second World War, populations of most of the most important mosquito vector, *Aedes aegypti*, were suppressed. The control campaigns, however, were abandoned in the early 1970s and the vector re-established itself in virtually all of the countries that had vector control campaigns and further expanded into a few new areas. This re-establishment of the vector has resulted in the dengue viruses spreading rapidly around the globe. During the last two decades, all countries in the tropical regions (Singapore included) have experienced a marked increase in the incidence of both DF and dengue haemorrhagic fever (DHF). Globally, an average of 25,000 cases of DHF per year were reported from 1956 to 1980. From 1981 to 1985, the number increased to 137,504. From 1986 to 1990, the average number of reported DHF cases per year increased to 267,692. The World Health Organization (in 2006) estimated that approximately two billion people are living in tropical and subtropical countries and an additional 120 million each year are travelling to these countries. Therefore a large share of the world population is at risk of contracting dengue.

The widespread distribution and rising incidence of dengue virus infection world-wide and the large numbers of people afflicted have resulted in dengue being classified by national and international public health authorities as an emerging or re-emerging infectious disease (Gubler and Clark, 1995; LeDuc, 1996). Although Tones (1997) argued that the estimated loss associated with the disease is in the same order of magnitude as tuberculosis, sexually transmitted diseases (excluding HIV/AIDS), Chagas disease, Leishmaniasis or intestinal Helminths, only rarely are studies found focusing on the disease burden of dengue. Estimates of the total direct and indirect costs from the 1977 epidemic in Puerto Rico are found ranging from US$6.1 million to US$15.6 million (Von Allmen *et al.*, 1979). The 1980 epidemic in Cuba, with 344,203 reported cases, cost US$103 million. Another outbreak in 1980 in Thailand was estimated to cost approximately US$6.8 million. Recently, a study (Tones, 1997) on the impact of an outbreak in rural Puerto Rico has shown a loss of income attributable to the disease of US$305 per household or US$125 per person. The direct costs of DHF in Thailand in 1994 were estimated to be US$13.36 million for 51,688 cases (Sommani *et al.*, 1995). When indirect costs were included, the cost of DHF was estimated to be between US$19.3 million and US$51.9 million.

4   Like many other countries, the incidence of the disease in Singapore has shown cyclical peaks and troughs since 1980. More importantly, every three to four years a reduction in dengue incidence is followed immediately by a two to three years increase in reported incidence. The new peaks in the incidence have been consistently higher than those observed in the previous cycles. For instance, when the first peak was observed in 1982, only 216 cases were reported. Subsequently, 436 cases were reported in 1987, followed by 2,878 cases in 1992, 5,258 cases in 1998 and more recently 14,209 cases in 2005. Despite the large number of victims, no comprehensive study has been found to estimate not only the disease burden of dengue but also the economic cost of dengue.

It is imperative to know the magnitude of the health consequences that are attributed to dengue as such knowledge is necessary for performing a CBA for devising cost-effective abatement strategies and guiding policy decisions. The objective of this study is to assess and evaluate the economic cost of dengue in Singapore using primary data from 1980 to 2007. Special attention focuses on the most recent cycle of 1999–2005. The estimated economic cost of dengue is provided for first, for a low incidence year in 2000, second, for a high incidence year in 2005 and third, the more recent medium incidence years of 2006 and 2007. The assessment and evaluation is the first step in developing a more consistent national approach to dengue management. In this study, a two-step procedure is adopted. First, the incidence of dengue is determined. Second, economic (monetary) values of mortality and morbidity are calculated to estimate the health impact in terms of an increase in mortality and morbidity due to dengue. Other costs, such as the cost of dengue prevention and control incurred by various government agencies, are also included. The cost from lost tourism is identified as an important economic cost of dengue to Singapore. However, as no formal study has been found showing the impact of dengue on the number of tourist arrivals, it is therefore viewed as an important cost but not included in our study. Figure 52.1 summarizes the estimation methodology.

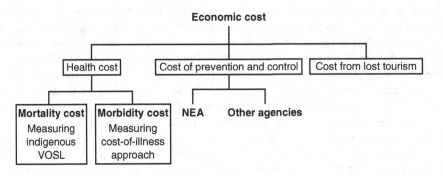

Figure 52.1 Estimation methodology

The study is structured as follows. Section two provides an overview of the incidence of dengue in Singapore. Section three describes the proposed methodology for estimating the economic cost associated with dengue. This section also details the baseline assumptions that are required for such estimations. Section four provides the results and discussions of the economic cost associated with dengue in the four cycles. The section also specifically compares the morbidity and mortality costs of dengue in low and high incidence years. Section five concludes the discussion.

5   Figure 52.2 splits the data into cycles. From the four cycles, three interesting observations are documented. First, the incidence of the disease has shown cyclical peaks and troughs since 1980. Second, the incidence of dengue transmission has increased significantly in Singapore. Since 1987, the number of reported cases of

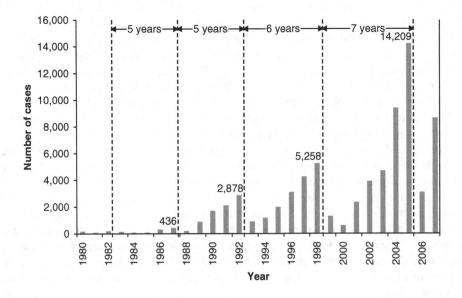

Figure 52.2 Dengue cycles, 1980–2007

DF has been significant. Importantly, every three to four years a reduction in dengue incidence is followed immediately by a two to three year increase in reported cases. Further, the new peaks have been higher than those observed in the previous cycle. For instance, from the peak of 436 in 1987, the incidence of dengue increased to 2,878 in 1992, to 5,258 in 1998 and up to 14,209 in 2005. Overall, the average annual DF incidence increased by 562.2 per cent (first to second cycle), by 76.3 per cent (second to third cycle) and 86.9 per cent (third to fourth cycle). Third, the length of each cycle has lengthened from five years to six years and then to seven years.

Figure 52.3 shows the number of deaths from 1999 to 2007. The highest number of deaths is observed in 2005. This is probably because of the significant outbreak of 14,209 cases reported in 2005. Anecdotal evidence from Singapore seems to suggest that the number of deaths was higher for adults aged 15 years and above. For instance, patients over 15 years old represented all the nine deaths reported in 2004, the 25 out of 27 deaths reported in 2005 and nine out of ten deaths reported in 2006.

The estimation in this study measures the health cost associated with dengue in terms of morbidity and mortality costs. The morbidity cost is estimated using a commonly known approach, the cost-of-illness (COI) approach, which concentrates on the aspects of the value of health that are well defined with observable quantities, as well as directly measurable. Medical expenditures and foregone earnings due to illness are considered. The COI approach regards people as productive agents who yield a continuing return in the future. The expenditure and value of any resources used in promoting health are referred to as the direct COI. The loss of labour earnings due to sickness and the lost product of labour are considered as the indirect COI. The mortality cost is measured using the VOSL in Singapore. Other costs, such as the cost of dengue prevention and control incurred by various government agencies, are also included.

6 In estimating the direct morbidity costs covering costs of treatment, the average number of days of illness and the cost of healthcare are estimated. Based on the

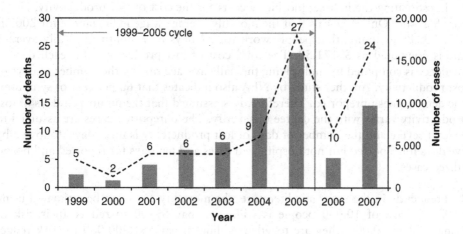

Figure 52.3 Dengue cycle 1999–2005

Table 52.1 Number of patients hospitalized on various types of wards (2006–2007)

Ward	Number hospitalized	%	Bill size per day 50th percentile S$	Total bill size 90th percentile S$
Ward A	164	17.41	438.95	1,624.11
Ward B1	108	11.46	321.17	1,188.34
Ward B2	263	27.92	126.55	468.25
Ward C	407	43.21	78.80	291.57
Total	942	100.00		

Source: Data obtained from website of the Ministry of Health, Singapore, www.moh.gov.sg/mohcorp/stat istics.aspx?id=242, between 1 May 2006 and 30 April 2007.

data provided by the Ministry of Health, the average number of days of hospitalization is 3.7 days per person admitted with dengue.

The level of expenditure on hospitalization bills is obtained from the website of the Ministry of Health. The data obtained is for the period of 1 May 2006 to 30 April 2007. The average bill sizes per day for various wards are calculated by dividing the total bill sizes by the average number of days spent at different hospitals. After calculating the average bill sizes per day for each hospital, the average bill sizes for different wards are computed and summarized in Table 52.1. The 50th percentile indicates that 50 per cent of patients pay this amount or less and 50 per cent pay more. This figure provides an estimate of the typical bill size for patients. For instance, a typical patient pays S$438.95 per day for Ward A, S$321.17 per day for Ward B1, S$126.55 per day for Ward B2 and S$78.80 per day for Ward C. The total bill sizes are obtained by multiplying the bill sizes per day by the average number of days of hospitalization, i.e. 3.7 days. Table 52.1 also shows that 17.41 per cent of patients stayed in Ward A, 11.46 per cent in Ward B1, 27.92 per cent in Ward B2 and 43.21per cent in Ward C. The weighted average of the total bill size is obtained. It is found that the weighted average bill size is S$675.70 for each incidence of dengue.

7 In estimating the indirect morbidity costs for the cost of lost productivity, Singapore Statistics Online reveals that the monthly average wage in Singapore for 2007 is S$3,773. By assuming that people work for 22 days in a month, the daily average rate is computed as S$171.50. The total cost of lost productivity for each dengue incidence is computed by multiplying the daily average rate by the number of days of lost productivity. Another study by NEA also indicates that 60 per cent of symptomatic dengue goes unreported. Therefore, it is assumed that the number of days of lost productivity varies with the degree of severity. The unreported cases are assumed to be least severe and the number of days of lost productivity is three days, followed by five days for reported but not hospitalized cases and ten days for reported and hospitalized cases.

8 Frequently in the economic literature, the mortality costs can be estimated using VOSL. If each of 10,000 people is willing to pay S$100 to reduce their risk of dying by 1 in 10,000, they are together willing to pay S$1,000,000 for risk reductions of that sum to one statistical life. The S$1,000,000 is the value of statistical

Table 52.2 Total cost of prevention and control

Year	Government agencies S$ million	NEA S$ million	Total S$ million
1999	1.47	14.70	16.17
2000	1.46	14.60	16.06
2001	1.62	16.20	17.82
2002	1.62	16.20	17.82
2003	2.50	25.00	27.50
2004	2.50	25.00	27.50
2005	5.15	51.50	56.65
2006	10.00	52.30	62.30
2007	88.40	63.50	151.89

Source: Based on data from the National Environment Agency (NEA), Singapore and other sources.

life. In estimating the mortality costs of dengue in Singapore, we use S$2.05 million as estimated by Quah et al. (2009).

9   Various government agencies in Singapore provided their estimated costs incurred in dengue prevention and control in 2007. Out of 21 government agencies, 16 responded. Additionally, the NEA managed to provide estimated costs from 1999 to 2007. Table 52.2 summarizes the estimated costs incurred by Singapore's government agencies in combating dengue.

It is noted that total costs of prevention and control increased substantially in the high incidence year of 2005 and the subsequent years.

10   In estimating the morbidity and mortality costs associated with dengue we calculate the costs for the four cycles of 1983–87, 1988–92, 1993–98 and 1999–2005 with special focus on the most recent cycle of 1999–2005. We also compute the morbidity and mortality costs for 2006 and 2007, respectively.

According to Ministry of Health records, 80–90 per cent of patients diagnosed with dengue were hospitalized before 2006. However, when a set of new admission criteria was implemented in 2006, only 68 per cent of patients diagnosed were hospitalized. Therefore, in estimating the economic costs associated with dengue, we take into consideration the following. First, the percentage of hospitalization varies from 80 to 90 per cent for the period 1980–2005. For a more conservative estimate, 80 per cent

Table 52.3 Total health cost of dengue

Cycle	Health cost of dengue (S$ million)
1983–1987	25.31
1988–1992	57.18
1993–1998	75.47
1999–2005	209.15
2006	27.09
2007	32.69

Source: Author's own calculations.

Table 52.4 Total economic cost of dengue, 1999–2005

Cost	2005 S$	2006 S$	2007 S$
Mortality cost	55.35	20.50	14.35
Morbidity cost	32.47	6.59	18.34
Cost of prevention and control	56.65	62.30	151.89
Total economic cost (S$ million)	144.47	89.39	184.58

Source: Author's own calculations.

of hospitalization is assumed for the period 1980–2005 and 68 per cent of hospitalization is assumed for 2006–2007. Second, mortality costs are estimated using the VOSL of S$2.05 million. Third, the average number of days of hospitalization is 3.7 days. The loss of productivity days varies from three days for unreported cases, five days for reported but not hospitalized cases and ten days for reported and hospitalized cases. Fourth, since formal study focusing on the effect of dengue on lost tourism is virtually non-existent, we are aware of the potential tourism loss but do not consider it in this study.

11   Table 52.3 summarizes the total morbidity and mortality costs. Total morbidity and mortality costs increase over the cycles. For the estimation using the VOSL of S$2.05 million, the total morbidity and mortality costs for the cycles 1999–2005, 1993–98, 1988–92 and 1983–87 are S$209.15, S$75.47 million, S$57.18 million and S$25.31 million, respectively.

Based on the above, it is concluded that the total and average morbidity and mortality costs of dengue show a significant rising trend.

12   Figure 52.4 shows the number of dengue cases reported and the morbidity and mortality costs for the cycle 1999–2005 using the VOSL of S$2.05 million.

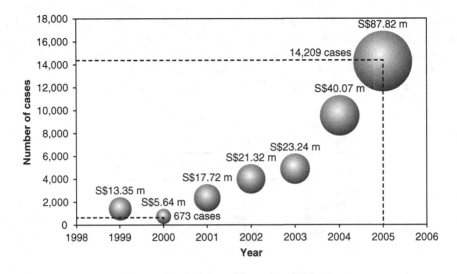

Figure 52.4 Total health cost of dengue, 1999–2005

It is noted previously from Figure 52.2, for the cycle 1999–2005, that 2005 is identified as a high incidence year where 14,209 cases were reported (with 8,525 cases unreported) compared to only 673 cases (with 404 cases unreported) in 2000. From Figure 52.4, the estimated morbidity and mortality costs increase with the number of cases reported. Using the VOSL of S$2.05 million, the costs are S$87.82 million in the high incidence year of 2005 compared to only S$5.64 million in the low incidence year of 2000. In other words, the morbidity and mortality costs of dengue in the high incidence year are approximately 15 times higher compared to the low incidence year, measured using the VOSL of S$2.05 million.

13 Based on the data provided, we estimate the overall economic cost of dengue in 2005. The costs include (1) morbidity cost, (2) mortality cost and (3) cost from prevention and control by various government agencies. Figure 52.5 shows the breakdown of costs of dengue in 2005 assuming no loss in tourism. The overall economic cost of dengue amounts to S$144.47 million. The cost of prevention and control, mortality cost and morbidity cost makes up 39.2 per cent, 38.3 per cent and 22.5 per cent of the economic cost of dengue, respectively.

Table 52.4 shows the overall economic cost of dengue using a VOSL of S$2.05 million. The economic cost is S$144.47 million in 2005, S$89.39 million in 2006 and S$184.58 million in 2007.

14 Dengue virus infection is without doubt one of the most common arthropod-borne diseases worldwide, representing a major health and economic burden for many tropical countries including Singapore. This study quantifies the economic cost associated with dengue for the four cycles of 1983–87, 1988–92, 1993–98 and 1999–2005. The morbidity and mortality costs for 2006 and 2007 are also estimated. The study may serve as an important guide for policy makers as the estimates indicate the magnitude of the problem and provide a necessary perspective, so that fighting dengue can be prioritized relative to other interventions that improve public health. Based on this study, several important findings have been identified. First, the morbidity cost per case covering the direct cost of hospitalization and medical care and the indirect cost of lost productivity is approximately S$1,495 before 2006 and S$1,380 after 2006. This is because of the observed reduction in the percentage of

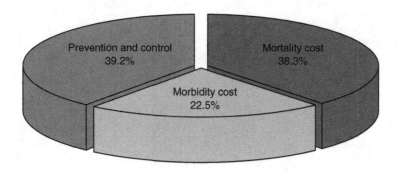

Figure 52.5 Breakdown of the economic cost of dengue in 2005

hospitalization from 80 to 90 per cent before 2006 to only 68 per cent after 2006. The mortality cost per case is estimated based on a VOSL of S$2.05 million. Second, when an estimation is made for the most recent cycle 1999–2005, the morbidity and mortality costs of dengue in a high incidence year are approximately 15 times higher compared to a low incidence year. Third, using a VOSL of S$2.05 million, the cost of prevention and control, mortality cost and morbidity cost makes up 39.2 per cent, 38.3 per cent and 22.5 per cent of the economic cost of dengue, respectively.

The overall economic cost associated with dengue may be small in magnitude compared to Singapore's GDP but it is an increasing trend. Hopefully, to some extent, it may gain sufficient attention from decision makers in setting health priorities and making budgetary decisions. The study suggests that when resources for research and control are allocated, dengue should be given a priority equal to many other infectious diseases that are generally considered more important.

Note

1 American Diabetes Association (2008). Economic Costs of Diabetes in the U.S. in 2007. *Diabetes Care*, 31(3): 596–615.

53 Cost-benefit analysis and the problem of locating environmentally noxious facilities (NIMBYs)

An informal discussion

1 A major concern of CBA is in the identification, quantification and valuation of environmental damage associated with proposed projects. Predominant among these external environmental effects are air pollution, water pollution and noise pollution causing hazards to human health and deterioration in environmental quality. These degradations in environmental quality are mainly the result of a lack of ownership rights such that there are no market transactions, and hence no market prices, to indicate values. People who have to put up with these noxious effects that are mainly the incidental by-products of a project go uncompensated. Therefore, it is the task of a CBA economist to measure these environmental disamenities as part of the social costs of a project.

The siting of locally noxious facilities such as sewage treatment works, city airports, electric power plants and incinerators is another important area where a CBA study would be helpful for decision makers. These are facilities that offer useful services to the general public and are often considered 'necessary' by society, but almost everyone agrees that they should be located at places outside their neighbourhoods: the so-called 'NIMBY (not in my backyard) syndrome' (Popper, 1983).

A CBA study of an environmentally noxious facility based on a national accounting stance rather than a local or regional one would, invariably in most cases, lead to acceptance of the facility, bowing to the demands of a greater general public.[1] People who live in the neighbourhood and are the direct recipients of the negative externality often go uncompensated under a Kaldor–Hicks efficiency criterion and, consequently, too many of these projects may be proposed.

2 What do garbage dumps, airports, sanitary landfill, sewage treatment plants, strip mines and nuclear power facilities all have in common? For one thing, these are facilities which, to a large extent, involve the public sector in full or partial ownership or have substantial government operating subsidies. Further, where the physical facility requires a fairly large tract of land, this would usually be acquired under the laws of compulsory acquisition. In the construction of hydroelectric power plants or any nuclear facility, a public utility regulatory agency is also typically involved. Thus, the public sector, whether acting as owner, financial supporter or regulator, must decide, first, on the merits of having the facility and, second, after having decided for the facility, where it should be located.

The second characteristic of these environmentally noxious facilities is that they generally impose non-exclusive negative externalities in the immediate neighbourhood. Examples of such disamenities are pollution, displeasing aesthetics and even potentially life-threatening hazards, as in chemical plants, nuclear facilities and electrical transmission stations. While the greater public (at regional or national levels) enjoys the goods and services newly created, or outputs, at reduced monetary costs, it is the local residents who must put up with such non-exclusive disamenities.

As these environmentally noxious facilities are becoming larger in size and operation, they are more likely to be sited in remote areas or areas with a rural background. It is also in these areas that the potential for environmental and ecological conflict of a much larger scale becomes likely.

Concern over social, economic and negative environmental impacts, from megaprojects, has led to the increasing adoption of more open processes for discussions on project evaluation. These processes normally involve public participation and open forums to ensure that all parties can express their concerns. In some cases, strong local opposition may even succeed in having a proposed facility relocated elsewhere or redesigned for mitigation of its more negative impacts. While these cases are rare, it is without doubt that the decision process can be time-consuming and, in most cases, a costly exercise. In cases where, on the one hand, the local residents are opposed to the siting of the facility, the larger public, on the other hand, demands a faster response in meeting its needs. The characteristics of these environmentally noxious facilities are such that the problem of location involves more than the usual standard cost-benefit calculations, and may require a time-consuming process searching for a conflict-resolution instrument acceptable to all.

3   There are six commonly suggested conflict-resolution instruments for the siting and local acceptance of an environmentally noxious facility in a particular neighbourhood. These are: local regulations such as zoning; public hearing and environment impact assessments; licences and permits; compulsory acquisition of land with market compensation; mitigation policies; and general compensation.

4   Local governments or municipalities in most countries have the authority to impose certain bylaws and regulations pertaining to environment and land use. Zoning, for example, involves the division of land into districts that have different regulations. These regulations are in the form of legal constraints under which land use, rights and entitlements are defined and can be exchanged. These regulations are usually formulated and based on a master or comprehensive plan designed to protect and promote the health, safety and welfare of the local population.

Public-sector economists tend to favour zoning as an effective regulatory measure for promoting efficient resource allocation in areas of incompatible land use, especially where public–private interests conflict. Zoning is supposed to correct market imperfection in the presence of negative externalities so that it results in prices of land that equal the true marginal product without causing the prices of similar land to differ. Two types of zoning exist: separation-of-land use zoning divides an area into zones and permits only certain land uses in each zone, for example, separate zones for residential, commercial and industrial use; exclusionary zoning restricts certain land uses altogether. For example, it may regulate the planting of trees and shrubs, billboards, colours, heights of buildings and other aesthetic considerations.

While zoning regulations do lessen conflicts in incompatible land uses, they do not by themselves extinguish any negative externalities emanating from an environmentally noxious facility imposed on the surrounding neighbourhood. To the extent that less favoured areas or municipalities are used for siting environmentally noxious facilities, the question is whether property owners in such areas should be compensated for bearing the negative externality. Zoning can also be too complex and costly a measure to result in optimal land uses because of lengthy and elaborate zoning processes.

Thus, zoning regulations neither protect nor compensate residents of less favourably zoned areas. Also, where mega-projects involving state or federal authorities are concerned, local governmental regulations become relatively ineffective: land can be re-zoned, special permits can be granted, the law can be invoked and political pressures can be applied.

5   International lending agencies (for example, the World Bank) increasingly require that explicit attention be given to the environmental impact of proposed projects and that this be included in any loan applications (Earth Summit, 1992). Environment impact assessments are a means to avoid post-facility consequences which have been unanticipated or underestimated (Fischer and Davis, 1973; Schofield, 1987). In the process of accounting, measuring and valuing environmental impacts of projects, opportunities are provided for informal public hearings, review and comments from professionals, and meetings with various interest groups. Although less than perfect solutions, environment impact statements are meant to identify negative environment changes early, so that mitigation, modification of the scale of the project, relocation of the facility or even dropping the proposed project entirely can be undertaken (Ortolano, 1997; Lee and Kirkpatrick, 2000).

To the extent that environment impact assessments are public information, environmental litigation by strong local opposition may not be uncommon. The cost of such actions (temporary injunctions) is the delay in initiating projects and, along with it, the project benefits. Often, a ready presumption is that citizen participation and judgement lack scientific rigour in estimating environmental impacts, but it must also be recognized that the values of planners or evaluators need not coincide with the values held by the people. The evaluations should reflect the values of all the people potentially affected by a proposed project or facility and not just some of the people, in this case, the planners and the outside residents.

While evaluation methods such as checklists, matrices, networks, map overlays and computer simulation provide very useful aids to decision making, assessment can be improved further by infusing them with information on public attitudes, and especially those of the local residents of a neighbourhood facility, *early* in the design and planning stages. Most environment impact assessments tend to overlook this useful view. Better and more informed decision making requires both quantitative and qualitative assessments (for example, more local public opinion surveys and forums). To the extent that forums are incorporated into an environment impact assessment, these are very useful conflict-resolution instruments. For large-scale projects involving government funding, environment impact assessments are now required in Indonesia and Malaysia.

6   As with all large-scale installations, environmentally noxious facilities normally require some form of building and operational licence or permit. This is another conflict resolution instrument which carries with it opportunities for public hearing and involvement. Depending on the strength of the arguments and evidence

provided by project opponents, the proposed facility may be reduced in scale, relocated or even abandoned.

Licensing and obtaining permits, however, requires considerable documentation and, at times, comprehensive surveys, such that delays in project benefits and outputs are inevitable. In the United States, for example, a study has shown that, in the extreme case of a proposed siting of a nuclear power facility, the construction-permit review or resolution stage may take up to eight years to be completed (Randall, 1987). While extreme care and effort must be taken in deciding on the location of nuclear facilities, in other less life-threatening situations the important question must be whether the demands of the larger society can afford the delays brought about by such procedures.

7   Compulsory acquisition of land where private owners are compensated with market values for their land is another widely used conflict-resolution instrument, which may, however, result in losses of welfare to private landowners. Compulsory acquisition recognizes the need for the legal–state machinery to compel reluctant landowners to dispose of their land for a public purpose. It is also used to prevent unjust enrichment on the part of private landowners who are only prepared to give up their land for a price several times higher than the market price of the land. Without such legal power, a private landowner would be 'in a position to hold the (proposed) scheme and name his price' (*Fraser v. R.* [1963] SCR 455).

In most instances, compulsory acquisition recognizes the comparative method of valuing property. This involves a comparison of data collected from various sales of similar properties in the same or similar localities.

It must be emphasized, however, that compulsory land acquisition can only be justified if the public benefits outweigh the private costs inclusive of the losses to dispossessed landowners. The rationale of paying market compensation is that the money sum awarded to the expropriated landowners would enable them to purchase a similar property and, consequently, be made no worse off. Society can then make use of the land resource for whatever public purpose it has in mind that would confer a positive net benefit, thereby increasing social welfare.

However, it is well known that land, unlike most goods and services traded in the market, is not identical, and hence the implicit assumption behind market compensation, namely availability of near or perfect substitutes, is clearly unrealistic. Land is unique. Apart from physical differences, neighbourhood qualities and length of occupancy, there would still be the psychological cost of relocation to a different community, for which disturbance damage awards do not presently allow.

Insufficient compensation payments would also mean too many public projects may be implemented. That market compensation for compulsorily acquired land may result in undervaluation is illustrated in Figure 53.1.

The vertical axis describes the varying levels of money income, while the horizontal axis shows the varying levels of real property services accruing to the landowner. Before the land was compulsorily acquired, the landowner enjoyed U^2 level of welfare with OX property services and OM level of money income or wealth. The property owned by the landowner has a market price given by the slope of the line P_1P^1. The landowner can sell the land OX at this price but has chosen not to do so, because he would be worse off. If he sold the land, he would end up

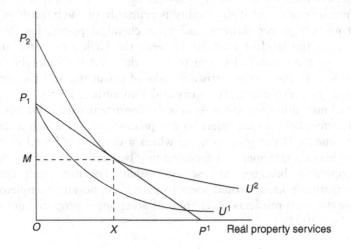

Figure 53.1

enjoying a lower welfare U^1, with zero property services and OP_1 level of money income. Thus, if the basis for compensation for compulsory acquisition of land is that of market value, the loss in welfare $(U^2 - U^1)$ may occur. Adequate compensation in OX land is, in fact, equal to OP_2.

This conflict-resolution mechanism can be highly efficient if a method can be devised to compensate dispossessed landowners for their actual loss incurred. Negative externalities imposed by an environmentally noxious facility can be internalized by also compulsorily purchasing adjacent land from their property owners and paying actual loss compensation. A buffer zone would then be created. More conscious efforts should be made to obtain property with compensation payments made agreeable to both sides: bid pricing from alternative locations may be made known to landowners so that unreasonableness and unwarranted enrichment can be minimized. A value-to-owner compensation standard may be applied (Knetsch and Borcherding, 1979). This conflict-resolution instrument has much potential and deserves more research by way of implementation acceptable to all affected parties.

8 Measures to mitigate environmental degradation and negative externalities are commonly relied upon as a useful conflict-resolution instrument in facility siting. These mitigation measures usually involve some redesigning of the facility or improved monitoring and decision procedures to reduce actual or perceived risks arising from the facility. Such measures may include the provision of a sealed covering for a sewage treatment facility (to reduce unpleasant odours and air pollution), the placing of reinforced materials around chemical storage tanks (to reduce chances of a leakage) or the installation of continuous monitoring devices within and around the facility.

Apart from those mitigation measures, which usually involve some kind of engineering or technological options, there are also mitigation measures which aim to regulate the operation of the facility through local residents' participation by way of their representation on the facility's governing board. This type of institutional mitigation measure is useful if the facility is primarily of the hazardous kind, as in the case of nuclear power stations and toxic chemical plants, for they represent efforts to reduce the level of mistrust between the facility operator and the host community. These measures also aim to raise the level of comprehension among local residents as to the actual statistical risks of accidents, and the measures that are being taken to prevent them (Gregory and Kunreuther, 1990).

Institutional mitigation measures seem to be consistent with what has been called 'procedural rationality', which refers to the processes upon which a decision outcome is determined. If the process upon which a decision is based is perceived to be flawed or biased, agreement on facility siting between the local residents and its owner or operator becomes almost impossible. Together with compensation schemes, mitigation policies would seem to play an important complementary role in promoting the local residents' likelihood of accepting a proposed noxious facility (Quah and Tan, 2002).

9   Concern over the negative external impacts arising from the siting of an environmentally noxious facility has led to the adoption of more open processes for project evaluation and, in some jurisdictions, for example, in British Columbia, Canada and in Massachusetts, United States, compensation schemes or mitigation actions are now required as part of local development. Existing compensation plans require public participation in the form of public hearings and submissions so as to identify, measure and internalize major worries and concerns held by local residents.

One simple compensation scheme proposal (scheme I) calls for local governments to submit sealed bids indicating the minimum compensation sum that they would be willing to accept from a higher-level government or quasi-government body to locate an environmentally noxious facility within their vicinity. The bids are then compared and the facility will be built in that jurisdiction which has submitted the lowest bid. This is consistent with the idea that efficiency is attained with the least-cost host provider. Each community's optimal bid will always be greater than the absolute valuation of siting the facility, such that the winning bidder will always receive a net gain from hosting the facility (Quah and Tan, 1998).

To illustrate, let v_i be the negative value to community $i(v_i < 0)$ from hosting the noxious facility in the backyard. Each community knows only its own valuation but not those of the other communities. Let us now consider how should community i should make its bid, b_i.

Let B be a monotonically decreasing bidding function. Community i assumes that any other community j will bid an amount $B(v_j)$ if its valuation of siting the facility is v_j. If community i bids an amount $b_i(b_i > 0)$ and wins, the community earns a surplus of $b_i + v_i$. If there are n communities bidding, the probability of community i winning with bid b_i is the probability that all $n-1$ other bidders have valuations such that $b_i < B(v_j)$, or $v_j > B^{-1}(b_i)$. From the properties of order statistics, this probability p_i is given by

$$p_i = \left\{ 1 - F[B^{-1}(b_i)] \right\}^{n-1},$$
(1)

where it is assumed that all the bidders' valuations are independently and identically distributed, and F denotes the probability distribution function of the valuations. Note that the probability bidder $j(j \neq i)$ has a valuation $v_j > B^{-1}(b_i)$, given by

$$p[v_j > B^{-1}(b_i)] = 1 - p[v_j < B^{-1}(b_i)] = 1 - F[B^{-1}(b_i)],$$

From the assumption of independent and identically distributed bidders, equation (1) is obtained. Community i will decide on its bid, b_i, with the view of maximizing the expected surplus, τ_i, where

$$\tau_i = (b_i + v_i)\{1 - F[B^{-1}(b_i)]\}^{n-1}. \tag{2}$$

Hence community i chooses the bid b_i such that

$$\frac{\delta \tau_i}{\delta b_i} = 0,$$

a necessary condition for an optimal solution.

Next, it is easily seen that by differentiating τ_i with respect to v_i using the chain rule we get

$$\frac{d\tau_i}{dv_i} = \frac{\delta \tau_i}{\delta v_i} + \frac{\delta \tau_i}{\delta b_i}\frac{db_i}{dv_i} = \frac{\delta \tau_i}{\delta v_i} = \{1 - F[B^{-1}(b_i)]\}^{n-1} \tag{3}$$

If rational behaviour among the bidders is assumed, at a Nash equilibrium (that is, the combination of strategies in a game such that neither player has any incentive to change strategies given the strategy of the opponent), $b_i = B(v_i)$ so that equation (3) becomes

$$\frac{d\tau_i}{dv_i} = [1 - F(v_i)]^{n-1} \tag{4}$$

Clearly, at equilibrium, all n communities must be simultaneously maximizing their expected surplus. Thus equation (4) must hold for each of the n communities.

Substituting the equilibrium condition into equation (2), we get

$$\tau_i = (b_i + v_i)[1 - F(v_i)]^{n-1};$$

that is,

$$B(v_i) + v_i = \frac{\tau_i}{[1 - F(v_i)]^{n-1}.} \tag{5}$$

Solving the differential equation (4) for τ_i (with the boundary condition that $\tau_i = 0$ when $v_i = 0$) and noting that $[1 - F(y)]$ is an even function, we obtain

$$\tau_i = \int_a^0 [1 - F(v_i)]^{n-1} dy,$$

where $a = v_i$. When this expression for τ_i is substituted into equation (5) we obtain

$$B(v_i) = -v_i + \frac{\int_a^0 [1 - F(y)]^{n-1} dy}{[1 - F(v_i)]^{n-1}} \tag{6}$$

Clearly, the last term on the right-hand side of equation (6) is non-negative. Thus,

$$B(v_i) > -v_i;$$

that is, at equilibrium, community i's optimal bid is always greater than the absolute valuation of siting the facility, so that the winning bidder will always receive a net gain from hosting the facility.

This result is consistent with that obtained by Kunreuther and Kleindorfer (1986). Using the sealed-bid auction mechanism where the community with the lowest bid gets to host the facility, they argued that the optimal bid from community i is given by

$$b_i^* = \frac{n-1}{n} \left[\min_{j \neq i}(v_{ij}) - v_i \right]$$

where $v_{ij} > 0$ denotes the value to community i of siting the facility in community $j (j \neq i)$. Again, the optimal bid $b_i^* > -v_i$.

If all the bids are perceived to be too high, plans for the facility will be shelved, reduced in scale and a rebid conducted or new sites proposed (O'Hare *et al.*, 1983; Randall, 1987).

Along similar lines, another compensation scheme (scheme II) might call for *all* municipalities to submit sealed bids, again indicating the minimum compensation sum that they would require for hosting the facility *but* compensation to be received would come from *all* the remaining non-host communities (Quah and Tan, 2002). Therefore, if community i is not selected to host the facility, then it will have to pay a tax of $b_i/(n-1)$ to help compensate the host community. As the community's WTP value is independent of the hosting community's WTA value, this auction mechanism is coalition free.

Thus, whether a particular community is geologically or physically suitable to host a noxious facility is immaterial or irrelevant to scheme II, as what is being recognized here is that the negative externalities imposed on the host community should be borne by *all* communities, because the output of the noxious facility is enjoyed by all. Just as in the case of a public good, where provision is normally made by government and paid for by general taxes, the same treatment applies here, where each municipality can be regarded as an 'individual entity' consuming the public good. As in scheme I, the eventual host community would be the one that offers to accept the facility at the *least* compensation sum.

Such a 'compensation auction' method would provide some means of assessing the actual and perceived external diseconomy brought about by the siting of the facility on the local residents and ensure that the optimal location was selected in terms of minimizing social cost. If the compensation auction method were to be conducted systematically, transaction costs in the form of delays and local opposition to the facility would be greatly minimized.

A major assumption of both compensation auction methods, however, is that local governments must have some idea how to estimate the actual and the perceived welfare loss on the part of their residents and their own municipalities. Such assessments can be difficult, and some losses are not readily identifiable. Aspects such as aesthetic nuisance and social pollution are intangible social costs. However, other items, such as the costs of treating pollution, expenditure on the required expanded infrastructure (roads, additional lighting, etc.) and compensation for land acquisition, are more easily measured and submitted for compensation. This, in turn, necessitates an agreed-upon structure and methodology for environment impact assessments and CBA between local governments and the federal or state government. Where disputes occur, an arbitration compensation board may be set up, whose decisions may be final.

However, both compensation auction schemes I and II may induce strategic bidding on the part of municipalities. In order to avoid hosting the proposed noxious facility, they may bid high. Concomitantly, there may also be municipalities bidding more than their true social costs, hoping to gain from compensation in the event that they are selected as the host community. However, at least in scheme II, there is an element of restraint in that, if a municipality strategically bids high, either to gain more than the social costs imposed or to avoid hosting the facility, the municipality may not be selected if there is at least a bid lower made by other municipalities and, worse still, the municipality concerned would have to pay for the social costs (on an equal basis with other municipalities) to the municipality that was selected under scheme II.

The above compensation auction schemes I and II can also take on different bidding formats, including first-price sealed-bid and second-price sealed-bid. Experimental findings suggest that despite the advantage of scheme II in restraining strategically higher bids, scheme II does not appear to be efficient for the siting of NIMBY facilities, because the winning bidders were often not the ones with the lowest social costs (Quah and Yong, 2008).

For more work on compensation auctions, see Quah and Tan (1999b).

10   Assuming that social costs to the local residents can be measured, there is also the question of whether the compensation received by the local government is equitably distributed to its residents in proportion to the harm suffered. Upon receiving the compensation, the local government may choose instead to reduce property taxes or provide increased services for its residents. Again, just as in the provision of some public goods, for which every individual pays through taxes, through the acceptance of a public bad, in this case a local bad, every individual receives a reduction in municipal taxes or property taxes or both. It might be argued, however, that those residents who are directly affected by the negative

externality as measured by their residential or business proximity to the facility, and those residents who lose their land through compulsory acquisition, should receive more compensation commensurate with their larger loss. And, while there are, admittedly, difficulties whenever actual compensation payments have to be made, say, to more than a few hundred families disturbed by aircraft noise, their dwellings being near an airport, one could think of compensation as being a function of decibel rating or distance to the airport.

Valuing intangibles such as peace and quiet, unpolluted air and water, aesthetic beauty and visibility is not an easy task. But to ignore such valuations or to ascribe descriptive features of them in some CBAs and environment impact analyses is to reduce them to a value of zero. The result is that people tend to take these intangibles for granted. There are quite a number of methods that have been devised by economists to measure and value such intangibles. Methods such as contingent valuation, hedonic pricing, travel cost and revealed preference have been used extensively and are continually being refined.

11   There is a crucial need to establish clear guidelines and criteria for compensation if claims are allowed. This is to minimize delays in the construction of the proposed facility by avoiding the probability or likelihood of entertaining a floodgate of claims or even litigation. Making the criteria known would also aid opponents of an environmentally noxious facility in understanding the basis upon which to make claims. A well-defined set of criteria will also avoid political controversies and rent-seeking behaviour of some parties, including municipalities.

Another advantage in establishing clear compensation criteria over negotiated claims with each party was suggested by Skaburskis (1988) in that, if the developer is a public utility, the executives, being less answerable to the market, would quite naturally be inclined towards overcompensation in order to maintain a more 'peaceful' environment and to speed up the construction of the facility. To make up for this, higher rates for the output produced would be charged to the utility's customers.

No compensation claim should be allowed for the fact that employees (consisting of outside residents) of the facility will be using existing public goods and services provided by the local government if congestion has not yet set in. Further, the savings made by the project developer because of proximity and accessibility to the local neighbourhood services should not be a factor in settling compensation claims. Using uncongested public goods and services does not create costs. Compensation should be paid only where impacts create real costs and not in cases where they involve a transfer of income or wealth. Changing the quality of the local environment and hence the reduction in values to local residents should be compensatable. Pecuniary externalities should not be compensated. The compensation scheme should require the project developer to pay for harmful effects arising from the facility, but it should also allow the owner of the facility to receive payment for beneficial impacts. Thus, only the net costs of the project should be included in the compensation package. Compensation claims should be based on significant external impacts. Those impacts that are small or remote relative to the required costs of assessing their magnitude should be excluded. Just as in standard CBA, double counting of project impacts should be avoided. For example, the owner of the facility should pay the damage done to local roads less the amount paid indirectly through the local tolls or taxes on its trucking or transport services. For more information on sets of efficiency criteria, see Skaburskis (1988) and Quah and Tan (2002).

12   Policy makers will, however, also be concerned with equity. If redistribution of income and wealth is an important goal of the federal or state government, the compensation sum received by the local government should be distributed and used more in favour of the welfare of the lower income groups, the elderly and the disabled in the local community. Ideally, people adversely affected by the negative environmental impacts should be compensated directly if they can be identified and the extent of their sufferings measured easily. Equity grounds alone would dictate that compensation claims by landowners adjacent to the facility should receive priority considerations.

Mishan (1977b: 250) has argued that the lower income groups are especially disadvantaged when it comes to spillover effects. This is because

> The rich have legal protection of their property and have less need of protection from the disamenity by others. The richer a man is the wider is his choice of neighbourhood ... In contrast, the poorer a family, the less opportunity it has for moving from its present locality. To all intents, it is stuck in the area and must put up with whatever disamenity is inflicted upon it.

One might argue, therefore, that it is the economically disadvantaged jurisdiction that would more often be the selected site for locating an environmentally noxious facility. The local residents would, in most likelihood, be unable to mount and sustain an effective opposition. This factor, together with the prospects of increased employment and money income, would almost certainly sway the arguments in favour of the location of the facility.

Notes

1 An application of Cost-Benefit Analysis is very relevant for understanding and resolving conflicts on siting issues in China's Belt and Road Initiative. For a more discussion on this subject, see Quah and Iuldashov (2020).

Part VIII

Further notes and advanced materials

54 Cost-benefit analysis analysis and the economist

1   A characteristic of the modern age is the inordinate respect which the production of figures commands. Nothing impresses people more than quantification of some sort, be it surveys, statistics, merit rankings, indices of economic or social trends, or money measures of gains and losses.

It is not surprising, then, that there is seldom a debate today about the propriety of some economic measure without someone calling for a CBA. Apparently, among politicians and the public at large, the belief persists that economists are also practitioners of a sort of black art, which enables them not only to rank economic alternatives, but also to calculate the actual magnitude of gains or losses arising from any proposed economic change.

Although the practising economist is, of course, aware that the regard in which he is held by the innocent public would not stand up well to close scrutiny, he accepts it as incumbent upon him to put himself out to go to some lengths in the attempt to produce reasonably reliable estimates of gains and losses of introducing economic measures, plus some idea of the confidence that can be reposed in his findings.

Bearing in mind such good intentions, let us now sum up our views on the practice of CBA by addressing ourselves briefly to three main aspects: (i) the methods adopted in CBA for selecting and processing the relevant data, in particular the economic concepts and techniques to be used; (ii) the ways and means of gathering data, whether from econometric studies, surveys or questionnaires; and (iii) the proposals for coping with uncertainty over the future of the movements of the relevant variables.

2   With regard to the second aspect, the ways of gathering the required data, ample space is given to it in several popular textbooks on CBA, the proposals being illustrated by innumerable examples. In this sixth edition, we depart from previous editions by including several frequently encountered topics in practical CBA where illustrations and cases are presented on how and what empirical data and methodology are often used in measuring and estimating the costs and benefits of several market and non-market goods. Also provided are a series of exercises intended to sharpen the student's understanding of the matter treated in successive chapters. Containing, as they do, a plethora of examples, tables, graphs, etc., there is much to be said for the usefulness of these quantitative illustrations and case studies.

Important as this second aspect is, we have nonetheless confined ourselves in this volume chiefly to the first and more controversial aspect – to both a detailed exposition and a critical assessment of the economic concepts and techniques that we have argued are proper to the practice of CBA. Our decision to concentrate on what may be called theoretical constructs may be justified in view of the fact that, in general, the existing treatment of this primary aspect is far from satisfactory and is, indeed, often misleading.[1]

3   Although the occasional textbook appears in which the authors vaunt their 'broad band' approach, we have no hesitation in rejecting as erroneous any manifestation of eclecticism in respect of techniques to be employed in CBA. No one doubts that a cavalier attitude in this respect makes it easier to come up with figures, indeed with sets of figures. But the question to be faced in such cases is that of the meaning to be attached to the figures.

As indicated earlier, our notion of the validity of the economic concepts and techniques that may be used in a CBA turns on its conformity with the maxims long accepted in mainstream economics, namely, (i) that the value the economist is to place on any good or bad affecting a person is no more or less than that which the person himself places on it, and (ii) that, within some defined community, the net social benefit of any economic change is equal to the algebraic sum of the individual valuations of all who, in one way or another, are affected by the change.

These maxims which go to form the only acceptable foundation on which CBAs can be raised also have the incidental but singular merit of making the findings of a cost-benefit calculation easily understood by the elected policy makers in the community. And this understanding must be augmented by making it clear that, although the calculation of a positive net social benefit may be *said* to meet a Pareto criterion, it is generally one that only realizes a *potential* potential Pareto improvement for the community.[2]

So informed, the community's decision makers are enabled to make, if not wise policy decisions, at least decisions that accord with their broad economic goals.

In this connection, moreover, we have sought to make it evident why, in any such calculation, the economist is to restrict himself to the economic data only. In particular, he is to eschew recourse to any weighting of money values, whether distributional weights or socio-political weights. The economist should, of course, be ready to inform policy makers about the distributional *consequences* of introducing specified economic measures. But it is entirely up to the policy makers themselves whether an otherwise beneficial project or measure should be rejected in consideration of the regressive distributional effects of its implementation, or vice versa.[3]

4   A penultimate word about those expected external effects that we know about yet which currently elude reliable methods of measuring their dollar value. Granted that the economist cannot include them in his calculus, he can at least make clear the area of ignorance. Thus, after seeking to measure all that can be measured with honesty, he can, first, also provide a physical description of these unmeasurable spillovers, and some idea of their significance. Second, he may offer a guess, or a range of guesses, at the value of damage to be expected. He will certainly want to avoid spurious quantification – spurious because based on invalid concepts.

Third, and as a development of the preceding suggestion, he can have recourse to what have been called elsewhere (Mishan, 1969a) 'contingency calculations', these being the estimates of a critical magnitude for these unmeasurable spillovers which will just offset the excess benefits of a project that is calculated in disregard of them.

To illustrate, if the cost-benefit calculation of a new airport produces an excess benefit over cost of some $10 million per annum for the next *t* years, but only by ignoring the aircraft noise it generates, the increased traffic congestion it causes and the increased loss of life that is expected to follow, the economist can impress the authorities and the public with the importance of these consequences by making hypothetical estimates of a critical *average* loss per person, or per family, based on rough calculations of the numbers of people likely to be affected. Thus, (a) if it were reckoned that about half a million additional families would suffer in varying degrees as a result of the newly located airport, an annual compensatory sum averaging as little as $20 per family would wholly offset the excess benefit. Again, (b) if the new airport becomes responsible for adding to the road congestion within the region of the airport, so as to cause an average delay of one hour a week to about one million motorists, this delay alone, if valued at 20 cents an hour, would wholly offset the $10 million of excess benefits of the project. Similarly for loss of life, and any other remaining side effects.

Even though the estimate of the number of people affected is speculative, provided it is not altogether implausible, the resulting contingency calculations may well cast doubt as to the economic feasibility of the scheme – enough doubt, at least, to delay a decision until estimates of these less tangible, but socially important, features of the scheme can be made with greater assurance. However, there may be instances in which the per person, or per family, valuation of the spillover deriving from the contingency calculation will be so large as to place the economic infeasibility of the scheme beyond doubt.

5 Turning to the third aspect of CBA entails removing the provisional acceptance of our estimates of annual net benefits over the future. Here we are bound to recognize the difficulties of coping with unavoidable uncertainties in the movements of the relevant prices and other variables in the years to come.

Clearly, one cannot expect the various proposals for coping with future uncertainty to be as satisfactory as those proposed for a valid framework of CBA. For one thing, of the variety of methods proposed for dealing with future consequence, none can be securely anchored in the individuals' own choices. In consequence, none can be vindicated by reference to the maxims of mainstream economics. However we may rank them, all methods proposed are, by necessity, arbitrary. The choice, in any given instance, of one technique rather than another for dealing with such uncertainty will therefore depend on the economist's own assessment of the project and the sorts of benefits and costs to be measured.

The fact that many public projects are directed to environmental improvements – to the reduction of pollution, of effluent, or to the creation of national parks, and the value of collective goods, which take the form of benefits in kind (much easier to calculate than the terminal value of annual cash payments) – the valuation of the former benefits over the future is less affected by the vicissitudes of the market or of economic events generally.[4]

6   Moreover, the 2017 Nobel Prize in Economics was awarded to Professor Richard Thaler for his contributions to behavioural economics. Professor Thaler's work essentially questions the economic dogma of the so-called 'rational man' as defined by classical economic theory, who makes decisions based on weighing the additional benefits against the additional costs of every single option.

Through a series of experiments, Professor Thaler and his colleagues (chiefly another Nobel laureate, Daniel Kahneman, and the late Amos Tversky) showed that people simplified decision making using mental shortcuts or heuristics. For example, they hold separate mental accounts for different types of income and expenditure, such as 'bills' and 'savings'. He termed this 'mental accounting'. Professor Thaler showed that people made decisions rigidly along each of these accounts.

Another significant contribution is his work on social preferences. He showed that, unlike standard economic assumptions, people value fairness and reciprocity. This is shown in many experiments and empirical work. One such experiment is known as the simple ultimatum game between two persons. The first person, or the allocator, is given a sum of money from which he or she is to share with the other person, the recipient. If the recipient refuses the amount being shared, there is no payoff for both parties. Conventional economics predicts that the recipient should accept any amount offered because of the marginal gain (since having a sum of money, no matter how small, is better than none).

However, the experiment revealed that most recipients will not accept just any amount – it must be a high enough amount. If the first person has $100 and offers to share $1, the second person is likely to reject it, although it is irrational to reject free money. Experiments show that when the offer is closer to parity, or about half of $100 in this case, the second person is more likely to accept it. Behavioural economists associate this behaviour with an innate sense of fairness, so that people would rather have no money than accept a disproportionately tiny share.

Professor Thaler's work has augmented classical or 'rational' economics, not overhauled it. In the wake of the behavioural revolution, economists have studied how to incorporate behavioural effects into existing economic models. And when some of these effects are accounted for, rationality again provides a good basis for explaining behaviour. For example, behavioural economists speak of choice overloading where a consumer will avoid making a purchase when faced with too many options. One might see this as an issue where a rational consumer is facing high transaction costs in decision making. In various versions of the ultimatum game, people make seemingly irrational choices that involve accepting a lower payoff to oneself in exchange for a fairer distribution of payoffs. These actions may be considered rational once the innate benefits from fairness are considered – essentially fairness is treated as a good with a value on it. Different individuals may set a different value on fairness. Likewise, transaction costs will differ among individuals. Seen in this light, behavioural economics is not necessarily in conflict with 'rational' economics.

Thus, policy makers must remain rationally agnostic in selecting the right policy tools. They must worship at neither the temple of rationality nor the shrine of behavioural economics. Economists have not thrown out standard economic models in response to behavioural economics. They have simply updated them. Similarly, nudges ought to augment existing public policy tools, not replace them. A rational approach of weighing the relative merits of each tool for a given purpose is required.

However, if the stakes are sufficiently high, such as in the treatment and disposal of toxic waste; or if conventional policy tools are more cost-effective, then the conventional tools ought to be used. Nudges are not inherently superior. The best policy instrument is context dependent. A rational view of behavioural economics requires us to also acknowledge that behavioural effects do have implications on a government's decision-making process. Unlike an individual, a government does not have inherent preferences for certain goods and services. Instead, a government needs to take society's preferences into account in prioritizing which goods and services to provide.

For example, in deciding whether to build a road through a nature reserve, the government needs to have a sense of society's preferences between convenience and greenery. The means of doing so is to conduct a CBA. Such an exercise puts a dollar value on otherwise non-monetary costs and benefits, allowing a holistic evaluation of the trade-offs that each option entails. And, these dollar values are computed using techniques that measure society's preferences for goods. Non-market goods, such as fairness and transaction (inconvenience) costs mentioned earlier, and others like national pride and aesthetics can be valued and included in the CBA as well.

However, precisely because CBA uses the subjective values that people place on the costs and benefits at hand, people's susceptibility to behavioural effects would also affect the computation of costs and benefits. The behavioural economics of loss aversion and the endowment effect is an example of this. There is evidence of large disparities between WTP and WTA (Horowitz and McConnell, 2002). People tend to value things more if they own them. Consequently, the amount one is willing to pay for gaining something is less than what one is willing to accept for losing it. Thus, the choice of measure matters. For example, assessing pollution damages with WTP to mitigate the pollution – rather than WTA compensation for the pollution – would produce a lower value for the cost of pollution. Thus, not taking behavioural biases into the framework of valuation may lead to serious misguidance in policy decision making. For example, the value of intervention that reduces likelihood of injury, the incidence of serious illness or environmental impact is understated if it is measured in terms of how much people are willing to pay for it rather than by how much people would demand to be denied such changes (Knetsch *et al.*, 2012).[5]

Additionally, since people value fairness, a CBA that does not explicitly take the impact of equity into account would be incomplete. CBA should include people's level of pro-social behaviour when evaluating the socio-economic impact of proposed projects.

Behavioural economics has certainly broadened the field of economics and has provided policy makers with another set of tools to use, but reminding ourselves that rationality in these insights and tools is equally important.

Notes

1 Among the more common errors still to be found in the many textbooks on the subject, we may mention: the alleged measure of 'excess loss' or 'deadweight loss' believed to be

incurred when a project is to be financed by raising excise (or even income) taxes; the measurement of 'producers' surplus' regarded as a sort of rent to producers; occasional blurring of the difference between resource cost and opportunity cost; the employment of a statistical measure of the value of a life lost, or of a disease, disablement or other misfortune; the licentious adding or subtracting of consumer surpluses without attention to the pertinent *ceteris paribus* clauses; a failure to emphasize the difference between the CV^{12} and CV^{21} measure of a good and bad which can be crucial to the cost-benefit calculation, especially in projects affecting the environment; the arguments purporting to show that the DPV method is to be preferred above the IRR method and, more generally, a naïve treatment of the ways future net benefits are to be discounted.

2 A project that affects the welfare of only a small community for a short period (no longer than three or four years) may be able, however, to realize a potential Pareto improvement.

3 It is perhaps unnecessary to remark that cost-effective analysis, which seeks to determine the lowest resource cost of meeting specified goals (or else the largest increase of some good, or largest reduction of some bad, for a given resource cost) has some affinity with the maxims of mainstream economics. Other than occasional recourse to a discounting or compounding procedure, cost-effectiveness is a less sophisticated discipline than CBA.

4 There are also other projects that wholly or in part create collective goods, yet whose benefits are far more difficult to evaluate, because they are also sure to generate a variety of externalities over the future. Included among such projects are the creation of dams, irrigation systems and canals.

5 See Knetsch *et al.* (2012) for more information on different measures of gains and losses, namely WTA losses, WTP for gains, WTA to forego reduction in losses and WTP to avoid reduction in gains.

Appendix 1
Cost-effectiveness analysis

1   The analysis of cost-effectiveness is effectively comprehended within the techniques of CBA. Yet, although a knowledge of cost-benefit techniques more than suffices for a calculation of cost-effectiveness, it is important to make explicit the difference in political constraints involved in the latter and therefore in its prescriptive significance.

First, let us highlight the basic distinction between the two by a simple illustration. Let V^a be the net value person (or group) A places on the project in question; say it is +100. And let V^b be the net value placed on it by B, say –80. For this project that affects only A and B, the cost-benefit calculation is simply $V^a + V^b$, or 100 –80 which equals +20. In contrast, a cost-effectiveness analysis would contain only V^b, a cost of 80, provided, however, that B enjoys no benefit but suffers only a loss of 80 and that A enjoys only a benefit of 100.

If, instead, A suffers a cost of 40 to be set against a gain of 140 (net gain of 100), and B suffers a loss of 110 to be set against a gain of 30 (net loss of 80), the aggregate cost of the project to A and B would be 40 +110, a total cost of 150. It should be manifest that we could equally have calculated only the benefits conferred on A and B by the project without any reference to the cost. Thus, in the preceding example the aggregate benefits alone would be 140 plus 30, a total of 170.

2   Although a benefit-effectiveness calculation may occasionally be required, a cost-effectiveness calculation is the more common. In the latter case, the problem facing the economist is that of discovering the lowest cost of achieving a particular objective regarded as desirable by the community. An example could be that of reducing the effluent poured into a river or lake to some predetermined level. Another example would be that of estimating the lowest cost of saving a life in undertaking a specific project.

A ready presumption of cost-effectiveness is that aggregate benefits must be so high as to make a project proposal desirable in itself and/or the fact that political considerations dominate the decision. For example, vaccination is probably the most cost-effective public health intervention that is undoubtedly net-beneficial to society. As shown in the study by Ozawa et al. (2011), the delivery of six life-saving vaccinations in 72 low and middle-income countries between 2011 and 2020 would prevent death of 6.4 million children under age five (or $231 billion dollars if VOSL is applied). At the same time, the benefit of policy intervention is not so obvious in cases of chronic and non-communicable diseases such as diabetes and cancer because there is a limited pool of resources but many competing health needs. Benefits need to be expressed in monetary terms for adequate comparison and assessment of policy options. Another problem arising from benefits expressed in non-monetary terms is disparity between the value of direct treatment costs and the value that the patient attaches to the treatment. For instance, it was revealed in Ubel *et al.* (2012) that the majority of oncologists surveyed agree that a new cancer treatment adding a year to a patient's life is only worthwhile when the cost is less than $100,000.[1] At the same time, another study by Seabury *et al.* (2012) has shown that patients value metastatic cancer therapy 23 times higher than its costs, which also reveals their WTP.

Whether or not the project in question will be undertaken may no longer depend upon a CBA which also calculates the benefit of the project. The decision whether to proceed may now depend only on the political process which takes account only of the information on costs.

3   It should be obvious that, in order for the problem to have an economic dimension, there must be more than one way of achieving the required change. In the first example, that of reducing effluent by a given volume, say *E*, we may suppose that there are two factories, A and B, pouring effluent into a lake, each having a distinct rising marginal cost curve of effluent-reduction. We assume that factory A is the more efficient in effluent-reduction in that its marginal cost for any given volume of effluent-removal is below that of factory B. Nonetheless, unless very little effluent is to be removed, it would generally be uneconomic to let factory A alone curb the entire amount of the effluent decided upon. The marginal cost of reducing effluent can be made lower by eventually bringing in factory B at the point where its initial marginal cost of effluent-reduction is just below that reached by factory A. As the student suspects – and as is illustrated in Chapter 19 – the optimal contributions of the two factories in reducing the required amount of effluent must be such that their marginal costs are equal. This condition ensures that the effluent is removed at least cost.

4   The same least-cost condition has to be met if, instead of a problem of removing effluent where two methods for doing so are available, the problem is that of preventing a given number of deaths from a particular disease. In such a case, however, the least-cost calculation will depend not only on the degree of risk reduction specified, but also on coverage of diseases; for, whatever the least cost happens to be, the economist is at liberty to point out that, for this same cost, a yet greater number of lives may be saved if some of this money, at least, were spent on other potentially fatal diseases.

Thus, suppose a test for lung cancer costs $1,000 per patient, and it is known from long experience that, on a first test, of every 10,000 patients tested, 100 will be shown to have the disease. Therefore, a first test costing $10 million reveals 100 of these 10,000 persons to be afflicted with lung cancer. Assuming there are no false positives and yet a slight chance of a false negative, a repetition of the test (or of a somewhat different test costing the same as the original) on the remaining 9,900 patients at a total cost of almost $10 million discovers yet another ten patients to be suffering from lung cancer. A third test on the remaining 9,890

Table A1.1 Cost of detection for lung cancer

Number of tests conducted on group of 10,000 patients	Total cost of test	Number of cancer victims discovered	Cost per detected cancer victims
1st test	$10 million	100	$100,000
2nd test	$10 million	10	$1 million
3rd test	$10 million	1	$10 million

patients, again at almost the same cost, reveals only one more patient with the disease. The decision makers may wonder whether the second and third tests are worthwhile, assuming always that there is a good chance of saving a person's life if lung cancer is detected by the test.

The economist can help in this respect by calculating the marginal cost of detecting lung cancer in a patient. A first test, which costs $10 million discovers 100 lung-cancer victims. The 'marginal cost' of a detected cancer (in such a case, marginal cost being the average cost of detecting cancer in the 100 patients suffering from lung cancer) is, therefore, equal to $100,000. A second test, which costs almost as much as the first, discovers an additional ten lung cancers with the 'marginal cost' of a detected cancer now being close to $1 million. A third test, which detects only one cancer, shows a marginal cost of nearly $10 million, as shown in Table A1.1.

Incurring a sum close to $10 million in order to save the life of one additional patient may gratify our humanitarian impulses, yet it would be economically inefficient if this sum could be used in some other way that would save more than a single life. Whatever the sum appropriated specifically for carrying out tests that would enable lives to be saved, the largest number of lives would be saved if that sum were allocated among the different disease tests on the equi-marginal principle.

5   It should be emphasized, however, that useful as a cost-effective analysis can be, a cost-*benefit* analysis is effectively superior. In our first example of effluent reduction, the economic calculation of the many benefits of reducing the level of effluent may reveal that it far exceeds the implicit value held by decision makers. In the second example, a calculation of the value of human life, or of reducing the risk of death, may warrant a far larger sum than is currently set aside for testing patients for fatal diseases. In sum, economic valuation of the benefits of a programme in addition to the calculation of its cost will provide all the relevant economic information necessary to enable policy makers to make more judicious decisions.

Note

1 At the same time, when given a hypothetical scenario of an individual patient seeking a hypothetical drug that costs $250,000, the oncologists also endorsed it. This is an example of doctors being insensitive to the healthcare costs due to omission or ignorance of cost-effectiveness information in their decision making.

Appendix 2
The alleged contradiction of the Kaldor–Hicks criterion

1   The once-famous critique of the Kaldor–Hicks criterion harks back to Scitovsky's demonstration in 1941 that the ranking from using the Kaldor–Hicks test could in fact be reversed: a movement from I to II, using the Kaldor–Hicks test would show position II to be economically superior; at the same time, having reached position II, a movement back to I would show the latter to be superior.[1]

Because this seeming paradox is familiar enough to the student of economics and in any case, it is pertinent only within a general equilibrium analysis – as distinct, that is, from a partial equilibrium context common to a cost analysis – we deal with it briefly.

What must be demonstrated here is how a movement from one collection of goods Q_1 to another collection Q_2 results in a potential Pareto improvement that is compatible with the reverse, one from Q_2 to Q_1, which also realizes a potential Pareto improvement.

2   The Scitovsky 'paradox' is easiest to illustrate and resolve using the geometry of goods space, measuring the amount of good X on the horizontal axis and the amount of good Y on the vertical axis. Let I_1 in Figure A3.1 be the community indifference curve passing through the initial collection of goods Q_1 comprising Y_1 of good Y and X_1 of good X. This collection of goods can be thought of as being divided between two persons (or two groups of persons), A and B, in a manner indicated by point d_1 on the contract curve from O to Q_1 of the box diagram, $OY_1Q_1X_1$. The tangency of d_1 between A's indifference curve I_A and B's indifference curve I_B is, by construction, parallel to the tangency of the community curve I_1 at Q_1.[2] As the alternative collection Q_2 is above the I_1 community indifference curve, it is possible to improve the welfare of everyone by moving to the Q_2 position (allowing always for sufficient divisibility). It is possible, that is, to make both A and B better off in Q_2 than in the Q_1 position.

However, *having moved* to Q_2 on this recommendation,[3] the resulting distribution of this Q_2 collection might be one such as is represented by point d_2 on the OQ_2 contract curve of the box diagram $OY_2Q_2X_2$, A's welfare (greater than it was in the Q_1 position) being represented by A's I'_A indifference curve, and B's welfare (less than it was in the Q_1 position) being represented by B's I'_B indifference curve. Again, the slope of the mutual tangency of I'_A and I'_B is, by construction, parallel with the tangent of the community indifference curve I_2 passing through Q_2. With this distribution resulting from the movement from Q_1 to Q_2, the slope at Q_2 is such that the I_2 curve passes below Q_1. And from this we infer that a movement

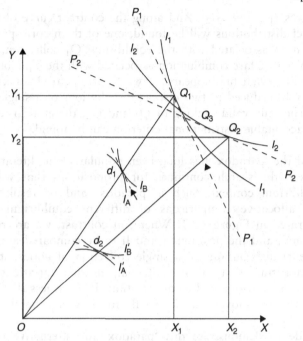

Figure A2.1

from Q_2 to Q_1 realizes a potential Pareto improvement: beginning with the d_2 distribution of Q_2, that is, a movement to Q_1 can make both A and B better off.[4]

The same apparent paradox results if, instead of community indifference curves, we make use of the relative prices arising from the respective distributions of the two collections of goods. The relative prices for Q_1 are represented by the slope of the line P_1P_1 tangent to the I_1 curve at Q_1 and, at these relative prices, it is clear that Q_2, being to the right of this price line, is valued more highly than the Q_1 collection of goods. Once the community has moved to Q_2, however, the resulting relative prices are represented by the line P_2P_2 tangent to the I_2 curve at Q_2. At these relative prices, it is equally clear that Q_1, being above the P_2P_2 line passing through Q_2, is valued more highly than the Q_2 collection of goods.

3 Now the likelihood of such a reversal actually occurring in an economy producing a large number of goods and with a population of millions of people is far smaller than that conveyed by the impression of a two-good two-person diagram. Nonetheless, it remains a disconcerting possibility and one that has to be taken seriously in attempts to prove such general economic propositions as, for instance, that international trade is better for a country than autarchy or that an optimal position is better for the community than a non-optimal one.

The resolution of this 'paradox' in 1973 is of some interest in this connection and results in a caveat about proofs of general welfare propositions. For in all such reversal cases, as illustrated in Figure A3.1, there will be a unique hypothetical collection of goods Q_3 (being the point of intersection in the Figure of community indifference curves I_1I_1 and I_2I_2). And along the contract curve of this Q_3 collection, two distinct distributions will be found, one of them corresponding with the welfare combination associated with the equilibrium Q_1 collection, the other corresponding with the welfare combination associated with the equilibrium Q_2 collection. It follows that, what first appears as two 'contradictory' collections of goods, Q_1 and Q_2, may be reduced to two distinct distributions of a single (hypothetical) collection Q_3. The only valid ranking of Q_1 and Q_2, therefore, is a distributional ranking – if an acceptable distributional criterion can be found.[5]

4 This form of the 'paradox' has long been popular in the literature on welfare economics, where the search continues for propositions that will hold within a general equilibrium context. Such a 'paradox' and its resolution, however, apply only to allocative comparisons of different equilibrium collections of goods, as illustrated in Figure A2.1. Where, in contrast, we are restricted to an exchange economy, and the positions I and II to be compared are no more than different (efficient) distributions of a single collection of goods, it is simply *not* possible to demonstrate that the sum of compensating variations is positive in the movement from distribution I to distribution II, much less that it is also positive for the reverse movement from II to I and, therefore, constitutes a 'paradox'.

Attempts made to demonstrate this 'paradox' for alternative distributions of a *single* collection of two or more goods founder on a logical inconsistency: it transpires that the exact compensating variations involved in the movement from distribution I to distribution II (or from II to I) entail amounts of the two or more goods for each person that, when added together, amount to a collection that is entirely different from the original collection. In sum, the alleged distributional comparison of a single collection is inadvertently transformed into a comparison of two collections of goods. And we already know that there is no difficulty in contriving a 'paradox' for two different collections of goods.[6]

Notes

1 Although this seeming paradox was first demonstrated by Scitovsky using the standard two-person two-good box diagram, it was, in fact, mentioned earlier by Pigou in his Economics of Welfare (1952).
2 A simple geometric technique for the construction of community indifference curves (that meet the optimal exchange condition) has been explained in Mishan (1957).
3 Though without intervening in the resulting distribution so as, by transfer payments, actually to make both A and B better off.
4 If, instead, we constructed Figure A2.1 so that I_1 passed above Q_2 and I_2 passed above Q_1, the reverse paradox is illustrated: that Q_2 is potentially Pareto inferior to Q_1, and also that Q_1 is potentially Pareto inferior to Q_2.
5 The complete exposition of this paradox resolution is found in Mishan (1973).
6 A detailed demonstration of the invalidity of the existence of a distributional 'paradox' for a single collection of goods can be found in Mishan(1976b).

Appendix 3
The problem of second-best

1   It is a commonplace that, within a general equilibrium context, the necessary conditions that result from maximizing a social welfare function subject only to a production-boundary constraint may be interpreted as equal to the marginal-cost pricing rule for all goods.[1] The Second-Best Theorem, as formulated by Lipsey and Lancaster (1956), concludes that, if but one additional constraint is imposed on the welfare function (and in the real world there will be many), the necessary conditions that emerge from the maximizing procedure are different from those identified with the marginal-cost pricing rule and, in general, are surprisingly complex.

In the simple mathematical proof of the theorem, the authors first confirm that the necessary conditions that emerge from the maximizing of a welfare function subject only to a production boundary can be shown as equal to the condition that the ratio of any two prices be equal to the *ratio* of their corresponding marginal costs, a condition that, of course, is also met when the price of each good in the economy is equal to its marginal cost. Nonetheless, the ratio condition implies that, if there is a constraint additional to the production boundary, say the price of good x alone is set irremovably 20 per cent above its marginal cost, optimality will only be met if all other goods in the economy are produced to the point where their prices are also 20 per cent above their corresponding marginal costs.[2]

It may be expedient to elaborate on this last statement, as it is occasionally asserted that for the stricter condition, prices for all goods be set *equal* to their corresponding marginal costs, since for overall optimality it is necessary to ensure equality also between the marginal product of the factor and its marginal valuation to the factor owner, say, to the worker.

If, for example, the hourly wage of a specific type of labour is $10, whereas the value of its marginal product is $12, it may be argued that, by allowing the worker to increase the number of hours he works, a net social gain can be affected. The worker, for instance, may agree to work an hour longer for $10.50, another hour for $11 and so on, until the wage he receives for the nth hour is equal to the social value of his marginal product. Hence, by adding this condition, both the worker and the consumers are made better off.

This argument would be valid if, in perfect competition, each worker could indeed determine the number of hours he works in each activity by reference to the wage offered. But whether he is paid by the hour or by piece rates, the worker never does, in fact, determine the weekly hours he will work – even if overtime work is offered, the number of additional hours is circumscribed. In general, then, the worker has to accept as a condition of his employment the number of hours per day and the number of days per week that go with the job (along with specific overtime opportunities, if any). The choice of the number of hours per week, and their distribution over each day and week, are not extended to the worker in the operation of modern industry. He has to measure the weekly pay package, along with other conditions, in one activity with those offered by another or, in the last resort, with remaining unemployed. Thus, he compares the alternatives open to him on an all-or-nothing basis.

It follows that marginal adjustments of the amounts produced by various firms are not by the hour, or by the piece, of one or more workers. They are in fact made only by the entrance of additional workers or by their departure from the firm.

Given this situation, an optimal position is attained – one in which no further 'reshuffling' of factors can increase the aggregate value of the output produced – when all goods prices are proportional to their corresponding marginal costs.

2   The Second-Best Theorem incidentally disposes, if it were ever necessary, of the naïve proposition that an excise tax imposes a 'deadweight' or an 'excess' loss on the economy – inappropriately demonstrated in a partial equilibrium context using a simple demand and supply diagram. From such demonstrations, it is occasionally alleged that a CBA must take account of such an excess loss when it is, in part at least, financed by the levying of (additional) excise taxes.

For such a proposition to be valid, it is necessary that every good in the economy, save that (or those) being taxed, be priced at marginal cost – a most unlikely situation. What is more, if it so happened that all other goods were already priced at m per cent above their corresponding marginal costs, the levying of an excise tax of m per cent on the good or goods originally priced at marginal cost would bring the economy into an optimal position: far from being a burden, it would be a benefit. This would be so, in some degree at least, if a weighted average of the prices of all other goods was about m per cent. In the absence of any such situation, however, it cannot be known whether the excise taxes in question will be a loss or a benefit to society, much less its measure.

3   We may take it for granted that, in any modern economy, there will be a number of irremovable constraints – arising from excise taxes and subsidies, from strong monopolies and from industries that exploit 'cheap' labour – at least for some time. It follows from the Second-Best Theorem that there is no longer a simple rule that, if followed by the remaining goods in the economy, will ensure a second-best solution. Worse, owing to the complexity and extent of the data required to formulate the valid second-best rule, we can never even hope to discover it.

To make matters still worse, there appeared in the same year as the Second-Best Theorem an article (Mishan, 1957) highlighting the problem of the 'First-Best' solution. Lancaster and Lipsey (1956), it will be recalled, developed their theorem by positing a unique welfare function. Where there is no more than a single boundary constraint, a unique optimal position will indeed emerge. Mishan's analysis, in contrast, showed the existence, in general, of a relationship between the distribution of welfare of any batch of goods and the relative prices resulting. In consequence, any point along some segment of the production boundary becomes a potential optimum for the economy, one that can be realized by a particular distribution of welfare among the members of the community. Indeed, it is this relationship between relative goods prices and distribution in each and every batch of goods within some segment of the production boundary that is responsible for what is known as the 'Scitovsky paradox', discussed in Appendix 2.

In view of the undue influence exerted by the Second-Best Theorem on economists concerned primarily with the allocation of resources, it is as well to emphasize that in CBA – where, within a partial economic context, the question to be addressed boils down to the magnitude of the net benefit to society of introducing one or several goods into the economy – one is no longer seeking a price–marginal cost ratio to be applied to *all* remaining goods in the economy, given as irremediable the ratios of the one or two deviant sectors that will bring the consequent suboptimal economy as close as possible to the assumed unique optimal position. Rather the contrary, the economist must now accept *as a constraint* the range of different ratios that prevail in *all* the goods in the economy. He must then select the ratio for the one or several goods to be produced by the project that will bring the economy as close as possible to an optimal position, given the existing level of employment.

In other words, given the level of social welfare pertinent to the existing suboptimal position of the economy, the cost-benefit analyst is to set the outputs of the project at marginal cost ratios that will maximize the increase in social welfare. Contrary to what may be expected, the solution to the problem is quite simple.

This is easily understood by breaking the problem into two parts. First, we measure the tangible *ceteris paribus* gain of the introduction of the one or several goods by the project, generally in terms of the increase of their consumer surplus when their outputs are extended to the point at which their social prices are *equal* to their corresponding marginal opportunity costs. We then turn to the more elusive measure of the increase, if any, of that given tangible measure of gain, by some adjustment in these project outputs so that their social prices are somewhat above, or else below, their corresponding marginal opportunity costs.

By employing the same calculus used in establishing the Second-Best Theorem, it also emerges that there is no feasible method of discovering which way the adjustment should go, much less by exactly how much.

This negative result can be made yet more telling by two further reflections. Even if, following some divine revelation, this 'ideal' social price–marginal opportunity cost ratio were then applied by the economist to the outputs of the project, the movement from the initial outputs (at which social price is *equal* to its marginal opportunity cost) cannot be expected to be really worthwhile. In a modern economy in which scores of thousands of finished and intermediate goods are produced, each with its own price–marginal cost ratio (more accurately, its social price–marginal opportunity cost ratio), the divinely indicated adjustment would make so negligible a difference that it would be virtually imperceptible to the individuals comprising society.

Add to this (bearing in mind that, in fact, we will not be able to discover this 'ideal' ratio) that the assumption of a unique optimal position of the economy, as assumed in the Second-Best Theorem, is unwarranted. As shown by Mishan (1957), any number of points on the production boundary of the economy can become an optimal position by a particular redistribution of income that will also, in general, alter all relative prices. Thus, there is no avoiding the conclusion that no perceptible gain may be presumed from any divergence from the cost–benefit analyst's habitually setting outputs at social price equal to marginal opportunity cost when measuring, over time, the gains in consumer surplus from the goods introduced by the project.

Notes

1 Other necessary conditions that are subsumed in an overall optimal position of the economy – the exchange optimum and the production optimum – are treated in detail in Mishan's 'A survey of welfare economics' (1960). See also his 'Second thoughts on second best' (1962b).

2 Their general proof proceeds as follows: in order to maximize some function

$$F(x_1, x_2, \ldots, x_m)$$

subject to a single constraint\hfill

$$\phi(x_1, x_2, \ldots, x_m)$$

using the Langrangian method, maximize $W = F - \lambda\phi$. The necessary conditions will include $F_i = \lambda\phi_i$ or $F_i/F_j = \phi_i/\phi_j$ $(i = 1,2, \ldots, m)$. However, if now an additional constraint is introduced, say $F_1/F_m = k\phi_i/\phi_m$, where $k \neq 1$, the Langrange method requires that we maximize the function

$$W' = F - \lambda\phi - \mu(F_1/F_m - k\phi_1/\phi_m)$$

and the necessary conditions become much more complex (Lipsey and Lancaster, 1956). Also see Ng (2004: ch. 9, s. 9.1 and 9.2).

Appendix 4
Origins of the Hicksian measures of consumer surplus

1 Marshall's (1924) definition of the individual's consumer surplus, the amount of money a person is willing to pay rather than go without the thing over that which he actually pays, though it has strong intuitive appeal, is not altogether satisfactory: for it implies a constraint on the quantity to be bought. The sum of money the consumer is willing to pay, say, for a licence to buy the good at some given price rather than go without it, depends on how much he is expected to buy. And if, as Marshall implicitly assumed, the amount of the good he is to buy – on paying for this licence – is the *same amount* as that which he buys at the price *in the absence* of any need for a licence, then he *will not*, generally, pay as much for the licence as he would if, instead, he were allowed to buy as much of the good as he wanted. His having to pay for a licence makes him worse off, and if his income effect were positive, he would then – at the same price – choose a smaller amount than if he could buy freely without a licence. Consequently, if he is constrained to buy the initial (larger) amount, he will pay less for the licence.[1]

2 Such considerations prompted Hicks's definition (1939) of a *compensating variation* measure of the consumer's surplus. For the privilege of being able to buy the good at the existing price, *in whatever amount he chooses*, the consumer is willing to pay some maximum sum – his compensating variation. In 1943, Henderson pointed out that the exact measure proposed by Hicks would differ according to whether the consumer had to pay for the opportunity of buying the good at the given price or whether, instead, he was to be paid for abandoning this opportunity. This distinction is illustrated by reference to the indifference curve for a single individual in Figure A4.1.

The good x is measured along the horizontal axis, to be introduced into the economy at a fixed price given by the budget line $Y_0 X_0$, OY_0 measures money income over a period during which the prices of all goods other than x remain constant. Prior to the introduction of good x, the individual's money income Y_0 corresponds to a real income indicated by the indifference curve I_0. Once x is introduced at the price given by the budget line $Y_0 X_0$, the individual chooses the point Q_1 on the higher indifference curve I_1, and therefore consumes OM_1 of x.

The difference made to the person's real income, $I_1 - I_0$, is unambiguous. Ambiguity arises simply because we are to measure the real gain in terms of money income, as defined, along the vertical axis. Hicks's compensating variation, CV, is equal to $Y_0 Y_1$, for if the consumer is made to pay this sum in order to be permitted to buy x at the price (given by the slope of $Y_0 X_0$), he could just reach Q_0 on his

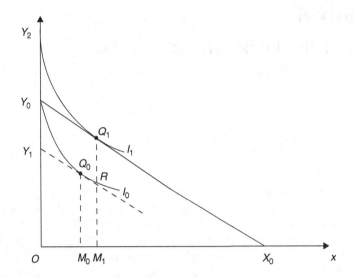

Figure A4.1

original indifference curve I_0. That is, if he is to be exactly as well off as he was originally before x was introduced, Y_0Y_1 is the maximum sum he can afford to pay for the privilege of buying x at the given price. And if called upon to pay this maximum, the amount of x that he would in fact buy is given here by OM_0.

Turning to Henderson's distinction, we now ask a different question: what is the minimum sum the consumer will accept to give up entirely the opportunity of buying the new good x at the market price, given by the slope of Y_0X_0? The answer is a sum equal to Y_0Y_2. For adding this sum to his initial income OY_2, his total income becomes OY_2 and this income, without any x, is on his indifference curve I_1. He is then just as well off as he would have been if, at his original income OY_0, he was able to buy x at the given price. This measure of consumer's surplus was called by Hicks (1944) the equivalent variation, EV, inasmuch as, in the absence of x, such a sum provides the consumer with an equivalent improvement in his welfare.

Provided the income effect is positive ('normal'), Q_1 will be to the right of Q_0 on the parallel budget lines. OM_1 will therefore be larger than OM_0, and Y_0Y_2 will be larger than Y_0Y_1.[2]

3   More generally, the definition of CV is the sum of money to be paid by the consumer when the price falls; or to be received by him when the price rises – which, following a change in the price, leaves him at his initial level of welfare. The EV, conversely, is that sum of money to be received by the consumer when the price falls; or to be paid by him when it rises – which, if he were exempted from the change in price, would yet provide him with the same welfare change. These two measures have already been illustrated in Figure A4.1 for the special case of the introduction of a new good x at a given price, rather than for a change in the

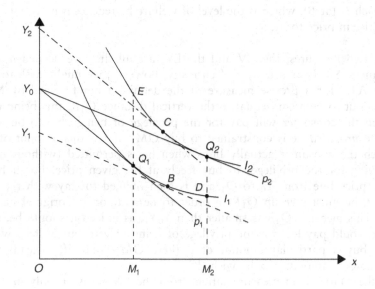

Figure A4.2

existing price of *x*. They are now illustrated in Figure A4.2 for the case of a fall in the existing price of *x*.

Initial money income is again represented by OY_0, initial real income being given by the indifference curve I_1 which is reached by the tangency of the price line p_1 at Q_1. If the price of *x* falls to p_2, the tangency of the p_2 price line at Q_2 raises the consumer's real income from I_1 to I_2. His CV is then equal to Y_0Y_1, this being the maximum sum he could afford to pay for the lower price p_2 without being any worse off. For if he pays this sum, so reducing his money income to OY_1, the now lower price p_2 enables him to reach B on his original I_1 curve. His EV, conversely, is equal to Y_0Y_2, this being the minimal sum he will accept to forgo the opportunity to buy what he wants at the lower price p_2, for with this sum, his total income would be equal to OY_2, and with this income and the old price p_1 he could just reach the higher indifference curve I_2 at C. This increase in his welfare is exactly equal to that which he could attain with this new price p_2 and with his original money income OY_0. Once more, Y_0Y_2 will exceed Y_0Y_1 for a 'normal' good *x*, as drawn, the reverse being true if *x*, instead, were an 'inferior' good.

We can now go through the same exercise for a rise in the price of *x*. With income OY_0, we begin with the consumer being faced with p_2 and, therefore, choosing point Q_2 on indifference curve I_2. A rise in the price of *x* to p_1 now induces him to take up the position Q_1 on the I_1 indifference curve. Our definitions would therefore measure the CV of such a price rise by Y_2Y_0, this being the minimum sum that would restore the individual's welfare to its original level I_2 when the price rises to p_1. The EV is now to be measured as equal to Y_0Y_1, this being the maximum sum the consumer is prepared to give up if he is exempted from the higher price p_1. For giving up this sum and retaining the old price p_2 would enable him to reach I_1 (at B), which is the level of welfare he reaches if he is not exempted from the rise in price to p_1.

4   These two measures, the CV and the EV, are all that are needed in ordinary circumstances. Solely as a matter of curiosity, however, we might wish to go back to Figure A4.1 for a precise measure of the definition put forward by Marshall. This turns out to be a sum equal to the vertical distance Q_1R, this being the maximum sum the consumer will pay for the privilege of being able to buy x at the given price *provided* he is constrained to buy OM_1 of x – this amount of x being that which the consumer actually buys when he is permitted (without having to pay anything for the privilege) to buy freely at the given price. For if he moves along the price line from Y_0 to Q_1 and is then obliged to stay with the quantity OM_1 of x, he must give up Q_1R in order to be at R on his original indifference curve I_0. This measure Q_1R is smaller than Y_0Y_1, as indeed it should be, since the consumer would pay less for the privilege of being able to buy x if he were compelled to buy a particular amount of it (here OM_1) than if, instead, he could choose whatever amount of x he wished.[3]

Thus, the Marshallian measure differs from the CV measure only in its having a quantity constraint attached to it. Extending the Marshallian-type measure to a change in the price, we return to Figure A4.2. For a fall in price from p_1 to p_2, the relevant quantity constraint is OM_2, and the quantity-constrained CV is therefore measured as Q_2D, A quantity-constrained EV, requiring the consumer to purchase only OM_1 of X – this being the amount he buys at the original price p_1 without receiving any compensation – is measured as Q_1E.[4]

Again, for a rise in price from p_2 to p_1 these measures are reversed. $Q_1 E$ becomes the quantity-constrained CV, and Q_2D becomes the quantity-constrained EV. Q_2D is smaller than Y_0Y_1, and Q_1E is larger than Y_0Y_2.

In this short account of the origins and development of Hicks's measures of consumer surplus, the reader will notice that we follow the contemporary literature in adopting the term proposed by Hicks, the equivalent variation, in this and the following three Appendices, whereas in the text we refer to it as the CV[21] – the compensating variation for the movement back from state 2 to state 1 is necessary to maintain the state 2 welfare.

Notes

1   Marshall's dissatisfaction, and eventual disillusion, with the concept of consumer surplus, arose from his utility analysis. Aware that the fall in the price of a good which made the consumer better off had some effect on the amount he would buy, Marshall tried to circumvent the problem by holding the individual's marginal utility of income constant. But this was plausible only for minute changes in the individual's welfare. Moreover, in extending the concept to the market, Marshall's choice of working in terms of cardinal and interpersonal utility proved cumbersome and unconvincing.

2   Once Hicks introduced the more operational distinction between income and substitution effects, it became evident that it was real income, and not the marginal utility of money, that was to be held constant. And despite popular belief to the contrary, these are not alternative methods of expressing the same condition. A constant marginal utility of money does not imply constant real income, and vice versa.

3   This is true (that is the Marshallian measure is smaller than the CV) irrespective of whether x is a 'normal' or an 'inferior' good.

4 It is clear from Figure A4.2 that the quantity-constrained CV measure Q_2D is smaller than the unconstrained CV measure Y_0Y_1, which is as it should be, because he would always pay less for a constrained privilege than for an unconstrained one. For the analogous reason that he would want to receive a larger compensation if he were to be constrained with respect to quantity than if he were not to be so constrained, the quantity-constrained EV measure EQ_1 is larger than the ordinary EV measure Y_0Y_2.

Appendix 5
Marginal curve measures of consumer surplus

1   The two more popular measures of consumer's surplus, CV and EV, can be represented on the marginal diagram, Figure A5.1. I_0' is the marginal indifference curve corresponding to indifference curve I_0 in Figure A4.1 in Appendix 4. In fact, I_0' is the curve of the first derivative of I_0 with respect to x. Similarly, the marginal indifference curve I_1' is the first derivative of the I_1 curve of Figure A4.1. For convenience, both marginal indifference curves are represented as straight lines in Figure A5.1. And, since in Figure A4.1 I_1 is indicative of a higher level of welfare than I_0, the assumption of a 'normal' good x requires that marginal indifference curve I_1' be drawn above (or to the right of) I_0'.[1]

If we regard individual welfare as continuously variable, the indifference curves are infinitely dense and so also, therefore, are the marginal indifference curves. For illustrative purposes, however, we could select an arbitrary number of marginal indifference curves, I_{01}', I_{02}', and so on, as indicated by the broken lines in Figure A5.1.

We shall return to this diagram presently, after taking a closer view of the origin and of the point M_1 by means of an incremental diagram, Figure A5.2. The story opens with no x being available and our consumer having I_0 welfare. The maximum sum he will pay for a single unit of x is shown as the first unit column, with height v_1. Let us suppose that he pays this maximum sum, in which case his welfare remains unchanged at level I_0. He is then offered a second unit of x. The maximum he can now afford to pay for this second unit is given by the height of

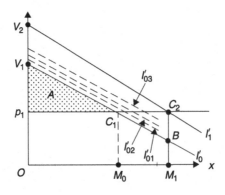

Figure A5.1

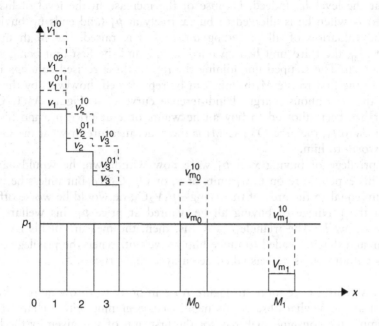

Figure A5.2

the second column, v_2. Again, we suppose that he is required to pay this maximum, so retaining his original welfare at I_0, and a third unit of x is offered to him, for which he can pay as much as v_3, the height of the third column. If we continue in this way, he will eventually, after purchasing M_0 units of x, have offered as much as v_{m0} for the M_0th unit of x.

If he buys M_0 units of x on these terms, he will be no better off after buying them than he was before he bought any x. His level of welfare, that is, remains at I_0. Now, let the price p_1 be set at height v_{m0}. The sum of the portions of the solid columns that stick up above the price line (their dotted segments) must now be interpreted. Since his payment of this sum, in addition to price p_1 per unit for OM_0 units of x, is such that he is no better off than he was originally without x, this sum is to be regarded as the CV for introducing x at a price p_1. It is the maximum sum he will be able to pay for the privilege of buying x at p_1 without his being any worse off than he was originally. In Figure A5.1, with continuous curves, this CV is represented as the area of the shaded triangle A.

2   Let us now return to our consumer in a more charitable humour and allow him to buy all the x he wants at the introductory price p_1. His welfare, or real income, increases from I_0 to I_1, and –because his real income effect is assumed positive – he buys more of x: in fact OM_1 of x in Figure A5.1.

Looking at things in the light of the incremental diagram Figure A5.2, we notice that, because of this increase in real income, the value of the final M_1th unit is now valued at v_{m1}^{10}, equal to price p_1, and not at the smaller value v_{m1} – the maximum he would have paid for the M_1th unit on the first procedure, which retained his welfare at the level I_0. Indeed, because of the increase in the level of his welfare from I_0 to I_1 when he is allowed to buy x freely at p_1 (and ends up buying OM_1 units), the valuation of all preceding units of x is raised; the M_0th unit being valued at v_{m0}^{10}, the third unit being valued at v_3^{10}, and the first unit being valued at v_1^{10}, and so on. The stepped line joining the top of these revised columns in Figure A5.2, from the first to the M_1th unit, can be represented, however, by the segment V_2C_2 of the continuous marginal indifference curve I_1' in Figure A5.1. Once the consumer has been allowed to buy all he wants of x at price p_1, and his welfare rises from I_0 to I_1, the area $OV_2\,C_2M_1$ is the exact measure of what the OM_1 units of x are worth to him.

If the privilege of buying x at p_1 were now withdrawn, he would have to be returned his expenditure on OM_1 units of x, or $Op_1C_2M_1$. But unless he were also paid a sum equal to the area of the triangle $p_1V_2C_2$, he would be worse off than he was with the privilege of buying all he wanted at price p_1; his welfare, that is, would be below I_1. The triangle $p_1V_2C_2$ is, then, the measure of his EV. It is the minimum sum that is needed to make him as well off when the privilege of buying x at p_1 is withdrawn as he was when he enjoyed that privilege.[2]

3 We now return, once more, to Figure A5.2 in order to throw more light on two issues that are somewhat obscure. As mentioned, beginning with welfare at level I_0, the maximum the consumer will pay for the first unit of x is given by the height v_1 of the first solid column. But if, instead of paying this maximal sum, he pays no more than the price p_1, he makes a surplus on this first unit equal to the column segment p_1v_1. As a result, his welfare rises, say, to I_{01} (greater than I_0), and the maximum he is now prepared to pay for the second, third and subsequent units of x is – on the assumption of a positive income effect – raised somewhat to v_2^{01} for the second unit, to v_3^{01} for the third unit of x and so on. Let him now be offered a second unit of x at the same price p_1, and he makes as a surplus on this second unit an amount equal to $p_1\,v_2^{01}$. His welfare has risen by another increment to, say, I_{02}, and the maximum sum he will pay for successive units also rises. For the third unit, he will now pay as much as v_3^{02} (above v_3^{01}, but not shown in the figure) and so on. Proceeding in this way, determining the resulting maximum sum the consumer will pay for each successive unit prior to allowing him to buy it at price p_1, we can trace a locus that has been called (Hicks, 1944), the 'marginal valuation', MV, curve. Its relation to the marginal indifference curves of Figure A5.1 could be shown here but, in order not to clutter up the picture, we have reproduced the main features of Figure A6.1 in Figure A5.3, and shown this MV curve as the line joining V_2 to C_2.

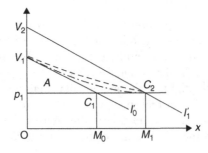

Figure A5.3

This MV curve is not, however, to be identified with the demand curve, for in order to generate a demand curve for x, we trace the path of consumer purchases by gradually *lowering the price* from V_1 to p_1. Although both the MV and the demand curves pass through C_2 when the price is p_1, for all previous quantities of x the MV curve (for a 'normal' good) is above the demand curve, shown as the *dotted* curve joining V_1 to C_2. The reason is simply that, in tracing the locus of the MV curve, the consumer is deemed to buy each successive unit of x, from the first onward, at the actual price p_1. In contrast, the demand curve is generated by having the consumer pay a price that is first equal to OV_1 and, though gradually lowered, remains above p_1 until the final M_1th unit is bought. As a result, the surplus of welfare gained in the purchase of the first, second, third and subsequent units of x (save for the final M_1th unit) is greater for the MV curve procedure than for the demand curve procedure. At each unit of x, save the final M_1th unit, the consumer's valuation is, therefore, higher for the *MV* curve than for the demand curve.

4 In order to broach the second issue, we return to Figure A5.2, and recall that the maximum sum the consumer will pay for the first unit is given by the height v_1 of the first column. If he is permitted to buy this one unit at p_1, his CV for that one unit is equal, as indicated, to the dotted segment of the column above the p_1 line. Suppose we now ask the question: what is the minimum sum he will accept in order to give up the privilege of buying this one unit of x at p_1? Now if this question is asked prior to his having bought any unit of x at a price (such as p_1) below his maximum valuation of a first unit, his welfare will still be at the I_0 level. The minimum sum he would accept to forego having the one unit of x might then be thought equal to the maximum sum he would pay for it. But whether in fact he has bought this x unit at p_1, and his welfare has risen to the level I_{01} (greater than initial level I_0), or whether he has *not* yet bought this unit of x, and his existing welfare is still at I_0, makes no difference. The minimum sum he will require to forgo the unit he bought at p_1, or the opportunity to buy it at p_1, is in either case the same, and larger than the maximum sum he would pay to be able to buy a unit of x at p_1. For assuming that he has not yet bought any x at p_1, and his welfare is still therefore at I_0, the individual must ask himself the question: what is the level of welfare I *could* reach if I were permitted to avail myself of the opportunity of buying this unit of x at p_1? And the answer, as indicated above, is the level I_{01}, greater than I_0. The sum of money which, therefore, exactly compensates him for *not* being able to attain this I_{01} level of welfare (through the purchase of a unit of x at p_1) is equal to the column segment $p_1 v_1^{01}$.

This description of the sum of money, however, corresponds exactly to the definition of the EV – the sum which, if he is exempted from the economic change in question, provides him with the equivalent change in his welfare.[3] More generally, if no constraint is placed on the amount of x the consumer would wish to buy, the EV necessary to induce him to forgo the opportunity of buying x at p_1 is equal to the area of triangle $p_1 V_2 C_2$ in Figure A5.3.

5 Let us summarize these interpretations. The CV for introducing x at price p_1 is given by the shaded triangle A in Figure A5.1. Once x is introduced at that price, the consumer, in the absence of constraint, will buy OM_1 units and achieve a welfare level corresponding to indifference curve I_1. In order to persuade him to

forgo this opportunity to buy x at p_1, which takes him to I_1 welfare, he must receive a minimum sum equal to the area of the large triangle, $p_1V_2C_2$. By definition, this is his EV.

If, however, he has already been given the price p_1, and the economic change consists of withdrawing it entirely, this same minimum sum, equal to triangle $p_1C_2V_2$, now represents the consumer's CV, being the sum that must be paid to him in order to maintain his existing welfare at I_1. His EV in this circumstance is the smaller triangle A, this being the maximum sum he would pay to be exempt from losing the opportunity to buy at p_1, which payment would in fact reduce his level of welfare to I_0,[4] the level prior to the introduction of good x.

Confining ourselves to the CV and EV of introducing a normal good x at price p_1, it is clear that the area between the price and EV, the individual's demand curve is greater than the CV area and less than the EV area, i.e. for 'normal' goods, CV < D < EV. It is obvious that the smaller is the income effect, the smaller will be the difference between these areas regarded as measures of consumer's surplus. In the limiting case of zero effect, the three areas coincide.[5]

6 Finally, we can translate the CV and EV measures of Figure A4.2, featuring a fall in the price from p_1 to p_2 onto the marginal diagram of Figure A5.4. At p_1 the consumer is buying OM_1 units. At p_2 he is buying OM_2 units. The marginal indifference curves I_0', I_1' and I_2', are indicated as solid lines, and the demand curve passing through VDH as the dotted line.

The CV of the fall in the price from p_1 to p_2 is equal to the cost difference for OM_1 units of x, or rectangle p_1p_2FD, *plus* the triangle DFG. The EV for that fall in price is equal to the cost-difference for OM_2 units, or rectangle p_1p_2HJ *less* the triangle HJK. These measures of CV and EV are, of course, reversed for a price rise from p_1 to p_2.

The horizontal slice of consumer's surplus under the demand curve, the area p_1p_2HD is an approximation to either of the exact measures, being clearly greater than the CV measure, and smaller than the EV measure, for a price fall. Again, the smaller the income effect, the closer is the coincidence of the three measures. For a zero income

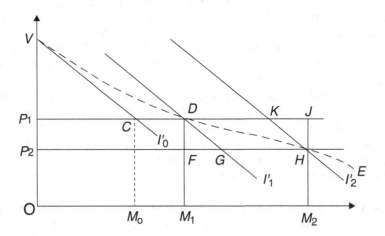

Figure A5.4

effect, the measures coincide. Goods with zero income effect are hard to come by, but for a great many purposes the income effect involved is small enough for economists to make use of the area under the demand curve as a close approximation of the relevant benefit or loss.

Notes

1 If, instead, the income effect on x were negative, the reverse would be true; the I_1' marginal indifference curve would be below the I_0' marginal indifference curve.
2 The reader might care to note that the quantity-constrained CV – corresponding to the Marshallian definition of consumer's surplus – is smaller than the Hicksian CV. In Figure A5.1, it can be represented as the shaded triangle A *less* the triangle C_1C_2B, because the quantity constraint requires of the consumer that, in paying a maximum for the privilege of buying x at p_1, he continues to buy OM_1 units (and not the OM_0 units he would have chosen to buy). Since the marginal indifference curve I_1' shows the maximum he is prepared to pay for these additional M_0M_1 units of x, and shows that this maximum for each such unit is below the price p_1, his welfare can be maintained – after paying a sum equal to the triangle A – only by refunding him the losses he must sustain on the additional M_0M_1 units, a total loss given by the triangle C_1C_2B.
3 If, however, the economic change being contemplated is the exact opposite of this, i.e. the *withdrawal* of the opportunity of buying a unit of x at p_1 and, as a result, a reduction of the consumer's welfare level from I_{01}, the payment of this sum is the appropriate CV for such an economic change, for it is the sum the consumer must receive in order to maintain his existing level of welfare, I_{01}, following such a change.
4 It should be self-evident that the maximum sum a consumer will pay to acquire a benefit (his CV) is the same maximum sum he will pay to hold on to it (his EV), i.e. to be exempt from its removal once he already has it.
5 If x had a negative income effect we should have EV < D < CV. Figure A5.3 would have to be revised by exchanging points M_0 and M_1, C_1 and C_2, V_1 and V_2. The demand curve joining the new V_1 to the new C_2 would then be steeper than either of the two marginal indifference curves. In the extreme case, the demand curve over a range slopes upwards from left to right.

Appendix 6
The concept and measure of rent

1 Although the concept of rent, in the specific sense of a surplus to factor-owners, is not so popular in CBAs as the concept of consumers' surplus, it is possible that, with growing awareness of allocation theory and growing refinements in techniques of measurement, it will become increasingly employed. The concept deserves more detailed treatment for another reason: the use of the area above the supply price of a factor is a less reliable proxy for the measurement of rent than is the area below the consumer's demand curve a proxy for his surplus. The reader will appreciate this remark more readily after the concept of rent has been defined.

Textbook definitions that are still in current use can be divided into two types. One conceives of rent as a payment in excess of that necessary to maintain a factor in its current occupation. The other would describe it as the difference between the factor's current earnings and its 'transfer earnings' – the latter term denoting its earnings in the next most highly paid use. As we shall see, the first type of definition is ambiguous because of the quantity constraint. The second type of definition is even more restricted, however, as its validity would require that, in the choice of occupation, men are motivated solely by pecuniary considerations. Indeed, it will transpire that, like consumer surplus, rent is a measure of change in a person's welfare and, again like consumer surplus, can have both a CV and an EV measure.[1]

2 As with the treatment of consumer surplus, our first recourse will be to the indifference map. Figure A6.1 indicates four quadrants of a diagram in which money income Y is again measured vertically, and the good L (which can be thought of as labour services) is measured horizontally. Any horizontal distance to the right of the origin O would measure the amount of L acquired by the individual; any horizontal distance to the left of the origin, the amount of L given up. Similarly, any distance above the origin measures the amount of income acquired, and any distance below it the amount of income given up. As distinct from the consumer goods' situation which is depicted in the north-east quadrant, the factor supplies' situation is here depicted in the north-west quadrant.[2]

If we construct a price-line p_1 passing through the origin and tangent at Q_1 to the indifference curve I_1, the individual is represented as in his chosen equilibrium position, giving up OL_1 of this particular sort of labour and, in exchange, acquiring OY_1 units of money income. Let the market supply price for this sort of labour rise from p_1 to p_2, and the individual's new equilibrium is given by the combination Q_2 on the I_2 indifference curve. The resulting change from Q_1 to Q_2 may be divided, in the usual Hicksian way, into a pure substitution effect – a movement

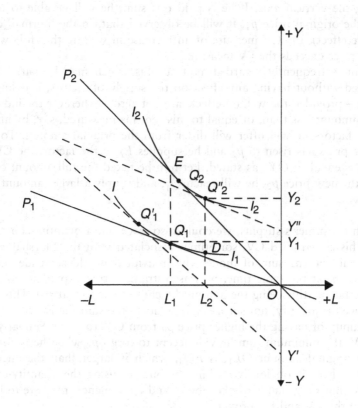

Figure A6.1

from Q_1 to Q'_1 – and a pure welfare effect – a movement from Q'_1 to Q_2. Although the welfare effect can, of course, go either way, it should be noticed that a positive welfare effect – implying a welfare-induced increase in the *demand* for a good or factor – constitutes a reduction in the *supply* of a good or factor. Thus, a positive, or 'normal' welfare effect, following a rise in the price of a factor, acts to reduce the amount put on the market. As we shall see, the 'backward-bending' supply curve of the factor owner is the outcome of a strong positive welfare effect overcoming the unambiguous substitution effect.

The increase in the individual's welfare that follows the rise in the price of his labour from p_1 to p_2 can be measured, first as a CV – here, the exact amount of money that has to be taken from him to restore his welfare to its original I_1 level. The measurement of the CV on the vertical axis is, therefore, OY'. It is the maximum sum of money he could give up for the opportunity of selling his labour at the higher price p_2. If he gives up this sum OY', he will have the negative income indicated by Y' and, with price p_2, he can just reach I_1 at Q'_1.

This increase in his welfare can also be measured as an EV – here, the exact amount of money which has to be given to him to ensure that, if the opportunity to sell his labour at p_2 is not extended to him he is still able to reach the new welfare level as indicated by indifference curve I_2. The EV is, therefore, measured as

OY'' along the vertical axis. If he is paid this sum, he will be able to reach I_2 at Q_2'', with the original price p_1. It will be observed that, in the 'normal' case (positive welfare effect), the CV measure of an increase in welfare that follows a rise in the supply price exceeds the EV measure.

Since rent is frequently regarded as a surplus which may be partly or wholly appropriated without having any effect on the supply of factors, it is important to notice that – provided the welfare effects are not zero – wherever the individual has to pay an amount less than, or equal to, his rent (as measured, say, by his CV), the amount of factors he will offer will differ from the original amount. To illustrate, if, after the price has risen to p_2 and he supplies L_2 of the factor, the CV measure of his rent is equal to OY', as stated. Let him be taxed the full amount of this rent and, with the new price p_2, he will reach Q_1', and supply a larger amount of factors than before.

3   As with consumer's surplus, we could also trace out a quantity-constrained CV and EV. This constrained CV, sometimes associated with the Marshallian concept of rent, would be the sum of money the individual would surrender in order to retain p_2 when, at the same time, he was restrained from providing no more than OL_2 of the factor (this being the amount he chose to supply at p_2). This restriction on his choice of quantity, not surprisingly, reduces the sums he is willing to pay for the opportunity of having the higher price p_2 from OY' to Q_2D. Similarly, the constrained EV, the minimum sum he will accept to forgo p_2 when he is compelled to supply the original amount OL_1, is EQ_1, which is larger than the unconstrained EV of OY'. There is obviously nothing 'wrong' in using the quantity-constrained CV and EV. But on grounds of plausibility and convenience, they are to be rejected in favour of the CV and EV proper.

4   It is instructive to turn briefly to the case of the supply of a factor in two alternative occupations A and B. Although the individual might choose to work part time in each occupation, this is not always feasible owing to institutional arrangements. We shall therefore confine the analysis to the case of placing his factor L entirely in occupation A or entirely in B.

Figure A6.2 represents a section of a three-dimensional indifference map, with the same vertical axis Y and two horizontal axes, L_a and L_b, crossing at right angles. If we imagine our three-dimensional figure were cut vertically into four equal parts, the figure is the space left after the removal of the vertical quarter in which L_a and L_b are both negative. Our attention is largely restricted to the upper, the positive, part of the diagram.

The rate of pay in A is given by p_a, which is higher than p_b. If he chose to work in A at p_a, his earnings OY_a would be higher than his earnings OY_b, in B. Nevertheless, the individual chooses to place his factors entirely in occupation B, his equilibrium being Q_b on the indifference surface I_2 which is above the indifference surface I_1 on which is found his alternative choice, Q_a. Compared with the equilibrium he could reach in the A occupation, the individual enjoys a positive economic rent which, as an EV, can be measured as OY' – this being the maximum sum he is prepared to pay to remain in B, for, after paying as much as OY', he can just reach the I_1 indifference surface – the new, lower, level of welfare which he would reach if he had to move into the A occupation. Conceived as a CV, the rent is measured

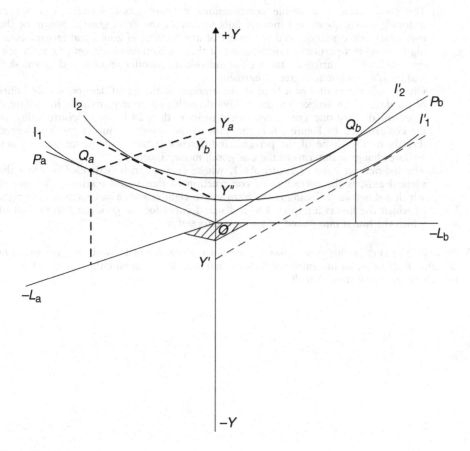

Figure A6.2

as a sum equal to OY'', this being the minimum sum the individual must be paid in order to induce him to transfer to occupation A, for, after receiving the sum OY'', he will be able, moving along p_a to reach the I_2 indifference surface – representing his original level of welfare.

It should be manifest that, because of his occupational preference for B, the positive rent from working in B rather than A is accompanied by a smaller money return. Indeed, the textbook definition of rent, turning on the difference between the factors' current earnings and their transfer earnings, would, in this instance, be negative for the worker who chooses the B occupation, whereas it is clearly a positive rent on the CV or EV definition.[3]

Notes

1 This account follows the treatment of rent proposed by Mishan (1958).
2 This construction has three advantages over the more common leisure–income diagram which is placed in the usual north-east quadrant.

(i) The choice among available combinations of two goods, leisure (regarded as a homogeneous good) and money, fails to convey the more general notion of the individual as a demander and a supplier of any number of goods and factors, electing to provide a particular combination of them according to market prices. In general, each of the variety of factors the individual can offer requires a different skill and entails a different degree of hardship.

(ii) One avoids the artifice of a limit to the amount of the 'good' leisure, say 24 hours of the day, which artifice has the awkward result that an improvement in welfare is represented along one axis as equivalent to more than 24 hours of leisure a day. In the construction of Figure A6.1, the limit to the supply of any factor is governed directly by the shape of the person's indifference curves, and the measure of any welfare change is in terms of the one good, money income.

(iii) The indifference map of Figure A6.1, whose curves can be extended to cross the vertical axis, is the correct prior construction to that useful textbook diagram in which a downward-sloping curve from left to right crosses a price axis, to the right of which the line is interpreted as a demand curve for the good, and to the left of which the line is interpreted as a supply curve of it.

3 By a *positive* rent in this connection we mean an *increment* in his welfare from being in B rather than in A; an increment of welfare that can be measured either as the EV or as the CV of the move from A to B.

Appendix 7
Marginal curve measures of rent

1 The marginal curves I'_1 and I'_2 in Figure A7.1 correspond to I_1 and I_2 in Figure A6.1, except that, for conventional reasons, they are drawn from left to right. The I'_0 marginal indifference curve in the figure corresponds to some original I_0 curve (not depicted in Figure A6.1) before any price was offered for the factor L. It is convenient, again, to draw these three curves as straight lines.

To fix our ideas, we shall suppose L to be labour of a given skill, measured along the horizontal axis in hours per week in a specific industry A, the prices of all other factors and goods being taken as constant.[1]

When the individual first contemplates employment in A, the I'_0 curve is the locus of minimal payments required to in, and no more, as he moves from left to right along the I'_0 he is no better off at any point along it than he is at the beginning, prior to his employment there. The introduction now of an hourly wage $p1$ enables us to represent triangular areas corresponding to his CV and EV.

2 The individual's CV is a sum of money equal to the area of the larger triangle $V_0 C_0 p_1$, determined as follows. The area beneath the I'_0 curve up to the M_0th unit, equal to $OV_0 C_0 M_0$, is the minimum sum of money needed to induce him to work

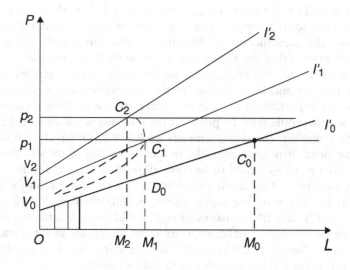

Figure A7. 1

the OM_0 hours, whereas the rectangular area, $Op_1C_0M_0$, is what he would be paid for working the OM_0 hours. The *excess* of this rectangular area over that minimum sum, equal to the triangle $V_0C_0p_1$, is therefore the maximum sum he can afford to pay for having the opportunity to sell his labour in A at p_1. For if he pays this maximum sum in exchange for this opportunity of selling his labour at p_1, he is just able – by choosing to work OM_0 hours – to maintain his welfare at the original I_0 level, being then no better off than he was before the p_1 opportunity was presented to him.

His EV, in contrast, is a sum that is equal to the area of the smaller triangle $V_1p_1C_1$, explained as follows. We put the question: having availed himself of the p_1 price to offer OM_1 units of labour and reached the I_1 level of welfare, what is the maximum sum he is willing to pay in order not to have to do any work in A?[2] This is equal to the area $OV_1C_1M_1$ under the I_1' curve. However, if he gives up the opportunity to sell his labour at p_1, the total income he foregoes is equal to the rectangular area $Op_1C_1M_1$. And this loss of income exceeds the most that he is willing to pay by the area of the triangle $V_1p_1C_1$. In order, then, to retain this I_1 level of welfare (which he was able to reach with p_1) when p_1 is no longer available to him, he must receive a sum equal to the area of this triangle.[3]

By starting with a supply price equal to V_1 in Figure A7.1, a price at which the individual supplies nothing, and gradually raising the price to p_1, at which he supplies OM_1 units, we generate the dotted-line supply curve of labour joining V_0 to C_1. For a 'normal' good or factor being offered (one for which *less* is offered as welfare increases), the supply curve will be steeper than the relevant marginal indifference curves. For an 'inferior' good or factor, in contrast, the supply curve will be flatter than the marginal indifference curves. In the 'normal' case, Hicks's marginal valuation curve (MV) will also be steeper than the marginal indifference curves. And since, for each successive unit offered, the welfare effect (until the M_1th unit is reached) is greater than that produced in generating the supply curve, the MV curve, indicated by the broken-line curve V_0C_1, will be above the supply curve.

3   We must now face the critical question: how well does the area between the price and the individual's supply price approximate the CV and EV measures of rent? Although the construction of diagrams of this sort can be somewhat arbitrary, it is well known that the supply curve can be much steeper than the marginal indifference curves and, indeed, can be backward bending – implying a welfare effect that is positive and large relative to the substitution effect. What makes the welfare effect so important in the factor market are the existing economic institutions under which people tend to place all their labour in single occupations. The welfare of each worker, therefore, depends exclusively, or largely, on the level of a single factor price. It is quite possible, in fact as well as in theory, that a further rise in price from p_1 to p_2 would (if he were allowed to choose) result in the worker's choosing to supply OM_2 units, a smaller amount of labour than the OM_1 units he supplies at p_1. The resulting supply curve, passing through $V_0C_1C_2$, though it lies between the CV and EV measures of rent, could be very different from either. This would be bad enough if either measure were acceptable as satisfactory for the purpose in hand. But in a CBA, guided by the criterion of a potential Pareto improvement, it is the CV measure that is usually employed.

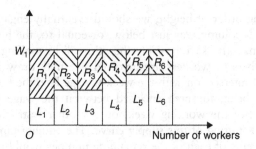

Figure A7. 2

Granted 'normal' welfare effects, a project that *raises* the supply price of the factor, on the one hand, produces a CV measure of rent that could be significantly *larger* than the area above the supply price. The consequent underestimation of the rent accruing to the factor-owner might, erroneously, preclude an economically feasible project. On the other hand, for a project that *lowers* the supply price of a factor, the area defined by the CV could be significantly *smaller* than the area above the supply curve. The consequent overestimation of the loss of rent resulting from using the area above the supply price as a proxy for the CV measure might then, again erroneously, preclude projects that are economically feasible.[4] How important is this consideration likely to be?

4   As indicated earlier, in modern industry it is the general practice to offer workers a 'package deal'; in its simplest form, a wage rate plus a constraint on the number of hours per day, and also on the number of days per week. Such constraints vary from industry to industry and in occupations within the industry, but this fact makes no difference to the analysis of rent in such circumstances.

Suppose the hours per week in the A industry are set at 40, except in the particular case in which the worker, when offered p_1 per hour, would have in any case chosen to work 40 hours, the constraint will be operative. If so, his CV under the 40-hour constraint will be smaller than it would be without it. Provided it is positive, however, he will accept the all-or-nothing offer and make some rent from it. The worker's CV under this constraint – the maximum sum he will pay in order to have the opportunity to work the 40-hour week in A at p_1 – is the excess of the weekly wage over the minimum payment he will require. And this minimum weekly payment he would accept is represented in Figure A7.2, as the area of a unit L column with height equal to such minimum sum. Since the figure ranks the columns in ascending order of height, column L_1 corresponds to the minimal sum of the first worker; he would accept a sum lower than all the others and, in consequence, makes the largest (constrained) CV rent. Letting the total pay for the 40-hour week be measured as OW_1 on the vertical axis, the CV measure of rent for the first worker is represented by R_1; the shaded extension of column L_1 to height W_1. Similarly, the areas of R_2, R_3, R_4, ... indicate the rents of workers 2, 3, 4 and so on.

Clearly, the stepped line obtained by tracing the tops of the L columns indicates the beginning of the supply curve of labour for that industry. If we continued adding workers in ascending order of height, we should eventually engage a worker, say the nth worker, whose L column was just below, or equal to, the height of the W_1 line. All workers in the industry, save possibly the nth, will be making a rent.

Where large numbers of workers are involved, we may draw a continuous supply curve to the point of intersection with the weekly wage line, the total rent to the workers in this industry being the area enclosed between the wage line and the supply curve. A lengthening of the working week, or any other restriction, would be represented as an upward shifting of this supply curve. The equilibrium number of workers would fall, and the rents of each of the remaining number would be reduced.

We may conclude, tentatively, that, notwithstanding the difficulties discussed in connection with the *individual* supply curve, the constraints imposed by industry are such that the area above the supply curve of a particular type of labour to an industry offers a good measure of the rent enjoyed by the number employed. The gain or loss of rent resulting from a rise or fall in the weekly wage can now also be measured in the conventional way.

Notes

1 We could have used a larger diagram to disclose the nature of the marginal indifference curve I_0' by taking hourly increments of this labour and – parallel with our treatment of consumer's surplus – constructing successive columns, the heights of which would indicate the individual's valuation of each successive hour offered. Having gone through this process in connection with consumer's surplus in some detail already, we shall not repeat it – though we have drawn in the first three columns under the I_0' to remind us of the process.

2 Along any marginal indifference curve, a movement *rising upward* (to the right, as drawn in the figure) implies a *giving up* of units, the vertical height therefore measures the *minimum* sums required for successive units offered. A movement *sloping downward* (to the left, as drawn in the figure) implies the *acquiring* of additional units – or the withdrawal of units once supplied. The vertical height therefore measures the *maximum* sums he will pay for additional units.

The same interpretation holds for the consumer's marginal indifference curves, although downward sloping is, in contradistinction to Figure A7.1, to the right, and upward-sloping is to the left.

3 The quantity-constrained CV, associated with the Marshallian measure, can also be represented in Figure A7.1. Once price p_1 is introduced, the amount the individual chooses to supply is OM_1. The most he is willing to pay to obtain this price p_1, while at the same time being constrained to purchase OM_1 units, is a sum equal to the area $V_0 D_0 C_1 p_1$, which is clearly smaller than the unconstrained CV, $V_0 C_0 p_1$, as indeed it has to be.

4 Under the same conditions, the conclusion for changes in the demand price is the opposite of that for the supply price. On the one hand, a project that *raises* the demand price of a good will, in the 'normal' case, have a CV (the minimum sum the consumer will accept as compensation) that is *larger* than the area under the demand curve. If the welfare involved is substantial, the consequent underestimation of the loss could result in a CBA admitting projects that do not meet the criterion.

On the other hand, for a project that results in a *reduction* of the price of a good to the consumer, the CV is smaller than the area under the demand curve. The consequent overestimate of the gain from using the area under the demand curve as a proxy for the CV might again admit projects that are not economically feasible.

Appendix 8
The limited applicability of property rights

1 Unfortunately the real world is less accommodating than free-enterprise econo-mists wish. Extending property rights to arable or pasture lands, to mineral and marsh lands, possibly also to some lakes and to stretches of a river, may work well to some extent. But in some cases it does not work well enough to prevent environ-mental damage occurring on a significant scale, and in others it is quite impracticable.

Property rights in forest lands, for example, do not work well – not unless trees are fast-growing and timber companies are restricted to areas so limited that, over the long term, profits depend upon continual re-afforestation.

Unfortunately, nearly all tropical rain forests, although officially under state con-trol, tend to be treated as a commons. They continue to be destroyed rapidly both by large tractor-using companies in search of quick profits from the exports of hardwood to industrial countries, and also by migrant peasants who use 'slash and burn' methods in levelling thousands of acres of tall-tree forests in order to clear a space for farming. No account, in these activities, is taken of the loss to be borne by present and future generations, not only the irreplaceable loss of fauna and flora[1] but also the cumulative effect such destruction has on the Earth's atmosphere and climate upon which our survival depends.

Deep-sea fishing is another instance where, although property rights are conceiv-able, they would be far too costly to enforce. Systems of rationing the fish catch with the aim of conserving the fish population may seem more practical, but they are wasteful, unpopular with fishermen and difficult to monitor.

2 In other cases, the idea of allocating property rights is a non-starter. There is no way in which the atmosphere over any area of the Earth's surface can be parcelled out to companies or people so as to make them responsible for its maintenance. And as it is impossible to confer distinct portions of air space on individuals or corporations, the atmosphere above the Earth will be used – as it always has been in the absence of prohibitions or regulations of emissions – as a common sewer.

Nor is anti-pollution legislation that effective. The required installation, say, of tall smoke stacks can reduce the amount of smoke and noxious particles suffered by the local population. But, as we now know, the wind-borne gases produced by burning fossil fuels move across national boundaries and settle in other countries in the form of acid depositions, so damaging their soil, forest lands and lakes.

Not only does our planet's atmosphere continue, in the main, to be used as a common sewer for a variety of man-produced gases, our oceans have also long been used for dumping waste and, in the past few decades, for extremely poisonous chemical and radioactive wastes.

Apart then from a few familiar instances – such as the cultivation of crops or of cattle and other animals – property rights have limited applicability, and none whatever to the more serious environmental problems.

Note

1 Loss of potential medical benefits from undiscovered use of plants.

Appendix 9
Deadweight loss or love's labour lost

1 When public investment is to be financed not by borrowing, but by taxation, wholly or partly – whether by excise taxes, income taxes or property taxes – an alleged consequence is the generation of a marginal Pareto loss, one that is referred to as a 'marginal excess tax burden' or 'deadweight loss'.

   This alleged burden does not address itself to the amounts transferred by the taxes – the gain in spending power of the government being exactly equal (if we ignore collecting costs) to the loss of spending power of the taxpayers, but to what is sometimes called the 'distorting' effects of taxes, tariffs, subsidies, etc. As this term 'distorting' effects is used somewhat licentiously, it makes for clearer thinking to focus directly on the relevant issue: will the taxation in question move the economy as a whole closer to, or further from, an overall optimal position? And if we can determine which way, can we also measure the change in total welfare? It should be obvious that answers to these questions are related to the analysis used in establishing the Second-Best Theorem, as discussed in Appendix 3.

2 Prior to the 1950s, economic textbooks occasionally illustrated the marginal excess tax burden of an excise tax t by a wedge, equal to height t, placed between the demand and supply curve of Figure A9.1. Originally, the equilibrium price was p_1 and the equilibrium quantity x_1. Following an excise tax equal to t, the equilibrium price rises to p_2, and the equilibrium quantity falls to x_2.

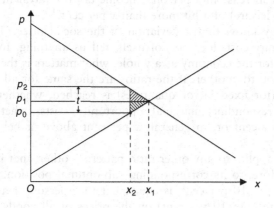

Figure A9.1

The amount transferred from consumers and producers together is then equal to $t \times Ox_2$ – with producers paying the amount equal to $(Ox_2 \times p_1p_0)$ and consumers paying the amount $(Ox_2 \times p_1p_2)$. But the loss to both producers and consumers together exceeds the sum transferred to the government by the amount measured by the shaded triangles, the upper shaded triangle being a loss of consumer surplus, and the lower shaded triangle being a loss of producer surplus. Hence, the excise tax t entails an excess marginal burden as measured by the shaded triangles.

All very neat, and all very misleading. Quite apart from the unwarrantable concept of producer surplus, as discussed in Part II, such a partical-equilibrium conclusion cannot be extended to a general-equilibrium conclusion. A validation of the apparent marginal loss of consumer surplus from imposing an excise tax would require that all the remaining goods in the economy continue to be priced as equal to their corresponding marginal cost, and also that there be no income taxes. If it happens that, in the absence of income taxes, the prices of all remaining goods were above their marginal costs by the same proportion, $\frac{p_1p_2}{Op_1}$, then a tax of p_1p_2 on good x would restore the economy to a full optimal position (given fixed factors) as compared with the original sub-optimal position before good x was taxed. In that case, the excise tax on good x would be an excess marginal gain rather than an excess marginal loss.

Inasmuch as it is virtually certain that, in a modern economy producing many thousands of items, at any moment in time their prices will be above or below their corresponding marginal costs in varying degrees, there can be no assurance whether an excise tax on good x or on several other goods also will move the economy as a whole closer to or further from an optimal position, much less that the gain or loss can be measured. This conclusion is reinforced when one bears in mind that in CBA it is not the ratio of market prices to their marginal costs that is relevant but (correcting for externalities) the ratio of the social valuation per unit (or 'social price') to the corresponding marginal opportunity cost.

It will be convenient in the remainder of this Appendix to refer to the former ratio as the market ratio and the latter as the social ratio.

3   An income tax, or rather an increase in income tax, is perhaps less elusive, if only an x per cent increase in a person's income tax is equivalent to a uniform tax on all goods (save leisure) of a bit more than x per cent.[1]

Now, we already know that a deviation of the social price of a good from its marginal opportunity cost does not, of itself, tell us anything. In connection with optimal positions for the economy as a whole, what matters is the difference of this ratio from one good to another. If the ratios are the same for all goods, an overall optimal position (for fixed factor quantities) is reached, whether all social prices are equal to corresponding marginal opportunity costs, whether they are all 5 per cent, 100 per cent or, in general, x per cent above or below corresponding marginal costs.

The same logic applies to any other ratio pattern – other, that is, than a uniform ratio – and, therefore, to its corresponding sub-optimal position. Thus an increase in income tax of, say 10 per cent, is equivalent to a person of a uniform increase (of something more than 10 per cent) on the prices of all goods (save leisure). By simply hiking up all prices by the same percentage for all persons the original sub-optimal position remains unchanged.[2]

4 The only warrantable conclusions that we can draw from the above considerations are as follows:

(i) In general, and bearing in mind that only the pattern of social ratios is relevant, it is uncertain whether the chosen range of excise taxes imposed to raise funds for the project will result, on balance, in a marginal excess burden or marginal excess gain for the community.

(ii) Even where there may reasonably be a presumption of marginal excess burden or marginal excess gain, it is unlikely to be significant. For instance, in the absence of a national emergency, an average increase in income tax exceeding 5 per cent would be unusual in any modern democracy. Yet, for most democracies, the resulting increase in revenue would be more than enough to finance one or two large public projects.

(iii) Whether the additional taxes raised to finance the public project(s) in question may be presumed, on balance, to issue in some deadweight loss or some 'deadweight gain', its *actual* figure will almost certainly elude measurement.

5 As a postscript, it may be added that, even if the economist were vouchsafed, by some divine power, the exact figure for the 'deadweight loss' or 'deadweight gain' from the raising of taxes specifically to fund the public projects in question, it is *most unlikely* – in view of the fact that the economist's measures of social gains and of opportunity costs are unavoidably only approximate, to say nothing of the allowances to be made for future uncertainties – that its inclusion in the cost-benefit calculation would materially affect the acceptability or otherwise of the public projects or of their ranking.

Notes

1 A tax of 1 per cent on a person's income is equivalent to him of $100x/(100 - x)$ per cent of all goods save leisure. Thus, an income tax of 1 per cent is exactly equal to a uniform tax on all goods (save leisure) of 1.02 per cent, an income tax of 5 per cent to a uniform excise tax of 5.26 per cent, and so on.

  If there is already a sizeable income tax but no excise taxes (or no comparable ones), an x per cent income tax is equivalent to a uniform excise tax of something more than 1.02 per cent.

2 It may, of course, be argued that the optimality condition which requires the value of a person's leisure to be equal to the social value of his marginal product is infringed by an income tax. We know, however, that perfect competition is not only possible with fixed factor quantities but also that in the modern economy fixed factors are generally the rule, not the exception. It follows that this labour–leisure condition is generally infringed, regardless of taxes: few workers can be offered the opportunity of choosing, each day, just how long they wish to work in a variety of different occupations.

  Hence, the introduction (or increase) of an income tax cannot be held to infringe a condition that is, in any case, already infringed in its absence.

Appendix 10
The value of human life

1   As Sir Thomas Browne solemnly observed in his *Religio Medici*, 'Heresies perish not with their authors but, like the river Arethusa, though they have lost their currents in one place, they rise up in another'. So also with the economist's valuation of life, the heresy being regression to the belief that the economic value of a human life is somehow to be related if not to the utility of his expected earnings, capital or consumption, then to some contrived economic index. Such recipes for cooking up an economic value of human life may bear comparison with the calculation of the value of a two-week honeymoon for a loving couple by reference to their anticipated outlays over the period (including foregone earnings) plus, perhaps, some allowance being made for the frigidity of one or other of the spouses. For the figure arrived at on this assumption of the relevant data bears no logical relation to the value that might be placed on the anticipated honeymoon experience by either of the enamoured couple.

When it comes to valuing human life by reference to the effects of the expected economic activity of the individual, three nominal models are of interest in order of technical sophistication: those of Usher (1985), Conley (1976) and Arthur (1981). It would be tedious to attempt a summary description of the construction of these models which, however, may be worth ploughing through for the intellectual diversion – testimony to an increasing tendency among academic disciplines of too much technique chasing too few ideas.

We may also mention in passing a number of other ambitious models such as those of Cook and Graham (1977), Jones-Lee (1980a) and Keeney (1980) that involve neither expected earnings, etc., nor yet direct WTP, yet contrive to produce an economic value for a person's life.

Most of these models contain a crucial magnitude, call it Q, which is incorporated into a mathematical expression from which the value of a person's life is to be calculated – or, at least, set within bounds.[1] But the usefulness of the magnitude Q cannot be independently determined without recourse to empirical data.

Certainly, no method has been devised by which such models can be tested.[2] Nor is the purpose of such models evident. Operationalizing them is very difficult and, however plausible their assumptions or their actual estimates of the economic value of human life, they can hardly be said, or expected, to influence economic policy.[3]

Notes

1 Thus Q would be H^T in Conley's paper, WE in Arthur's paper and RL in Jones-Lee's paper. To be sure, the paper by Jones-Lee also introduces the concept of maximum acceptable risk, but he cannot obtain it from his RL figure. He must discover it from direct estimates or guess at it or else accept it as a residual from a direct estimate of his $\Delta v/\Delta p$, always assuming he can also place a reliable figure on his RL.

2 The value of a life calculated from such a model may, of course, be 'tested' by reference to a CV^{12} for a given change in risk (as indicated, and criticized in Chapter 50), but in that case, the model is superfluous.

3 Guided by such models – or else by (unwarranted) inferences from some average compensation required for accepting a given (additional) risk of death or injury in a particular activity – calculations have indeed been made for the value of a human life and, also, for the value of a range of injuries sustained by a person.

For instance, the value, or 'shadow price', of a human life has been calculated as equal to about $4 million, that of a brain injury equal to $119,000, that of a drowning or near-drowning $100,600, and so on for a range of injuries.

Accepting the mainstream economic principle that the value of an item (good or bad) to a person is that which he himself places on it, in order for such calculations to be valid, we should have to discover, say, that in 1989 a person would have been indifferent as between remaining alive and the receipt of about $4 million (which presumably he would donate to family and friends or charities). If he received $5 million in exchange for his life, his welfare would therefore have been increased. Similar remarks, of course, apply to all such calculations.

Needless to remark, no interviews have been reported that confirm the validity of such calculations. (See also Chapter 50, section 5.)

Appendix 11
The rate of time preference

1   It is commonly alleged that the individual's rate of time preference, when positive – a preference for $100, say, this year rather than $100 next year – arises from impatience or myopia, allowing that he expects to be alive and well over the near future.

It is correct to state that, if a person is indifferent between receiving an additional 100 this year and an additional 105 next year and an additional $105(1.05)^2$ the year after, his rate of time preference is 5 per cent. If such individual were to receive 100 each year until some terminal year T, the value of this stream of benefits would be equal to $100(1.05)^T + 100(1.05)^{T-1} + \ldots + 100$, or $\Sigma_1^T 100(1.05)^t$ in the Tth year. Yet, from such statements, we are not able to infer whether, with respect to income or consumption over time, a person is impatient, prudent or overcautious.

Ignoring the problem of uncertainty, let us consider the distribution of income over a number of years of a person A in an economy where there is no market for loans of any sort. We simplify further by representing person A's indifference curves as between only two years, y_1 measured along the horizontal axis of Figure A11.1, and y_2 measured along the vertical axis. (A third year y_3 is suggested by an arrowhead marked y_3, emerging from the origin, allowing the imaginative student to conceive of three-dimensional indifference surfaces covering a three-year time span which can, mathematically, be extended to any n years.)

Allowing the sum of, say, $40,000 to be distributed between years 1 and 2, all the possible divisions are indicated by all possible points along the 45 degree line D, person A can choose to take all the available $40,000 in year 1, all of it in year 2 or, more likely, some of the $40,000 in year 1, and the remainder in year 2. If person A is a prudent person, he will choose to distribute the available income so as to receive $20,000 in each of two years, a division indicated by point Q_3, at which his highest indifference curve I_3 is tangent to the distribution line D. For at any other point along line D, he will be on a lower indifference curve.

Thus, at Q_3 on his I_3 indifference curve, person A is indifferent to receiving a given increment of income, say $100, in year 1 or receiving the same $100 increment of income in year 2. In so far as person A remains equally prudent – irrespective of the total available income dividing it equally between the two years – all points of tangency between his indifference curves and the relevant D lines will lie along a 45 degree ray, OR, passing through the origin. This OR ray, being equidistant at any point from each of the axes, is what identifies person A as being

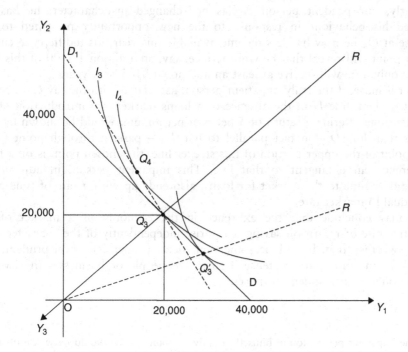

Figure A11.1

prudent – as valuing an additional dollar in year 1 as being exactly of value to him as an additional dollar in year 2.

Were person A an impatient person, he would instead have chosen a point Q'_3 along the D line, a point below Q_3, so as to have more income available in year 1 than in year 2. He being an impatient person would be represented by a ray OR' (the broken line in the figure) that is below the ray OR.[1]

2   Returning now to our prudent person A who chooses Q_3 division of his income between this year and the next, we suppose a loans market springs up, one that offers $105 next year for every $100 received this year – a return of 5 per cent per annum. Our prudent person A is now faced with a new opportunity to improve his welfare: in the absence of this new opportunity, he would be just as well off if, for parting with $100 of this year's income, he were to receive an additional $100 next year. If, instead, he were to receive an additional $105, he would certainly be better off.

In Figure A11.1, the new opportunity line facing person A at Q_3 once the loans market is introduced is shown by the broken line D_1 through Q_3, which is steeper than the original line D. In consequence, person A moves to Q_4 on line D_1, this being on a higher indifference curve I_4. Once at Q_4 on his I_4 indifference curve, his rate of substitution will be 105 next year for 100 this year – his rate of time preference, that is, becomes 5 per cent per annum, equal then to the rate offered by the market.

Clearly, our prudent person A has not changed his character: he has only changed his behaviour in response to the new opportunity presented to him. Because at Q_4 he now has less income available this year, his indifference curve I_4 at that point will reveal that he will sacrifice, say, an additional $100 of this year's income only if he will receive at least an additional $105 next year.

What is more, if the truly impatient person, associated with the ray OR', chooses point Q_3' along line D in the absence of a loans market, the introduction of such a market, one offering a return of 5 per cent per annum, would be shown by a line steeper than line D – in fact parallel to line D_1 – passing through point Q_3'. At some point of the upper portion of this steeper line, the chosen point is on a higher indifference curve tangent to that line. This impatient person, in adjusting his income over time to the market for loans, also ends up with a rate of time preference equal to market rate.

We may conclude that the existence in the economy of a market offering a positive rate of return on savings can arise independently of the character of the savers, whether they be, all or some, impatient, prudent, or over-prudent. Such a market can come into existence if there are people or businesses that want to borrow only for investment purposes.

Note

1 If the impatient person found himself initially at point Q_3, he would be worse off than if he were at Q_3'. Moreover, the slope of his indifference curve passing through point Q_3 along the D line would be steeper than 45 degrees, indicating that if he has to give up, say, $100 this year he will require more than $100 next year if his welfare is to be maintained.

Appendix 12
Selecting a set of investment projects for given political objectives

1 In selecting from a number of technically feasible investment projects that set which maximizes the excess terminal benefit, $TV(B) - TV(K)$, subject to a budget constraint, the method proposed here assumes normalization of the alternative investment options unless otherwise stated.

The features of the selection problem are, first, that there are several objectives to be achieved, single or complex, and second, that each of these objectives can be achieved by several alternative investment projects. For example, one of the objectives could be that of pest control over a certain area. Another could be that of flood control plus electricity generation.

Assuming the existence of a competitive economy with a high level of employment, with a ρ greater than r, the problem becomes that of choosing from the array of all the technically feasible investment projects available – a number of alternative projects (not necessarily the same number) for each of the political objectives – those that together produce the largest excess terminal benefit subject to the budget constraint. We must bear in mind, however, that, although we are to ensure that all the investment projects to be compared have the same time span, as indicated in the preceding chapter, they will not necessarily have the same initial outlay.

2 In setting up the problem, some general guidelines should be followed:

(i) The same objective to be realized in more than one area is to count as a different objective.
(ii) If, within a single area, two or more objectives are achieved by only one of the investment options, these two or more objectives are to be treated as a single objective.
(iii) If, for any objective that provides two or more services, there are m alternative investment options providing these services but in different proportions, they are to count as m alternative investment options.

If, for example, it is possible that, within the same area, one investment project provides flood control alone, another provides both flood control and electricity and a third provides flood control and electricity also, but in different proportions, there are three investment options to be counted.

Turning to the question of finance, the more general approach is that the finance to be made available for the investment projects selected, no greater than the politically determined budget constraint, may be raised by taxation or borrowing or both. But, beyond the budget, some additional finance may be provided by not renewing some of the already existing public enterprises (their amortization funds then becoming available to contribute to the outlay of one or more of the investment options).

3   Restricting ourselves first to a budget that is raised only by taxation and/or borrowing, we proceed by dividing the *excess* terminal benefits (ETB) of each investment option by the terminal value of its outlay, which gives us the per dollar ETB for each investment option, its DETB.

We now place in a single row all the DETBs of those investment options that are able to provide one particular objective, there being as many rows as there are objectives. The array of the resulting DETBs forms the data that we have to work with.

We can illustrate the selection process under the simple assumption that there are but three political objectives to be attempted: (A) a passenger and traffic bridge across the river Flo in a particular locality for which there are three alternative investment options, as shown in Table A12.1; (B) a dam across the river Flo that will generate electricity for a nearby urban area, for which there are five investment options, as shown in Table A12.1; (C) a dam further down the river Flo that provides both flood control and electricity to another urban area, for which there are four alternative investment options.

To the right of the array of DETB figures in Table A12.1 are bracketed figures giving the terminal value, in $ million, that is required for that particular investment option – 12 in all in Table A12.1. The DETB figures themselves are all positive as, indeed, they have to be if the investment option is Pareto efficient, i.e. each of the investment options included in the table produces a greater terminal value than that of its terminal opportunity cost.

Suppose the budget available is $5 million, inasmuch as the figures in the brackets are the terminal values of the outlays, this initial budget of $5 million must be compounded forward to the common terminal year T at P to become, say, $7 million. Thus, the problem reduces to that of choosing no more than one of the alternative options in each row of the table so as to produce the highest aggregate terminal value of outlays that does not exceed $7 million.

If, for instance, we pick the DETB of 0.22 in row C and that of 0.30 in row A, the two options together require a terminal outlay equal to $5 million plus $2 million, altogether $7 million, which exhausts the terminal value of the budget. The excess terminal benefit of using these two investment options comes to (0.22 × $5 million) plus (0.30 × $2 million), a total excess terminal value of $1.7 million. We could, instead, pick the DETB of 0.5 in row B and the DETB of 0.35 in row

Table A12.1 Investment options

A	0.05(4.8)	0.20(1.5)	0.30(2.0)		
B	0.10(4.5)	0.20(4.0)	0.40(4.0)	0.45(3.0)	0.50(3.5)
C	0.22(5.0)	0.25(4.0)	0.30(2.5)	0.35(3.0)	

C which together produce a larger excess terminal benefit of $2.8 million while using up terminal outlays equal to $6.5 million.

And so we could continue picking other sets of one, two or three investment options, but no more than one from each row, to obtain the highest excess terminal benefit subject to the terminal budget constraint of $7 million. It would be quicker, however, to devise a computer program wherever there were a large number of objectives and many alternative investment options for each objective.[1]

4   We now turn to the case in which the budget, $7 million in the above example, may be supplemented by the funds made available by a discontinuing of a number of existing public projects that could otherwise be renewed. To simplify, we shall continue to suppose the existence of the data in Table A12.1 but, in addition, we suppose that there are three existing public projects, X_1, X_2 and X_3, that have now reached their terminal year and which therefore can either be renewed or else their recouped outlays be used instead to finance one or more additional investment options. If, at most, all three of these existing public projects were discontinued, the terminal value of their outlays would, let us say, add $3 million to the $7 million budget.

Clearly, it would be economically inefficient to discontinue X_1, X_2 or X_3 (so as to make additional funds available for achieving the objectives) if its DETB, which has to be foregone, exceeds that of the one or more investment options it supplants. To illustrate, if the X_1 renewable public project is the only one with a lower DETB than any of the 12 investment options being considered for the three objectives *A*, *B* and *C*, it would certainly be economic to discontinue it first and to use the amortized funds, amounting to its initial outlay, to finance one or more of the investment options. Should it so happen that the terminal value of X_1's outlay were equal to $4 million, this much of the available budget would be enough to finance one or more of the investment options, or possibly less than enough.

Consequently, some juggling about to alight upon the best mix of investment options that does not exceed a maximum terminal value of $10 million must be anticipated.

Once there were a large number of objectives to meet, each attainable by quite a few alternative investment options, it would be advisable to design a computer program.[2]

Notes

1   The problem can be formalized, bearing in mind that for each of the Qi objectives (*i* = 1, 2, ..., *n*) there can be many Ij alternative investment options (*j* = 1,2, ..., *m*), where *m* is the largest number of alternative investment options for any one or more objectives); also that we can admit *no more than one* of the alternative investment options for any one objective.

If *Tij* denotes the DETB of the *j*th investment option that can achieve the *i*th objective, *Kij* the terminal value of its outlay, and *K* the terminal value of the budget that is available (equal to $7 million in the above example), then we are to maximize

$$\sum_{i=1}^{n}\sum_{j=1}^{m} T_{ij}K_{ij} \leq K.$$

2 The problem can again be formalized (using the notation and caveats in note 1) as follows:

$$\text{maximise} \sum_{i=1}^{n}\sum_{j=1}^{m} T_{ij}K_{ij} \leq K + M \tag{A12.1}$$

And *also*

$$\text{maximise} \sum_{q=1}^{g} T_{q}M_{q} \leq M \tag{A12.2}$$

(g being equal to 1 *or* 2 *or*, ..., or g, as required by the problem.)

Where M_1, M_2, ..., Mg are the respective terminal values of the outlays of public projects X_1, X_2, Xg that may be renewed or *discontinued*, their corresponding DETB being T_1, T_2, ..., Tg. The maximum allowable for the terminal values of those public projects that are discontinued is (politically) fixed at M. Moreover, economic efficiency requires that each of the Tq chosen in (A12.2) not be greater than any of the Tij selected in (A12.1).

Appendix 13
Why cost-benefit analysis is useful for regulatory reform[1]

1   In Singapore, at least until the 1980s, CBA was not the main tool used for evaluation by the public sector. Instead, something called cost-effectiveness analysis (CEA) was the main instrument for analysis of projects, programmes and policies. It was used widely at the time, and is still relevant now.

While the terms sound very similar, there is one crucial difference between the two. CEA ranks projects and policies in terms of which yields the least cost to achieve a certain targeted outcome. But it cannot indicate whether something is more worthwhile to do. Conventional CEA usually does not measure social costs, unlike CBA. An example of a social cost is a cost such as traffic congestion that is borne by society. CEA may, for example, analyse a new redevelopment project in an area in terms of the value it adds to the economy and the increase in land use efficiency – but may not take into account the effect of congestion in the area. In that sense, CBA provides a more holistic appraisal of a project or policy.

In such circumstances, CEA falls short of CBA, as it does not capture all the costs. Furthermore, CEA provides no information or evaluation as to why certain policies or projects should be adopted in terms of benefits. Rather, the benefits are taken as a given.

2   Why this slightly academic discussion of CBA today? It is my belief that there is a need to return to some rigour in discussing the pros and cons of projects and policies, at a time when so much public discussion is driven by opinion and political posturing, rather than more objective assessments. In a recent book by the celebrated Harvard law professor Cass Sunstein, *The Cost-Benefit Revolution*, he explains why policies should be considered carefully on the basis of their costs and benefits, rather than on mere subjective opinions, lobby groups and intuition.

CBA began life in the United States Flood Control Act of 1936 which required government agencies to use CBA to estimate benefits over costs.

A series of standardized CBA practices was provided by the then US Bureau of the Budget in the 1950s, followed by the Transport Ministry of the United Kingdom in evaluating highways and airports in the 1960s.

International agencies followed in deciding whether to support some projects in developing countries using CBA. From the mid-1990s, government agencies in Asia became more interested in knowing whether there were significant net benefits of a proposed project or programme. With rising demands for various expenditure projects, a careful consideration of which projects to support, given constraints on budget, became paramount.

3 Regulatory reforms in environmental, health and safety regulations have become more prevalent. These days, another instrument, called regulatory impact analysis (RIA), has come into fashion. RIA takes into account distributional and equity considerations, going beyond pure economic considerations. In that sense, it is in fact a kind of CBA.

CBA in its complete form covers similar ground with its repertoire of mandatory questions. These include: who is the reference target group; what and which costs and benefits have to be accounted for; how to estimate these costs and benefits; whether equity considerations are important (especially relevant to developing countries); what to do with uncertainties over long-term policies and projects; and what investment criteria to use to calculate the overall viability of the project.

4 One area where CBA has played an important regulatory role is air quality.

Some years ago, when the World Health Organization (WHO) raised its guidelines for air quality, making them more stringent, countries all over the world, including Singapore, had to consider whether they would implement the new guidelines.

Fortunately, this was not an all-or-nothing choice as there were several interim air quality levels provided by the WHO. Countries had to consider the cost of implementing these guidelines, such as the higher costs of doing business as well as of living. This in turn meant higher transport cost, and higher monitoring and enforcement costs.

If some countries follow the guidelines and others do not, those which do may incur higher costs and lose cost competitiveness. However, these higher costs have to be compared with the benefits of having better air quality, such as better health and increased productivity. A cleaner environment can also boost tourism and make a city more attractive to skilled manpower. CBA provides a framework for a careful analysis of these benefits and costs in meeting the various interim guidelines.

In yet another example, in 2012, the US Environmental Protection Agency and the transportation department came up with plans to increase the fuel economy of cars. This regulatory reform was shown to have huge positive net benefits. Such benefits include savings in fuel and time costs for motorists in not having to refill frequently and perhaps higher work productivity. The lower fuel consumption also means less environmental pollution. These benefits would have to be compared against the increased cost of manufacturing such fuel-economy cars.

Careful CBA can benefit many areas of policy through the gathering of empirical data and rigorous assessments. In the area of competition and anti-trust, many jurisdictions must consider the economic efficiency gains against the losses in competition when entities merge. In workplace safety, in areas which involve the risk of lives and injury, the use of CBA in estimating the value of a statistical life is common. In establishing workplace regulations, the benefits have to take into account the reduced number of accidents and hence lives that would be saved. Economists calculate this by means of how much people would be willing to pay to reduce the risk of death, and this is compared against the increased costs that employers have to bear to meet higher workplace safety requirements.

Legal courts also use CBA in the assessment of damages where some quantitative valuation is required. In environmental regulations, we tend to underestimate the cost of meeting higher environmental obligations. The cost of environmental pollution is not just the cost of damages but also the cost of controlling such damages. It is the total cost that matters.

CBA can be used to answer questions that may seem intractable. For example, if we were to cut emissions, and thus raise air quality, what will be the public health benefits? If we save five lives per year from a road-widening project or health safety regulations in the workplace, how do we convert this information of five lives into some monetary equivalence?

If we were to reduce incarcerations of people involved in certain types of crime and have more probations and perhaps even house arrests of the offenders, by changing legal regulations, what would be the net savings to society from incarceration compared to non-incarceration penalties? Should we raise the level of employment training for certain industries – and how does this translate into monetary returns for society?

These issues and questions can to a large extent be answered by CBA, and there are many more. CBA, however, is a normative tool for decision making in that it prescribes what should be done, but does not specify how it should be carried out.

5   While it provides a good objective framework, CBA does have limitations.

For example, if it is used to analyse a long-term policy, uncertainty over the estimated benefits and costs in the future will affect the quality of its assessments. Also, concerns for intra- versus inter-generational equity often involves some philosophical issues.

The choice of methods for valuing benefits and costs can attract some controversy. The lack of local or indigenous studies may render some measurements of benefits and costs challenging. The costs of doing a full and proper CBA often requires expertise, funding and time. And while the principles of CBA do not vary between developed and developing countries, differences in labour, output and financial markets between these countries mean methodologies for measuring benefits and costs have to be adapted to suit the conditions of these countries.

It is not the answer to a question that is most important, but rather the process of getting to the answer that matters more. And because governments' budgets have limitations, CBA provides a strong argument for rational and informed decision making.

As Professor Sunstein wrote in a *Bloomberg* article:

> It is not exactly news that we live in an era of polarised politics, but Republicans and Democrats have come to agree on one issue, the essential need for cost-benefit analysis in the regulatory process. In fact, cost-benefit analysis has become part of the informal constitution of the US regulatory state. This is an extraordinary development.

In Singapore, the Centre for Public Project Management unit was established in 2011, within the Ministry of Finance, and supports the ministry in ensuring an efficient and effective use of public resources. However, this centre provides advice only on major development projects.

What is perhaps needed is an extension of this to encompass CBA of proposed or amended regulations across a variety of public policies. CBA should also be considered for use by financial regulators. Besides rationality, CBA is often hailed as a check on arbitrary and incomplete regulatory actions. As budgets continue to be constrained and demands for expenditure become greater, the need for justification for new projects and policies means that CBA is here to stay.

Note

1 This appendix note is based on an article in the *Singapore Straits Times* by Quah, 2019.

Appendix 14
Valuing household production

1   The economic values of household production (such as the daily services of cooking, cleaning and the multitude of other regular home maintenance chores that are demanded by the household) are not to be neglected in CBA. Consistent with other non-market goods, household production has to be valued, where it could constitute a benefit arising from a policy in question, or the opportunity cost of moving homemakers into the workforce.

   Most of the difficulties encountered in valuing household production lie in the fact that no records are kept on such time consumption, and second, that the amounts taken by households are generally not purchased in market transactions where prices would then indicate their value at the margin. The lack of a market mechanism and market price in no way makes household production any less economically significant. It only means that household production valuation necessitates their imputation through some indirect methods. However, the success of these indirect methods in producing meaningful estimates will depend on, among other things, the definition given to household production; the method of dealing with joint production activities; and the method's consistency with economic theory (Quah, 1986).

2   Problems of definition add difficulties to obtaining accurate assessments. Even with careful precautions in survey design, as in time–budget studies, concerning what is and is not to be included, people's responses with respect to time spent and the economic value of household production can deviate widely depending on how they perceive the different household activities. For some, cooking, general household repairs and gardening may be viewed as pleasures or hobbies, while others look on them as differing little from cleaning, ironing and after-meal clean-up. In other words, how do we distinguish between household work and leisure? A clear definition of what constitutes household production is required to avoid any ambiguity concerning what is meant by the term 'household work' and if any meaningful set of estimates of the quantity and economic value of household production are to be derived.

3   Another major problem in household production research concerns the measurement of multiple activities which occur simultaneously within the household. Some tasks, such as laundry and caring for children can often be done concurrently with other activities, raising ambiguities of how such time is to be reported. To simply allow for these simultaneous activities can lead to a gross exaggeration of

the total amount of time spent performing household work. Such overstatements of time devoted to household work usually arise when it is the case that while performing one activity, the individual gives only intermittent attention to the other. Thus, for example, a household member may be doing some cooking, while occasionally glancing over or tending a child. The latter activity could hardly be given the same amount of time as the former. A more accurate method of accounting for time use in households where joint production activities are concerned is to ascribe the time entirely to the major task. In other words, time is recorded only for the major household task performed and the other activity is ignored. This appears to be a solution to accounting of such time where simultaneous activities are involved.

4   Household production valuation methods should produce meaningful estimates consistent with economic theory. Methods of valuing household production revolve around two general approaches; the replacement cost method and opportunity cost method (see Quah, 1989 for details).

There are two variations of the replacement cost method. The first, called the replacement cost by housekeeper method (RCHK) takes the value to be equal to the wage payment that would be necessary to hire a person to spend a like number of hours performing all household tasks (equation 1).

$$H = \sum_{i=1}^{N} W^{RA} = W^{RA} \times N \tag{1}$$

where H = value of household production in an economy
  W^{RA} = annual average gross wage of a hired help
  N = number of households in the country.

The second variation, called the replacement cost by specialized function (RCSF), applies an appropriate wage rate for comparable services offered in the market to the average amount of time that is devoted to different types of activities (equation 2).

$$H = \sum_{i=1}^{N} \left(52 \sum_{j=1}^{n} \sum_{l=1}^{m} T_{jl}^{ph} W_L^R \right) \tag{2}$$

where T_{jl}^{ph} = time spent in household work per week by the jth household member in household item l
  W_L^R = simple or weighted average of hourly wage rates of the various market services equivalent to housework item L
  m = the number of housework items
  n = the number of household members in a family.

Another means of valuing household production is to ascribe the time devoted to household production to the opportunity income given up when time is devoted to producing household services rather than earning money income from paid employment outside the home. Called the opportunity cost method, it has three variations. The first, known as the opportunity cost before taxes (OCBT), utilizes the gross market wage rate per hour foregone in the production of household services (equation 3).

$$H = \sum_{i=1}^{N} \left(52 \sum_{j=1}^{n} T_j^{ph} W_j^m \right) \tag{3}$$

The second variation subtracts the marginal income tax from the gross market wage, and is known as the opportunity cost net taxes (OCNT) method (equation 4).

$$H = \sum_{i=1}^{N} \left[52 \sum_{j=1}^{n} T_j^{ph} \left(W_j^m - t \right) \right] \tag{4}$$

where t = marginal income tax on an additional hour of work

The third variation, which allows for work-related costs to be subtracted from net income, is also known as the opportunity cost net costs (OCNC) method (equation 5).

$$H = \sum_{i=1}^{N} \left[52 \sum_{j=1}^{n} T_j^{ph} \left\{ W_j^m (1 - t_r) - C_j^m \right\} \right] \tag{5}$$

where t = marginal tax rate

C_j^m = work-related costs per hour of work.

5   As with other non-market goods, other valuation techniques, such as the contingent valuation method, are also options for valuing household production (Quah, 1987). Within each valuation method lie further refinements, such as adjusting for occupation-specific experience (e.g. see Lowen and Sicilian, 2015). The appropriate method ultimately will depend on the purpose of the valuation: whether it is for national income accounting, matrimonial property settlements or the valuation for compensation questions (see Quah, 1986 for details). This, in turn, depends on the objective and motivation of the CBA conducted, and the policy in question.

Bibliography and further reading

Aabø, S. (2005). 'Are Public Libraries Worth Their Price? A Contingent Valuation Study of Norwegian Public Libraries', *New Library World*, 106(11/12): 487–495.

Abelson, P. (2003). 'The Value of Life and Health for Public Policy', *Economic Record*, 79: 2–13.

Adler, M. and Posner, E. (eds.) (2000). *Cost-Benefit Analysis: Legal, Economic, and Philosophical Perspectives*, Chicago, IL and London: University of Chicago Press.

Alberini, A., Cropper, M.L., Fu, T.T., Krupnick, A., Liu, J.T., Shaw, D. and Harrington, W. (1997). 'Valuing Health Effects of Air Pollution in Developing Countries: The Case of Taiwan', *Journal Environmental Economics and Management*, 34: 107–126.

Amirnejah, H., Khalilian, S., Assareh, M.H. and Ahmadian, M. (2006). 'Estimating the Existence Value of North Forests of Iran by Using a Contingent Calculation Method', *Ecological Economics*, 58(4): 665–675.

Anderson, R.J. and Crocker, T.D. (1971). 'Air Pollution and Residential Property Values', *Urban Studies*, 8: 171–180.

Arkes, H.R. and Blumer, C. (1985). 'The Psychology of Sunk Costs', *Organizational Behavior and Human Decision Processes*, 35: 124–140.

Arrow, K.J. (1966). 'Discounting and Public Investment Criteria', in Kneese, A.V. and Smith, S.C. (eds.), *Water Research*. Baltimore, MD: Johns Hopkins University Press.

Arrow, K.J. and Lind, R.C. (1970). 'Uncertainty and the Evaluation of Public Investment Decisions', *American Economic Review*, 60(3): 364–378.

———. (1972). 'Uncertainty and the Evaluation of Public Investment Decisions: Reply', *American Economic Review*, 62(1): 171–172.

Arthur, W.B. (1981). 'The Economics of Risks to Life', *American Economic Review*, 71(1): 54–64.

Balassa, B. (1974). 'Estimating the Shadow Price of Foreign Exchange in Project Evaluation', *Oxford Economic Papers*, 26: 147–168.

Bateman, I.J., Day, B.H. and Lake, I. (2004). The Valuation of Transport-Related Noise in *Birmingham, Technical Report to the Department for Transport*, retrieved 15 June 2011 from www.dft.gov.uk/pgr/economics/.

Baumol, W. (1968). 'On the Social Rate of Discount', *American Economic Review*, 58: 788–802.

———. (1972). 'On Taxation and the Control of Externalities', *American Economic Review*, 62: 307–322.

Beal, D.J. (1995). 'A Travel Cost Analysis of the Value of Carnarvon Gorge National Park for Recreational Use', *Review of Marketing and Agricultural Economics*, 63(2): 292–303.

Becker, G. (1965). 'A Theory of the Allocation of Time', *Economic Journal*, 75: 493–517.

Beesley, M. (1965). 'The Value of Time Spent in Travelling: Some New Evidence', *Economica*, 32: 174–185.

Bierman, H. and Smidt, S. (1988). *The Capital Budgeting Decision: Economic Analysis of Investment Projects* (7th edn), New York: Macmillan.

Blaug, M. (1985). *Economic Theory in Retrospect* (4th edn), Cambridge: Cambridge University Press.

Blomquist, G.C. and Whitehead, J.C. (1998). 'Resource Quality Information and Validity of Willingness to Pay in Contingent Valuation', *Resource and Energy Economics*, 20: 179–196.

Boardman, A., Greenberg, D., Vining, A. and Weimer, D. (2001). *Cost-Benefit Analysis: Concepts and Practice* (2nd edn), Upper Saddle River, NJ: Prentice-Hall.

———. (2006). *Cost–Benefit Analysis: Concepts and Practice* (3rd edn), Harlow: Pearson.

Bradford, D. (1975). 'Constraints on Government Investment Opportunities and the Choice of Discount Rate', *American Economic Review*, 65: 887–899.

Brent, R. (1990). *Project Appraisal for Developing Countries*, Hemel Hempstead: Harvester Wheatsheaf.

———. (1996). *Applied Cost-Benefit Analysis*, Cheltenham: Edward Elgar.

Broome, J. (1978). 'Trying to Value a Life', *Journal of Political Economy*, 9: 91–100.

Buchanan, J. (1965). 'An Economic Theory of Clubs', *Economica*, 32: 1–14.

Buchanan, J. and Stubblebine, W. (1962). 'Externality', *Economica*, 29: 371–384.

Burrows, P. (1979). *The Economic Theory of Pollution Control*, Oxford: Martin Robertson.

Campbell, H. and Brown, R. (2003). *Benefit–Cost Analysis: Financial and Economic Appraisal Using Spreadsheets*, Cambridge: Cambridge University Press.

Campen, J. (1986). *Benefit, Cost, and Beyond: The Political Economy of Benefit-Cost Analysis*, Cambridge, MA: Ballinger.

Carson, R., Meade, N.F. and Smith, V.K. (1993). 'Contingent Valuation and Passive-Use Values: Introducing the Issues', *Choices*, 8(2): 5–8.

Champ, P.A. and Loomis, J.B. (1998). 'WTA Estimates Using the Method of Paired Comparison: Tests of Robustness', *Environmental and Resource Economics*, 12: 375–386.

Chia, W. (2011). 'Value of a statistical life'. In E. Quah (Ed.), *Cost-Benefit Analysis Cases and Materials*, London, UK: Routledge.

———. 'Estimating the economic cost of air pollution on health'. In E. Quah (Ed.), *Cost-Benefit Analysis Cases and Materials*, London, UK: Routledge.

Chin, A. and Knetsch, J.L. (2008). 'Values Depend on the Measures: Are Many Transport Project Valuations Seriously Biased?' Mimeo.

Chuenpagdee, R., Knetsch, J. and Brown, T. (2001). 'Coastal Management Using Public Judgments, Importance Scales, and Predetermined Schedules', *Coastal Management*, 29: 253–270.

Clawson, M. (1959). 'Method of Measuring the Demand for and Value of Outdoor Recreation', in *Resources for the Future*. Washington, DC: Brookings Institution.

Clawson, M. and Knetsch, J. (1966). *The Economics of Outdoor Recreation*, Baltimore, MD: Johns Hopkins University Press.

Coase, R. (1960). 'The Problems of Social Cost', *Journal of Law and Economics*, 3(1): 1–44.

Cohen, D. and Knetsch, J.L. (1992). 'Judicial Choice and Disparities between Measures of Economic Values', *Osgoode Hall Law Journal*, 30: 737–770.

Coleman, J. (1984). 'The Possibility of a Social Welfare Function', *American Economic Review*, 56: 1105–1122.

Conley, B.C. (1976). 'The Value of Human Life in the Demand for Safety', *American Economic Review*, 66(1): 45–55.

Cook, P.J. and Graham, D.A. (1977). 'The Demand for Insurance and Protection: The Case of Irreplaceable Commodities', *Quarterly Journal of Economics*, 91: 143–156.

Cropper, M. and Oates, W. (1992). 'Environmental Economics: A Survey', *Journal of Economic Literature*, 30: 675–740.

Currie, J., Murphy, J. and Schmitz, A. (1971). 'The Concept of Economic Surplus and Its Use in Economic Analysis', *Economic Journal*, 81: 741–799.

Dardis, R. (1980). 'The Value of a Life; New Evidence from the Marketplace', *American Economic Review*, 1970: 1077–1082.

Dasgupta, P. and Heal, M. (1979). *Economic Theory and Exhaustible Resources*, Cambridge: Cambridge University Press.

Dasgupta, P., Marglin, S. and Sen, A. (1972). *Guidelines for Project Evaluation*, New York: United Nations.

Davis, O. and Whinston, A. (1965). 'Welfare Economics and the Theory of Second Best', *Review of Economic Studies*, 32: 1–14.

Day, B., Bateman, I. and Lake, I. (2007). 'Beyond Implicit Prices - Recovering Theoretically Consistent and Transferable Values for Noise Avoidance from a Hedonic Property Price Model', *Environmental and Resource Economics*, 37(1): 211–232.

Dewenter, R., Haucap, J., Luther, R. and Rötzel, P. (2007). 'Hedonic Prices in the German Market for Mobile Phones', *Telecommunications Policy*, 31(1): 4–13.

Dinwiddy, C. and Teal, F. (1996). *Principles of Cost-Benefit Analysis for Developing Countries*, Cambridge: Cambridge University Press.

Dixon, J.A., Scura, L.F., Carpenter, R.A. and Sherman, P.B. (1994). *Economic Analysis of Environmental Impacts*. London: Earthscan Publications.

Dorfman, R. (1962). 'Basic Economic and Technological Concepts', in Maass, A., Hufschmidt, M.M., Dorfman, R., Thoms, H.A., Marglin, S.A. and Fair, G.M. (eds.), *Design of Water Resources Systems*. London: Macmillan.

Dorfman, R., Samuelson, P.A. and Solow, R.M. (1958). *Linear Programming and Economic Analysis*, New York: McGraw-Hill.

Dreze, J.H. (1974). 'Discount Rates and Public Investment: A Postscriptum', *Economica*, 41: 52–61.

Duesenberry, J. (1949). *Income, Saving and the Theory of Consumer Behaviour*, Cambridge, MA: Harvard University Press.

Dupuit, J. (1844). 'De La Mesure De L'utilite Des Travaus Publics', *Annales Des Points Et Chaussées*, translated by R. Barback (1952) in *International Economic Papers*, 2: 83–110.

Eckstein, O. (1958). *Water Resources Development*, Cambridge, MA: Harvard University Press.

Ehrenkranz, N.J., Ventura, A.K., Guadrado, R.R., Bond, W.L. and Porter, J.E. (1971). 'Pandemic Dengue in Caribbean Countries and the Southern United States – Past, Present and Potential Problems', *New England Journal of Medicine*, 285: 1460–1469.

Einio, M., Kaustia, M. and Puttonen, V. (2008). 'Price Setting and the Reluctance to Realize Losses in Apartment Markets', *Journal of Economic Psychology*, 29: 19–34.

Eisner, R. and Strotz, R. (1961). 'Flight Insurance and the Theory of Choice', *Journal of Political Economy*, 69: 355–368.

Ellis, H. and Fellner, W. (1943). 'External Economies and Diseconomies', *American Economic Review*, 33: 493–511.

English, M. (1984). *Project Evaluation: A Unified Approach for the Analysis of Capital Investments*, New York: Macmillan.

European Commission (2000). *Analysis of the Fundamental Concepts of Resource Management*, retrieved from http://ec.europa.eu/environment/enveco/waste/pdf/guarport.pdf.

Farrell, M. (1958). 'In Defence of Public Utility-Price Theory', *Oxford Economic Papers*, 10: 109–123.

Feldstein, M. (1964a). 'Net Social Benefit Calculation and the Public Investment Decision', *Oxford Economic Papers*, 16: 114–131.

———. (1964b). 'The Social Time Preference Discount Rate in Cost-Benefit Analysis', *Economic Journal*, 74: 360–379.

———. (1972). 'The Inadequacy of Weighted Discount Rates', in Layard, R. (ed.), *Cost–Benefit Analysis: Selected Readings*, pp. 311–331, Harmondsworth, Penguin.

Fischer, D. and Davis, G. (1973). 'An Approach to Assessing Environmental Impacts', *Journal of Environmental Management*, 1: 207–227.

Fisher, A. (1973). 'Environmental Externalities and the Arrow–Lind Public Investment Theorem', *American Economic Review*, 63(4): 722–725.

Fix, P. and Loomis, J. (1997). 'The Economic Benefits of Mountain Biking at One of Its Meccas: An Application of the Travel Cost Method to Mountain Biking in Moab, Utah', *Journal of Leisure Research*, 29(3): 342–352.

Fleming, C.M. and Cook, A. (2008). 'The Recreational Value of Lake McKenzie, Fraser Island – An Application of the Travel Cost Method', *Tourism Management*, 29(6): 1197–1205.

Flowerdew, A. (1971). 'The Cost of Airport Noise', *The Statistician*, 13: 23–35.

Foster, C. and Neuburger, H. (1974). 'The Ambiguity of the Consumer's Surplus Measure of Welfare Change', *Oxford Economic Papers*, 26: 66–77.

Freeman, A. (1971). 'Air Pollution and Property Values: A Comment', *Review of Economics and Statistics*, 53: 415–416.

———. (1977). 'A Short Argument in Favour of Discounting Intergenerational Effects', *Futures*, 4: 7–9.

———. (1993). *The Measurement of Environmental and Resource Values: Theory and Method*, Washington, DC: Resources for the Future.

Friedman, M. and Savage, L.J. (1948). 'Utility Analysis of Choices Involving Risks', *Journal of Political Economy*, 56: 279–304.

George, I. (1978). *Modern Cost-Benefit Methods*, Basingstoke: Macmillan.

Gibbs, C., Guttentag, D., Gretzel, U., Morton, J. and Goodwill, A. (2017). 'Pricing in the Sharing Economy: A Hedonic Pricing Model Applied to Airbnb Listings', *Journal of Travel & Tourism Marketing*, 35(1): 46–56.

Glaister, S. (1974). 'Generalised Consumer Surplus and Public Transport Pricing', *Economic Journal*, 84: 849–867.

Gramlich, E. (1990). *A Guide to Benefit–Cost Analysis* (2nd edn), Upper Saddle River, NJ: Prentice-Hall.

Green, H.A.J. (1961). 'The Social Optimum in the Presence of Monopoly and Taxation', *Review of Economic Studies*, 29: 66–77.

Gregory, R. and Kunreuther, H. (1990). 'Successful Siting Incentives', *Journal of Civil Engineering*, 60: 73–75.

Groothuis, P.A. (2005). 'Benefit Transfer – A Comparison of Approaches', *Growth and Change*, 36(4): 551–564.

Gubler, D.J. (1991). 'Dengue Hemorrhagic Fever – A Global Update (Editorial)', *Virus Information Exchange News*, 8: 2–3.

Gubler, D.J. and Clark, G.G. (1995). 'Dengue/Dengue Hemorrhagic Fever – The Emergence of a Global Health Problem', *Emerging Infectious Diseases*, 1: 55–57.

Gubler, D.J. and Trent, D.W. (1994). 'Emergence of Epidemic Dengue/Dengue Hemorrhagic Fever as a Public Health Problem in the Americas', *Infectious Agents and Disease*, 2: 383–393.

Gürlük, S. and Rehber, E. (2008). 'A Travel Cost Study to Estimate Recreational Value for A Bird Refuge at Lake Manyas, Turkey', *Journal of Environmental Management*, 88(4): 1350–1360.

Haab, T., Whitehead, J.C. and McConnell, T. (2000). 'The Economic Value of Marine Recreational Fishing in the Southeast United States – 1997 Southeast Economic Data Analysis', *NOAA Technical Memorandum NMFS-SEFSC-446,Deparment of Economics*, East Carolina University and Department of Agricultural and Resource Economics, University of Maryland, retrieved 15 June 2011 from www.st.nmfs.noaa.gov/st5/RecEcon/Publications/SE_vol2.pdf.

Halstead, S.B. (1980). 'Dengue Hemorrhagic Fever – A Public Health Problem and A Field for Research', *Bulletin of the World Health Organization*, 58: 1–21.

Halstead, S.B. (1992). 'The 20th Century Dengue Pandemic – Need for Surveillance and Research', *World Health Organization Statistics Quarterly*, 45: 292–298.

Hammack, J. and Brown, G.M. (1974). *Waterfowl and Wetlands: Toward Bio-Economic Analysis*, Baltimore, MD: Johns Hopkins Press.

Hammitt, J.K. and Zhou, Y. (2006). 'The Economic Value of Air-Pollution-Related Health Risks in China – A Contingent Valuation Study', *Environmental and Resource Economics*, 33(2): 399–423.

Hanemann, W. (1991). 'Willingness to Pay and Willingness to Accept: How Much Can They Differ?' *American Economic Review*, 81: 635–647.

Hanemann, W.M., Loomis, J., and Kanninen, B. (1991). 'Statistical Efficiency of Double-Bounded Dichotomous Choice Contingent Valuation', *American Journal of Agricultural Economics*, 73(4): 1255–1263.

Hanley, N. and Barbier, E.B. (2009). *Pricing Nature: Cost-Benefit Analysis and Environmental Policy*, Northampton, MA: Edward Elgar.

Hanley, N. and Spash, C. (1993). *Cost–Benefit Analysis and the Environment*, Cheltenham: Edward Elgar.

Harberger, A.C. (1968). 'On the Opportunity Cost of Public Borrowing', *Economic Analysis of Public Investment Decisions: Interest Rate Policy and Discounting Analysis*, Hearings before the Joint Economic Committee, 90th Congress, 2nd Session, USGOP, Washington, DC.

———. (1971a). 'On Measuring the Social Opportunity Cost of Labour', *International Economic Review*, 89: 23–33.

———. (1971b). 'The Three Basic Postulates for Applied Welfare Economics: An Interpretive Essay', *Journal of Economic Literature*, 9: 785–797.

Hause, J.C. (1975). 'The Theory of Welfare Cost Measurement', *Journal of Political Economy*, 83: 1145–1182.

Haveman, R.H. and Krutilla, J.V. (1968). *Unemployment, Idle Capacity and the Evaluation of Public Expenditure*, Washington, DC: Resources for the Future.

Henderson, A. (1941). 'Consumers Surplus and Compensating Variation', *Review of Economic Studies*, 8: 117–121.

Hicks, J.R. (1939). *Value and Capital* (2nd edn, 1944), Oxford: Clarendon Press.

———. (1944). 'The Four Consumers' Surplus', *Review of Economic Studies*, 11: 31–41.

———. (1956). *A Revision of Demand Theory*, Oxford: Clarendon Press.

Hicks, R., Steinbeck, S., Gautam, A. and Thunberg, E. (1999). Volume II – The Economic Value of New England and Mid-Atlantic Sportfishing in 1994, *NOAA Technical Memorandum NMFS-F/SPO-38*, retrieved 15 June 2011 from www.st.nmfs.noaa.gov/st5/RecEcon/Pubhcations/tm_f-spo-3-1999.pdf.

Horowitz, J. and McConnell, K. (2002). 'A Review of WTA/WTP Studies', *Journal of Environmental Economics and Management*, 44: 426–447.

Ibarra, A., Minerva, A., Chuenpagdee, R., Charles, T. and Cima-Velázquez, A. (2010). Assessing Natural Resource Values Using the Damage Schedule Approach: Fishing and Other Resource Uses of the Maya People in Quintana Roo, Mexico. In: Proceedings of the Fifteenth Biennial Conference of the International Institute of Fisheries Economics & Trade, July 13-16, 2010, Montpellier, France: Economics of Fish Resources and Aquatic Ecosystems: Balancing Uses, Balancing Costs. Compiled by Ann L. Shriver. International Institute of Fisheries Economics & Trade, Corvallis, Oregon, USA, 2010.

Ironmonger, D.S. (2001). 'Household Production', in Smelser, N.J. and Baltes, P.B. (eds.), *International Encyclopedia of the Social and Behavioral Sciences*, vols. 20.69, pp. 34–39. Oxford: Pergamon.

Jeong, H. and Haab, T. (2004). The Economic Value of Marine Recreational Fishing: Applying Benefit Transfer to Marine Recreational Fisheries Statistics Survey (MRFSS), *AEDE Working Paper AEDE-WP-0039-04*, Department of Agricultural, Environmental, and Development

Economics, The Ohio State University, retrieved 15 June 2011 from http://ageconsearch.unm. edu/bitstrean/28322/1/wp040039.pdf.

Jeuland, M., Lucas, M., Clemens, J. and Whittington, D. (2010). 'Estimating the Private Benefits of Vaccination against Cholera in Beira, Mozambique – A Travel Cost Approach', *Journal of Development Economics*, 91(2): 310–322.

Jiao, L. and Liu, Y. (2010). 'Geographic Field Model Based Hedonic Valuation of Urban Open Spaces in Wuhan, China', *Landscape and Urban Planning*, 98: 47–55.

Johansson, P.O. (1993). *Cost-Benefit Analysis of Environmental Change*, Cambridge: Cambridge University Press.

Johnson, E.J., Hershey, J., Meszaros, J. and Kunreuther, H. (1993). 'Framing Probability Distortions, and Insurance Decisions', *Journal of Risk and Uncertainty*, 7: 35–51.

Jones-Lee, M. (1980a). 'Maximum Acceptable Physical Risk and a New Measure of Financial Risk Aversion', *Economic Journal*, 90: 49–72.

Jones-Lee, M. (1980b). 'Maximum Acceptable Physical Risk and a New Measure of Financial Risk Aversion', *Economic Journal*, 90: 550–568.

Kachelmeier, S.J. and Shehata, M. (1992). 'Estimating Risk Preferences under High Monetary Incentives – Experimental Evidence from the People's Republic of China', *American Economic Review*, 82: 1120–1140.

Kahneman, D., Knetsch, J.L. and Thaler, R.H. (1986). 'Fairness as a Constraint on Profit Seeking – Entitlements in the Market', *American Economic Review*, 76: 728–741.

Kahneman, D., Knetsch, J.L. and Thaler, R.H. (1990). 'Experimental Tests of the Endowment Effect and the Coase Theorem', *Journal of Political Economy*, 98: 728–741.

Kahneman, D., Ritov, I. and Schkade, D. (1999). 'Economic Preferences or Attitude Expressions? An Analysis of Dollar Responses to Public Issues', *Journal of Risk and Uncertainty*, 19(1–3): 203–235.

Kahneman, D. and Tversky, A. (1979). 'Prospect Theory: An Analysis of Decisions Under Risk', *Econometrica*, 47: 263–291.

Kaldor, N. (1939). 'Welfare Propositions of Economics', *Economic Journal*, 49: 549–552.

Keeney, R. (1980). 'Equity and Public Risk', *Operations Research*, 9: 45–56.

Khatun, F.A. (1997). 'The Cost of Particulate Air Pollution in Dhaka City', *The Bangladesh Development Studies*, XXV(1 and 2): Bangladesh Institute of Development Studies.

Klocek, C.A. (2004). Estimating the Economic Value of Canaan Valley National Wildlife Refuge: A Contingent Valuation Approach, *Dissertation*, Davis College of Agricultural Forestry and Consumer Sciences, West Virginia University.

Knetsch, J. (1989). 'The Endowment Effect and Evidence of Nonreversible Indifference Curves', *American Economic Review*, 79: 1277–1284.

———. (1990). 'Environmental Policy Implication of Disparities between Willingness to Pay and Compensation Demanded Measures of Values', *Journal of Environmental Economics and Management*, 18: 227–237.

———. (1995). 'Asymmetric Valuation of Gains and Losses and Preference Order Assumptions', *Economic Inquiry*, 33: 134–141.

———. (2003). 'Environmental, Ecological, and Behavioural Economics', in Dovers, S., Stern, D.I. and Young, M. (eds.), *New Dimensions in Ecological Economics: Integrative Approaches to People and Nature*. Cheltenham: Edward Elgar.

———. (2011). 'Behavioural effects and cost-benefit analysis: lessons from behavioural economics'. In E. Quah (Ed.), *Cost-Benefit Analysis Cases and Materials*, London, UK: Routledge.

Knetsch, J.L. (2000). 'Environmental Valuations and Standard Theory – Behavioural Findings, Context Dependence, and Implications', in Tietenberg, T. and Folmer, H. (eds.), *The International Yearbook of Environmental and Resource Economics 2000/2001*, pp. 267–299. Cheltenham: Edward Elgar.

Knetsch, J. and Borcherding, T. (1979). 'Expropriation of Private Property and the Basis for Compensation', *University of Toronto Law Journal*, 29: 237–240.

Knetsch, J., Riyanto, Y. and Zong, J. (2012). 'Gain and Loss Domains and the Choice of Welfare Measure of Positive and Negative Changes', *Journal of Benefit–Cost Analysis*, 3(4): Article 1.

Knetsch, J. and Sinden, J. (1984). 'Willingness to Pay and Compensation Demanded: Experimental Evidence of an Unexpected Disparity in Measures of Values', *Quarterly Journal of Economics*, 99: 507–521.

Kong, F., Yin, H. and Nakagoshi, N. (2007). 'Using Tire GIS and Landscape Metrics in the Hedonic Price Modelling of the Amenity Value of Urban Green Space – A Case Study in Jinan City, China', *Landscape and Urban Planning*, 79: 240–252.

Krupnick, A.J., Harrison, K., Nickell, E. and Toman, M. (1993). The Benefits of Ambient Air Quality Improvements in Central and Eastern Europe – A Preliminary Assessment, *Discussion Paper ENR93-19*, Washington, DC: Resources for the Future.

Krutilla, J. (1967). 'Conservation Reconsidered', *American Economic Review*, 54: 777–786.

Krutilla, J. and Eckstein, O. (1958). *Multiple Purpose River Development, Studies in Applied Economic Analysis*, Baltimore, MD: Johns Hopkins Press.

Kunreuther, H. and Kleindorfer, P.R. (1986). 'A Sealed-bid Auction Mechanism for Siting Noxious Facilities', *American Economic Review*, 76: 295–299.

Layard, R. and Glaister, S. (eds.) (1994). *Cost-Benefit Analysis* (2nd edn), Cambridge: Cambridge University Press.

LeDuc, J.W. (1996). 'World Health Organization Strategy for Emerging Infectious Diseases', *Journal of the Amend Medical Association*, 275: 318–320.

Lee, N. and Kirkpatrick, C. (2000). *Sustainable Development and Integrated Appraisal in a Developing World*, Cheltenham: Edward Elgar.

Leibenstein, H. (1966). 'Allocative Efficiency Vs X-Efficiency', *American Economic Review*, 56: 392–415.

Linnerooth, J. (1979). 'The Value of Human Life: A Review of the Models', *Economic Enquiry*, 17: 52–74.

Lipsey, R. and Lancaster, K. (1956). 'The General Theory of Second Best', *Review of Economic Studies*, 24: 11–32.

List, John A. (2003). 'Does Market Experience Eliminate Market Anomalies?' *The Quarterly Journal of Economics*, 118(1): 41–71.

Little, I.M.D. (1957). *A Critique of Welfare Economics* (2nd edn), Oxford: Oxford University Press.

Little, I.M.D. and Mirrlees, J. (1968). *Manual of Industrial Project Analysis in Developing Countries, Vol. 2*, Paris, France: OECD.

Loehman, E.T., Berg, S.V., Arroyo, A.A., Hedinger, R.A., Schwartz, J.M., Shaw, M.E., Fahien, R.W., De, V.H., Fishe, R.P. and Rio, D.E. (1979). 'Distributional Analysis of Regional Benefits and Costs of Air Quality Control', *Journal of Environmental Economics and Management*, VI: 222–243.

Loomis, J., Hanemann, M., Kanninen, B. and Wegge, T. (1991). 'WTP to Protect Wetlands and Reduce Wildlife Contamination from Agricultural Drainage', in Dinar, A. and Zilberman, D. (eds.), *The Economics and Management of Water and Drainage in Agriculture*, pp. 411–429. Norwell, MA: Kluwer Academic Publishers.

Loomis, J. and Walsh, R. (1997). *Recreation Economic Decisions: Comparing Benefits and Costs* (2nd edn), State College, PA: Venture Publishing.

Loomis, J.B., Peterson, G.L., Champ, P.A., Brown, T.C. and Lucero, B. (1998). 'Paired Comparison Estimates of Willingness to Accept versus Contingent Valuation Estimates of Willingness to Pay', *Journal of Economic Behaviour and Organization*, 35: 501–515.

Lowen, A. and Sicilian, P. (2015). 'An Alternative Valuation Method for Household Production Using American Time Use Survey Data', *Journal of Legal Economics*, 22(1): 1–23.

Lvovsky, K., Huges, G., Maddison, D., Ostro, B., and Pearce, D. (2000). *Environmental Costs of Fossil Fuels*. Washington, DC: The World Bank.

Lyon, S.F., Merrill, N.H., Mulvaney, K.K., and Mazzotta, M.J. (2018). 'Valuing Coastal Beaches and Closures Using Benefit Transfer: An Application to Barnstable, Massachusetts', *Journal of Ocean and Coastal Economics*, 5(1): 1.

Marglin, S. (1963a). 'The Opportunity Costs of Public Investment', *Quarterly Journal of Economics*, 77: 274–289.

———. (1963b). 'The Social Rate of Discount and the Optimal Rate of Investment', *Quarterly Journal of Economics*, 77: 95–111.

Marglin, S.A. (1976). *Value and Price in Labour Surplus Economies*, New York: Oxford University Press.

Margolis, J. and Guitton, H. (eds.) (1969). *Public Economics*, London: Macmillan.

Marshall, A. (1924). *Principles of Economics* (8th edn), London: Macmillan.

Mayer, M. and Woltering, M. (2018). 'Assessing and Valuing the Recreational Ecosystem Services of Germany's National Park Using Travel Cost Models', *Ecosystem Services*, 31C: 371–386.

McKean, R. (1958). *Efficiency in Government through Systems Analysis, with Emphasis on Water Resource Development*, New York: John Wiley.

Meade, J. (1962). 'External Economies and Diseconomies in a Competitive Situation', *Economic Journal*, 64: 54–67.

Mishan, E. (1952). 'The Principle of Compensation Reconsidered', *Journal of Political Economy*, 60: 312–322.

———. (1957). 'A Reappraisal of the Principles of Resource Allocation', *Economica*, 24: 324–342.

———. (1958). 'Rent as a Measure of Welfare Change', *American Economic Review*, 49: 386–394.

———. (1960). 'A Survey of Welfare Economics 1939–1959', *Economic Journal*, 70: 197–265.

———. (1962a). 'Welfare Criteria: An Exchange of Notes', *Economic Journal*, 72: 234–244.

———. (1962b). 'Second Thoughts on Second Best', *Oxford Economic Papers*, 14: 205–217.

———. (1963). 'Welfare Criteria: Are Compensation Tests Necessary?', *Economic Journal*, 73: 342–350.

———. (1965a). 'Reflections on Recent Developments in the Concept of External Effects', *Canadian Journal of Economics and Political Science*, 31: 3–34.

———. (1965b). 'The Recent Debate on Welfare Criteria', *Oxford Economic Papers*, 17: 219–236.

———. (1967a). 'Interpretation of the Benefits of Private Transport', *Journal of Transport Economics and Policy*, 1(2): 184–189.

———. (1967b). 'Pareto Optimality and the Law', *Oxford Economic Papers*, 19: 255–287.

———. (1967c). 'A Normalisation Procedure for Public Investment Criteria', 77: 777–796.

———. (1969a). *Welfare Economics: An Assessment*, Amsterdam: North-Holland.

———. (1969b). 'The Relationship between Joint Products, Collective Goods, and External Effects', *Journal of Political Economy*, 77: 329–348.

———. (1969c). *Welfare Economics: Ten Introductory Essays*, New York: Random House.

———. (1970). 'What Is Wrong with Roskill?', *Journal of Transport Economics and Policy*, 4: 221–234.

———. (1971a). 'Pangloss on Pollution', *Swedish Journal of Economics*, 73: 1–27.

———. (1971b). 'The Postwar Literature on Externalities: An Interpretative Essay', *Journal of Economic Literature*, 9(1): 1–28.

———. (1971c). 'Evaluation of Life and Limb: A Theoretical Approach', *Journal of Political Economy*, 79(4): 687–705.

———. (1973). 'Welfare Criteria: Resolution of a Paradox', *Economic Journal*, 83: 747–767.

———. (1974). 'Flexibility and Consistency in Project Evaluation', *Economica*, 41: 81–96.

———. (1976a). 'Choices Involving Risk: Simple Steps toward an Ordinalist Analysis', *Economic Journal*, 86: 759–777.

———. (1976b). 'The New Welfare Criteria and the Social Welfare Function', *Economisch En Sociaal Tijdschrift*, 30(5): 775–783.

———. (1977a). 'The Plain Truth about Consumer Surplus', *Zeitschrift Für Nationalökonomie*, 37(1): 1–24.

———. (1977b). 'Property Rights and Amenity Rights', in Dorfman, R. and Dorfman, N.S. (eds.), *Economics of the Environment: Selected Readings*. New York: W.W. Norton.

———. (1977c). 'Economic Criteria for Intergenerational Comparisons', *Futures*, 9(5): 383–404.

———. (1977d). *The Economic Growth Debate: An Assessment*, London: Allen & Unwin.

———. (1980a). *Introduction to Normative Economics*, New York: Oxford University Press.

———. (1980b). 'The New Welfare Economics: An Alternative View', *International Economic Review*, 21: 691–705.

———. (1981). 'The Value of Trying to Value a Life', *Journal of Public Economics*, 15: 133–137.

———. (1982). 'The New Controversy about the Rationale of Economic Evaluation', *Journal of Economic Issues*, 16: 29–47.

———. (1985). 'Consistency in the Valuation of Life: A Wild Goose Chase?', *Social Philosophy and Policy*, 2: 133–137.

———. (1988). *Cost-Benefit Analysis: An Informal Introduction* (4th edn), London: Unwin Hyman.

———. (1993). *The Costs of Economic Growth* (2nd edn), London: Weidenfeld & Nicolson.

Moeltner, K. and Woodward, R. (2009). 'Meta-Functional Benefit Transfer for Wetland Valuation: Making the Most of Small Samples', *Environmental and Resource Economics*, 42(1): 89–108.

Montgomery, M. and Needleman, M. (1997). 'The Welfare Effects of Toxic Contamination in Freshwater Fish', *Land Economics*, 73(2): 211–223.

Moore, P.G. (1968). *Basic Operation Research*, London: Pitman.

Mullarkey, D. (1997). Contingent Valuation of Wetlands: Testing Sensitivity to Scope, *Dissertation*, Department of Agricultural and Applied Economics, Madison: University of Wisconsin.

Mulligan, P. (1977). 'Willingness to Pay for Decreased Risk from Nuclear Plant Accidents', Working Paper No. 3, Energy Extension Program, Penn State University.

Mumy, M. and Hanke, E. (1975). 'Public Investment Criteria for Underpriced Products', *American Economic Review*, 66: 289–300.

Musgrave, R.A. (1963). *The Theory of Public Finance: A Study in Public Economy*, New York: McGraw Hill.

———. (1969). 'Cost-Benefit Analysis and the Theory of Public Investment', *Journal of Economic Literature*, 7(3): 797–806.

Nash, J. (1950). 'The Bargaining Problem', *Econometrica*, 18: 155–162.

Needleman, L. (1976). 'Valuing Other People's Lives', *Manchester School*, 44: 309–342.

Nellthorp, J., Bristow, A.L. and Day, B. (2007). 'Introducing Willingness-to-Pay for Noise Changes into Transport Appraisal – An Application of Benefit Transfer', *Transport Reviews*, 27(3): 327–353.

Ng, Y.K. (2004). *Welfare Economics: Towards a More Complete Analysis*, Basingstoke: Palgrave.

———. (2016). 'Welfare-Reducing Growth and Cost-Benefit Analysis: Essay in Memory of E. J. Mishan', *The Singapore Economic Review*, 61(3).

Nichols, A. (1969). 'On the Social Rate of Discount: Comment', *American Economic Review*, *American Economic Association*, 59(5): 909–911. December.

Nichols, D.A. (1970). 'Land and Economic Growth', *American Economic Review, American Economic Association*, 60(3): 332–340. June.

Nwaneri, V.C. (1970). 'Equity in Cost-Benefit Analysis', *Journal of Transport Economics and Policy*, 4: 238–256.

O'Hare, M., Bacow, L. and Sanderson, D. (1983). *Facility Siting and Public Opposition*, New York: Von Nostrand Reinhold.

Odean, T. (1998). 'Are Investors Reluctant to Realize Their Losses?', *The Journal of Finance*, 53: 1775–1798.

Ong, Q. and Quah, E. (2014). Welfare Perceptions of and Public Expenditure on Environmental and Non-Environmental Goods (with Qiyan, Ong), Theoretical Economics Letters (USA), 4, 457–464

Ong, Q., Quah, E., Tan, K.C., Ho, K.W. and Knetsch, J. (2008). Happiness and Cross Category Paired Comparison of Public Amenities, *Working Paper*, Nanyang Technological University.

Ortolano, L. (1997). *Environmental Regulation and Impact Assessment*, Chichester: John Wiley.

Ostro, B. (1994). Estimating the Health Effects of Air Pollutant – A Method with an Application to Jakarta, *Policy Research Working Paper*, No. 1301, Washington, DC: World Bank.

Otto, D., Monchuk, D., Jintanakul, K. and King, C. (2007). *The Economic Value of Iowa's Natural Resources*, retrieved 15 June 2011 from www.card.iastate.edu/environment/items/DMR-Amenity.pdf.

Ozawa, S., Stack, M. L., Bishai, D. M., Mirelman, A., Friberg, I. K., Niessen, L., Walker, D. G. and Levine, O. S. (2011, June) 'During The 'Decade Of Vaccines,' The Lives Of 6.4 Million Children Valued At $231 Billion Could Be Saved', *Health Affairs*, 30(6): 1010–1020. doi: 10.1377/hlthaff.2011.0381.

Page, T. (1977). *Conservation and Economic Efficiency*, Baltimore: John Hopkins University Press.

Paul, M. (1971). 'Can Airport Noise Be Measured in Money', *Oxford Economic Papers*, 23: 297–327.

Pauwels, W. (1977). 'The Possible Perverse Behaviour of the Compensating Variation as a Welfare Ranking', *Zeitschrift Fur Nationalokonomie*, 38: 369–378.

Pearce, D. and Nash, C. (1983). *The Social Appraisal of Projects*, Basingstoke: ELBS and Macmillan.

Pearce, D.W. (1996). 'Economic Valuation and Health Damage from Air Pollution in Tire Developing Countries', *Energy Policy*, 24(7): 627–630.

Pearce, D.W. and Crowards, T. (1995). *Assessing the Health Costs of Particulate Air Pollution in the UK*, CSERGE Working Paper GEC 95–27, Centre for Social and Economic Research on tire Global Environment, University College London and University of East Anglia, retrieved 12 June 2011 from www.uea.ac.ukenv/cserge/pub/wp/gec/gec_1995_27.pdf

Pearce, D.W., Whittington, D. and Georgiou, S. (1994). *Project and Policy Appraisal: Integrating and Environment*, Paris: OECD.

Peterson, G. and Brown, T. (1998). 'Economic Valuation by the Method of Paired Comparison with Emphasis on Evaluation of the Transitivity Axiom', *Land Economics*, 74 (2): 240–261.

Pigou, A.C. (1952). *Economics of Welfare* (5th edn), London: Macmillan.

Pinheiro, F.P. (1989). 'Dengue in the Americas 1980–1987', *Epidemiological Bulletin of the Pan American Health Organization*, 10: 1–8.

Pinto-Prades, J.L., Loomes, G. and Brey, R. (2009). 'Trying to Estimate a Monetary Value for the QALY', *Journal of Health Economics*, 28(3): 553–562. https://doi.org/10.1016/j.jhealeco.2009.02.003.

Poor, P.J. (1999). 'The Value of Additional Central Flyway Wetlands: The Case of Nebraska's Rainwater Basin Wetlands', *Journal of Agricultural and Resource Economics*, 24(1): 253–265.

Popper, F. (1983). 'The Political Uses of Risk Analysis in Land Use Planning', *Risk Analysis*, 3: 255–263.

Portney, P. and Weyant, J. (eds.) (1999). *Discounting and Intergenerational Equity*, Washington: RFF Press.

Prest, A.R. and Turvey, R. (1965). 'Cost-Benefit Analysis: A Survey', *The Economic Journal*, 75: 683–735.

Putler, D.S. (1992). 'Incorporating Reference Price Effects into a Theory of Consumer Choice', *Marketing Science*, 11: 287–309.

Puttaswamaiah, K. (ed.) (2000). *Cost-Benefit Analysis: Environmental and Ecological Perspectives*, Piscataway, NJ: Transaction.

Quah, E. (1986). 'Persistent Problems in Measuring Household Production: Definition, Quantifying Joint Activities and Valuation Issues are Solvable', *The American Journal of Economics and Sociology*, 45(2): 235–245.

———. (1987). 'Valuing Family Household Production: A Contingent Evaluation Approach', *Applied Economics*, 19: 875–889.

———. (1989). 'Country Studies and the Value of Household Production', *Applied Economics*, 21: 1631–1646.

———. (1993). *Economics and Home Production*, Singapore: Ashgate.

———. (2013). 'Cost-Benefit Analysis in Developing Countries: What's Different?' in Livermore, M.A. and Revesz, R.L. (eds.), *The Globalization of Cost-Benefit Analysis in Environmental Policy*. New York: Oxford University Press.

———. (2016). 'Editor's Comments on Special Issue in Honor and Memory of Professor Ezra J. Mishan', *The Singapore Economic Review*, 61(3): 1602002.

———. (2017a). 'Using Cost–Benefit Analysis In Developed And Developing Countries: Is It The Same?' *Special Feature C of Annual Macroeconomic Review*, 92–97.

———. (2017b, November 25). 'Why Thaler Matters: A Rational Look at Behavioural Economics' *Straits Times, Singapore*. Retrieved from www.straitstimes.com.

Quah, E. and Boon, T.L. (2003). 'The Economic Cost of Particulate Air Pollution on Health in Singapore', *Journal of Asian Economics*, 14(1): 73–90.

Quah, E. and Chia, W. (2019, September 17). 'What the 2015 Haze Cost Singapore: $1.83 Billion' *Straits Times, Singapore*. Retrieved from www.straitstimes.com

Quah, E., Chia, W.M. and Sng, H.Y. (2009). 'What is Human Life Worth?' In Sng, H.Y. and Chia, W.M. (eds.) (2010), *Singapore and Asia: Impact of the Global Financial Tsunami and other Economic Issues*. Singapore: World Scientific.

Quah, E., Choa, E. and Tan, K.C. (2006). 'Use of Damage Schedules in Environmental Evaluation – The Case of Urban Singapore', *Applied Economics*, 38: 1501–1512.

Quah, E. and Nursultan, I. (2020). Why CBA and NIMBY Syndrome Are Important Challenges to China's BRI? *Journal of Asian Economic Integration*, 2(1): 97–114. https://doi.org/10.1177/2631684620916043

Quah, E. and Tan, K.C. (1998). 'The Siting Problem of NIMBY Facilities: Cost-benefit Analysis and Auction Mechanisms', *Environment and Planning C: Government and Policy*, 16: 255–264.

———. (1999a). 'Economics of NIMBY Syndrome: Siting Decisions', *Environment and Planning C: Government and Policy*, 16: 255–264.

———. (1999b). 'Pricing a Scenic View – The Case of Singapore's East Coast Park', *Impact Assessment and Project Appraisal*, 17(4): 295–303.

———. (2002). *Siting Environmentally Unwanted Facilities: Risks, Trade-Offs and Choices*, Cheltenham: Edward Elgar.

Quah, E. and Tan, T.T. (2019). 'Valuing the Environment', in Huang, B. and Yu, E. (eds.), *Ways to Achieve Clean Asia*. Japan: Asian Development Bank Institute.

Quah, E. and Toh, R. (2011). *Cost-Benefit Analysis Cases and Materials*, London: Routledge.

Quah, E. and Yong, J. (2008). 'An Assessment of Four Popular Auction Mechanisms in the Siting of NIMBY Facilities: Some Experimental Evidence', *Applied Economics*, 40: 841–852.

Rabin, M. (1998). 'Psychology and Economics', *Journal of Economic Literature*, 36: 1146.

Ramsey, D.D. (1969). 'On the Social Rate of Discount: Comment', *American Economic Review*, 59: 919–924.

Randall, A. (1987). *An Economic Approach to Natural Resource and Environmental Policy* (2nd edn), New York: John Wiley.

Roberts, L.A. and Leitch, J.A. (1997). Economic Valuation of Some Wetland Outputs of Mud Lake, Minnesota-South Dakota, Agricultural Economics Reports, Department of Agricultural Economics, North Dakota State University.

Rosenberger, R.S. and Loomis, J.B. (2003). 'Benefit Transfer', in Champ, P.A., Boyle, K.J. and Brown, T.C. (eds.), *A Primer on Nonmarket Valuation*, pp. 445–452. London: Kluwer Academic Publisher.

Rowe, R., Lang, C., Chestnut, L., Latimer, D., Rae, D., Bernow, S. and Write, D. (1995). The New York Environmental Externalities Cost Study – Summary of Approach and Results, *European Commission, International Energy Agency and Organization for Economic Cooperation and Development Workshop on External Cost of Energy*, 30–31 January, Brussels.

Rutherford, M., Knetsch, J. and Brown, T. (1994). 'Assessing Environmental Losses: Judgments of Importance and Damage Schedules', *Harvard Environmental Law Review*, 20: 51–101.

Salensminde, K. (2004). 'Cost-benefit Analyses of Walking and Cycling Track Networks Taking into Account Insecurity, Health Effects and External Costs of Motorised Traffic', *Transportation Research Part A*, 38: 593.

Samuelson, P.A. (1954). 'The Pure Theory of Public Expenditure', *Review of Economics and Statistics*, 36: 387–389.

———. (1963). *Foundations of Economic Analysis* (2nd edn), Cambridge, MA: Harvard University Press.

Sandmo, A. and Dreze, J.H. (1971). 'Discount Rates for Public Investment in Closed and Open Economies', *Economica*, 38: 395–412.

Schmitz, H. and Westphal, M. (2013). 'Short- and Medium-Term Effects of Informal Care Provision on Health', *SSRN Electronic Journal*. 10.2139/ssrn.2304088.

Schofield, J. (1987). *Cost-Benefit Analysis in Urban and Regional Planning*, London: Allen & Unwin.

Scitovsky, T. (1941). 'A Note on Welfare Propositions in Economics', *Review of Economic Studies*, 9: 77–88.

Scott, M.F.G. (1974). 'How to Use and Estimate Shadow Exchange Rates', *Oxford Economic Papers*, 26: 169–189.

Seabury, S.A., Goldman, D. P., Ross Maclean, J., Penrod, J. R. and Lakdawalla, D. N. (2012, April). 'Patients Value Metastatic Cancer Therapy More Highly Than Is Typically Shown Through Traditional Estimates', *Health Affairs*, 31(4): 691–699. doi: 10.1377/hlthaff.2012.0174.

Sewell, W.R.D., Davis, J., Scott, A.D. and Ross, D.W. (1965). *Guide to Benefit-Cost Analysis*, Ottawa: Queen's Printer.

Shrestha, R.K., Stein, T.V. and Clark, J. (2007). 'Valuing Nature-Based Recreation in Public Natural Areas of the Apalachicola River Region, Florida', *Journal of Environmental Management*, 45(4): 977–985.

Sinden, J.A. (1967). 'Review', *World Agricultural Economics and Rural Sociology Conference*, Abstracts, 9: 1–16.

Skaburskis, A. (1988). 'Criteria for Compensation for the Imports of Large Projects', *Journal of Policy Analysis and Management*, 7: 668–686.

Small, K., Winston, C. and Yan, J. (2003). 'Preferences for Travel Time and Reliability', Working Paper, University of California (Irvin).

Soh, C. (2011). 'Benefit Transfers'. In E. Quah (Ed.), Cost-Benefit Analysis Cases and Materials, London, UK: Routledge.

Solow, R.H. (1974). 'The Economics of Resources or the Resources of Economics', *American Economic Review*, 64: 1–14.

Sommani, S., Okanurak, K. and Indaratna, K. (1995). *Social and Economic Impact of Dengue Hemorrhagic Fever in Thailand*, Bangkok: Mahidol University, Social and Economic Research Unit.

Squire, L. and van der Tak, H. (1975). *Economic Analysis of Projects*, Baltimore, MD: Johns Hopkins Press.

Sugden, R. and Williams, A. (1978). *The Principles of Practical Cost–Benefit Analysis*, Oxford: Oxford University Press.

Sund, B., Svensson, L., Rosenqvist, M. and Hollenberg, J. (2012). 'Favourable Cost-Benefit in an Early Defibrillation Programme using Dual Dispatch of Ambulance and Fire Services in Out-of-Hospital Cardiac Arrest', *European Journal of Health Economics*, 13: 811–818.

Supreme Court of Canada. *Fraser v. The Queen*, [1963] S.C.R. 455, 1963-10-02.

Sydsaeter, K. and Hammond, P. (2005). *Further Mathematics for Economic Analysis* (2nd edn), Harlow: Pearson Education.

Takayama, A. (1994). *Analytical Methods in Economics*, Hemel Hempstead: Harvester Wheatsheaf.

Tang, S. (1991). *Economic Feasibility of Projects: Managerial and Engineering Practice*, New York: McGraw-Hill.

Thaler, R.H. (1999). 'Mental Accounting Matters', *Journal of Behavioural Decision Making*, 12: 183–206.

Thaler, R.H. and Benartzi, S. (2004). 'Save More Tomorrow – Using Behavioural Economics to Increase Employee Saving', *Journal of Political Economy*, 112: S164–S182.

Throsby, D. (1970). *An Introduction to Mathematical Programming*, New York: Random House.

Thurstone, L.L. (1927). 'The Method of Paired Comparisons for Social Values', *Journal of Abnormal Social Psychology*, 21: 384–400.

Tipping, D.G. (1968). 'Time Savings in Transport Studies', *Economic Journal*, 78: 843–854.

Tkac, J.M. (2002). Estimating Willingness to Pay for the Preservation of the Alfred Bog Wetland in Ontario: A Multiple Bounded Discrete Choice Approach, *Masters Thesis*, Department of Agricultural Economics, Gill University.

Tones, M. (1997). 'Impact of an Outbreak of Dengue Fever – A Case Study from Rural Puerto Rico', *Human Organization*, 56: 19–27.

Ubel, P.A., Berry, S. R., Nadler, E., Bell, C. M., Kozminski, M. A., Palmer, J. A., Evans, W. K., Strevel, E. L. and Neumann, P. J. (2012, April). 'In A Survey, Marked Inconsistency in How Oncologists Judged Value of High-Cost Cancer Drugs in Relation to Gains in Survival', *Health Affairs*, 31(4): 709–717. doi: 10.1377/hlthaff.2011.0251.

United Nations Conference on Environment and Development, and Johnson, S. (1992).*The Earth Summit: The United Nations Conference on Environment and Development (UNCED)*. London: Graham & Trotman/Martinus Nijhoff.

US Environmental Protection Agency. (2000). *Guidelines for Preparing Economic Analyses*, Washington, DC: Environmental Protection Agency.

US Federal Inter-Agency Subcommittee on Evaluation Standards (1958). *Proposed Practices for Economic Analysis of River Basin Projects*, retrieved 12 June 2011 from ftp://ftp-fc.sc. egov.usda.gov/Economics/Technotes/1958cAnalysisOfRiverBasinProjects.pdf.

Usher, D. (1985). 'The Value of Life for Decision Making in the Public Sector', *Social Philosophy and Policy*.

Viscusi, W. and Aldy, J. (2003). 'The Value of Statistical Life: A Critical Review of Market Estimates Throughout the World', *Journal of Risk and Uncertainty*, 27: 5–76.

Von Allmen, S.D., Lopez-Correa, R.H., Woodall, J.P., Morens, D.M., Chiriboga, J. and Casta-Velez, A. (1979). 'Epidemic Dengue Fever in Puerto Rico, 1977 – A Cost Analysis', *American Journal of Tropical Medicine and Hygiene*, 28: 1040–1044.

Walsh, R. (1986). *Recreation Economic Decisions: Comparing Benefits and Costs*, State College, PA: Venture Publishing.

Walshe, G. and Daffern, P. (1990). *Managing Cost–Benefit Analysis*, Basingstoke: Macmillan.

Weale, M. (2011). 'A Cost-benefit Analysis of Cataract Surgery Based on the English Longitudinal Survey of Ageing', *Journal of Health Economics*, 30(4): 730–739. doi: 10.1016/j. jhealeco.2011.05.008.

Weisbrod, B.A. (1964). 'Collective-Consumption Services of Individual-Consumption Goods', *The Quarterly Journal of Economics*, 78(3): 471–477.

Weisbrod, B.A. (1968). 'Income Redistribution Effects & Benefit–Cost Analysis', in Chase, S. B., Jr (ed.), *Problems in Public Expenditure Analysis*. Washington, DC: Brookings Institution.

Wilkinson, R.G. (1973). *Poverty and Progress: An Ecological Model of Economic Development*, London: Methuen.

World Bank (2018). The World Bank Annual Report 2018 (English). Washington, DC: World Bank Group. http://documents.worldbank.org/curated/en/630671538158537244/The-World-Bank-Annual-Report-2018

World Health Organization (1998). Report of the Bi-regional Workshop on Health Impacts of Haze-Related Air Pollution, Report RS/98/GE/17(MAA), Manila, World Health Organization, Regional Office for the Western Pacific.

World Health Organization (2006). *Report on Dengue*, 1–5 October 2006, Geneva, Switzerland.

Writehead, J.C. and Blomquist, G.C. (1991). 'Measuring Contingent Values for Wetlands: Effects of Information about Related Environmental Goods', *Water Resources Research*, 27 (10): 2523–2551.

Xie, B.C. and Zhao, W. (2018). 'Willingness to Pay for Green Electricity in Tianjin, China: Based on the Contingent Valuation Method', *Energy Policy*, 114: 98–107.

Yildirim, S. and Philippatos, G. (2007). 'Competition and Contestability in Central and Eastern European Banking Markets', *Managerial Finance*, 33(3): 195–209.

Yu, X. and Abler, D. (2010). 'Incorporating Zero and Missing Responses into CVM with Open-Ended Bidding: Willingness to Pay for Blue Skies in Beijing', *Environment and Development Economics*, 15(5): 535–556.

Zeckhauser, R. (1975). 'Procedures for Valuing Lives', *Public Policy*, 23: 419–464.

Zhuo, X., Zhang, P., Gregg, E.W., Barker, L., Hoerger, T.J., Pearson-Clarke, T. and Albright, A. (2012). 'A Nationwide Community-Based Lifestyle Program Could Delay or Prevent Type 2 Diabetes Cases and Save $5.7 Billion in 25 Years', *Health Affairs*, 31(1): 50–60.

Index

Printed in the United States
By Bookmasters